THE GOLDEN YEARS
*Hibernian in the Days
of the Famous Five*

Dedication

To my late brother Kenny, a great Hibby.

Acknowledgements

Special thanks should go to my good friend Phil Thomson, who was a constant source of enthusiasm and encouragement and without whose help and confidence this book would never have been finished.

Thanks must also go the staff at the National Library of Scotland in Edinburgh, whose endless patience and assistance was of immense help.

Thanks also to Tommy Preston and Lawrie Reilly for the use of their scrapbooks. My main sources of information have been: *The Edinburgh Evening News*, *The Scotsman*, *Sunday Mail*, *Daily Record*, and *Evening Times*. Also, *The Scottish Football Book*, *100 Years of Hibs* (Thomson and Docherty), *The Hibees*, and *Hibernian: The Complete Story*, both by John Mackay, the Hibernian official programmes 1946–1961, and many other publications far too numerous to mention.

THE GOLDEN YEARS
Hibernian in the Days of the Famous Five

Tom Wright

First published in Great Britain in 2010 by
The Derby Book Publishing Company Ltd,
3 The Parker Centre, Derby, DE21 4SZ.

ISBN 978-1-85983-788-7

Printed and bound by DZS Grafik, Slovenia.

Contents

Foreword

The post-war years were arguably the most exciting in the history of the Scottish game. During this time Hibernian Football Club exploded onto the scene to become the best side by far in the entire country. Soon the illustrious all-international forward line of Gordon Smith, Bobby Johnstone, Lawrie Reilly, Eddie Turnbull and Willie Ormond, collectively known as the 'Famous Five', would, in time, become revered throughout the land and widely recognised as the best forward line ever produced by a Scottish side. But Hibs were much more than the Famous Five. Although the magical quintet would terrorise defences the length and breadth of the country, many other players who would become famous wearing the green-and-white jersey would break through to become internationals or major personalities in their own right.

This is the story of how a football team on the brink of extinction in the early years of the 1930s rose from the ashes under the leadership of a sometimes brash, but energetic and charismatic young chairman. Under the stewardship of an experienced manager, the club took the football world by storm in the years immediately following the end of the war. These were exciting times. The general public had been starved of entertainment during the war years, particularly the many thousands who had been serving abroad, and the clamour to watch competitive football created an almost unprecedented crowd boom, which lasted well into the following decade.

It was a time of great change. Within a few short years would come the advent of competitive European football, the development of floodlights and the arrival of televised football, which would perhaps have the biggest long-term impact on the game. This book covers not only all the major events, but also the sometimes less important, but no less interesting, happenings at the club during this time.

The Golden Years covers the definitive period in Scottish football, through the phenomenon of the Famous Five and the wider changes in the Scottish game. This was the period when visionaries shaped the world game that we know today.

In the Beginning: Harry Swan

In the summer of 1931 Harry Swan was elected to the board of directors of Hibernian Football Club. The event would have far-reaching consequences, not only for Hibs but also for the whole of Scottish football. Under his leadership the club would come to the fore during what is generally considered to be the greatest period of the Scottish game. In order to fully appreciate the golden post-war years at Easter Road that encapsulated the great days of the 'Famous Five', when the club won three League Championships within a five-year period, it is perhaps important to examine the part played by Swan in the renaissance of Hibernian in the years immediately preceding World War Two.

Henry Scott Swan was born at No.4 Breadalbane Street in Leith on 13 January 1896 to father George, a slater journeyman, and mother Catherine, a few weeks before Hibs faced Hearts just several hundred yards away at Logie Green in the only Scottish Cup Final to date to be played outside Glasgow. A master baker by trade, who at first worked at and later owned the well-known baker's shop and restaurant Littlejohn's in the Leith Street area of the city, Swan had seen brief service with the Royal Scots during World War One before being discharged in 1915 on health grounds on account of his flat feet. Originally with sympathies that lay towards Leith Athletic, he and a relative would visit Tynecastle and Easter Road on alternate Saturdays, and it is said that it was before a Derby game between Hearts and Hibs in Gorgie one day that Harry declared that he would become a firm supporter of the winning side. How football history might have been different had Hearts emerged victorious!

Swan first came to prominence at Easter Road when he became a debenture shareholder of the club in 1924 when funds were required to finance the building of a new grandstand to house the crowds that were flocking to watch the great Hibs side of Harper, McGinnigle, Dornan, Kerr, Miller, Shaw, Ritchie, Dunn, McColl, Halligan and Walker, which reached consecutive Scottish Cup Finals in 1923 and 1924. But by the end of the decade the great side of just a few years earlier was in decline, culminating in relegation at the end of the 1930–31 season. Swan's reputation as an intelligent, astute and ambitious no-nonsense figure had meanwhile impressed several of his fellow debenture holders, and that same year many of these shareholders, who had been concerned for some time by the running of the club, and were anxious for a return for their investment, were eventually successful in their bid to have representation at board level. At the AGM that year three new members were elected to the board, one of them Swan, who became the first-ever non-Catholic to become a director of the club. Less than a year later, however, after the team had failed in its bid to clinch promotion at the first time of asking, Swan resigned, accusing his fellow directors of lacking ambition and of employing small-minded penny-pinching measures which were not consistent with his forward thinking ideas for the club.

On the football front things looked better for Hibs the following season, and they were eventually promoted back into the top division as champions; but although the team made a reasonable start to the 1933–34 season, their form soon slid and it required a late fight to avoid a return to the Second Division. At that year's AGM, following the resignation of a director, Harry Swan was again nominated for election to the board by a body of debenture holders and was duly elected for a second time. To his astonishment, at a meeting of the newly-elected committee later that evening, he was informed that although Owen Brannigan wished to remain on the board, he was relinquishing his position at the head of the committee, and that at a vote taken earlier the rest of the directors had elected him chairman. He was 38 years old at the time.

Swan inherited a team that was in the doldrums when he first became chairman at Easter Road, but within the time span of a 10-year prophesy that he would make Hibs great again, they had started to fulfill that promise. Just a few years later the transformation would be complete. Under his leadership and well-recognised legislatory skills Hibernian would burst to the forefront of Scottish football during arguably the game's finest-ever period, the golden post-war years. He would help mould a side that would become associated with fast-flowing, attractive and intelligent football, not only at home but further afield, which would epitomise all that was good in the game, before going on to become the most successful side ever to grace the famous colours of Hibernian in the long and distinguished history of the club.

In the summer of 1936 Harry Swan made arguably his greatest-ever appointment. Unknown to all but a trusted few, during the previous season the effervescent Willie McCartney, who had been manager of Hibs' greatest rivals Hearts for 16 years before resigning 12 months before in mysterious circumstances that have never been satisfactorily explained, had been approached to take over from temporary manager Johnny Halligan during the season. McCartney, however, refused to accept the position until the relegation issue had been settled; providing that the club was still in the top division. Despite some heart-stopping moments, safety was eventually achieved, the club finishing 17th in a League of 20, and Willie McCartney was duly installed as manager.

Although Hibs' form during the following three seasons, the last before World War Two, was again inconsistent, it was clear that there were definite signs of improvement, both on and of the field. It was also evident that a strong bond was growing between the chairman and the manager, who were both highly ambitious and wanted nothing but the best for the team and its supporters.

The ebullient and flamboyant McCartney cut a magnificent figure. Impeccably dressed, usually in a pinstriped suit with Crombie-style overcoat and sporting either a bowler or Homburg hat, he was rarely seen without the characteristic carnation in his buttonhole. Looking every inch like a showbiz impresario, his was a figure that commanded immediate respect, and the sight of his impressive frame filling the tunnel on the rare occasions he felt the need to venture trackside during a match, was the guarantee of extra effort from his players. Much shorter in stature than the manager, Swan was also rarely seen without his trademark apparel, the Homburg hat. Fast gaining a deserved reputation as a man of vision and a great legislator, he had an endearing sense of humour but was also a man who did not suffer fools gladly and was not without his enemies in the game.

It was soon after the appointment of Willie McCartney that Harry Swan made the bold, and some thought rash, promise that if given 10 years he would make Hibs a great side again. Although he would be out by a few years, time would prove the astute Swan right. One of the first tasks undertaken by the new manager was to appoint Hugh Shaw as first-team trainer. Shaw had been a member of the brilliant Hibs side of the mid-1920s, before travelling west in 1926 after a dispute with the club to continue his playing career in the colours of Glasgow Rangers. Transferred to Hearts in 1928, where he played under the management of Willie McCartney, he had short spells with East Fife and Leith Athletic before eventually becoming manager of Highland League side Elgin City. Shaw was already at Easter Road on McCartney's arrival, having rejoined the club in 1934 as assistant to trainer Johnny Halligan, and when former Hibs centre-forward Jimmy McColl, yet another member of the great 1920s side and the first Hibs player to score 100 goals in all competitions, was appointed as assistant trainer in 1937, the off-field partnership of Harry Swan, Willie McCartney, Hugh Shaw, Jimmy McColl and later as trainer, after a long career as a player wearing the green and white, Sammy Kean, all of whom would serve the club so well for many distinguished years, was complete. Director Tom Hartland was already on the board of directors. One other board member who would have a significant part to play in the Hibs story, Wilson Terris, would join the club much later.

Another task undertaken by McCartney was to install a first-class scouting system, and in the years immediately preceding the outbreak of hostilities this led to an exciting crop of youngsters, such as goalkeeper Jimmy Kerr, Tommy McIntyre, Arthur Milne, Sammy Kean, Davie Shaw, Willie Clark and Willie Finnigan, joining the club.

At the start of the 1939–40 season, Hibernian would play only five League games, winning two and losing three; the most notable defeats by Queen of the South and Albion Rovers, before war was declared on Germany. On 3 September 1939, League football was annulled and players' contracts invalidated. Sammy Kean had the distinction of scoring Hibs' last peacetime goal for seven years in the surprise 5–2 defeat by newly-promoted Albion Rovers at Easter Road the previous afternoon.

The liner *Athenia* was torpedoed by a U-Boat off the coast of Ireland en route to America on the opening day of the war, and the battleship *Royal Oak* sunk by submarine with a heavy loss of life at Scapa Flow a few weeks later. But even when the Forth Bridge and Rosyth dockyard were attacked from the air two days after the Scapa Flow disaster, in the first attack on the British mainland of World War Two, there still existed a phoney conflict in which little appeared to be happening. Consequently, within a few weeks it was felt safe enough to recommence football, a move designed to help boost morale, but this was purely on a part-time basis with no reserve sides. With Leagues divided into East and West sections, and crowds initially limited to a maximum of 8,000, the players were allowed to earn no more than £2 per week excluding bonuses, which, however, was 10s more than their English counterparts. The higher wages on offer in Scotland, not including any alleged under-the-counter payments, often encouraged players working or serving in the Armed Forces in the North of England to travel over the border to guest for Scottish clubs, a situation that would be of great benefit to Hibs in the years ahead. The East and West regional Leagues proved unsuccessful and unpopular, not least because of the absence of games against Celtic and Rangers for the sides in the East section, and near normality returned to League football with the formation of the Southern League in 1940–41. The new set-up involved most of the pre-war sides, with the exception of Aberdeen, presumably because of the travelling involved, Kilmarnock, whose ground at Rugby Park had been requisitioned by the military authorities, and Queen of the South.

The War Years, a Quite Extraordinary New Year's Derby and 'The Gay Gordon'

At the beginning of 1940 a game took place, which well deserves a mention due to the uniqueness of the occasion. Games against near neighbours Hearts were always keenly anticipated by the fans and players of both sides, and a quite remarkable Edinburgh derby took place at Easter Road on 1 January 1940. Special permission had been granted to extend the wartime crowd limit to 15,000, and regardless of the fact that a thick blanket of fog that had hung over the city all morning would make it likely that visibility would be at a premium, over 14,000 had still paid to see the game. Once the match started, the poor visibility made it extremely difficult for the newspaper reporters covering the event to follow the proceedings taking place in the murky gloom, and at times they and the spectators could only determine the identity of the players nearest to them, being forced to rely on hand signals from 'messengers' in the crowd to pass on the names of any goalscorers. Hibs were leading 3–2 at half-time, but with the players of both sides making the most of the interval break, which was taken on the field, the referee discovered that he had brought the first half to an end two minutes early. Ordered to complete the missing two minutes, Hearts scored twice during the period to take a 4–3 lead. The high-scoring game eventually finished 6–5 in Hearts' favour, with several goals from either side falling into the 'dubious' category due to the poor visibility.

If things had been bad for the newspaper reporters, they were as nothing compared to the task facing the famous journalist and radio commentator Rex Kingsley, who had been hired to broadcast the entire second half for the *Home Services Radio Programme*. Normally, during similar climatic conditions the broadcast would have been cancelled, but because wartime regulations prohibited the mention of any inclement weather, which might alert the listening enemy to the atmospheric conditions prevailing throughout the country, Kingsley was forced to commentate on 45 minutes of fictitious action, with his field of vision limited only to a few yards either side of the stand-side touchline. Reporting on mostly exaggerated or imaginary incidents and action, with goals signalled by louder roars from the crowd, he too was informed of the scorers by 'couriers'. Miraculously he somehow managed to complete the 45 minutes of action taking place unseen under the blanket of fog, keeping up the coherent but fake broadcast right to the final whistle.

In the visitors' changing room, some minutes after the game had ended, it was discovered that the Hearts outside-left Donaldson was missing. A search party discovered the player, still at his station, peering into the gloom ready to collect the ball, completely unaware that the match had finished.

There was an amusing ending to this highly unusual affair. After the game, Kingsley, who had been concerned by the quality of the coverage, was placated by a passing policeman with the advice, 'Dinnae worry Rex, judging by some of the reports of yours I've read in the *Sunday Mail*, this'll no be the first game you huv'nae seen very well'.

In a final postscript to this remarkable affair, several days later Rex received a letter from Hearts player Duncan McLure, who, on the advice of relatives who had listened to the game on the radio, thanked the commentator for crediting him with a better game than he had actually played.

In the spring of 1941, manager Willie McCartney made certainly his and probably Hibernian's greatest-ever signing. Only days before, 16-year-old Gordon Smith, playing at centre-forward for a Scottish Junior XI against a combined Hibs-Hearts Select XI to celebrate the opening of Lochee United's new ground at Beechwood Park in Dundee, scored a hat-trick against Hibs' pre-war Scottish international centre-half Bobby Baxter in the Junior side's 3–2 victory. Watched by Easter Road manager Willie McCartney and Hearts chairman Alex Irvine, the youngster gave an all-round impressive performance as he ran the Edinburgh select defence ragged throughout the entire 90 minutes. Newspaper reports suggested that Hearts had arranged to sign the player after the game, and although he had signed nothing, Smith himself accepted the fact that he was now a Hearts player. It later transpired that he had only been offered a trial by the Gorgie side, and it was this news that prompted the intervention of the Hibs manager. The following Sunday the owner of the lemonade factory next to the players' home in Mill Lane, Montrose, coincidentally – or perhaps prophetically No.7 – called to say that a Willie McCartney from Hibs was on the phone wishing to speak to the youngster. Gordon himself had no wish to talk to the Hibs manager, as his mind was made up and he wanted to sign for Hearts, the team he had supported since he was a boy – if they wanted him. His father encouraged him, if only for the sake of civility, to speak to the Hibs manager. On being told of Hearts' offer of a trial, McCartney, in characteristic fashion, bellowed that a trial match was not necessary to see his obvious potential, and that he had more than demonstrated his worth in the select match and Hibs wanted to sign him there and then. Such were the legendary powers of McCartney's persuasion that after an initial meeting with the player in an Arbroath hotel, Gordon travelled down to Edinburgh the following day, Monday 28 April 1941, to put pen to paper and collect his £10 signing-on fee before joining his new teammates at Tynecastle, where they were preparing to face city rivals Hearts in a rearranged New Year's Day League game. He was 27 days short of his 17th birthday.

Completing a wonderful day's business for the club, 17-year-old Bobby Combe, a lifelong Hibs supporter, was signed by McCartney just after the game, and both he and Smith were joined at Tynecastle that evening by 17-year-old Jock Weir, still registered with Leith Renton, who was making only his second appearance for Hibs' first team. That same afternoon the local newspapers had carried a story that a deputation from Hearts had watched 17-year-old Combe score two fine goals for Inveresk Athletic in a Cup Final against Leith Renton at Easter Road the previous Saturday. Combe had been training at Tynecastle, so it was therefore something of a shock for the Hearts officials to discover that both he and Smith, who were listed respectively on the team lines as Trialist and Junior, would be lining up against them that evening.

Replacing centre-forward Willie Anderson, who had been injured in Hibs' game against Dumbarton two days before, and using borrowed boots as his own had not arrived in time, Gordon Smith again scored a hat-trick in the rearranged 5–3 Spring Holiday victory with Combe and Adams scoring the others as Hibs gained revenge for a recent Southern League Cup defeat by Hearts. With newspaper headlines declaring, 'Hibs super tactics bring success as Hearts flop', there was particular praise for newcomers Smith and Combe as well as Willie Finnigan, who was described as having a quiet but forceful game. Although they could not know it at the time, both Gordon Smith and Bobby Combe would play an integral part in Hibernian's glory years of the late 1940s and early 50s, and between them they would give the club 34 years of sterling service. The rest, as they say, is history.

It was after this game that Gordon Smith was approached in the street outside Tynecastle by a 12-year-old Hibs fan inviting the player to his house for a cup of tea. Smith politely declined the offer, but during the following years he would visit Lawrie Reilly's house many times as a teammate and friend.

The teams at Tynecastle were:

Hibs: Kerr, Shaw, Hall, Kean, Baxter, Rice, Weir, Trialist, Junior, Finnigan, Adams. (Scorers: Smith 3 Combe and Adams)
Hearts: Waugh, McClure, Miller, Philip, Dykes, Brown, Dougan, Walker, Whalley, Hamilton, Christie. (Scorer: Walker 3)

Although living in the Angus market town of Montrose at the time, Gordon Smith had, in fact, been born in Edinburgh, at No.4 Springvalley Terrace in the middle-class Morningside area of the city on 26 May 1924. The second eldest of a family of six, five boys and a girl, born to father Robert, a grocer's assistant, and mother Christina, née Sutherland, who had married exactly one month after Armistice Day in 1918, the family had moved to Montrose when Gordon was only two years old after his father had accepted a position in a grocer's shop in the town.

Passionate about his football from an early age, Gordon Smith played for his school side Montrose Academy, gaining two Schoolboy international caps against Ireland and England, lining up alongside future teammate Bobby Combe before progressing through the ranks of amateur football with Bromford and Kirriemuir Harp juveniles, eventually signing as a semi-professional with Montrose Roselea. At the time of the game against the combined Hearts-Hibs Select XI he had moved on to another junior side, Dundee North End.

At the end of the 1940–41 season there would be only a short break from football for the young Smith and his new teammates. Concerned at the major loss of revenue created mainly by the absence of games against the 'Old Firm' in the wartime regional Leagues that had been in place the previous season, Hibs chairman Harry Swan was instrumental in the setting up of an initially experimental Summer Cup competition featuring the top 16 sides in the country. Based on a home and away knockout format designed to provide clubs with much-needed income during the summer months, it would be only one of many innovative moves that the far-seeing Swan would initiate to the benefit of the game in almost 30 years at the helm at Easter Road.

This, then, was the situation during the summer of 1941. The draw for the first round of the Swan-inspired Summer Cup had initially paired Hibs at home against Celtic, the second leg to be played at Parkhead four days later, but with none of the eight ties providing a game in Glasgow on the opening day, the authorities immediately recommended that the Hibs v Celtic, St Mirren v Partick Thistle, and Albion Rovers v Third Lanark fixtures be reversed. There was yet another problem. Many of the clubs that had allowed their players to appear as guests for other sides during the season now refused to allow this arrangement to continue for the new competition, although this did not apply to East Fife, who still allowed Hibs the use of Tom Adams, and it was only through the intervention of SFA secretary George Graham, who strongly advised that this arrangement should continue, that the situation was eventually resolved.

Against Celtic at Parkhead in the opening round, the clever and enterprising play of the Hibs forwards, particularly that of hat-trick hero Arthur Milne, home on leave from the services, and two-goal Bill Anderson, allowed the visitors to leave Glasgow with a convincing 5–3 victory. In the return leg at Easter

Road on the Wednesday, watched by the biggest crowd of the day including Hibs transfer target, Sgt Instructor Matt Busby (who had recently been posted to the Scottish Command), and the legendary English outside-right Stanley Matthews (who would soon join the RAF and turn out occasionally for both Morton and Airdrie), saw the visitors somewhat surprisingly run out 1–0 winners. The defeat was not enough, however, to prevent Hibs from progressing into the next round. Interestingly, Celtic's share of the gate money from the Easter Road fixture amounted to £150, while Hibs had received only £100 from their visit to Parkhead four days earlier. By comparison, Hearts had left Hampden Park after their game against Queen's Park that same day with the princely sum of £17.

In competition with several other sides, Hibs were keen to take Scottish international Matt Busby on loan from Liverpool, and although there was an initial problem over Liverpool's insurance valuation of the player, he eventually signed on at Easter Road. Curiously, Celtic failed to take the war years nearly as seriously as city rivals Rangers, and some say it was this lack of foresight that was to prove expensive for the club in a barren post-war period. One example of this lack of desire was the rejection of local boy Busby, born in nearby Bellshill, who while keen to guest for the Parkhead side was given little encouragement. The snub was to prove of immediate advantage to Hibs, who were to benefit from almost two years of sterling service from a player who would win wartime caps for Scotland while at Easter Road before moving to Orkney with his unit in 1942. Interviewed several years later, Hibs wartime centre-half Bobby Baxter recalled that as well as signing Busby, Hibs were keen to sign Stanley Matthews, and the player was interested in playing at Easter Road. Unlike Busby, however, Matthews was stationed too far away to make playing in Edinburgh a viable proposition.

Busby made his debut for the club in the 2–1 replay victory over Clyde in the Summer Cup, Anderson and teenage prodigy Gordon Smith scoring the goals, and a narrow 1–0 victory over Dumbarton in the semi-final at Tynecastle earned Hibs a passage into the Final. Somewhat predictably, there had been talk of an all-Edinburgh Final against Hearts, the first since the clubs had met at Logie Green in 1896, but these hopes were dashed when Rangers defeated the Gorgie side in the other semi-final at Hampden.

In the week leading up to the Final, Hibs signed outside-right Jimmy Caskie on loan from Everton after protracted negotiations between the parties. Rangers and several other Scottish clubs, including Falkirk, were also keen to sign the player, but Easter Road was his preferred destination. Caskie and another player had earlier been fined and banned from turning out again for St Mirren after having been found guilty of receiving illegal under-the-counter payments. The Paisley club had also been fined for its part in the matter and several of its directors suspended from the game. Part of the Caskie deal had been the promise of a place in the line up for the Final, which meant exclusion for Gordon Smith, and it was left to manager McCartney to break the heartbreaking news to the youngster, who had featured in three of the six earlier games in the competition, scoring twice. In later years Smith would confess that missing the Final remained one of the biggest disappointments of his long and distinguished career.

The Final took place at Hampden on Saturday 12 July 1941, in front of a crowd of 37,200, including a 13-year-old Lawrie Reilly, who saw Hibs break Rangers' wartime monopoly by recovering from a two-goal half-time deficit to take the Cup by the odd goal in five. Early on it had all seemed so different as Rangers, by far the better side in the first half, raced to a 2–0 interval lead, although Hibs had been denied a couple of good penalty claims. After the break there was only one side in it as the Edinburgh side rallied magnificently to level things, Willie Finnigan scoring twice before the unlikely hero of the hour, centre-half Bobby Baxter, scored the winner just minutes from the end. Hibs' resurgence had been inspired by yet another half-time change by manager McCartney, who switched Caskie to the left wing and Nutley to the right, and the Edinburgh side, well led by centre-forward Arthur Milne, literally ran the Glasgow side ragged, and by the end they were a disjointed and dispirited outfit. With time running out and the score level, the tension became too unbearable for manager McCartney, who spent the closing minutes pacing nervously behind the Hampden stand.

The Hibs side that defeated Rangers was: Kerr, Shaw, Hall, Busby, Baxter, Kean, Nutley, Finnigan, Milne, Combe, Caskie.

At the after-match victory dinner at the Central Hotel in Glasgow, attended by an obviously still disappointed Gordon Smith, Harry Swan thanked his victorious players for their efforts, not only in the Final itself, but for the entire Cup run, which had resulted in pride being restored at Easter Road. Swan was surprised, however, when manager Willie McCartney rose to suggest that owing to the chairman's part in the revival of Hibs, and his involvement in the inauguration of the Cup itself, the trophy should be presented to him, and it was left to Football League President Mr W. Cuff to hand over the trophy, watched by no less a distinguished personage than the famous FA secretary Stanley Rous.

As a matter of interest, the total drawing for the entire competition had been £10,400, a not inconsiderable sum at the time. The winning team were informed that as well as their £2 wages they would each receive £10 in War Savings Certificates and be allowed to accept up to £8 in bonus money from the club.

As already mentioned, Hibs more than held their own against Rangers during the war, and this was never more clearly demonstrated than in the Southern League game at Easter Road on 27 September 1941 when the home side recorded a famous 8–1 victory over their Glasgow rivals, Gordon Smith this time playing a prominent part in the proceedings. It was Rangers' heaviest-ever defeat in a competitive match, and it remains so to this day. Only three times before in their long and illustrious history had the Ibrox side conceded even six goals in a domestic game, two of these defeats coming in the early 1890s during the infancy of Scottish League football.

Milne opened the scoring for Hibs after just seven minutes, before Combe put his side two ahead 13 minutes later. Venters scored from the spot after a rather soft award midway through the half, but Smith himself restored Hibs' two-goal lead shortly before the break when he headed a Caskie free-kick past Dawson in the Rangers goal. Three goals to one ahead at the interval, Hibs had been so dominant that the famous journalist and radio broadcaster Rex Kingsley, writing in the *Sunday Mail,* thought that the only thing that could possibly save Rangers from complete humiliation would be a Nazi invasion. Centre-half Willie Woodburn, who would face the Easter Road side in many a titanic struggle during the immediate post-war years, was injured in the first half and reappeared after the interval on the wing, but he was a virtual spectator as Hibs went to town in the second half, scoring five more goals including three in a three-minute spell on the hour mark. Venters was ordered off after committing a reckless and cynical foul, shortly before Gordon Smith ended the goal rout by scoring Hibs' eighth. The shell-shocked Blues were left hanging on in desperation, before the final whistle ended an afternoon of abject misery for the Ibrox side and their followers. Rangers had been completely out-played in every position, and never before in their history had they been so comprehensively and thoroughly thrashed. So much in the ascendancy were Hibs, that they could easily have scored at least another five or six. Three times the ball was cleared from the visiting goalline, and several terrific saves by Dawson prevented an even greater embarrassment. The injury to Woodburn and the dismissal of Venters had had little bearing on the eventual result, with the outcome a foregone conclusion long before either event.

Hibernian: Crozier, Shaw, Hall, Hardisty, Baxter, Kean, Smith, Finnegan, Milne, Combe, Caskie. (Scorers for Hibs: Combe 4, Smith 2, Milne 2.)
Rangers: Dawson, Gray, Shaw, Bolt, Woodburn, Little, McIntosh, Gillick, Smith, Venters, Johnstone. (Scorer: Smith)

At this time Gordon Smith was still living and working in Montrose, only commuting by train to Edinburgh on match days. Often he would have a hectic race to the station by bicycle in time to catch his train to the capital, leaving little sister Rachael to collect the abandoned transport and return it home, ready for the next occasion. This arrangement was obviously far from ideal, and with the encouragement of Willie McCartney the player moved to Edinburgh and a reserved wartime occupation in Henry Robb's shipyard in Leith.

With Smith a by now almost automatic choice for Hibs, either at centre-forward or outside-right, the season after their Summer Cup success Hibs again met Rangers at the ultimate stage of the competition, but this time a no-score draw was decided by the toss of a coin. There was to be yet another disappointment for the teenage Smith when a correct call by the Rangers captain meant the Cup made its way to Ibrox.

The Edinburgh side contested a third wartime Cup Final and it will be no surprise to learn that the Light Blues were again the opposition. The Southern League Cup had been initiated in the 1940–41 season, and only once in the six seasons of its existence did Hibs advance beyond the sectional stage. In 1943–44, after beating Third Lanark, Albion Rovers and Morton, a 5–2 victory over Clyde in the semi-final ensured another tense and gripping Final against the Glasgow side. It had earlier been decided that no extra-time would be played, and that in the event of a draw, the side that had won the most corners would be the winners. With 89 minutes played the game was still goalless and the flag kick tally even, when the Rangers defence conceded a corner from a Jimmy Caskie move and Hibs won the Cup by six corners to five.

Not only had Hibs beaten Rangers in two of the three Finals contested between the sides, they, more than any other, had challenged the dominance of the Glasgow giants in League fixtures throughout the war, finishing in second place twice, third three times and fifth once. The skilful crop of youngsters signed pre-war by McCartney, allied to other up-and-coming young players who had signed since, such as Jock Govan, Hugh Howie, Peter Aird and Bobby Nutley, to say nothing of Gordon Smith himself, would learn much from a mixture of experienced players acquired on loan, such as Matt Busby of Liverpool, Alec Hall of Sunderland, Jimmy Caskie of Everton and Middlesbrough's Bobby Baxter, who had earlier guested with Hearts until falling out with the Tynecastle club. Another player acquired under the loan system was Bob Hardisty, then stationed at nearby Dalmahoy, who would later become famous as captain of the well-known non-League side Bishop Auckland, who would gain an illustrious Amateur Cup pedigree during the 1950s. Bob's first game for Hibs created a major headache for the club when there was difficulty in providing the player with a pair of football boots to fit his unusually large feet. The problem was eventually overcome, however, and Hardisty went on to play many times for the Edinburgh side.

It has often been said that, but for the outbreak of World War Two, Harry Swan would have achieved his aim of making Hibs great within the time span of his 10-year prophesy, but in reality, it was probably the war and the influence of the experienced guest players that would be responsible for the blossoming and development of the latent talent of the younger players already at the club, having a positive and lasting effect on the young men who would become post-war icons of a golden age. Gordon Smith in particular would benefit greatly by playing in front of the vastly experienced and intelligent Matt Busby and alongside the shrewd Willie Finnigan.

Throughout the war years, with Smith playing a major part, Hibs had competed vigorously with Rangers, who while providing several players for active service themselves, also had the advantage of a greater number of players to select from, either signed or on loan, due mainly to the enormous number of men who were in reserved wartime occupations in the shipyards and the multitude of other works that dominated Clydeside. In the six seasons of the Southern League Championship, the results between the sides had ended level, with five wins each and two games drawn, although the Glasgow side had scored the most goals, 26 to Hibs' 24.

The Easter Road side had fared better during the war years against their near neighbours and bitter rivals Hearts, winning seven, drawing two and losing only three of the 12 matches contested, scoring 10 more goals than the 16 conceded. Hibs' results against Celtic during the same period were five wins, four draws and three defeats, scoring 24 goals to the Parkhead side's 15.

The war years had also been a productive time for Gordon Smith. In the four years since signing for the club he had been overall top goalscorer twice, notching an impressive total of 108 goals in all competitive games, more than double that of any other player, although it must be remembered that the great majority of Smith's colleagues, unlike him, did not have the security of a war reserved occupation, many often finding great difficulty in attending the fixtures, even, that is, if they were still in the country at the time.

Nevertheless, since signing for the club Gordon Smith had quickly built up a well-deserved reputation as a skilful, dangerous and respected opponent, both on account of his goalscoring abilities and phenomenal ball control. Inspired by his magical play, Hibs started the 1944–45 season with an unbeaten run of seven games, a sequence that had only been bettered by the 10 wins and four draws of two years earlier, and there were now calls to cap the elegant winger. Smith had already become a figure of near adoration among the Hibs fans, and his growing reputation gained its just reward when he won the first of his three wartime and 18 full Scotland caps against England at Wembley in October 1944.

As Hibs were drawing 1–1 with Celtic at Parkhead courtesy of a strike by Bill Anderson, Smith was one of four Hibs players, not counting former colleague Matt Busby, who lined up against the Auld Enemy. The Scotland forward line was an all-Edinburgh affair. Smith, centre-forward Arthur Milne and outside-left Jimmy Caskie of Hibs were joined by inside-forwards Tommy Walker and Andy Black of Hearts. Remarkably, all had been signed at one time or another by the Hibs manager Willie McCartney. Like his teammate Smith, Arthur Milne was also making his international debut. They were joined in the Scotland line up by Easter Road centre-half Bobby Baxter, who captained the side. It was the 13th game between the teams since the start of the war, and although Scotland had been beaten by England at Hampden earlier in the year, and had lost three of the five games between the sides at Wembley during this time, it was generally felt that this would be the Scots' best chance of success against their oldest enemy for some time. It was not to be, however. Even without the influence of England's famous half-back line of Brittain, Cullis and Joy, England were still far too good for the visitors and they eventually ran out easy 6–2 winners. An impressive display of power football by the home side shattered the Scots, and although the final scoreline flattered England, it was nevertheless an embarrassing defeat. Smith himself was a distinct success, one of the few in the Scotland side on the day, his performance even outshining that of his opposite number Stanley Matthews. Teammate Caskie proved a disappointment, as did Milne, although it has to be said that the centre-forward had suffered through lack of decent service. Centre-half Baxter started brightly, but he too, like his teammates, quickly faded, eventually failing completely to subdue his opposite number Tommy Lawton, who scored twice.

After the disappointment of Wembley, there would be one final wartime Cup Final appearance for Hibs and Gordon Smith, but this time the Easter Road side were beaten 2–0 at the ultimate stage of the Southern League Cup in 1945 by a Partick Thistle team featuring guest player Bill Shankly, who would make over 60 wartime appearances for the Firhill side, and a soon-to-be Hearts stalwart Bobby Parker.

This, then, was the situation at the end of the war, and no one at Easter Road could have guessed that Hibernian, and Harry Swan, were about to come into their own in a big way.

A Debut for Lawrie Reilly, Victory Cup Final and a Trip to Czechoslovakia

Just a few days after the disappointment of the Cup Final defeat by Partick Thistle, yet another player who would go on to achieve legendary status at Easter Road made his first appearance in a green-and-white jersey. In those pre-television days, athletic and sports events were a popular attraction for the often entertainment-starved public, frequently drawing large crowds. One of the most popular was the annual Press Charities Sports Gala, which had become a feature of the Edinburgh Trades Holiday period. Held that year at Tynecastle on Saturday 6 July 1945, fine summer weather helped swell the crowd to well in excess of 10,000, who paid a record sum of £750 for the privilege. All proceeds would be shared equally after expenses, between the Royal Infirmary and Leith Hospitals, and the Press Benevolent Fund.

After the earlier athletics events, and, of all things, the novelty of a sheepdog display, came the eagerly awaited main event of the afternoon, the popular and keenly contested five-a-side tournament featuring sides from Hibs, Hearts, Rangers, Leith Athletic, Falkirk, a composite side from Fife, an Army XI and a Lothian Juniors Select XI. The Hibs team consisted of experienced campaigners Gordon Smith, Jock Weir, Bobby Baxter, Willie Finnigan and a 16-year-old Lawrie Reilly, listed in the newspaper reports of the time as Laurie Riley, who was making his first-ever appearance for the club. Although beaten 3–2 by Rangers in the Final, Reilly had scored twice in Hibs' 5–2 victory over Fife in the opening round, the first of many goals he would score for the club during the next 13 years.

Although the family home was at No. 33 Bryston Road, in the Polworth area of Edinburgh, only a few hundred yards from Tynecastle Park, the home of Hibs' great rivals Hearts, Lawrance Reilly was, in fact, born in his grandmother's house at No. 67 Raeburn Place on 26 October 1928, a brother for elder sister Rita who was three years his senior. Originally to be called Lawrence with the usual spelling, the registrar mistakenly entered the name on the birth certificate as Lawrance, and so Lawrance it remained. Father John, a railway worker, had been a keen amateur footballer with Edinburgh club Corinthians and several other minor clubs in the city and was also a boxing enthusiast, but his main interest was a lifelong passion for Hibs, a passion he would have no difficulty in passing on to his son. Although as a youngster the young Reilly would occasionally visit Tynecastle to watch the last 15 minutes of the action when the gates were opened to allow fans to leave the ground early, he had, in fact, accompanied by his father, visited almost every ground in Scotland watching Hibs before he had left primary school, a pastime made easier because of the free railway passes allowed his father.

As well as Gordon Smith's Tynecastle debut, Lawrie also remembers watching Hibs defeat Rangers 8–1 in 1941 and the Summer Cup Final defeat of the same side at Hampden earlier in the year. A pupil of North Merchiston primary school, it was there that the young Reilly started playing organised football, both for the school side and also the Boys Brigade XI, before moving on to Boroughmuir secondary where, unfortunately for him, only the rugby code applied; although he did feature occasionally in the school cricket XI. It was around this time, however, that he joined the well-known juvenile side Edinburgh Thistle, which was run by Hibs' renowned groundsman Harry Reading. Scoring 106 goals in 55 games from the centre-forward position, Reilly formed a prolific partnership with inside-forward Archie Buchanan, who would be a teammate at both juvenile and senior level over the next 13 years, as Edinburgh Thistle embarked on a successful streak, winning several trophies including the Scottish Secondary Cup in an unbeaten 55-game run. The impressive form of the young Reilly soon drew the attention of Hearts, where an uncle had an involvement, but there was only ever going to be one destination for the player, and that was Easter Road. Both he and teammate Archie Buchanan joined Hibs in the summer of 1944, but because they were still only 16 they could not be secured on a professional contract until their 17th birthday, so in the meantime they were both allowed to continue their football development with the juvenile side.

Victory in Europe had been secured in May 1945, but because the fight against the Japanese in the Far East had continued until the August of that year, there was insufficient time to reorganise League football on a normal basis and it was decided to continue the Southern League for yet another season.

The new football season kicked-off at Tynecastle with English First Division side Huddersfield facing an Edinburgh Select XI in only the second of what was to become a regular fixture over the next few years. Representing Hibs that day in the Select's 4–0 victory were Gordon Smith, Bobby Baxter, Jock Govan, Sammy Kean and Willie Finnigan, with the added novelty of Harris of Queen's Park appearing at centre-forward. Huddersfield took the field wearing numbered jerseys, a fact that created no little interest among the fans.

Just before the start of the season proper Hibs were disappointed to learn that Middlesbrough were refusing to allow centre-half Bobby Baxter to continue to feature as a guest signing at Easter Road and demanding a fee for the Edinburgh-born player. While definitely interested in retaining the services of the experienced defender, chairman Harry Swan was of the opinion that the suggested transfer fee was excessive for a 34-year-old. In a move as unexpected as it was sudden, the international defender stunned the city by rejoining Hearts, whom he had left in August 1940 after falling out with the Tynecastle club, for a fee believed to be in the region of £2,500. Baxter, born in the Gilmerton area of the city, had spent eight seasons at Ayresome Park before the war since signing from Musselburgh Bruntonians, and had represented Scotland three times during this period and twice in wartime internationals while guesting for Hibs.

There were, however, several new signings, including two players who would make a first-team breakthrough in the coming season, inside-forward Alex Wright and 26-year-old Jimmy Cairns from Dunipace Juniors, recently discharged from the Royal Navy. Joining them at Easter Road was 18-year-old defender Matt McNeil from Maryhill Juniors, who would later play an indirect part in the coming together of the Famous Five.

For Hibs there was to be a disappointing start to the new campaign, losing 3–0 away to Queen of the South on the opening day, but a convincing 4–1 win over Hearts in the Wilson Cup at Easter Road, followed by a 2–1 victory over Rangers at the same venue three days later, Arthur Milne netting both the Hibs goals, set the Easter Road side on their way to an undefeated seven-game unbeaten run. Two games into this unbeaten sequence, as the first team faced Hamilton Academicals at Douglas Park on 25 August 1945, both Lawrie Reilly and Archie Buchanan made their competitive debuts for the club in the corresponding reserve fixture at Easter Road. Both players, still listed under the auspices of Edinburgh Thistle as they were then still too young to sign full professional forms, performed well, particularly Buchanan, who scored in Hibs' 3–1 win. Buchanan's impressive performance earned the youngster almost immediate promotion, and he made his first-team debut three weeks later in the 1–1 draw with Aberdeen at Easter Road; although it was back to the reserves the following week for the lanky inside-forward.

Lawrie Reilly would not have too long to wait for his own first-team start. With outside-left Caskie injured and both Combe and Brown back in the forces, Hibs were forced to make changes to the side due to travel to Kilmarnock on Saturday 13 October 1945. As it turned out Caskie was fit enough to play, and although Reilly had been initially chosen to feature in the second team that day, and the first-team forwards to be selected from Smith, Devlin, Milne, Peat, Weir, Docherty and Collins, the youngster found himself lining up at inside-right alongside boyhood hero Gordon Smith in Hibs' 4–3 victory. The Hibs front line that day was Smith, Reilly, Milne, Bogan and Caskie. The 16-year-old did well enough on his first start without drawing particular attention, the highlight of the afternoon being a speculative 55-yard effort by Sammy Kean, which evaded the desperate attempt of the goalkeeper who tried to punch clear, but only succeeded in helping the ball into the net for Hibs' winning goal near the end. Nevertheless, the youngster was included in the first-team squad for the home game against Motherwell a week later, but there would be no place for him in Hibs' no-score draw, the inside-right position being filled by the more experienced Bobby Combe, forming Hibs' seventh right-wing pairing since the start of the season.

Hibs' game against Third Lanark in Glasgow seven days later was watched by the Scotland selectors in view of the forthcoming game against Wales at Hampden, and there was absolutely no surprise when Gordon Smith, then playing some of the best football of his career, and at the time described in one newspaper as being 'Rightly and freely acclaimed as one of the brightest stars in the game', was selected to face the Welsh, with teammate Jock Govan listed as a reserve. It was Smith's inclusion at inside-right to Willie Waddell of Rangers, however, that caused a few eyebrows to be raised. Although he had once temporarily filled the position at club level after an injury to Bogan and performed well, the consensus of popular opinion was that the country would be robbed of the 'Best advantage of the outside-right's undoubted skill' if reduced to playing in the unfamiliar position. As it turned out, after a quiet start, Smith, making only his second international appearance, eventually improved to create a more-than-able partnership with the Rangers player, who scored the second goal in the home side's 2–0 win, Scotland's first victory since 1942.

It was at around this time that Hibs' regular pre-war outside-right Tommy McIntyre, recently returned from the armed forces, posted a transfer request after realising he had little chance of dislodging Gordon Smith from the right-wing position. McIntyre had played many fine games for the club since signing from Portobello Renton in 1936, impressing enough to warrant a place in the SFA XI that toured Canada in the close season of 1939, but like so many others his promising career had been interrupted by the war when he was called up to the forces, one of 30 or more Hibs players who saw service in uniform during the hostilities. McIntyre had only managed six appearances for the club during the years of conflict and would soon join Kilmarnock, where he would make an immediate impression by scoring twice inside a minute against St Mirren on his debut.

For the young Reilly it was back to the as yet unbeaten second team, but not for long. As Gordon Smith lined up for Scotland against Wales at Hampden in mid-December, Reilly wore the number-nine jersey in a Hibs side much depleted by injuries in the 3–2 defeat of St Mirren. He had celebrated his 17th birthday only three weeks before and was now a full professional. It was the second of only 10 first-team appearances he would make that season. That same afternoon, as Hibs finished the match at Easter Road with 10 men due to injury, Hibs reserves registered an impressive 7–1 victory at Love Street. The results comprehensively underlined a remarkable vindication of manager Willie McCartney's recruitment policy.

Reilly, who would eventually score a total of 234 competitive goals for Hibs, ending his career as the club's all-time record goalscorer, scored his first senior goal, the only one of the campaign as it would turn out, in Hibs' emphatic 6–1 win over Partick Thistle seven days later. With his side two ahead at the interval, the former Edinburgh Thistle player demonstrated his predatory skills 13 minutes after the break by taking advantage of a defensive slip to crash his shot past the despairing dive of the goalkeeper.

The popular Jimmy Caskie, who had played such a huge part in the resurgence of Hibs since joining the club on loan from Everton in 1941, was transferred to Rangers at the end of November. He made his first start for the Ibrox club against his former Easter Road teammates in Glasgow at the beginning of the following month in a 3–2 home victory. Gordon Smith, by now rightly acclaimed as the best outside-right in the country, scored Hibs' opening goal. Smith always seemed to reserve his best performances for games against the Ibrox side, and he chose this game to display his by now sublime and scintillating talents. The winger, the best player on the field by far, had what the newspapers of the day described, somewhat lyrically, as a 'grand game' as he tormented and teased the Light Blue defence throughout, although unfortunately for him his brilliant performance did not result in the victory his mesmeric skills had deserved.

Smith took particular delight in performing well against Rangers, a side he had little time for. He would confess in later years that this dislike stemmed from one of his first games against the Ibrox side during the war, when, after a tackle by future Rangers manager Scott Symon, with the ball at the other end of the park, he felt an excruciating pain across both thighs as he attempted to rise, Symon's kick accompanied by the warning that there would be more of the same to come, a fact confirmed during many of his tussles against the Glasgow side in coming seasons.

Just before the turn of the year, the New Year's Day games, always a popular holiday fixture with the Scottish football fans, came under threat with the warning that the players would withdraw their labour on that day unless they were allowed an increase in wages. The £2 maximum wage introduced by the football authorities as a wartime measure in 1939 had by this time been increased to £3 per week with £1 bonus for a win and 10s for a draw, but the players were still dissatisfied. They wanted the maximum increased to £6 per week with £2 for a win and £1 for a draw. The League management committee agreed a temporary £1 per week increase to £4 with a £2 and £1 bonus, and the proposed one-day strike was put on hold.

A Willie Peat goal gave Hibs a 1–0 home victory over Hearts on the first day of 1946 to bring to an end a run of poor form that had resulted in only one win from the previous five games. It was the Greens' first double over their nearest rivals since 1941, but any premature euphoria was quickly brought to an abrupt end the following day when they crashed to a humiliating 4–1 defeat at Cappielow. Three days later Jimmy Cairns made a scoring debut at inside-left against home-town team Falkirk, and Hibs would remain undefeated in the League for the remainder of the season. Inside-forward Tommy Bogan, meanwhile, had been finding it increasingly difficult to hold down a first-team place, and at the beginning of February he was transferred to Celtic. Like Caskie before him, Bogan's first game for his new club was against his former colleagues, but with Smith again playing a major part, a goal by centre-forward Weir ensured there would be no victory celebrations for the new Celt. Bogan had created history of a sort when in April 1945, only a few days before the end of the war, he played for Scotland against the Auld Enemy at Hampden. Breaking his leg in a clash with England goalkeeper Frank Swift inside the opening 40 seconds, he was carried off and never played for the full side again. Because the game was still classed as a wartime international, future Hibs player Leslie Johnstone, then with Clyde, was allowed to replace the unfortunate Bogan, and it was he who scored Scotland's solitary goal in a 3–1 defeat. Although only a wartime fixture, this must still rank as the shortest international career on record. Bogan earned one more representative honour when he was chosen for the Scottish League against the English League in 1948, but by this time he was wearing the colours of Celtic.

A 3–0 away victory against St Mirren in the penultimate game of the season, with only a rearranged game against Queen's Park to come, meant that only one more point was required to ensure Hibs finishing in second place behind Rangers for a second successive year, this time at the expense of Aberdeen. Jock Weir took the opportunity to cap a tremendously productive spell, in which he had scored 11 times in seven games, by scoring all three of his side's goals. Only the previous week the Newcastle United manager Stan Seymour had been at Easter Road, one of several visits that season, his target believed to be Gordon Smith, but he would undoubtedly have left the ground also impressed with the strong and speedy Weir. That same afternoon, at Easter Road, Hibs' outstanding second team, which included Lawrie Reilly, Archie Buchanan, Bobby Nutley, Arthur Milne and pre-war Scotland goalkeeper Jock Brown, deservedly won the Reserve League Championship with a win against the Paisley second string. The reserves had competed neck and neck with Hearts throughout most of the season, but had scored more than double the goals of their Edinburgh rivals and richly deserved the success. It was not to end there. Victory over Clyde gave them the Second XI Cup and only a ridiculous decision by the SFA to hold back the permit for the Reserve League Cup Final against Rangers until the following season denied the young Hibs the opportunity of winning the treble in the same season.

In the rearranged game against Queen's Park at Hampden, the necessary point was eventually secured with a 4–2 win, Gordon Smith scoring two of Hibs' goals to cap what for him personally had been a tremendously successful season, finishing equal top goalscorer alongside Arthur Milne, both with 14 goals. Smith had earlier received the reward that his consistent performances throughout the season had richly deserved when he was selected for the Scotland side to face Belgium at Hampden. This time he was in his normal position on the right wing to the exclusion of Waddell, but the Scots, including the Hibs player, who failed dismally to reproduce his club form, were unimpressive in a 2–2 draw and the entire forward line was replaced for the game against Ireland 10 days later. Smith was listed among the reserves for the game but did not travel.

In the ultimate Southern League Cup competition, Hibs took their place in a section that included Partick Thistle, Kilmarnock and Aberdeen, but two defeats from the home and away fixtures meant Aberdeen progressing through to the quarter-finals and a game against Ayr United at the expense of the Edinburgh side, who finished in second place.

Later in the same competition, Hearts were drawn against Rangers in the semi-final, the game originally arranged to be played at Easter Road, but in a move that provoked outrage among the majority of Hearts fans the Tynecastle directors insisted that the game be moved to Hampden. There was absolutely no doubt that the motive was purely financial, with Hampden then capable of accommodating almost double the capacity of Easter Road, but a somewhat absurd statement released by the Gorgie side insisted that the proposed move to Glasgow had only been initiated because of a desire to avoid a clash with a minor fixture that had been arranged at Tynecastle that same evening. As can be imagined, the Hibs directors were not best pleased at being denied the income from the fixture, but despite repeated pleas by the Hearts fans the game was played in Glasgow, Rangers eventually winning 2–1. The controversy did not end there. Perhaps to placate the Edinburgh side it was initially announced that any replay between Aberdeen and Airdrie in the other semi-final at Ibrox would take place at Easter Road, but in what was seen as another major snub to the city, Hibs complained bitterly to the SFA after it was announced that the replay would also be played in Glasgow. Both incidents had no small bearing on Hibs' determination to increase the capacity of the ground as soon as possible.

There would again be no place for Smith in the forthcoming Victory international against England at Hampden, the absence of the talented and versatile forward only explained, in the opinion of one newspaper reporter, as: 'the Glasgow complex of the selectors at work'. With Waddell again at outside-right, Smith, Sammy Kean and Davie Shaw were selected in reserve, but injury to Stephen, the Bradford right-back, saw Davie Shaw lining up alongside brother 'Jock' of Rangers, with the 'mobility of the Hibs player a direct contrast to the more robust and solid qualities of his brother'. The Hibs Shaw was a distinct success in the 1–0 victory over the Auld Enemy, his overlaps down the right wing creating danger to the English goal on numerous occasions, and he could be well pleased with his contribution; one that suggested further international recognition was sure to follow.

Johnny Aitkenhead was signed from Queen's Park at the beginning of May, just in time to take his place in the Hibs party that made its way to Celle in Germany to entertain the occupation army troops with a game against a BAOR representative side. Several of the players had visited the area before, among them Gordon Smith, who had played for a representative side the previous year. In those less politically correct days one newspaper reporter also reported that Bobby Nutley, DFM had 'passed over the area several times during the war on the way to drop bombs on Hamburg'.

Another move took place around this time that passed almost unnoticed by the Edinburgh public when Wilson Terris, a solicitor in the city, was elected to the Easter Road board. Terris, along with Harry Swan and Tom Hartland, would have a major part to play in Hibs' success during the next few years.

It had earlier been decided to rename that year's Summer Cup competition the Victory Cup, and after wins against Dundee (Gordon Smith scoring his first hat-trick of the season), Hearts and Partick Thistle in the earlier rounds, a 2–1 victory over Clyde in the semi-final at Tynecastle saw the Greens make yet another appearance at the decisive stage of a national tournament. The opposition in the Final was Rangers. This time there was to be no fairytale ending. Hibs' recent signing Johnny Aitkenhead, already a huge favourite of the Easter Road fans, scored late in the first half to cancel out an earlier goal by Rangers, which had deflected off Finnegan, but over the piece the Light Blues were the far superior side and well worthy of their 3–1 win. The Cup became the permanent property of the victors and can still be seen in the Ibrox trophy room.

The Hibs line up for the Final was by this time taking on a more familiar look, particularly in defence:

Hibernian: Kerr, Govan, Shaw, Howie, Aird, Finnegan, Smith, Peat, Milne, Aitkenhead, Nutley.

On the eve of the Cup semi-final just a few weeks earlier, 23-year-old inside-forward Eddie Turnbull had become Hibs' latest acquisition. Turnbull was born at No. 16 Bothy Rows in the small mining village of Carronshore, just a few miles from Falkirk, on 12 April 1923. He was the youngest of five children, two girls and three boys, born to father James, who worked in the local pit, and mother Agnes, née Jenkins, who had married in September 1907. Like most children at that time he honed his early footballing skills playing either in the street or local park before progressing to organised football at primary school. He gained early representative recognition when he was selected at inside-left for the Falkirk and District Primary Schools side that won the East of Scotland and County Cups during the 1936–37 season, as well as finishing runners-up in the Scottish Cup. Teammates included future Scottish internationals Bobby Brown and George Young of Rangers and Davie Lapsley, who would go on to star for St Mirren. Recently demobbed from the Royal Navy, he had seen service on the Russian convoys as a torpedo man aboard the destroyer HMS *Bulldog*. Just before Turnbull joined the ship the *Bulldog* had gained fame when several of its crew, at great personal risk, boarded a sinking German submarine to capture an Enigma code machine, the incident having no small part to play in shaping the later course of the war.

Spotted playing in only his first game for nearby Grangemouth Junior side Forth Rangers, against Dunipace in a local Cup semi-final at Brockville, Turnbull was invited to Easter Road the following day for signing talks with Hibs' legendary manager Willie McCartney. On the instructions of an older brother who had accompanied him on the trip to Edinburgh, Turnbull had no intention of signing a contract, but potent McCartney arguments and the go-ahead from the brother (who had meanwhile been fortified by several large whiskies by the astute manager) had convinced him that he would be doing the right thing. With the offer of a £20 signing-on fee, and a suggestion that he could be taken on the forthcoming tour of Czechoslovakia, he duly signed and was promptly left at home as the Hibernian party made its way overseas for the club's first continental tour since the 1920s.

It had been Swan's idea to take the team abroad, and once again he was far ahead of his time. While other sides either stayed at home or arranged pre-season tours to the Scottish Highlands, he started a habit that would continue for many years. Swan felt that playing foreign teams of stature – and Hibs usually played against top class opposition on these trips – could do nothing but enhance the experience and skill of the side, to say nothing of improving camaraderie among the players. He saw himself and his team as soccer missionaries, travelling throughout war-ravaged Europe, helping to 'cement relationships', as he often put it. Indeed, so often did he use the phrase on one trip abroad, that in the end both the players and the other members of the party were fed up hearing it. The upshot was that a journalist deposited a small bag of cement in his bed one night, in place of the usual pig-iron hot water bottle. It is not known if Harry enjoyed the joke.

By now Swan had gained deserved respect and a reputation as a man of vision, and there would be few innovations in the game in which he would not play a major part right up until the day he retired as a director at Easter Road. Like most mortals, he was occasionally wrong, but far more often right. Among the many predictions he would make, long before they came to pass, were sponsorship within the game, European competition, the use of floodlights, deconstruction of the Leagues (the 10-team Premier League would come almost two decades later) and later, after a particularly tousy Hibs versus Hearts game at Easter Road in the early 60s that had been blighted throughout by crowd trouble, he stated that perhaps they, the chairmen of the First Division clubs, had a duty to consider the construction of all-seater stadiums which would, he felt, alleviate the problem. It would be nearly 30 years before the all-seater stadium would be considered the norm.

The tour of war-devastated Czechoslovakia in the summer of 1946 was hailed as a fantastic success despite Hibs winning only two of the four games played. The Scots were credited with re-establishing the good reputation of British sport after a visit to the country a few months earlier by FA Cup-winners Derby County. The English side had been warmly received by their hosts but had proved disappointing guests, with displays of petulance and unexpected bad sportsmanship on the field. According to local newspaper reports, Hibs, even when losing, 'never once resorted to rough, foul, or unfair tactics, and maintained a discipline and dignity throughout the four game visit'. The club was gaining a fine reputation for Scotland, and the people of war-ravaged Czechoslovakia took the Scottish side to their hearts. Refereeing standards had been poor, but the visitors had accepted the officials' decisions at all times, although manager McCartney, less than diplomatically, suggested later that perhaps British referees should travel abroad to show their foreign counterparts how it should be done.

The trip itself had started ominously when, on the journey between Amsterdam and Prague, the sound of an explosion was heard, accompanied by a blinding flash of flame. The plane suddenly dropped several hundred feet before the pilot eventually regained control. The cause of the explosion was never discovered, but the experience had a disconcerting effect on the passengers, many of whom had never flown before, including manager Willie McCartney.

Hibs' first game ended with an excellent 3–1 victory over the illustrious Sparta Prague. The fixture had generated incredible excitement and fully 40,000 had packed into the stadium in anticipation. After this game, and also after the final fixture of the tour against Slavia Prague, McCartney had broadcast a match report back to the people of Scotland over the airwaves. The other tour results were Brno 3–Hibs 1, Vitkovice 1–Hibs 7, and Slavia 3–Hibs 2.

Wherever they went the Scots were fêted, attending several official receptions and banquets. There had also been a visit to the circus and several of the party had attended the trial of a suspected wartime collaborator in the people's court in Prague Town Hall. The tour was not without its humour, however. On the coach journey between Brno and Ostravia, the party had stopped at a small town for lunch. As there was a local football match in progress, Harry Swan, manager McCartney and some of the players decided to take a look. Their appearance, particularly that of McCartney, created great excitement among the locals, who mistook the manager for Winston Churchill, surrounding him brandishing 'V' signs in his direction. Joining in the spirit of the occasion, Harry Swan made a concerted but vain attempt to obtain a cigar to perpetuate the joke.

There would be a sad ending to the tour for one player. Only after arriving back in London would goalkeeper Jimmy Kerr learn of the death of his mother.

Enter Eddie Turnbull and Willie Ormond, and Scottish Cup Final Defeat

The first official post-war League Championship, now called the 'A' Division, kicked-off on 10 August 1946. The freshly painted Easter Road glistened in the warm summer sunshine as a large crowd gathered in the ground well before the kick-off in great anticipation for the match with Queen of the South. They were not to be disappointed. Kicking down the famous slope, 35,000 saw John Cuthbertson score Hibs' first post-war goal in the very first minute of the game when he smashed an Aitkenhead cross high into the roof of the net. Four-goal Jock Weir, who was so fast his feet sometimes acted quicker than his brain, was Hibs' star performer as he led the Greens to a 9–1 rout of the unfortunate Dumfries side. Three goals ahead after just 20 minutes, and four in front at the interval, Hibs, and Weir in particular, resumed where they had left off in the second half as Smith and 'Cubbie' taunted the poor Queens defence, who had no answer to the fast and decisive play of a superior team who scored another five times before the end.

Hibernian: Kerr, Howie, Shaw, Kean, Aird, McCabe, Smith, Cuthbertson, Weir, Buchanan, Aitkenhead.

That same afternoon, at Palmerson, the reserves were also in goal-hungry mood, running out 7–2 winners. Among the goalscorers were the teenage Lawrie Reilly and inside-left Eddie Turnbull, who was playing his first-ever competitive game for Hibs.

Billy Houliston, soon to win a Scotland cap while playing for the unfashionable club, scored one of the Doonhamers' goals. For the record, the second XI that day, several of whom would become first-team regulars, were: Brown, Govan, Ross, Fraser, Waldie, Cairns, Reilly, Wright, Milne, Turnbull and Nutley.

A post-war relaxation of the entertainment tax brought in as a wartime measure in 1940 had allowed terracing admission charges to be reduced from 1s 6d to 1s 3d, but not if you lived in Scotland. Clubs north of the border refused point blank to implement the change, irrespective of the tax cut, claiming that the perilous financial state of the game justified the retention of the previous admission charge. It was a standpoint that irritated Chancellor Dalton enough for him to threaten to 'exercise his prerogative' to force the change. Always at the forefront of any issue involving Scottish football, Harry Swan thought it 'unfortunate that the Chancellor had not sought the reasons for the Scottish clubs' recalcitrance in the matter'. Denying any allegation of profiteering, Swan added that 'The increase in wages and overhead charges, make it a financial necessity for the retention of the former rate of admission'. The average wage in Scotland for a top-class professional footballer at that time had risen from the wartime maximum rate of £4 per week to £10. The situation was closely monitored by the Treasury, but even a change of chancellor would make no difference to the Scottish clubs' attitude, although it would not be the last that was heard of the matter. All the teams south of the border had initiated the new cut rates immediately, but, somewhat ludicrously, several had also retained a few gates at the former admission price for 'anyone wishing to use them', or should that be daft enough to use them?

In the second League game of the season, important only for the fact that they were facing old adversaries Rangers at Ibrox, the Light Blues were awarded a penalty in the very first minute, which was converted by George Young. According to the press at the time, 'The large crowd inside the ground was mystified when referee Jackson awarded the home side a penalty when a harmless Gillick shot clearly hit Cuthbertson on the knee'. The suspect award did Rangers no good, however, as goals from Aitkenhead and Weir gave Hibs a 2–1 victory.

If any confirmation of Hibs' rising stature was still required, the Rangers official handbook that afternoon declared 'that a challenge was welcomed from half a dozen sides in the coming season, but in our opinion, only Hibs look capable of ending our domination'. Whether they desired only a challenge, or would have welcomed an end to their near monopoly of the Scottish game, is open to interpretation.

A great sadness hung over Easter Road at the end of August, with the news of the death of Paddy Cannon. Paddy had been associated with Hibs for over 50 years, joining the club in 1896, the year of Harry Swan's birth. Previously an athlete, or pedestrian as it was known at the time, this former great of the track served Hibs faithfully first as trainer, then groundsman for most of this time, and had still been involved at the stadium on a daily basis until a short while before. He was in his 90th year.

The following day, as Hibs were beating Hamilton Accies at Easter Road, the Airdrie players took the field at Broomfield for their match against Albion Rovers wearing numbered shirts, an event that created considerable interest among the spectators and members of the press. The numbering of players' jerseys had first been used at the 1933 FA Cup Final between Everton and Manchester City and had been compulsory in England since 1939. Third Lanark would soon follow the trend, as would Hearts and Dundee United, but as yet it was an innovation that was not a widely accepted feature north of the border.

In the game against Aberdeen, Gordon Smith was injured after only eight minutes, leaving him a virtual passenger on the wing. He failed to reappear after the interval, leaving Hibs in those pre-substitutes days to play the entire second half with only 10 men as they went down to their first defeat of the season. He would miss the next few games, but Smith's misfortune would give the young Reilly, whose form in the reserves had continued to impress, his first start of the current campaign, and he was on the right wing in time for the first Edinburgh derby of the season at the beginning of September. After a hard-fought 90 minutes at Easter Road, watched by a larger-than-average crowd, many of whom had come to witness Tommy Walker's farewell performance in a maroon shirt before his impending transfer to Chelsea, a goal by McRae gave the visitors a narrow win and both points.

By this time Bobby Nutley had been transferred to Portsmouth for £2,500, and the unsettled Arthur Milne had moved to St Mirren for almost the same figure. In 1937 the highly rated Milne, then with Dundee United, had been on loan at Liverpool, but taking advantage of a registration slip-up between both clubs, Hibs stepped in to secure the services of the £2,000-rated player for nothing. Even allowing for the fact that an SFA committee later ordered the Edinburgh club to pay Dundee United £750 compensation, nine years service in a green-and-white shirt, during which he scored over 100 goals, and a large profit at the end to satisfy treasurer Kenny McIntyre, represented a fantastic piece of business for the club.

At the end of the month Rangers eventually won the Reserve League Cup Final held over from the previous season after a replay at Easter Road. The drive of the injured Turnbull, which had been inspirational in helping his side recover from a 2–0 deficit in the first game at Hampden to force a

3–3 draw, was badly missed in the replay as the home side went down 4–0 to deny the Edinburgh youngsters a clean sweep of the previous season's honours.

It was around this time that a new-look League Cup competition was launched, with a trophy donated by the Clyde chairman and Scottish League president John McMahon. A four-week break from the League programme allowed the initial section matches of the tournament to be staged. The League Cup was actually a continuation of the Southern League Cup that had been contested during the war, but this time included sides from the lower League. As before, teams in the new competition were divided into groups of four, playing each other on a home and away basis, the top side in each group going forward to the quarter-finals. Hibs' inaugural tie in a tournament that exists to this day was against Celtic at Easter Road, on Saturday 21 September 1946. Celtic had failed to recapture the pre-war form that had seen them win two League titles inside three years, and one newspaper reporter opined that this game would give 'the Edinburgh public the opportunity to see this amazing Celtic side which had descended to depths hitherto unknown in the club's history'. It would not be as easy as many first thought, but a crowd of 30,000 saw the home side eventually triumph 4–2 despite being level at the break, after a strike by former Hib Tommy Bogan in the 25th minute had cancelled out an earlier counter from Aitkenhead.

The reserves had been in great form in recent weeks and now topped the League table with eight wins and a draw from their first 10 games, and in the corresponding reserve fixture between the sides at Parkhead, four goals from Reilly set his side well on the way to an impressive 7–0 win. Both Turnbull and Reilly had played particularly well, and on current form it was clear that they could not be held back much longer.

For the first team, encouraging wins against Hamilton, twice, and Third Lanark, with a 1–1 draw at Parkhead sandwiched in between, left Hibs needing just one point from their final section game against Third Lanark at Hampden (Cathkin at that time was unavailable) to progress into the later stages of the inaugural competition.

Eddie Turnbull made his competitive debut for the club at Hampden in the 2–1 League Cup win over Thirds on Saturday 26 October. By this time Gordon Smith had returned to the side after missing seven games through injury, with Reilly back in the reserves. The newcomer was Hibs' Man of the Match, making an immediate impact by forcing a great save from the 'keeper in the very first minute, before setting up the opening goal for Smith and scoring the winner himself. He would rarely be out of the first team again, barring injury, during the next 14 years. Turnbull had actually made his first full appearance at Easter Road 11 days earlier in Hibs' friendly match against Sparta AC, Lawrie Reilly deputising for Archie Buchanan at half-time, and had given a good account of himself. It was a momentous day for other reasons. Earlier that morning the Nazi war criminals found guilty of crimes against humanity at Nuremberg after an eight-month trial that had both gripped and horrified the world made the short walk to the gallows, bringing closure to one of the worst periods in world history.

On 18 November, shortly after the club had denied a rumour of a bid by Blackburn Rovers for both Gordon Smith and Jock Weir, Hibs were involved in surprise transfer activity, but this time as buyers. After protracted talks at Ochilview that lasted well into the night, 21-year-old outside-left Willie Ormond, like Turnbull a native of the Falkirk area who had also seen service with the Royal Navy during the war, was signed from Second Division Stenhousemuir for a fee around the £2,000 mark. Ormond first saw the light of day at No. 32 Napier Place in Falkirk on 23 February 1926, born to father Robert, an ironmoulder in a local foundry, and mother Margaret, née McNaughton, who had married the previous year. He was one of four brothers, the youngest of whom would die from natural causes during the war aged just 17. Football ran in the family and brothers Robert and Gilbert would both later see service with Airdrie in the late 1950s. The former Gairdoch Juveniles player had joined Stenhousemuir 17 months before on leaving the Royal Navy, and he had quickly gained a tremendous reputation with the Second Division side as a difficult and extremely dangerous opponent.

This was not to be the end of the Hibs manager's travels. As well as signing the former Hutchison Vale goalkeeper George Farm from Armadale Thistle, in fierce competition with both Hearts and Newcastle United, just a few days after the acquisition of Ormond, Willie McCartney motored to the Borders on Monday 25 November to sign 17-year-old Selkirk player Bobby Johnstone. Johnstone at the time was at the centre of a signing controversy between Selkirk and juvenile side Newtongrange Bluebell, who both claimed the player's registration. With the SFA involved in the dispute, the matter was eventually settled to the satisfaction of both parties, leaving the way open for the player to accept the terms offered by McCartney, and he became a Hibs player soon after. No one could possibly know it at the time, but the final cog in a machine that would in time combine to form arguably the greatest forward line Scotland has ever seen was now in place.

Bobby Johnstone was born at No.11 Cannon Street in the sleepy Border town of Selkirk on 7 September 1929, the only boy of five children born to father George and mother Elizabeth. At the time George played full-back for the local Selkirk side, but unlike his son in later years, he was not blessed with a fantastic football brain and sublime skills, his talents being of the more rugged and robust variety. Like most young boys at that time Bobby was keen on many sports, gaining his early football education either kicking a ball about in the street or the local park. A Hearts supporter from an early age, Johnstone first played organised football with the school sides and also the local youth club. On leaving school he worked for a time as an apprentice painter and decorator for a local firm, and he had by then progressed to a better class of football with both Newtongrange Star and Newtongrange Bluebell. It was at this time that fate, Willie McCartney and Hibs entered the scene to the eternal benefit of the Scottish and, in time, English game.

It is said that chance often plays a major part in destiny and, while there is absolutely no doubt that Willie Ormond would have made the breakthrough to the Easter Road first team sooner rather than later, providence would have a part to play in him making an earlier than expected debut. Ormond had played his first game in Hibs colours, forming a left-wing partnership with Archie Buchanan, with Reilly on the right, against Partick Thistle reserves at Firhill five days after signing for the club, and he had scored his first goal in a 4–0 victory over St Mirren's second team at the end of the month. An injury to regular outside-left Johnny Aitkenhead at Love Street that same afternoon proved worse than was first thought, and after only a handful of reserve-team outings Willie Ormond made his first-team debut on 7 December 1946, replacing Aitkenhead on the left wing in Hibs' 3–1 victory over Queen of the South in Dumfries. For the popular Johnny Aitkenhead the injury would not only require surgery and a lengthy spell in plaster, but it would also eventually spell the end of his Easter Road career.

Even at this stage Ormond's left foot was being 'favourably admired', and a newspaper report of the game stated somewhat prophetically that although the former Stenhousemuir player 'had had a severe test in his first League outing, he had the capabilities to make it in the big time'. That afternoon Ormond had formed a left-wing partnership with Eddie Turnbull, and with Gordon Smith at outside-right, three-fifths of what was soon to become a legendary five were already in place.

Seven days after his first appearance, Ormond became an instant hero with the home fans when he scored his first senior goal for the club in a 1–1 draw with Rangers at Easter Road, a game that saw both Shaw brothers, Davie of Hibs and Jock of Rangers, captaining their respective sides. With the gates due to open at 12.30, large queues for the 2.15 kick-off had started forming as early as 11 o'clock in the morning for a match regarded by many, even that early, as possibly the most decisive of that season's Championship race. Behind at the interval, a Smith and Weir-inspired Hibs mounted a storming comeback in the second half, and their efforts were rewarded with a share of the points. The home side were furious to be denied a stonewall penalty after Turnbull had clearly been brought down from behind as he raced into the box late in the game, but the referee adjudged the offence to have taken place outside the area. Justice was done, however, when Ormond smashed home a deserved last-minute equalising goal from the resulting free-kick, to the obvious delight of the home fans among the huge 42,000 crowd. The match programme for the game had reminded us that 'Fans were becoming more and more seat minded, and it is incumbent on club boards to provide more cover and better facilities for the supporters'. It was a topic that had no doubt already been considered by the ever-vigilant Harry Swan.

At Tynecastle on New Year's Day, sweet revenge was gained over bitter rivals Hearts for the earlier League defeat at Easter Road. The 3–2 victory, with Hibs scoring twice in the space of a minute, saw 1947 off to a great start, followed 24 hours later by a 3–1 home win against Queen's Park; although a 1–1 draw against a Morton side that included goalkeeper Jimmy Cowan a few days later cost second-placed Hibs the chance to leapfrog League leaders Rangers, who also drew that afternoon.

Football took a back seat to tragedy on 8 January, with the news that 14 miners had lost their lives underground in the West Calder shale mine disaster. After a goalless draw at Hamilton a few days later, Harry Swan announced that Hibs would be contributing 100 guineas to the disaster fund.

Later that month, an 8–0 away win over Alloa saw the beginning of a sequence of Cup victories that would ultimately end in Hibs reaching the first post-war Scottish Cup Final. A capacity 14,000 all-ticket crowd watched the right-wing trio of Smith, Finnegan and Weir inspire the visitors to an easier win than many expected, with four-goal Jock Weir, just returned to the side after a four-week absence owing to injury, the hero of the hour.

Weir arrived at the ground for training on the Monday to be notified by trainer McColl that he was wanted 'upstairs'. Rejoining his colleagues a short while later, clutching a one-way railway warrant, he collected his already parcelled boots and left. He had been transferred to Blackburn Rovers for £10,000, the deal being completed in the Caledonian Hotel that evening. When Harry Swan wanted you to go, you went, and quickly. The figure was a record-equalling fee for a transfer between Scottish and English clubs, with Blackpool reported to have paid Celtic a similar figure for inside-forward Willie Buchan in 1937. Although failing to complete the final three months of the season at Easter Road, Weir would still finish as Hibs' top goalscorer with 23 goals in all competitions. A few weeks after Weir's move south, newspaper readers were astonished to read that, following yet another big transfer deal, Blackburn had fielded a forward line (five players) costing an amazing £33,000 to assemble.

Lawrie Reilly replaced the transferred Weir for the game against Motherwell at Easter Road the following Saturday. With Finnigan in his usual place at inside-right, it was the first time that four of the soon-to-be-famous quintet had lined up together. It was not an auspicious occasion, however, with Hibs losing 2–1 to a better team. Although the home side took great credit for their endeavour, somewhat surprisingly the forwards were criticised for their reluctance to take a chance in front of goal.

Well aware that the first-team squad needed strengthening, particularly after the sale of Weir, McCartney travelled to England to sign wing-half John Wardlaw from Third Division Ipswich Town, a player who would fail to make an impact at Easter Road, and two weeks later Hibs paid Clyde £9,500, then a record fee between two Scottish clubs, for the services of Leslie Johnstone. Cup-tied Johnstone, who had taken over as an agreed substitute for leg-break victim Tommy Bogan in the wartime international against England in 1945, would have to exercise patience before making his debut, with Hibs playing only Cup games during the next few weeks.

The winter of 1947 was one of the worst on record, heavy falls of snow and freezing conditions during the month of February playing havoc with the fixture list. During this time Hibs managed to fit in only one game, a no-score third-round Scottish Cup tie against Rangers at Ibrox on 22 February. The match between the best two sides in the country at that time generated enormous interest among the supporters and at the kick-off there were almost 100,000 spectators packed inside the ground. With both Shaw brothers again captaining their respective sides, the visitors had by far the best of the action, and only goalline clearances by Young and 'Tiger' Shaw gave Rangers a somewhat fortunate second chance in Edinburgh.

In the boardroom after the game, Harry Swan was surprised to be approached by a delegation of Rangers directors led by chairman James Bowie, who sounded out the possibility of the replay being played back at Ibrox, with the guarantee of another six-figure gate, if the necessary permission could be gained, perhaps under the wartime emergency regulations which were then technically still in place. Not only was the suggestion dismissed out of hand, but Swan also insisted bluntly that 'Hibs will play Rangers at Easter Road, and will beat them'.

In the Ibrox dressing room, shortly after the intriguing discussion with the Rangers directors, Harry Swan presented the players concerned with their runners'-up medals from the previous season's unsuccessful Victory Cup Final. Only Milne and Nutley were absent from the 11 that had played that day, and their medals were duly forwarded on to them.

So great was the demand for the forthcoming all-ticket Scottish Cup replay with Rangers at Easter Road, that several outlets in the city, including the well-known sports shop Thornton's in Princes Street, were used to distribute the precious briefs. Fans had started queuing outside the sports shop on the evening before the sale, and by eight o'clock in the morning a crowd estimated to be in the region of 2,000 lined the pavement four or five deep. Before the replay, however, there was still the business of the League Cup quarter-final ties against Airdrie, which had been carried over from October.

The first leg at Broomfield produced a cracking match despite being played on a treacherous snow-covered pitch, the game ending four apiece. A heavy fall the previous night had left the field covered with a blanket of snow 6-10in deep in places, and only the work of several bulldozers and the sterling efforts of over 100 volunteers managed to clear the playing surface sufficiently to allow the match to proceed. Hat-tricks by both Gordon Smith for Hibs and Bobby Flavell for the home side whetted the fans' appetite for another exciting clash in the return leg in Edinburgh. Well ahead in the first half, the visitors fell away after the break as Airdrie mounted a revival to take the lead, only for Smith to score his third goal of the game when heading home a Peat cross near the end to earn a draw. There had been great joviality during the interval when a snowball fight between the fans took place using ammunition from the huge mounds of snow piled high on the trackside. As the teams returned to the field the fans turned their attentions to the policemen on duty, much to the consternation of the boys in blue, one young constable reportedly ending up resembling a snowman.

The second leg at Easter Road had created its own piece of football history. The powers that be had earlier decided that in the event of the scores finishing level after 90 minutes of play and extra-time, a 'golden goal' rule would apply. With the match still goalless after extra-time, Willie Finnegan was on hand to score the only goal of the game in the 125th minute to send Hibs into the semi-finals and yet another meeting with their arch rivals from Govan.

Meanwhile, for the Scottish Cup replay with Rangers, it was reported that just under 52,000 tickets had been sold, a new ground record for Easter Road, beating the previous best of 43,000, and such was the incredible interest in the game that it was said that 50,000 more could well have been sold. On the advice of the police, the game was held up for several minutes to allow the thousands of fans still outside the ground at kick-off time to gain access into the stadium, and those who were able watched another keenly contested game between the sides that looked certain to extend into extra-time with the match still goalless near the end. With just five minutes remaining, Gordon Smith, who had been a thorn in the side of the Rangers defence all afternoon, started a great run down the slope, and his pass to Cuthbertson was transferred to Ormond, who steadied himself momentarily before crashing a great left-foot drive past Brown in the Rangers goal to bulge the net. Sixty seconds later the game was over and Hibs were in the quarter-finals after Cuthbertson had driven home Hibs' second from close range after the visiting 'keeper could only parry a vicious Smith free-kick.

While the game was still in progress countless spectators had left the ground, unable to see any of the action taking place on the pitch, and the volunteer ambulance men were kept busy dealing with a seemingly endless procession of minor injuries. One attendant related the otherwise humorous tale of a fan who had sustained a suspected fracture of the leg. On hearing the call for an ambulance, the supporter limped away, insisting that he had come to see the match and that was what he fully intended to do.

A 2–0 Scottish Cup quarter-final victory over Dumbarton, whose late arrival at Easter Road due to adverse weather conditions ensured that the game kicked-off 23 minutes late, was good enough to send Hibs through to their second Cup semi-final in 10 days. Smith opened the scoring after just 30 seconds when he finished off a great three-man move by smashing an unstoppable thunderbolt into the top corner of the net, and although Dumbarton made a fight of it, a spectacular 30-yard drive from Cuthbertson midway through the second half ended the game as a contest.

Both the League Cup and Scottish Cup semi-finals were played on consecutive Saturdays in March. In the first, against Rangers at Hampden, a second-half goal by Cuthbertson was little consolation against the three scored by Rangers in the first period, and Hibs were out of the League Cup. Again there had been much talk in the city of a possible all-Edinburgh Cup Final, including the use of Murrayfield for the game; indeed, Swan had made provisional enquiries about its use, but the 'best laid plans…'. Hearts were beaten 6–2 by Aberdeen that same afternoon.

In the Scottish Cup semi-final against Motherwell, also played at Hampden, a goal against the run of play by Eddie Turnbull, wearing the number-nine jersey, gave Hibs a first-half lead, and only a magnificent performance by Hibs goalkeeper Kerr enabled the sides to change ends with the Edinburgh men still in the lead. The second period was played at a breathtaking pace, but despite both sides coming close on several occasions, the scoreline remained the same until 12 minutes from the end when Howie was adjudged to have handled inside the box while trying to protect his face from the ball. Motherwell scored from the resulting spot-kick to force extra-time. There was no more scoring during the extra 20 minutes, and for the second time in just over three weeks the golden goal rule came into operation. It was almost poetic justice when Howie made amends for his earlier penalty mistake by scoring the winning goal in the 142nd minute. Motherwell 'keeper Johnstone had come right to the edge of his box before clearing from his hands. Howie, who was just inside his own half, caught the goalkeeper's punt first time, and the ball soared over the bemused custodian and into the net, sending Hibs into their first Scottish Cup Final for 23 years. There was some doubt as to who was the most surprised, Howie or 'keeper Johnstone.

The golden goal ruling against both Airdrie and Motherwell had come into operation because the wartime 'emergency regulations', brought in to reduce travelling difficulties in the case of replayed matches, still applied if both clubs agreed. The ruling meant that if the game was still level at the end of 90 minutes, then extra-time in the shape of two periods of 10 minutes would be played. If the game was still level, then extra 10-minute periods would be played until one side scored what would be deemed the winner. Hibs' Cup Final opponents Aberdeen had also encountered the golden goal regulation in an earlier round, but in their case they had been let off lightly, 'only' being required to play 129 minutes against Dundee in the quarter-final. Both games, however, paled into insignificance compared to the wartime FA Cup tie between Cardiff City and Bristol City. Drawing 3–3 at the end of the regulation 90 minutes, the deciding goal was scored at 6.40, 220 minutes after first kicking-off.

The golden goal proved highly unpopular with players and supporters alike, and it was soon replaced by 'normal' extra-time, with a replay if necessary. The Scottish authorities had favoured a return to the wartime ruling of the use of corner-kicks to settle matters, but thankfully they had been outvoted by the other Home associations.

Because of the consecutive Cup-ties, Leslie Johnstone had been forced to watch from the sidelines for several weeks, and he finally made his debut for Hibs against Falkirk at Brockville at the beginning of April. Unfortunately, the rain that had been falling steadily all day developed into a deluge, causing the game to be abandoned goalless with 15 minutes remaining. Three other senior games in the area had also been called off, and indeed the weather had been so bad during the match that a Falkirk player had collapsed and been taken from the field, said to be suffering from hypothermia.

Meanwhile, Cup fever had gripped the green half of Edinburgh. Several days before the Cup Final there was even an unlikely show of support from Mr Alec Irvine, chairman of Hearts, who offered to display the Cup to the crowd before Hearts' friendly match with Chelsea at Tynecastle the following week if Hibs were to return from Hampden victorious.

On Saturday 19 April, Hibernian faced Aberdeen in the 1947 Scottish Cup Final. Supporters were required to cough up the grand sum of 2s for admission to the ground, with prices ranging from 3s for the enclosure to £1 15s for the Centre Stand. There were no special pre-Cup Final training routines for Hibs in those days and the players trained as normal in Edinburgh during the week, although Aberdeen took advantage of several days stay at Largs in the run-up to the game.

The players were said to be in confident mood as they made their way by road from their normal pickup point at the corner of Picardy Place in the capital on the morning of the game, and they emerged from the coach outside Hampden 'singing lustily as though hurling defiance at all comers'. At the pre-match meal, chairman Swan reminded them 'that not only their personal prestige was at stake during the game, but that of the city and the club as well'.

McCartney had selected 12 players for the Cup Final squad, but unfortunately for the youngster, 18-year-old Lawrie Reilly was omitted from the starting 11 and he watched the game from the stand.

In front of 82,140 fans basking in the brilliant summer sunshine, Hibs got off to the best possible start. Aberdeen 'keeper Johnstone allowed a pass back from Taylor to spin through his legs, and 'Cubbie' was on the spot to score the opening goal with less than 60 seconds on the clock. The Dons, however, were in rampant mood, and despite another brilliant performance from Kerr in the Hibs goal, they scored twice in the first 45 minutes, the second a brilliant strike from what looked an impossible angle near the byline by centre-forward Stan Williams, who had guested for Hibs on more than 20 occasions during the war. In the second half Kerr conceded a penalty when he sent Williams crashing to the ground, but the 'keeper redeemed himself by saving the spot-kick. The Edinburgh side failed to find their recent form and in truth Aberdeen were well worth their lead and really should have been ahead by more than one goal. A late switch, with Smith moving to centre-forward, saw Hibs showing some signs of improvement, but in the end there was no doubt that the better side had won.

As the victorious Aberdeen players received the Cup on the field in front of their jubilant fans, the first time the trophy had been presented in public (before then it had been handed to the winning side in the dressing room) the dejected Hibs fans made their weary way back to Edinburgh, wondering if the departed Jock Weir, still at that time Hibs' top goalscorer, might have made a difference had he not been transferred to Blackburn. It was also the first time that medals had been awarded to the losing side in a Scottish Cup Final. Meanwhile, the official party gathered for a somewhat subdued reception at the Central Station Hotel in Glasgow. During the after-match reception the 70 or so assembled guests, including the Hearts chairman Alec Irvine, who had attended the game as a guest of the club, were joined by the reserve-team players who had beaten a strong Morton second team at Cappielow that afternoon. It was later discovered that Willie Finnegan had broken his jaw during the Cup Final while attempting to force the ball and goalkeeper Johnstone over the line, a tactic allowed at the time. The injury was serious enough to require surgery and this was carried out in the Western General Hospital on the Sunday. Finnegan was joined in the same ward by teammate Willie Clark, who had been injured playing for the second team against Morton.

Hibernian: Kerr, Govan, Shaw, Howie, Aird, Kean, Smith, Finnigan, Cuthbertson, Turnbull, Ormond.
Aberdeen: Johnstone, McKenna, Taylor, McLaughlin, Dunlop, Waddell, Harris, Hamilton, Williams, Baird, McCall.
Referee: R. Calder (Rutherglen).

The legendary Bobby Calder had been handed the honour of refereeing the first post-war Scottish Cup Final. Calder, a railway worker from Glasgow, would later find fame as the brilliant Aberdeen chief scout under the stewardship of Eddie Turnbull, and later he was credited with unearthing such gems as Arthur Graham, Jim Smith and Charlie Cooke for the Grampian side. Later, while manager of Hibs in the early 70s, Eddie Turnbull would try unsuccessfully to lure Calder to Easter Road.

A few days after the Final, Hibs signed inside-forward Mick Gallagher from Alloa Athletic. Gallagher had been at Recreation Park only a few months, and although it would take the player some time to establish himself in the League side, he would eventually collect two League Championship medals while at Easter Road and become only the second Hibs player to be capped for the Republic of Ireland when lining up against Luxembourg in 1954.

In the League there were still four games left to play, including the rearranged game against Falkirk, which had been abandoned earlier due to the waterlogged pitch. There was also a Saturday evening match against Third Lanark at Hampden played just a couple of hours after the Great Britain side had defeated the Rest of Europe at the same ground. The Hibs players had been interested spectators as the British side triumphed 6–1 to confirm that there was nothing the foreigners could teach us – sadly an attitude that would prove expensive in the future – before lining up a few hours later on the same pitch, although in front of a much smaller audience than had watched the game that afternoon. All eight points were secured, but it was just not enough to force themselves to the top of the table, and for a third successive season Hibs finished in second place to Rangers, two points behind the champions. Young Reilly had played a few games during the campaign, as had Peat. Bob Stirling had been purchased late in the season from Dumbarton, and although the centre-forward appeared in the final few games of the season he was not the answer, and he was soon on his way. Although he had missed a large part of the season, Jock Weir had prevented Gordon Smith from becoming Hibs' top goalscorer for a fifth consecutive season. Weir had scored 14 times in the League and 23 in all competitions compared to Smith's six and 12 overall, although it should be mentioned that Smith had missed several games because of injury.

On the international front Davie Shaw had played for the full Scotland side against Wales and Northern Ireland, while Gordon Smith had been recalled to the side for the 1–1 draw with England at Wembley. As well as both players, Hugh Shaw had been selected as trainer for the England match and the game against the Rest of Europe. The club had also been well represented in the Scottish League side that faced the Irish League in Belfast. As well as Ormond, who was winning his first representative honour, Kean, Turnbull, Kerr and Govan had been chosen in reserve.

At the end of the season seven players, all youngsters, were given free transfers. Thirty-seven were retained, including leg-break victim Johnny Aitkenhead. As some indication of the talent available to manager Willie McCartney at that time, the second team had made a clean sweep of all the honours available to them, winning the Reserve League Championship, the League Cup, and, just days before the end of the season, they had beaten Rangers in the Final of the Second XI Scottish Cup.

The players, fans and everyone concerned with the club, although desperately disappointed that the first team had ended the season empty-handed, had taken certain comfort from the fact that notice had been served that they were a side to be reckoned with. Confidence remained high that the following season would bring its just rewards.

As a reward for the hard campaign just ended, the club embarked on a five-game tour of Norway and Sweden during the close season, in which 29 goals were scored and just five conceded, including a 3–1 reverse by Norkopping, the only defeat of the trip.

The Death of Willie McCartney and League Championship Success

First contested between Hearts and Arsenal in 1941 to raise money for deserving wartime causes, an 'Edinburgh Select' committee had been formed in 1944 and the fixture had since become an annual event against prominent top-class English sides. Comprising players from both Edinburgh sides and occasionally a guest player, and played on alternate years between Easter Road and Tynecastle, over £9,000 had been raised to date. Now 1946 FA Cup holders Derby County were the visitors to the capital in a precursor to the new season, one that was to prove eventful as far as Hibs were concerned. The popularity of the fixture at that time could be gauged by the fact that fully an hour before kick-off there were 10,000 inside Easter Road, a number that had swelled to well over 30,000 as the teams took the field. Under the captaincy of the legendary English international Raich Carter, who scored one of his side's goals, the visitors won a thrilling match 5–4.

In a change of format for the start of the 1947–48 season, the new campaign began with the League Cup qualifying ties, as opposed to the previous year when the inaugural competition had been played during the season. Hibs paraded new signing Alec Linwood, a £10,000 buy from Middlesborough, at centre-forward in their first game against Hearts at Easter Road. Linwood had been signed on the recommendation of centre-half Peter Aird. In the market for a centre-forward, manager McCartney had quizzed Aird on who had been his most difficult opponent. The defender wasted little time in naming the former international and McCartney moved quickly to secure Linwood's services at Easter Road. Interest in the game against Hearts had been fantastic, so much so that at one point the queuing crowds had lined four deep stretching all the way from the stadium, along both sides of Albion Road, down Easter Road to Drum Terrace,and up as far as Edina Place. During the war, many supporters had been starved of regular football, large numbers of them serving overseas throughout the duration, and now, with little in the way of Saturday afternoon recreational alternatives, the game was enjoying a post-war crowd explosion.

Christened by the press the '£50,000 forward line', Gordon Smith, Leslie Johnstone, Alec Linwood, Eddie Turnbull and Willie Ormond took their places at the kick-off, and it was former Stenhousemuir player Ormond who cancelled out an early opener by Urquhart. Linwood, a wartime Scotland cap, impressed the home fans in his first outing for the club, but a spirited performance by Hearts saw them take both points when Kelly scored the winner two minutes from time to defy a Hibs side that had been reduced to 10 men for most of the second half through injury. Although still not a universal innovation, the Hibs players were now displaying large white numbers on the back of their jerseys.

In the other section games, rampant Hibs scored five against both Airdrie and Clyde at Easter Road, and four more against the latter in the return game, but this meant nothing when another 2–1 defeat by Hearts, this time at Tynecastle, meant the Greens failed to reach the quarter-finals. No one tried harder than Gordon Smith to encourage his side to victory at Tynecastle, but for all his valiant efforts, the outside-right could make little headway against Hearts left-back Tam McKenzie, always a difficult opponent for Smith, while centre-half Parker and wing-half Laing shackled the twin threat of Linwood and Johnstone. There was no luck involved in the victory and Hearts finished worthy winners.

The Championship trail commenced with a Wednesday afternoon visit to Aberdeen, when over 40,000, a record attendance for a midweek game at Pittodrie at that time, crammed into the ground, the huge crowd spilling over onto the running track. More than 200 watched the game from the roof of the enclosure behind the King Street goal, with the police powerless to remove them. Inspired by a dazzling display from Gordon Smith, who was the mastermind behind every Hibs attack, goals by Turnbull and Smith himself gave the visitors a 2–0 victory and some small semblance of revenge for the Scottish Cup Final defeat in April.

The first League game of the season was between the Edinburgh rivals and took place at Tynecastle on 20 September, ending in yet another 2–1 victory for the Gorgie side, the third of the season so far. Although having most of the first-half pressure, Hibs just could not convert their superiority into goals, and the teams turned around at the interval with the score level. In the second half, two late goals from Hearts left the Greens chasing the game, and a goal by Ormond in the final minute was a mere consolation. The scoreline left the Hearts fans asking the facetious question: 'What's the Hibs phone number?' The answer: 'Abbeyhill two-one, two-one!'

The annual report for the previous 12 months, released at the beginning of September, showed that a profit of £16,636 had been made from a gross income of over £82,000, proof that Hibs were on a solid financial footing and had moved into the big money league. As was expected, despite the huge profit, it was again recommended that no dividend should be paid to shareholders. One interesting issue arose from the directors' report when it was revealed that five acres of land had been purchased adjacent to the main terracing that would allow a 'development of the amenities'. Even before the war it had been felt that an extension to the existing terracing was essential, but now it had become absolutely vital to accommodate the huge football-starved post-war crowds that were attending Easter Road. According to the report, the acquisition of this land was the first step towards what was eventually hoped to be a near 100,000 capacity stadium. The perceived snub by the SFA the previous season that had seen Easter Road overlooked as a neutral venue for the originally promised Scottish Cup semi-final matches between Hearts and Rangers, and the Aberdeen and Airdrie replay, now made the Hibs board more determined than ever to go ahead with these ambitious plans. The hope was that the increased capacity of the ground would make it a more attractive location for not only Cup semi-finals, but also the occasional less important international game. A major stumbling block to the scheme, however, was the difficulty in obtaining a building permit. Although the war had ended over two years before, building materials were still in extremely short supply, and with the rebuilding of war-damaged housing a priority it would be some time before the necessary permit could be obtained.

With Lawrie Reilly making his first appearance of the season on the wing as a replacement for the injured Smith, Leslie Johnstone scored his last goal for Hibs at the beginning of October in a 3–2 win over Queen's Park at Hampden. Johnstone had experienced great difficulty in settling in at Easter Road, and rumours of his unhappiness had been circulating for some time. There had been suggestions that resentment towards Johnstone by some of his more experienced teammates, jealous of the record fee paid for the player, had caused him worry, but these remain unsubstantiated. Reports of a bid by Hearts for the player were firmly denied, and the following Friday Johnstone rejoined Clyde for a fee similar to that paid to the Shawfield club eight months before.

With Linwood down with flu, Reilly replaced Johnstone at the centre of the attack, and he scored his first hat-trick for the club in a 6–0 home drubbing of Queen of the South. Both sides took the field wearing black armbands as a mark of respect for Willie McGinnigle, a teammate of both Hugh Shaw and Jimmy McColl in the great Hibs side of the 1920s, who had died earlier that morning. Jimmy Kerr had still not recovered from a hand injury received against Clyde, and his replacement Jock Brown took over for a dozen games, although this was not enough to qualify the giant goalkeeper for a League Championship medal at the end of the season. The win over the Doonhamers saw Hibs move to the top of the table on goal average from both Partick Thistle and Motherwell.

Hibs were now the leading goalscorers in Division A. Smith had scored nine, Leslie Johnstone (then with Clyde), Ormond and Turnbull notched five each, and Reilly had his hat-trick against Queen of the South.

At that time, Hibs' newly-formed third team, playing in the East of Scotland League and based at Whitestone Park in Peebles, were leading the table, as were the reserves, who had been defeated just once so far that term. The third, or C team, had taken the Border League by storm in this, their first season, and at the time they were averaging six goals per game, many being notched by the tiny Border Terrier Bobby Johnstone. Johnstone had made his first appearance for Hibs in the C team's 5–1 victory at Chirnside on Saturday 16 August, alongside fellow newcomer John Ogilvie, who had been signed from Thorniewood United during the summer. Johnstone scored his first goal in Hibs colours in a 4–0 victory over Berwick Rangers at Easter Road seven days later, and he followed this up by scoring four times in a comprehensive defeat of Airdrie the following midweek. There was also a 10–2 victory over Civil Service Strollers, Bobby scoring twice, played at the Inch public park in Edinburgh and watched by only a few dozen spectators, a far cry from the day just a few years in the future when Johnstone would face the might of England at Wembley in front of 100,000 fans. The at times mesmeric ball control and goalscoring prowess of the diminutive inside-right earned him quick promotion to the reserves, and he made his first appearance for the second team against Motherwell at Easter Road on Saturday 1 November 1947. As the diminutive Johnstone was impressing the home fans at Easter Road, over at Fir Park his soon-to-be teammate Gordon Smith was scoring what was described at the time as one of the most spectacular goals of his career in Hibs' 2–0 victory. Collecting the ball in midfield, Smith proceeded to bear down on the Motherwell goal at speed, beating man after man, before splitting the full-backs to prod the ball past the goalkeeper as he fell. The goal was acclaimed by thunderous applause from both sets of supporters.

For Johnstone it would be back to the third team, with only occasional appearances for the reserves, often failing to feature in either team during the latter part of the season due to the fact that he had been among the first to be called up for National Service. Conscription had been reintroduced during the Korean troubles in 1947 for men between the ages of 18 and 26, unless in full-time education or learning a trade. Initially for a six-month period, it was in time increased from one year's service to two, and it remained in place until the end of the 1950s. A major inconvenience for football managers, and not least the players themselves, it was seen by many as a waste of time, disrupting not only work, social and family life, but often also hindering a player's progress into the League side. Lawrie Reilly escaped conscription in rather strange circumstances. Initially exempt because of his apprenticeship as a painter and decorator, he would normally have expected to receive his call-up papers at the end of his training, but somewhat bizarrely, due to the excessive number of inductees that year, the military authorities had decided to exempt those born in the month of October 1928. Both Reilly and teammate Archie Buchanan, born 24 days before the Hibs centre-forward, took full advantage of the unexpected ruling to become full-time players at Easter Road.

Between then and the turn of the year, there would be only one League reverse, a 3–1 defeat at Brockville. This sparkling form was never better illustrated than on 8 November when Gordon Smith, at his brilliant best, scored five goals against Third Lanark, a feat never before accomplished by a wing player in Scotland, although it had been achieved twice in England. Assisted by an Alec Linwood hat-trick, Hibs demolished poor Thirds 8–0, and such was Hibs' superiority that the scoreline flattered Thirds considerably. The win meant that Hibs were now lying handy in second place, only one point behind leaders Partick Thistle. Smith's amazing goalscoring record would not be broken until April 1959, when Harry Melrose scored six from the left-wing position in Dunfermline's 10–1 home win against Partick Thistle. Incredibly, Melrose's goals had been scored in a relegation battle as the Pars battled to beat the drop, eventually securing safety by just one point.

The international selectors had been present at Fir Park when Gordon Smith scored his spectacular strike in Hibs' 2–0 victory earlier in the month, and both he and full-back Jock Govan, thought by many to be the first proper overlapping full-back in the country, were selected for the Scotland side to face Wales at Hampden later in the month. Against Motherwell Smith had tormented full-back Shaw throughout the 90 minutes, with wing colleague Willie Ormond, Hibs' other goalscorer, also in magnificent form against right-back Kilmarnock. Ormond's scintillating performance that day compelled the Motherwell manager to describe the player as 'the best outside-left in Scotland without doubt' and earn the former Royal Navy man his first international recognition when he was named in the reserve side for Scotland's game against Wales. Even this early in his Easter Road career, the consistently brilliant performances of Ormond had attracted a long list of admirers on both sides of the border. Representatives from Preston North End and several others were believed to have had the player watched, although as yet no formal bid had been received.

The Scotland game would end in disappointment for the Hibs contingent. Like Smith, who yet again failed to recapture his club form while wearing the dark blue jersey, Govan was a disappointment, and it was a humiliating night for both as tiny Wales humbled the Scots 2–1 on their own ground.

On the field things were going well, but the large Hibs support were stunned just a few days before Christmas when the recently capped Jock Govan tabled a transfer request after a dispute with the club over a benefit payment. This was closely followed by a similar demand from Sammy Kean for the same reason. According to Scottish League regulations at that time, players were entitled to a loyalty payment by the club after five years' service, usually about £650 less tax, later rising to £750, although the amount was at the discretion of the club. The authorities had already informed both players that service during the war years did not count, as a separate payment had already been made to cover this period. Consequently, Hibs, or Harry Swan, considered that both Govan and Kean had failed to qualify for the payment, hence both players' unrest. The dispute was eventually settled, but the transfer demands were just two of an epidemic of similar requests then sweeping the country, all for the same reason. With transfer fees beginning to spiral out of control, and £10,000 transactions becoming common, another reason for discontent among players at the time was the derisory amount paid to those involved in the deals, which bore little relation to the high fees paid to the clubs. More enlightened times would eventually see the players receive a fairer share of any transaction, but it would be almost 15 years before the change.

Sweet revenge was gained for the defeats earlier in the season when odds-on favourites Hibs beat Hearts 3–1 at Easter Road on New Year's Day, a result that left the Gorgie side in a perilous position near the foot of the League table, only two points above bottom-placed Airdrie. The gates had been opened two hours before the 2pm kick-off to accommodate the expected huge crowd, but all was not well among a section of the support. For some time there had been complaints regarding the 'inflated prices' charged by Hibs and many other clubs for entry to the grandstand for the all-ticket 'bigger' games. At that time, because a guaranteed percentage of the gate, not including the stand or enclosure, was required to be paid to the visiting side, the authorities regulated prices for the terracing. Clubs, however, were free to charge whatever they liked for entry into the other areas. The practice led 'Disgusted' to complain in the newspapers that 'the football public were being exploited. The increase in prices for selected matches is part and parcel of a commercial racket that should be condemned by all who love the game'.

Free-spending Blackburn Rovers were again involved in transfer speculation, this time linking them with an interest in either Govan or Davie Shaw, but this was immediately denied by manager Shaw. At that time hardly a week went by without interest from some club or other in one of the Easter Road players. Smith was an obvious target, and as already mentioned Preston North End were credited with an interest in Ormond. Both Newcastle United and Sunderland were keen to sign Eddie Turnbull. Smith himself would relate in later years that the club had seriously considered selling Turnbull to Newcastle, but that he, recognising the value of the player to the team, had strongly advised against it. Whether Smith's influence made any difference or not, Turnbull stayed at Easter Road for the rest of his career, and although perhaps lacking the individual talents of his other front-line colleagues, his value during the League Championship years and later cannot be underestimated.

Hibs, however, were involved in the transfer market when goalkeeper Jock Brown was sold to Dundee. Brown, father of future Scottish rugby internationals Gordon and Peter, had won a Scottish Cup medal with Clyde when they defeated Motherwell in the 1939 Final after disposing of Hibs in the semis, and had been capped for Scotland against Wales that same season. Joining Hibs in 1942, the 'keeper had been unable to hold down a regular first-team place despite deputising for the injured Kerr earlier in the season. Brown would soon be involved in end-of-season drama at Dens Park, when visitors Celtic, who required both points to guarantee First Division survival, were drawing 2–2 in the final minute of the match. In the dying seconds former Easter Road colleague Jock Weir, now playing for the Parkhead side, forced the ball over the line to ensure Celtic's safety from relegation for the first time ever, breaking Brown's thumb in the process, an injury that was evident until to the end of his days.

On 12 January 1948, the annual Dinner Dance was again held in the North British Hotel in Princes Street. Shortly after midnight, the players, dignitaries and invited guests joined in an impromptu rendition of *Happy Birthday* in honour of chairman Swan, who was celebrating his 52nd birthday. Manager Willie McCartney, giving one of his last-ever addresses on behalf of the club, spoke of the 'good fortune of Hibernian Football Club in possessing such a happy spirit'.

The following Saturday, as Hibs were defeating Queen of the South 3–0 at Palmerston to stay in the Championship race, goalkeeper Jock Brown was in unbeatable form at Tynecastle as Dundee defeated bottom-of-the-table Hearts. In midweek the Gorgie club had refused Hibs' offer of assistance in the shape of players on loan. Hearts were reminded that the offer was still open, but again a polite refusal was offered. Relegation for either Edinburgh side would also be a serious financial setback for the other, and in the interest of neither. It was not the first time such a transaction had been proffered. In a similar but reversed situation in the 30s, Hibs had accepted the use of a Hearts player, namely goalkeeper Willie Waugh, to stave off a similar threat of relegation.

The Scottish Cup campaign got underway on 24 January 1948 when Hibs travelled to Cliftonville to face Albion Rovers. It was a bitterly cold day, and as his team was struggling to an unconvincing 2–0 victory against resolute opponents, thanks to two goals from the recalled Cuthbertson, manager McCartney complained of feeling unwell near the end of the game. It was thought best that he should leave immediately and director Wilson Terris and Eddie Turnbull, who was not playing that day because of injury, accompanied him to his home at No.44 Hillpark Avenue (now Queensferry Road) in Edinburgh. It was only later that evening, when Turnbull was leaving an Edinburgh dance hall, that he discovered that McCartney had died from a massive coronary, leaving a widow, a son and three daughters. Scanning the billboards of the late-night editions of the following day's newspapers, Turnbull was stunned. McCartney had been larger than life, and it seemed inconceivable that the person who along with Harry Swan had done so much to force Hibs to the forefront of the Scottish game, was gone.

After a private ceremony at his home on the Tuesday morning, the funeral took place at Warriston Crematorium, the coffin being carried into the main chapel by senior players Finnigan, Govan, Kerr, Kean, Combe and captain Davie Shaw. A large crowd, many from the world of football, including the president and secretaries of both the SFA and the Scottish League, were in attendance to pay their own tribute to a giant of a man who would be sorely missed throughout the game. Hearts had laid on a bus for the players and officials of the Gorgie club, including former greats Alec Massie, Barney Battles and Jack Harkness, who had all come to pay their last respects to a former colleague. Almost 100 wreaths and other floral tributes were on show, many from football clubs throughout the country.

Although various names including Matt Busby, who was now in charge at Manchester United, had been touted as possible candidates for the vacant position of manager at Hibernian, Swan and his fellow directors lost no time in offering the job to popular choice Hugh Shaw, and the former trainer was duly installed in the hot seat in time for the club's next fixture, a home game against their by now nearest League challengers, Rangers.

On the Saturday at Easter Road, the players of both sides took the field wearing black armbands as a mark of respect for the popular Willie McCartney, and the huge 52,750 crowd, a new home record, stood in the time-honoured minute's silence in his memory. Billed as a possible League decider, the match started in dramatic fashion when Rangers' Young was forced into a goalline clearance in the opening seconds. Developing into a tense and thrilling struggle, Hibs were well on top throughout, apart from a sticky spell in the first half, and they well deserved their victory when Cuthbertson scored the winner in the very last minute of the game. Leaders Rangers were now just one point ahead of Hibs but still had two games in hand over their Edinburgh rivals.

Manager Shaw wasted no time in promoting Jimmy McColl to first-team trainer, and both were on the bench for the 4–0 Scottish Cup victory over Arbroath at Easter Road to set up a repeat of the previous season's Cup Final against Aberdeen in the third round.

As in the Cup Final 10 months before, Cubbie again opened the scoring in the first minute, but this time it was to be Hibs' day despite Ormond being carried off with a broken leg after 33 minutes. Shortly after this Kerr also had to leave the field after injuring his hand, leaving Hibs, in these pre-substitute days, to soldier on with nine men. The goalkeeper's return just before the interval was greeted by loud applause from the large Hibs support. The final 4–2 victory, secured by a badly-depleted side, bore testament to the spirit, determination and dedication that was to be found in plentiful supply at Easter Road at the time.

For Harry Swan there was to be no respite from the ticket controversy. A crowd of 37,000 had attended the Aberdeen game, with again only the Stand reserved. Many supporters were unhappy, not only at the increased Stand and Enclosure charges, but also at the selling arrangements for the coveted briefs, which could only be purchased at times thought to be 'inconvenient' for most ordinary fans who would be at work during the day. There was also the well-held belief that too many of the tickets were being received by 'middlemen', or people in the know. Swan, while showing sympathy with many of these complaints, made the valid point that it was impossible to please everyone, pointing out that the pay-as-you-come system also had snags in that supporters who worked on Saturday mornings were unable to take advantage of the early opening of the gates and therefore were disadvantaged by those who did not.

An offer by the directors to consider any system that would solve the problem brought a deluge of mail, but none that would solve the difficulties. Instead Swan and his backroom staff were heartened by the huge amount of support from fans indebted to the board for putting the club, and Edinburgh, on the football map.

Johnny Aitkenhead, one of the players who had earlier been offered to Hearts on loan, replaced leg-break victim Ormond in the side for most of the remainder of the season. Ironically, it was only because of the broken leg suffered by Aitkenhead in November 1946 that Ormond had made a premature first-team debut. Goalkeeper George Farm replaced the injured Kerr.

There were more changes of personnel at around this time. Unable to break into the first team, Bob Stirling was transferred to Third Lanark, and he was followed out of Easter Road shortly afterwards by Willie Brown, who joined Airdrie for around £5,000. George Robson, an ex-Hearts player and former manager of Leith Athletic, was appointed second-team trainer to replace the promoted Jimmy McColl, but Robson's time at Easter Road was short as he left shortly afterwards to scout for Burnley.

In the fourth round of the Scottish Cup, St Mirren were defeated 3–1 in Edinburgh, the victory allowing Hibs to face Rangers in the semi-final at Hampden. The Ibrox line up included former Easter Road favourite Jimmy Caskie, who had since been transferred from Everton. A record crowd of 143,000, still the highest attendance between club sides outside of a Cup Final or international match in British football, saw a first-half mistake by young goalkeeper George Farm, playing only his fifth game for the club and soon to sign for Blackpool, gift Rangers the only goal of the match and a passage into the Final. The youngster, who played well otherwise, failed to gather an easy-looking cross, dropping the ball at centre-forward Thornton's feet, who took immediate advantage of the error to score the winning goal. In an exciting tussle, the Edinburgh men went down fighting, but their efforts were not nearly good enough against a Rangers side back to their best, and the Cup exit allowed Hibs to concentrate single-mindedly on the Championship race. With only four games remaining, they were now three points ahead of Rangers, but the Glasgow side still had two games in hand. A visit to Parkhead saw Hibs collect both points in a 4–2 victory, with Turnbull and Linwood both scoring twice despite the Easter Road men trailing 2–1 at the interval, and a surprise defeat by Queen's Park at Ibrox that same afternoon, Rangers' second successive home reverse, gave Hibs' title hopes a huge boost.

The outstanding form of Gordon Smith had made it difficult for the selectors to ignore the Hibs man and he was selected for the Scottish League side to face the English League at Newcastle later in the month. A fit Willie Ormond would almost certainly also have been chosen. As it turned out, injury would force Smith's withdrawal from the game, his place taken by former Easter Road colleague Tommy Bogan of Celtic.

A tight and tense 1–0 win against Partick Thistle at Easter Road in front of 30,000, with Hibs showing 'League Championship nerves', saw them needing only three points from their last two games against Motherwell at home and Dundee away to secure the flag. On Monday 19 April 1948, the title was effectively won when a rampant Hibs defeated Motherwell 5–0 at Easter Road, leaving Rangers needing to win all three remaining games and score 26 goals without reply to overtake the Edinburgh side. Only once, in the 44 years since Third Lanark had won the Championship in 1904, had it been won by a side outside the Old Firm, and by a remarkable coincidence, it was Hibs' opponents Motherwell who had broken the Glasgow giants' dominance in the 1931–32 season.

The Hibs team that fateful day was: Farm, Govan, Shaw, Finnegan, Howie, Buchanan, Smith, Combe, Linwood, Turnbull, Reilly.

Five days later, on a blank Saturday for the capital side, the best Rangers could manage was a 1–1 draw with Motherwell and the Championship was mathematically secured, which was perhaps just as well. With the pressure lifted Hibs were expected to finish the season in style, but they were beaten 3–1 in the ultimate game of the season at Dens Park almost two weeks later. It was all immaterial anyway, and at Ibrox the following week a sparse crowd of under 10,000 saw Rangers lose 2–1 to Hearts.

After a wait of 45 years, the League Championship was back at Easter Road. Under the leadership of Harry Swan, Hibs had come a long way since the dark days of the early 1930s, when things had been so bad that rumours of a complete takeover by a Glasgow-based syndicate had been rife in the city. Swan could perhaps be excused, if on a match day he surveyed the ground from the director's box feeling extremely and justifiably proud of just what had been achieved at Easter Road since he took over the running of the club. During the season that had just ended, all three Hibs sides had won their respective Leagues, the reserves for a third consecutive year. They had also won the Second XI League Cup by defeating Falkirk in the Final, the young Lawrie Reilly playing a prominent part in the final outcome.

For the fifth time in eight seasons Gordon Smith had finished as the club's top marksman, notching 18 of the 86 League goals scored. Linwood had 15, Ormond 12, Turnbull 11, Cuthbertson 10, Combe eight, Leslie Johnstone five, Reilly four and Aitkenhead and Buchanan one each. One had been courtesy of an own-goal.

The teenage Lawrie Reilly had made several first-team appearances during the season, mostly at outside-left, but unfortunately for the youngster this was not enough to justify the award of a League Championship medal.

In midweek, all 41 senior players were notified that they had been retained for the following season, but for 11 youngsters there was the heartbreaking news that they had been released.

On the international front, the growing stature of Hibs had been reflected when full-backs Govan and Shaw were selected to represent their country against England at Hampden along with teammate Bobby Combe. Two weeks later there was a greater accolade for the club when Govan, Shaw, Smith, Combe and Turnbull were all chosen to face both Belgium at Hampden and Switzerland in Berne. There was a further Hibs connection in those games. Former Hibs player Leslie Johnstone was at centre-forward, with Hugh Howie a travelling reserve. Scotland's 3–0 defeat by France in Paris a few weeks later saw both Jock Govan and Davie Shaw again provide the full-back pairing, with Gordon Smith wearing the number-nine jersey. Eddie Turnbull, initially selected as the travelling reserve for the game along with teammate Bobby Combe and former Hibs player Leslie Johnstone, was a last-minute inclusion into the side at inside-left after a late withdrawal shortly before the start. Most record books fail to acknowledge Turnbull as having taken part in the game but documents at the Scottish Football Museum at Hampden confirm that the Hibs man did indeed play, and consequently another full cap should be added to his recorded total of eight, an omission in most, if not all, lists of international statistics.

It had been a truly marvellous season for the club, who had come so close to winning the coveted double. 'Tron Kirk' of the *Evening News* summed the situation up perfectly when he wrote: 'Hibernian had done Edinburgh proud, and Edinburgh should be proud of the Hibs'.

The Scottish League presented the club with an 8ft by 5ft white flag with green trim, bearing a huge central red lion rampant and the legend 'Hibernian League Champions 1947–48'. Flown over the grandstand on match days during the following 12 months, regrettably the banner has since disappeared from Easter Road.

So Near Yet So Far

It had been a busy summer for the new champions. As well as a five-match tour of Belgium, winning just one of the five games and drawing another, the players and officials had also been guests of Lord Provost Murray at a civic reception at the City Chambers to honour the club's historic success.

A large squad of full-time players reported for pre-season training under the watchful eye of Jimmy McColl, including the recently called-up youngsters, goalkeeper Tommy Younger from Hutchison Vale, Angus Plumb from Armadale Thistle, and Jimmy Bradley, signed from Port Glasgow juniors. Leg-break victim Willie Ormond, now fully recovered from the injury received against Aberdeen the previous season, had made his comeback in a 2–1 defeat by Liège in the first game of Hibs' tour of Belgium during the summer. There was an early setback for the player, however, when he injured the same leg during a pre-season five-a-side tournament at the coaching classes that were being run by the SFA at Abington, a misfortune that resulted in a further confinement at the Western General Hospital in Edinburgh.

There was still considerable suspicion within the game regarding coaching, a subject that had largely been conspicuous by its absence up until then. Indeed, the late manager Willie McCartney's preferred method of pre-match instruction had been to implore his side to go out and give the opposition the 'Reels of Bogie,' the 'Reels of Tulloch' or some other Scottish air. As always, never slow in realising any advancement that would be to the benefit of the game, Harry Swan, then chairman of the SFA Coaching Committee, lambasted the lack of interest shown by the majority of the clubs: 'There have recently been amazing strides in technique through intensive coaching, and he wished to clear up any misapprehension that the courses in any way interfered with any coaching received at club level. The courses were simply the best way to pass on the methods learned'.

Govan, Shaw, Howie, Smith, Combe, Linwood and Aitkenhead were selected as the Hibs contingent to wear the maroon of Hearts in the latest of the series of Edinburgh Select challenge matches against visitors Blackpool at Tynecastle. Combe opened the scoring in the first half, but it was Gordon Smith at his best who showed the opposition outside-right Stanley Matthews how the game should be played, testing the goalkeeper on several occasions with lightning strikes. As at Hampden in April, Davie Shaw again completely subdued the legendary Matthews, but that year's losing FA Cup finalists, spurred on by captain Harry Johnston and Stan Mortensen, more than deserved a share of the spoils in the 1–1 draw.

Hibs began their bid to retain the title with a 5–2 win over newly promoted 'B' Division winners East Fife at Easter Road. Before the game, Scottish League president McMahon, watched by Lord Provost Andrew Murray, unfurled the League Championship flag at the south end of the Main Stand in front of 35,000 cheering fans before the trophy was paraded around the ground. Sadly, there was to be no repeat of the previous season's triumph. In a game that fell well below expectation, all the excitement was packed into a 15-minute first-half spell that allowed the home side to change ends 3–1 to the good. The newcomers clawed a goal back in the second period while Turnbull was off the field receiving treatment for a head wound, but on his return to the action both he and two-goal Aitkenhead stepped up a gear, and Hibs finished convincing winners. George Farm had performed reasonably well in goal during the final games of the previous season, with rumours regarding the future of the experienced Jimmy Kerr doing the rounds, but the Ormiston custodian was between the sticks as usual at the big kick-off, and young Farm was back in the reserves. In the corresponding reserve fixture at Methil that same afternoon, Reilly, Plumb and Bobby Johnstone, then still in the forces, were the stars of the show as the second team defeated East Fife's 3–2 in front of 2,500 fans.

Irishman Mick Gallagher, signed from Alloa in 1946 after only five games for the Clackmannanshire side, made his first-team debut in a 3–1 victory over Hearts at Easter Road, and after four games Hibs were in a now familiar position at the top of the table, one point ahead of St Mirren, Dundee and Rangers. The victory over their nearest rivals meant that Hearts were now firmly anchored at the foot of the table.

At that time third-choice goalkeeper Lewis Goram, father of future Hibs and Scotland star Andy, was on loan at Leith Athletic and was said to be attracting interest from Blackpool, who were in urgent need of a 'keeper, so it was something of a surprise when the Seasiders switched targets and signed George Farm instead. In time Farm would become a stalwart of the English club, with an illustrious career at Bloomfield Road lasting many years. As well as winning several Scotland caps while at Bloomfield Road, he would appear in the famous 'Matthews' Cup Final against Bolton Wanderers in 1953, before eventually returning north of the border to manage Dunfermline, Raith Rovers and Cowdenbeath.

In yet another change to the format, the third in three years, the League Cup had again reverted back to its original configuration, with the six section games being played during September, and for the third year running Hibs' involvement in the competition was confined to the preliminary stages. Two four-goal wins against Clyde proved immaterial, when only three points were secured from the four games against the Old Firm, with the Ibrox side, the eventual winners of the competition, progressing to the quarter-final stages.

In the game against Celtic at Easter Road, only a stunning display by Scottish international goalkeeper Miller had saved the visitors from an even more embarrassing defeat than the 4–2 scoreline would suggest. Just under 53,000, a new crowd record, were inside the stadium at kick-off, but after a long wait to gain admission, hundreds were seen to leave the ground shortly after the start, unable to even catch a glimpse of the pitch. An angry crowd numbering well over 100 tried in vain to contact a representative of the club to complain about the situation, but were moved on by the police, a response that provoked many letters of protest being received by the club. Twice in the past few months attendance records had been broken at the ground, and it had now become a major priority that the capacity be extended. As would be expected, a number of letters were sent to the newspapers criticising the appalling overcrowding on the terracing. 'Safety First' wrote that 'far too many spectators had been allowed into the ground. I and several hundred others acted as a human retaining wall at the eastern embankment opposite the stand, and many were pushed down the slope followed by rubble and stones aimlessly kicked down on to supporters trying to find an exit.' Another complained that he was: 'one of the last few thousand admitted to the ground. Arriving late via a very long queue, I would have had no complaint if the gates had been closed, but there were at least 3,000 who paid at the turnstiles with almost no chance of even seeing the field. Advised by the police, we were convinced that the situation was hopeless and, accompanied by many others, I left the ground.

Financially the club continued to be in good shape. As confirmed by the above example, the large crowds then attending Easter Road, attracted by the at times breathtaking football on display, enabled a healthy profit of £10,053 being declared at the AGM from a gross income of £73,581 the previous year. This surplus would enable the club to continue with their ambitious plans to increase the capacity of the ground. At that time many Hearts supporters were unhappy about the numerous delays to proposed plans for the long-awaited development of Tynecastle, but for several months now work had been steadily progressing at Easter Road to build up the banking behind the main terracing, a project which when completed was expected to increase the capacity of the ground to more than 80,000.

Letters of complaint to the newspapers were not confined to the overcrowding situation. Many fans were still angry at Hibs' continued custom of raising the admission charges to both the enclosure and stands for 'big' games, a practice not then in evidence at Tynecastle or the majority of First Division grounds at the time. The club itself received a wide variety of correspondence, but not always of complaint. Many were received from supporters suggesting that the excellent form of Bobby Johnstone, the undoubted star of the reserve team and recently outstanding in a British Army XI against an FA representative side at Ipswich, warranted a first-team debut for the young inside-right.

On Wednesday 22 September 1948, Matt Busby brought FA Cup-holders Manchester United north to Edinburgh for a testimonial match in aid of the Willie McCartney benefit fund, which was expected to raise around £6,000 for the dependants of the late manager. A huge crowd of 30,225 watched the game, those in the ground paying 2s for the privilege, and as a measure of the respect held for McCartney within the game the fund was further boosted by generous donations from several other Scottish clubs including Rangers and Hearts.

For the first time at Easter Road the fans witnessed the novelty of the use of a white ball, which was merely a normal brown leather ball painted white and changed regularly to be cleaned as it gathered dirt. The plastic-coated white ball was not far in the future, but, incredibly, for some time regulations prohibited the introduction of a white ball during a game unless it had been used from the start, a ridiculous state of affairs in those pre-floodlight days when it was not unusual for a game to finish in virtual darkness.

On the day, Manchester United proved too good for the home side and were well worthy of the 1–0 win. After the game the players and officials of both teams attended a post-match banquet in the North British Hotel in Princes Street. In his after-dinner speech, Matt Busby, to accompanying applause, recalled that his wartime days at Easter Road had been the happiest of his playing career.

Hibernian: Kerr, Howie, Shaw, Finnigan, Aird, Kean, Smith, Cuthbertson, Linwood, Turnbull, Ormond.

Manchester United: Crompton, Ball, Carey, Anderson, Chilton, McGlen, Delaney, Morris, Rowley, Pearson, Mitten.

Before the game there had been an unexpected but welcome bonus for Lawrie Reilly. While waiting at the junction of Henderson Terrace and Dundee Street for a tram to take him to Easter Road, the youngster was stunned to learn from a passing fan that he had been selected for the Scottish League side to face the League of Ireland at Ibrox, his first international honour. The pre-season injury to Ormond had given Reilly an opportunity to secure an extended run in the side on the left wing, and a hat-trick in a 4–4 draw against Albion Rovers was his second first-team treble for the club. Reilly's wholehearted all-action style had drawn an ever-increasing circle of admirers, all well aware of the youngster's potential, but even so it was something of a surprise when the player was selected for the Scottish side. Reilly would let neither himself nor the country down. He scored his first goal in a dark blue jersey as the home side cantered to an easy 5–1 win, with teammate Bobby Combe scoring twice. According to one report: 'The tenacity, speed and bewildering footwork of the Hibs youngster captivated the huge 60,000 crowd inside Ibrox as he made an excellent impression in this his first representative game'.

Hugh Howie became the 11th player then at Easter Road to gain international recognition when he was selected at right-back for Scotland's match with Wales at Cardiff at the end of October, alongside teammates Davie Shaw and Lawrie Reilly, who would also be winning his first full cap. Despite his recent effervescent displays for Hibs there would be no place in the side for Gordon Smith. Smith had lined up at centre-forward in Scotland's previous game, a 2–1 defeat by Switzerland in Berne, but in fairness to the selectors, at that time he rarely reproduced his club form wearing the country's dark blue jersey. Teammate Reilly would take Smith's place against Wales. Govan, Shaw, Smith, Combe, Linwood, Turnbull, Howie and now Reilly had represented the full side, with Kean, Cuthbertson and Ormond all capped at inter-League level. In addition, both Aird and Kerr had been chosen as reserves in the past. Jock Govan, Scotland's regular right-back at the time, had missed the last few games for Hibs and consequently the game against Wales because of dental problems, and with Howie's inclusion it was most unusual for the same club to have two current players capped in the same position. In his one and only full international appearance, Howie would score one of Scotland's goals in a 3–1 victory, Willie Waddell of Rangers scoring twice.

Howie's exhilaration at joining the international ranks was destined to be shortlived. Within the space of a few weeks the lanky defender began to feel unwell and was eventually diagnosed as suffering from tuberculosis, then a far more serious disease than it is now. Part of the treatment consisted of spending many months in the pure clean air of Switzerland, and, financed by the club, the player was promptly dispatched to the town of Davos in the Alps to recuperate. Howie would in time recover from the debilitating illness, but it would be a long while before he would be well enough to engage in the rugged vigour of professional football. Meanwhile, the absence of Howie from the side had created the opportunity for defender Jimmy Cairns to make the left-back position his own, and the Falkirk man enjoyed an extended run to the end of the season.

A League Championship celebration dinner was held in the North British Hotel on Monday 18 October 1948. Handsome nine-carat gold Championship medals depicting the club name and the crests of both Edinburgh and Leith set in green and white enamel were presented to the 14 players – Kerr, Govan, Shaw, Howie, Buchanan, Finnigan, Kean, Aird, Smith, Combe, Linwood, Turnbull, Cuthbertson and Ormond – who had qualified for the award. Goalscoring sensation Lawrie Reilly had failed to make the stipulated number of appearances during the Championship season and, like goalkeeper Jock Brown, consequently missed out on receiving the coveted award. Manager Shaw and trainer McColl also received the prestigious decorations. Harry Swan and the other directors were presented with specially struck medals as a token of appreciation by fellow shareholders. In a glittering night of celebration, the members of both the reserve side and the third team were also presented with engraved silver tankards, the reward for winning their respective League titles.

By this time inconsistent League results had begun to be of concern. Victories against Third Lanark, Dundee and Rangers were negated by defeats at the hands of Celtic, Partick Thistle and Morton, a spate of poor results that culminated in a surprise but decisive 5–1 reverse at Fir Park. Gordon Smith, however, had made the critics who said he never played well at Ibrox eat their words with a magnificent two-goal display against Rangers at the beginning of November. Hibs were without the services of both Davie Shaw and Alec Linwood, who were on Scottish League duty against the Irish League in Belfast, but replacements Cairns and Cuthbertson played their part in a real team effort as the visitors raced to a 4–1 interval lead. Smith's first goal was from a tremendous drive that was past goalkeeper Bobby Brown before he could move, and the second was a quite brilliant swerving shot that hit the bar on its way into the net. Rangers managed to claw back a goal late in the game, but the 4–2 final scoreline allowed the Greens to leapfrog their nearest rivals to top the table.

Hibs, more than any other club in the country at that time, were involved in transfer speculation concerning various players, sometimes on a daily basis. Smith was an obvious subject of regular enquiries from several sources; Turnbull was linked with a move to Chelsea; Linwood to Partick Thistle; Govan to both Aston Villa and Sheffield United; and, according to Hugh Shaw, there was the quite ridiculous story doing the rounds that Wolves were lining up an exchange deal involving Lawrie Reilly and an unnamed English player. The interest was not confined to the first team. Such was the depth of talent then at Easter Road that most of the games involving the reserve and third teams were well attended by a host of scouts from other clubs, the elusive skills of Bobby Johnstone in particular catching the eye. Like Johnstone, defender John Paterson had also been in great form for the reserve side, and in mid-November he made his first-team debut when replacing Peter Aird at centre-half in a 1–1 draw with Falkirk at Brockville, a position he would hold until the end of the season.

In October, former Hibs player Leslie Johnstone became the most expensive player in Scottish football when Celtic paid Clyde £12,000 for his services. In a little under two years, Johnstone had been involved in three transfer deals in transactions totalling over £30,000. The prolific Alec Linwood was seen by Clyde as a natural successor to Johnstone, and he joined the Shawfield club just before the turn of the year. Linwood himself related that: 'Reilly had latterly come into the side on the left wing as a replacement for the injured Ormond. The return of the fit again Ormond, who immediately returned to his old position, coincided with me picking up an injury myself. Young Reilly was moved to centre-forward and that was the beginning of the end for me at Easter Road'.

Reilly, however, was not the immediate answer. Angus Plumb took over from Linwood, scoring nine goals in nine starts before it was decided that he too was not the answer. It would seem a lot was expected of you in those days. Gordon Smith was switched back into the centre of the attack for a couple of games with Reilly again deputising on the right wing, before the youngster, eventually and permanently, as it would turn out, reverted to centre-forward, a position he would occupy for Hibs and Scotland for the next 10 years.

Despite dropping a point at home against Queen of the South on Christmas Day, John Ogilvie making his debut at left-half, the result meant that all three Hibs teams now topped their respective Leagues.

Four days later the popular Johnny Aitkenhead, earlier placed on the transfer list at his own request after being unable to recapture his first-team place permanently after his return from injury, was transferred to Motherwell. It would prove a productive move for the player, who would win Scottish Cup and League Cup-winners' medals with the Lanarkshire side.

It was business as usual at Tynecastle on New Year's Day, Hibs going down 3–2 to Hearts, but there was better news for the Easter Road fans a few days later when Willie Ormond, now completely recovered from injury, made his long-awaited first start of the season in the reserves' 1–0 victory against their Edinburgh rivals. His energetic performance proved he had fully recovered from his injury and the Falkirk man was in his usual position a few days later as the first team secured a 3–2 victory at Methil.

At the end of the month questions were raised in Parliament by Sir Stafford Cripps, who had replaced Dalton as the Chancellor of the Exchequer, regarding the continued refusal of the Scottish clubs to implement the recommended reduction of admission charges caused by the lowering of the entertainment tax as far back as 1946, a situation which infuriated the Scottish League Management Committee. Cripps pointed out that when the entertainment tax had first been raised in 1940 the clubs, not surprisingly, had not been slow to raise the charges immediately, but Harry Swan again insisted that clubs north of the border, many of whom did not show a profit, could not afford to reduce their prices. Furthermore, he insisted that football was a community service that should not only be exempt from the ruling, but should also warrant a special consideration by way of tax relief. Despite its airing before such salubrious company, no further action was taken regarding the matter. It is worth remembering that it was not only the first-team games that would be affected by any reduction, but also those of the reserves. Although admission for those games was significantly less than for the League side, at times the second team were attracting substantial crowds and any shortfall could well represent a considerable loss to the club.

In the Scottish Cup it was the same old inconsistent and equally uninspiring story. After a 4–0 win at Forfar, Hibs struggled to beat Raith Rovers after a replay, received a bye in the third round and were defeated at home by East Fife in the quarter-finals. On a quagmire of a pitch the Fifers were more direct, took their chances and in the end well deserved their 2–0 victory. It was a black day for Edinburgh's Cup aspirations, as Hearts were beaten 4–2 by Dundee at Tynecastle the same afternoon.

After 11 years at Easter Road, Willie Finnigan made his last-ever first-team appearance in a green-and-white jersey in a 1–0 home defeat by arch rivals Rangers on 19 February 1949. Part-timer Finnigan, a pre-war signing from Bo'ness Cadora in 1938, who worked in St Cuthbert's Co-operative warehouse in Richmond Place during the week, had been a mainstay of the team for several years. Recognised as the schemer behind most of Hibs' moves from midfield, the chain-smoking Willie was respected by teammates, fans and opponents alike.

The second team continued to earn rave reports and were regularly attracting crowds of six or seven thousand to Easter Road to see them display their own brand of breathtaking football. Bulldozing the opposition into benign submission with their bewitching play, they again dominated the Reserve League Championship. No one took the eye more than young Bobby Johnstone, soon to be demobbed early from National Service with a little 'help' from the club. For some time the player had been the subject of numerous letters sent to the manager from supporters urging that the scrawny Selkirk lad be selected for the first team, but Shaw was already well aware of the youngster's capabilities.

On 2 April 1949, Johnstone and centre-forward Bruce made their first-team debuts at Paisley in a side weakened by injuries to Smith and Cuthbertson. Johnstone himself made a promising start to his senior career, the *Evening News* of the opinion that 'the slightly built youngster has all the makings of a star', but an overall poor performance from Hibs saw their Championship challenge all but disappear as they stumbled to a 2–0 defeat.

A week later at Wembley, Reilly, playing at outside-left, scored the best goal of the game as Scotland demolished favourites England 3–1 in a match that would become known forever as the 'Jimmy Cowan international'. The Morton goalkeeper was in immense form, repulsing everything the home side could throw at him until the dying minutes of the game. By that time it was far too late, as the Scots led 3–0. Young Reilly scored Scotland's third in true *Boy's Own* style, when he rifled a diving header from a Waddell cross past Frank Swift in the England goal.

As Reilly basked in the glory of Wembley, that same afternoon at Easter Road goalkeeper Tommy Younger was making an impressive start to his Hibs career. In a slender 2–1 victory over Partick Thistle, Younger did all that was required of him, and a match report of the game recorded that 'it appears that Hibs have unearthed two stars of the future in the goalkeeper and inside-right Bobby Johnstone'. With Younger and Johnstone taking the first faltering steps to success, another career was nearing its end. Like Finnigan before him, time had finally caught up with Sammy Kean, and he made his farewell appearance as a Hibs player on the day of Younger's debut. Unfortunately for both Kean and Finnigan, they had been two of many hundreds of professional players who had been robbed of the best years of a full and relatively lucrative career by the intervention of World War Two. Countless thousands of others, however, had been robbed of much more.

Younger retained his place for the final three matches of the season and looked a prospect in each, but at the end of the day Hibs were forced to settle for third place in the table, seven points behind champions Rangers, who had completed the first clean sweep of all three major honours, and six behind second-placed Dundee, who had proved a surprise packet since their promotion to the top division only two years before.

As far as the League was concerned, an expensive price had been paid for a lack of consistency, particularly in the latter months of the year when they had unexpectedly dropped points to the likes of St Mirren, Partick, Morton, Motherwell and Queen of the South, who had all finished in the bottom half of the table. Twenty-five players had been used during the League campaign, with two positions in particular proving a major problem. Six different players had been tried at centre-forward, and only one less at centre-half as the manager desperately struggled to discover the ideal blend. Illness and injury to key players such as Howie, Smith and Govan at crucial times of the season had not helped, but in truth a side as rich in terms of numbers and quality as the Easter Road outfit should well have been able to overcome this handicap. Nevertheless, a season that had promised so much had delivered so little, and as the expectations of the fans diminished as the season wore on, there were some who wondered if this fantastically talented team were to be a one-season wonder.

The Birth of the Famous Five and a Record Attendance at Easter Road

As the start of the 1949–50 season loomed ever nearer, Sammy Kean decided to retire from the playing side of the game to take over the duties of assistant first-team trainer, a position that had been specially created by the management for the veteran player, a pre-war signing from Kirkintilloch Rob Roy.

The close-season break, the first without an overseas tour since the war, seemed far in the past as the players arrived at the ground at the end of July for the dreaded first day of pre-season training. A surprise face among the crowd was that of Hugh Howie, now well on the way to full recovery from his illness, although it was some time before he could even contemplate a first-team comeback. Supervised by McColl and Kean, the players were put through their paces, either with the now traditional jogs around Kings Park, or else with lively runs to Seafield and Portobello before enduring vigorous training sessions at Easter Road in the afternoon. As a change of routine, an alternative method of punishment was to be taken by coach to Gullane to undergo agonising sessions comprising of repeated sprints up and down the sand dunes. During the 1970s, the then Rangers manager Jock Wallace would be credited by the media as the man who discovered the sand dunes of Gullane as the perfect place for training, but Hibs, and Hearts too for that matter, had been using the area as part of their fitness regime since well before the war.

By this time, the part-time Cuthbertson, unable to hold down a regular first-team place, had joined Third Lanark for a reported 'substantial fee'. Simon Waldie, like Cuthbertson, had also struggled to establish himself in the League side, and he moved on to further his career at Queen of the South. There was also the usual transfer speculation regarding Smith, this time a reported offer from Newcastle United, but despite the abundance of talent already at the club, which was the envy of most other sides in the country, the offer was instantly rejected, and all sights were focused firmly on the recapture of the League title.

That year the visitors to Easter Road for the annual Edinburgh Select game were FA Cup holders Wolverhampton Wanderers, a team containing such illustrious names as England captain Billy Wright and his international colleague goalkeeper Bert Williams. A disappointment for many of the supporters was the absence through injury from the Wolves side of centre-forward James Dunn, son of the legendary former Hibs star Jimmy of 'Wembley Wizards' fame. Two goals by Alfie Conn of Hearts were not enough to prevent a 3–2 defeat for the home side, and the guests became the winners of the Allison Cup, which was presented to the victors each year. To the embarrassment of the organisers, the Cup could not be found in time for the presentation, and the captain of Wolves was presented, albeit temporarily, with the Reserve League Cup won by Hibs' second team the previous season. Dignity was restored, however, when the Allison Trophy was eventually located and presented to the visitors before they left the city. It had been anticipated beforehand that there would be only mild interest in the game, but the 46,077 spectators who paid the then colossal sum of £5,496 for the privilege was a new record for a charities match in Edinburgh. Many of the large crowd had taken advantage of the huge mound of earth that was beginning to tower behind the main terracing. For months the back of the stadium had been used as a dumping ground in order to create the necessary banking for the construction of an extension to the existing terracing opposite the grandstand, which when completed would increase the capacity of the ground to just under 70,000. These were exciting times for the previously entertainment-starved Edinburgh sporting public, and at the time even the speedway at Meadowbank and the greyhound racing at Powderhall were well capable of attracting crowds in the region of 15,000 and 10,000 respectively.

It was also around this time that a new match programme was introduced. Under the leadership of editor Magnus Williamson, who had been given the remit by Harry Swan to produce the best programme in the country, the new-look larger format publication was an instant success, proving extremely popular with the fans. The eight page layout which replaced the old four-page design was well ahead of its time, as was its use of photographs and content matter. Its most prominent features were the large black-and-white action photograph that dominated the front page, an innovation at the time, and a green pitch layout listing the team line ups in playing formation across the centre pages. Although at 3p it was a penny dearer than its predecessor, the publication was thought well worth the increase in cost.

The League Cup had been steadily growing in popularity with players and supporters alike, and the section games were once again moved to act as a precursor to the League programme. Younger had shown enough promise in the four games he had played the previous term to now be regarded as Hibs' first-choice goalkeeper, and the youngster was between the posts when the 1949–50 season got underway at Easter Road with a single-goal victory over Falkirk. Centre-half Matt McNeil, seen as the answer to what had proved to be one of the previous season's problem positions, made his debut in the middle of a new-look half-back line. A deputation from Newcastle United had again watched Smith, but left with the now almost obligatory declaration ringing in their ears that the outside-right was not for sale at any price. The Hibs team on the opening day was: Younger, Govan, Cairns, Buchanan, McNeil, Ogilvie, Smith, Combe, Reilly, Turnbull, Ormond.

That same afternoon the high-flying reserves continued where they had left off the previous season with a 10–1 away victory at Dunfermline, the outstanding Bobby Johnstone scoring Hibs' fifth goal. This was closely followed by a 6–1 victory against Montrose, Johnstone netting twice, and a convincing 8–2 victory against Leith Athletic, Johnstone this time scoring five, which could well have been more had it not been for several fantastic saves by the opposition goalkeeper. Johnstone would make nine appearances for the second team that season, scoring 16 goals.

Five wins and a single reverse suffered at Brockville when the Bairns gained revenge for an opening day defeat, were enough to guarantee Hibs' first team a meeting with Partick Thistle in the quarter-finals. In the section game against Queen of the South at Easter Road, a 5–3 win, with Bobby Combe scoring his first hat-trick for the club since netting four in the famous 8–1 rout of Rangers in 1941, was part of a goal-crazy weekend for the club, as the reserves went on the rampage to thrash Alloa 11–1 and the third team Murrayfield Amateurs 8–1.

Goals were the name of the game at this point, and a rampant Hibs attack scored their 13th first-team goal in three matches, Turnbull and Reilly both collecting doubles, as Raith Rovers suffered a 6–0 thrashing at Starks Park before the resumption of League Cup business against Partick Thistle.

The first leg of the quarter-final tie at Firhill saw an uninspired Greens go down 4–2. Bobby Johnstone, who had been staking a claim for a regular first-team place for some time, made his first appearance of the season when he deputised for the injured Smith, scoring one of Hibs' goals, his first for the first team. Although there was plenty of effort from the Edinburgh side, they badly missed the imagination Smith would undoubtedly have provided. In the return leg four days later, another two goals by Reilly, his second a real beauty that brought the house down, and one each from Combe and Ormond, gave Hibs a passage into the semi-final and renewed confidence for the forthcoming derby at Tynecastle the following Saturday. Like so many times in the recent past, this confidence was soon found to be badly misplaced, as the Maroons inflicted a humiliating 5–2 defeat over their Easter Road rivals in what was described as one of the cleanest and most sporting contests ever seen at the stadium. This fact would presumably be of little consolation to the disappointed visiting supporters as they made their weary way home.

In a letter to the *Evening News* a supporter calling himself 'Hibs Aye' wondered at the policy then being pursued by those in charge of the club. 'First we sell the best centre we have ever had at the club in Linwood, then Cubbie, then last week we drop a promising goalkeeper and centre-half for no apparent reason.' The latter was a reference to both Younger and Paterson missing the second leg of the League Cup quarter-final.

The unpredictable form continued with Hibs recording a fine win over Aberdeen, before facing Second Division Dunfermline in the League Cup semi-final at Tynecastle, one of the first games to be played in front of Hearts' recently reconstructed terracing. Gordon Smith, who had missed the previous Saturday's game against the Dons because of injury, was again an absentee, and once again young Tommy McDonald, who had made his debut as Smith's stand-in only seven days earlier, was wearing the number-seven jersey.

Two goals by former Hib Gerry Mayes gave the Second Division side a surprise but fully merited 2–1 extra-time win. The victory was no fluke, and against a half-back line that was found to be woefully weak, Dunfermline could easily have run out more convincing winners. McDonald, Reilly and Ormond all tried manfully but without support, and even when a breakthrough was threatened they found goalkeeper Johnstone a formidable barrier.

Although the season was only a dozen games old, the half-back line had been giving problems since the start, and despite numerous permutations being tried, none had really proved effective. The semi-final was McNeil's eighth and last game for Hibs, and before too long he would be on his way to Newcastle in a £5,000 deal.

To their credit, there were no excuses offered by Swan or manager Shaw for the humiliating defeat, except that a complacent attitude shown by several members of the side had not helped the cause. They now wished Dunfermline the best of luck in the Final. The supporters were not as easy to placate, and again there were numerous letters sent to the local newspapers, most complaining about the woeful performance of the half-back line. 'Dunbar end' went even further, complaining that 'despite the belief in some quarters that young Reilly will make the grade as a centre-forward, he and 30,000 others say no, the youngster's place is on the wing'. This was something of an understatement, considering that Reilly would end his career having scored more goals for Hibs than any other player in the history of the club, and win more international caps by far than anyone else at Easter Road, before or since, almost all of them while playing in his favoured centre-forward position.

As a final footnote to the Tynecastle semi-final, if a warning on the perils of gambling was required, one might look no further than the experience of Eddie Turnbull. Encouraged by a relative to visit a local dog track on the Thursday evening before the semi-final, he was persuaded to have a bet. Deciding to wager the bonus that he was sure to collect after the game against the lower division team on the Saturday, Turnbull lost out on both counts and would think long and hard about gambling in the future.

Seven days after the Tynecastle débâcle, manager Shaw replaced the entire half-back line, and chose a mid-line that would, barring injury, become the established line up for some time to come: Combe, Paterson and Buchanan; or Buchanan, Paterson and Combe, as it would shortly become. Combe's move to right-half left a vacant position in the forward line, and this position was filled, permanently as it would turn out, by Bobby Johnstone. In a dour and uninspiring 2–0 victory against Queen of the South at Easter Road all eyes were focused nervously on the new half-back line, who performed their duties more than adequately, the fans completely unaware at the time that they were witnessing the first-ever appearance in a competitive game of a forward line that would soon achieve immortality: Smith, Johnstone, Reilly, Turnbull and Ormond, 'The Famous Five'. The quintet had only narrowly missed making a competitive first start on the day of Johnstone's debut against St Mirren the previous season. Only a late call-off by Gordon Smith due to injury had prevented this happening, and they made their first appearance as a complete unit in a friendly against Nithsdale Wanderers in Sanquhar on 21 April and again in a fundraising match in Belfast against an Irish League XI a few weeks later.

Although Bobby Combe would become an integral part of the Hibs success story during the following few years playing at left-half, the experienced player was unhappy at losing his place at inside-right. Having won three full Scotland caps and several inter-League call-ups during the previous few months in the forward position, the player felt that a move to wing-half would potentially cost him his place in the international set-up. A £10-per-month wage rise helped to placate his fears, but he never represented his country at full level again.

The Hibs line up against Queen of the South was: Younger, Govan, Cairns, Combe, Paterson, Buchanan, Smith, Johnstone, Reilly, Turnbull, Ormond.

At that year's AGM, it was revealed that a profit of £12,034 had been made from a gross income of £73,581 during the previous 12 months, figures that suggested prudent bookkeeping within the organisation. These figures, however, while impressive for a Scottish club at that time, paled into insignificance compared to several English clubs who declared a profit several times higher. For anyone interested, a paragraph in the Hibs accounts placed a value of £29,041 on the ground, stands and other buildings, while £21,536 was held in reserve at the bank.

Only one point would be dropped between the two disasters at Tynecastle and the turn of the year. While Dunfermline were losing 3–0 to East Fife in the League Cup Final at Hampden, Hibs fought out a 2–2 draw against Celtic at Parkhead in front of 35,000 spectators, a game the visiting side thoroughly deserved to win.

A week later, at Easter Road, another huge crowd of 54,000 saw Turnbull score the only goal of the game, but the strike was enough to take both points from Rangers. As the match kicked-off there were still thousands of fans outside queuing to get in, a definite indication, if any were still needed, that exciting things were happening at Easter Road. Again, several thousand spectators had made use of the unfinished mound of earth now towering behind the main terracing that gave an excellent, if precarious, view of the proceedings.

At the end of November goals from Bobby Johnstone and Lawrie Reilly gave Hibs a comfortable win against Third Lanark at Cathkin. As the spectators were exiting the ground at the end of the game, hundreds took advantage of the extra entertainment on offer as they watched the Glasgow Fire Brigade battle manfully to extinguish a fire in the press box, which was situated adjacent to the main stand. The fire had started accidentally when an open brazier used to heat the compartment was knocked over, resulting in the complete destruction of the press box and severe damage to part of the main stand. At least this fire had been started accidentally. A few weeks later at the same ground, hundreds of fans invaded the pitch, with several attempting to set fire to the grandstand after a second-round Scottish Cup tie between Thirds and Celtic had been called off a short time before the start owing to the lines being obliterated by the falling snow, with an estimated 18,000 inside the ground. The clubs offered to play a friendly, but this did little to appease the dissatisfied supporters of both sides, who demanded their money back, and only the intervention of the police prevented a serious incident. Both clubs were later censured for attempting to play a friendly match, which was strictly against the rules. This was not the first case of its kind, however. As far back as February 1912 a Scottish Cup replay between Hibs and Hearts at Easter Road was played amid a heavy downpour of hail and snow, which had threatened to obscure the lines from the start. Hibs had been leading 1–0 at half-time but, with the fans completely unaware of the decision, during the interval owing to the atrocious conditions both clubs had agreed to finish the match but that the result would stand as a friendly. Both Hibs and Hearts were later fined £25 for what was seen as a serious breach of the regulations.

After a home win against Raith Rovers on Christmas Eve, the board members were surprised to be summoned to the dressing room by the players. As club captain, Gordon Smith presented the directors with an onyx clock in the club colours inscribed 'To the management of the Hibernian FC as a token of appreciation from the players – Christmas 1949'. Harry Swan, accepting the gift on behalf of his fellow directors, made mention of the happy relationship that existed between the playing staff and the board. That there existed a tremendous spirit at the club at that time is undeniable. Talk today to any player from that era, and it is clearly evident that they were indeed happy times. Most could not wait to get to the ground, and before and after the training sessions there would be games of badminton, head tennis and numerous other pastimes, which all helped to forge a great team spirit. There were even a couple of pairs of boxing gloves, and many a laugh was to be had at the antics of the Joe Louis wannabes.

In the week that saw the passing in Dublin of the Hibs trainer to the great 1920s team Di Christopher, five of the top eight players in the goalscoring charts belonged to both the Edinburgh clubs. Willie Bauld led the way with 21 goals, with Smith and Wardhaugh next best with 14. Conn and Reilly had scored 13 each, and two players no longer on the books at Easter Road, Linwood and Cuthbertson, had 12 and 11 respectively.

A few days before New Year, McCabe and Plumb were transferred to Falkirk in a joint deal reputed to be worth £5,000 to the Easter Road club. McCabe had earlier been out on loan, while Plumb had become dissatisfied with reserve football after sampling first-team action the previous season. There was good news for the fans, however, on New Year's Eve. While the first team was winning 1–0 at Shawfield, at Easter Road captain for the day Hugh Howie made his long-awaited return from illness in the reserve side's 6–1 victory over Stirling Albion.

Both capital clubs had shown a rich vein of form in the run-up to the New Year's Day derby, played on 2 January that year because the 1st fell on a Sunday, and a tremendous sense of anticipation and excitement had been steadily building in the city for several weeks. At the halfway stage of the campaign prior to the game with Hearts, Hibs were in a much better position points-wise than during their Championship year and were popular favourites to win the all-Edinburgh clash. The huge mound of earth behind the Easter Road terracing had still not been landscaped, but this failed to deter the fans from using it for an elevated view, and it helped accommodate Edinburgh's biggest-ever football crowd as 65,840, including Lord Provost Sir Ian Murray, crammed into Easter Road to watch the traditional holiday fixture between the city's oldest rivals.

To act as a windbreaker and help contain what was predicted to be a record crowd, new 7ft-high fencing had been rushed into operation at the south or 'Dunbar end' of the ground in the days leading up to the match. Sizeable queues had started to form over an hour before the gates opened at 12 o'clock for the 2.15pm kick-off, and 15 minutes before the start the gates were closed with thousands still locked outside desperately trying to gain admission. Of those fans fortunate enough to have gained entry, hundreds made their way to the exits after finding it impossible to even see the pitch.

Mounted police had been urgently called to the ground in an attempt to maintain order and they struggled to control the masses while ambulance attendants battled manfully to treat several casualties on the pitch. The thousands of supporters attempting to gain a tentative foothold on the mass of loose earth towering behind the main terracing, described in one newspaper as 'table mountain', was an accident waiting to happen, and it was only good fortune that no serious injuries resulted from the numerous human landslides. The volunteer ambulance men found themselves overworked transporting the (thankfully mostly minor) injury victims to the makeshift casualty station inside Albion Road School, although five people were later taken to hospital. It is reported that two people died due to the effects of the crushing, one at the game itself and the other shortly after arriving home. The queues at one stage had stretched four or five deep along both sides of Albion Road, up Easter Road as far as the junction with London Road and down as far as Dalmeny Street, resulting in the kick-off being delayed for several minutes.

The game eventually got underway with hundreds of spectators lining the trackside, threatening on occasion to spill over on to the playing surface. Those that were able saw Hearts win a thrilling game 2–1, to inflict on Hibs their first home League defeat of the season. The visitors were forced to withstand severe first-half pressure, with goalkeeper Brown in outstanding form, and it was during this period that Hibs took the lead. With his side well on top, a splendid left-wing run by Ormond left a line of defenders sprawling in his wake, before sending over a hard head-high cross from the left that found the in-rushing Gordon Smith perfectly placed to brilliantly fire a header past the Hearts 'keeper from an acute angle. After the break, Hearts were the better side as they battled back to take the lead, but in the closing stages only several magnificent saves by Brown in the Hearts goal denied the home side a deserved share of the points. The result, however, still left Hibs at the top of the table with 29 points from 16 games, four points better off than second-placed Hearts, who had played a game more.

Before and after the match, there had been the now almost monotonous letters of complaint regarding Hibs' pricing policy and ticketing arrangements. With 7s 6d Centre Stand tickets changing hands for as much as £2, there were numerous allegations that when the tickets for the game had gone on sale, individuals, particularly young boys, had been paid to queue for tickets for others, and there was even the ludicrous complaint by one supporter that many of the people that had been seen queuing for the precious briefs had 'neither looked like football people, nor dressed like they could afford to pay the prices'.

The work to expand the main terracing was just the latest in a line of developments intended to increase the capacity of the stadium, which had been ongoing for many years. Before the war the area had been increased to accommodate just under 60,000, and the latest extension would add approximately 8,000 to that figure when completed. Plans to increase the maximum capacity to 98,000, with part of the terracing covered, had been in place since early 1948, but fortunately, with the post-war attendance boom soon to be over, these plans failed to materialise.

To accommodate the construction of the extension behind the main terracing, it had been necessary to purchase, from owners Redpath Brown, just over four acres of land that lay between the stadium and the railway line to the east. It also meant moving the bowling green that lay in the middle of this area, surrounded by a putting green and allotments, a hundred yards or so, from its original position directly behind the terracing to a new location at the south-east corner of the ground. One legal proviso attached to the purchase of the land was that it was 'to be used only in connection with the playing of the game of football', a condition that has often been breached throughout the years, usually to the despair of the supporters!

There had been some opposition to the intended purchase of the property, and this led to a quaint letter being forwarded to the owners. It is perhaps difficult with the passing of time to fully appreciate that even several years after the end of the war food was in still in relatively short supply, and it was this situation that prompted the Department of Agriculture for Scotland to intervene on behalf of several long-term allotment lease holders in July 1947, by writing to request that Redpath Brown, 'in light of the present food shortage, defer the sale of the land to Hibernian until the food situation becomes less stringent, or at least until the present growth cycle has been completed'.

As a matter of interest, the construction of the Easter Road grandstand and renovation of the standing areas began in 1924. Prior to this the main stand and a separate directors' box containing the changing rooms had been on the opposite side of the ground to the present structure, with an unstepped banking surrounding the other three sides of the playing surface. (The 1924 structure has since been demolished, and a new West Stand constructed in its place.) The original seated area was built in 1902 complete with a roof-mounted press box, and an adjacent directors' box was added in 1913. As far back as 1906, plans had been in place to move to a brand-new stadium at Piershill, just east of what is now Northfield Broadway, capable of holding over 50,000 spectators. Although a playing pitch, surrounded by a cycling and running track, was *in situ* complete with a small covered enclosure, it is not thought that any games were ever played at the new ground. It would appear that a planned more substantial grandstand was never built and the scheme eventually come to nothing when the North British Railway Co. obtained a compulsory purchase order to use part of the grounds for a new rail layout, which itself was never completed. The petition initially lodged with the local authorities, regarding the building of a new grandstand at Northfield, was for permission to 'Dismantle the existing grandstand situated at Hibernian Park, Easter Road. To re-erect at Piershill and alter same by the forming of a pavilion and press box and to construct open grandstands on either side of same'. It is almost certain that construction of the grandstand at Piershill was never undertaken as the stand and directors' box at Easter Road remained in use until replaced in 1924.

There was a postscript to the record attendance game. More than a year later Hibs were sued by a 71-year-old supporter for injuries received at the game. William Brand, a retired pub manager who lived in Rossie Place, just off Easter Road, claimed £750 compensation for his injuries. According to Brand, he was knocked unconscious, breaking several ribs and suffering severe shock when he was crushed against a retaining wall as he attempted to climb to safety from the swaying crowd. He further alleged that the police and stewards were unable to contain the 'grossly excessive number of spectators at the match'. According to him it was obvious even before the kick-off that it was dangerous to remain inside the stadium, and with no passages free from the crush he had no alternative than to attempt to scale the wall to safety, when he received his injuries. He was taken to hospital the following day and not released for almost a month. Denying the claim, lawyers for the football club insisted that all precautions had been taken, with more than the normal number of stewards on duty inside the ground, and that the number of injuries were not excessive for the size of the crowd. The court case was initially postponed and it is not known if further proceedings ever took place.

At the turn of the year, Hibs' third goal, scored by Jimmy Bradley, in an emphatic 6–1 win over Alloa at Easter Road, was the all-conquering reserve side's 100th of the season, and despite the first team's New Year defeat by Hearts, all three Hibs sides again topped their respective League tables. After the defeat by Hearts on 2 January, Hibs were to lose only one more League game that season.

A few weeks later, on 4 February 1950, Celtic were defeated 4–1 in a quite incredible match at Easter Road. Goalkeeper Tommy Younger was injured just before half-time in a clash with an opponent, forcing the home side to play the whole of the second half with 10 men. Eddie Turnbull often went in goal during training sessions and he fully expected to be called upon to replace the goalkeeper, but for some reason full-back Willie Clark was nominated and remarkably managed to keep a clean sheet for the final 45 minutes. The game was even more remarkable for the fact that Eddie Turnbull scored all Hibs' goals, three of them from the penalty spot, a feat unique in Scotland and only ever achieved three times before in England. The fourth was a typical Turnbull 'beezer' from fully 20 yards that screamed past goalkeeper Bonnar before he had the chance to move. Celtic's goal in the first half was also from the penalty spot by Collins after a retake. Goalkeeper Tommy Younger demonstrated the character and resolve that was prevalent throughout the club at that time when, although still far from recovered from his injury, he insisted on returning to help his short-handed teammates for the last 20 minutes of the game, a demand that was wisely rejected out of hand by manager Hugh Shaw.

In the Scottish Cup, hopes that the 48-year wait for the trophy would soon be over were brought to a swift end when Hibs were beaten 1–0 at Easter Road by Partick Thistle in the first round. In the opening 45 minutes, the home side did everything but score, but they were shocked when Thistle scored the only goal of the game 30 seconds after the restart. Thereafter Jags 'keeper Henderson was in unbeatable form, stopping everything that was thrown at him, and once again the home side were left to wonder if the elusive trophy would ever make its return to Easter Road.

A comprehensive 6–1 victory over Motherwell in mid-February was Hibs' best performance by far for some time. Yet another treble by Gordon Smith, the Greens' fifth of the season so far, and goals from Turnbull, Ormond and Reilly, saw Hibs overtake Hearts as the League's top scorers with 63, two more than their Edinburgh rivals. Rangers had managed only 43, but characteristically had conceded the least with 20, a tribute to their resolute 'Iron Curtain' style that often saw them adopt a strong defensive attitude once they had secured a lead. Bobby Johnstone had been Hibs' best player by far against Motherwell, the only one of the five not to figure on the score sheet, but his artistic promptings were behind most of Hibs' best moves.

At the beginning of March Hibs went down 1–0 to Third Lanark at home, a defeat that would eventually cost them dear. It is well recorded elsewhere that playing against them that afternoon was goalkeeper Lewis Goram, father of future Hibs and Scotland star Andy. Goram was still a registered Hibs player, but after a spell on loan at Leith Athletic he had been farmed out to the Cathkin club. It was Goram's one and only first-team appearance at Easter Road, and the result was a severe setback for the Edinburgh side, who were overtaken at the top of the table by fellow challengers Rangers.

There was a surprise in store for the fans the following week when Hugh Howie made a dramatic comeback to first-team action in place of the injured Combe after an absence of over 14 months in a 4–2 home win over Dundee, a victory that left the Championship challenge a two-horse race between Hibs and (predictably) Rangers. Again made captain for the day, the fans reserved a special cheer for the gangly international defender as he led the side out of the Easter Road tunnel.

A few weeks later, yet another event took place that further demonstrated the ambitious, imaginative and innovative thinking of Harry Swan. Tested almost a month before when several trainloads of Dundee fans had arrived before the match on 11 March, Hibs' new Easter Road Halt, which was situated on the Edinburgh to Granton railway line just behind the main terracing adjacent to the car park, was officially opened before the game against Clyde on Saturday 8 April 1950. A delegation from Easter Road, which included the directors and their wives, welcomed their counterparts, with captain Gordon Smith on hand to meet the players and fans of the Shawfield side who had travelled through from Glasgow by train. Thanks to the visionary Harry Swan, in conjunction with the North British Railway Company, many of the significant number of fans then attending Easter Road could now travel by 'football special' trains directly to the stadium. With only one platform, the Halt lacked facilities for return travel, and the supporters were required to make their way to either Abbeyhill Station or Waverley for the outward journey. In front of the gathered guests a short ceremony took place to officially open the new station, with Mrs Harry Swan formally cutting a green ribbon at the exit, then it was on to the game, where 25,000 watched Hibs run out convincing 6–3 winners, all of the soon-to-be-named 'Famous Five' scoring, Ormond twice. Sadly, Easter Road Halt now lies buried under thousands of tons of waste from the modern renovation of the stadium, the land now covered by a new housing estate.

With just two games left to play the Easter Road side were now three points ahead of the Light Blues who, however, still had three games in hand, and it was evident that the destination of the Championship would revolve around the clash of the titans at Ibrox.

As the big day dawned, Rangers still had a game in reserve over their nearest challenger, but if Hibs could return to Edinburgh with both points, then the title would be theirs. It was not to be. As Arsenal were beating Liverpool 2–0 in the FA Cup Final at Wembley, an unimpressive game in Glasgow ended 0–0, with one newspaper report of the time headlining the fact: 'No goals, no thrills, and for Hibs, no flag'. The Ibrox side had won the Scottish Cup the previous week, beating East Fife 3–0 in the Final, and the trophy was paraded around the ground before the teams took the field. With the gates locked well before kick-off time, and the kick-off delayed five minutes, a capacity crowd of over 105,000 saw Rangers make the better start, and although Hibs improved in the second half, the quality overall was such that the fans found it difficult to remind themselves that the game was a Championship decider. It could all have been so different. Only five minutes after the start Ormond missed a glorious chance to give his side the lead when he blasted wide with the goal gaping, and he and his teammates would rue the lost opportunity at full-time. A bitterly disappointed Swan would later declare: '49 points from any Championship is a great achievement. Rangers embarked on a what we have we hold attitude and must be deemed responsible for the poor quality of the game.'

The Light Blues still needed at least a draw the following week against Third Lanark to give them the flag and they succeeded. Thirds, with on-loan Goram still in goal and Johnny Cuthbertson at centre-forward, missed a penalty with only 15 minutes of the match remaining to deny themselves a victory and Hibs the League Championship trophy for the second time in three years. The decisive one-point lead gave Rangers the first-ever treble of League, League Cup and Scottish Cup.

It was while they were in London preparing for a friendly match against old adversaries Tottenham Hotspur that Hibs learned of Rangers' title success, before leaving for a six-game summer tour of Germany, Austria and Switzerland. At White Hart Lane a Willie Ormond goal from a wicked shot that deflected off future England manager Alf Ramsey and past his own goalkeeper was enough to give the visitors a winning start to the series of friendly games. The redoubtable Jimmy Cairns, who had survived the sinking of the destroyer HMS *Ghurka* in the Mediterranean after it had been torpedoed by a German U-Boat in 1942, had been injured during the League decider at Ibrox after a clash with Ian McColl, and it was only after arriving in London for the Spurs match that it was discovered that Cairns had cracked his fibula in the incident, playing almost 75 minutes against Rangers with a broken leg. Although 'Sailor' could still have accompanied his teammates to the Continent, the player elected to make his way home in order to recuperate in time for the new season.

The six-game Continental tour was deemed a brilliant success, with Hibs ending on the losing side only once, to Rapid Vienna, at that time considered one of the best teams in Europe. Overall 25 goals were scored and only seven conceded. It was during this trip that Hibs first experienced the novelty of playing under floodlights. During the last match of the tour, a 1–0 victory over Berne in Switzerland, Swan had initially been unhappy at not being informed beforehand that his side were to perform under the new medium, but it did not take the astute chairman long to realise the obvious potential of football under lights and the enormous advantages to be gained from their use. On his return to Scotland Swan made it a priority to discover more about this innovation.

During the long summer months, the thoughts of the Hibs fans kept returning to a season that had promised so much, only to end in bitter disappointment again. This time, however, with the gap between the top two sides much closer than in the previous campaign, it was widely felt that better things lay not too far in the future. Finishing six points in front of third-placed Hearts, Hibs had once again ended the season as top scorers in the League. Of the 86 Championship goals, Smith, Johnstone, Reilly, Turnbull and Ormond had been responsible for 80 of them, the others coming from Combe, who had scored four, and Buchanan with two. Since his reintroduction against Queen of the South in October, Bobby Johnstone had quickly settled into the side to become an automatic first choice. Looking every inch a future Scottish international, his astute football brain, tremendous passing ability and intricate dribbling skills complemented perfectly the individual talents of his more experienced teammates, particularly those of his incomparable wing partner Gordon Smith. History has seen the Famous Five receive most of the plaudits for Hibs' rise to prominence as the best side in the country during the late 1940s and early 1950s, but the often maligned rearguard, who were frequently criticised for their defensive failings, had conceded only 34 goals, the second lowest in the League, which was not bad going for a team so committed to attacking football. One unnamed forward would often complain that '"they" would concede three, leaving us to score four', but the back division could not have been all that bad, comprising on many occasions four players who were, or would become, full internationals, and one a League cap.

League Cup Final Defeat and Another League Triumph

During the summer months tremendous progress had been made on the extended terracing, now called 'Hill 60' by the players. Although the top level had not as yet been landscaped, the construction of a dividing wall to separate the top and bottom sections of the new enclosure was well underway and the entire project was expected to be completed shortly. It would soon be revealed, at that year's AGM, that the improvements to the stadium over the past couple of years had already cost the club almost £9,000, and the final total was expected to rise to around £14,000 before work would be completed. A top player at the club at that time would earn around £12 per week, so the final cost of the improvements represented a considerable outlay.

Just before the start of the forthcoming campaign there was the surprise announcement that Davie Shaw had left the club. A serious injury and the impressive form of Jimmy Cairns, an ever present the previous season, had limited Shaw's first-team appearances to just over a dozen outings, and the former club captain had been transferred to Aberdeen during the summer, ending 11 years' sterling service at Easter Road. Shaw had made a return to first-team action after his cartilage operation, ironically replacing the injured Cairns for the friendly match against Spurs at the end of the previous season, but with Sailor now well on the way to a full recovery from his broken leg, manager Hugh Shaw was placing his faith in the younger player. Davie Shaw continued to train with his erstwhile colleagues for some time, and the first day of pre-season training saw him take part in the opening exercises with the 30 or so full-timers under the watchful gaze of McColl and Kean. One familiar face missing from the line up was that of the popular Willie Finnigan, who had joined Dunfermline for a nominal fee a few days before, he too ending a long association with Easter Road that stretched back to well before the war.

As usual, several promising youngsters had been called-up to Easter Road during the summer break, including some who would have a prominent part to play in the coming years such as Jimmy Mulkerrin, John Grant, Lawrie Higgins, Willie McFarlane and the very much in demand Jimmy Shields, who had been signed from Shawfield Juniors.

In those less enlightened days, pre-season training consisted almost solely of running and exercises without a ball, so it was something of a relief for the players to take part in the numerous five-a-side competitions that marked the start of the forthcoming season. These contests were very popular with the fans, so much so that in those pre-television days, with pubs closing at 2.30 in the afternoon, Hibs won the Meadowbank Sports 'Fives' by a solitary corner, watched by a crowd in the region of 14,500, a figure that just failed to beat the record attendance for the ground.

The backroom staff were of the opinion that these competitions were a great supplement to normal training, giving the players a competitive edge and physical sharpness, and so popular were they with the players that one weekend alone Hibs entered five separate sides in various competitions, four of the teams reaching their respective Finals, three of them winning the tournament. Another popular activity that broke the monotony of training was the annual charity challenge match against Leith Franklin cricket club, which helped to raise funds for the nearby Eastern General Hospital, and on a beautiful summer's evening well over 5,000 spectators turned up at Leith Links to watch the fun, with the hospital fund the winners to the tune of £35 after a collection among the crowd.

As usual the new season was eagerly awaited, and a press report in the local *Evening News* at the time assured the Hibs fans that 'Gordon Smith promises to maintain his place unchallenged as the most complete club winger in the game today. Rangers fans will perhaps disagree, but with all due respect to a galloping and penetrative Willie Waddell, the Hibs outside-right has them all licked for sheer artistic ball control and well directed shooting'.

Once again the annual Edinburgh Select Charities game was used as a curtain-raiser to the new season, this time at Tynecastle, and seven days after the 1–1 draw with Newcastle United, who would go on to win the FA Cup that season, Jackie Milburn and all, it was down to the serious business of the League Cup.

Hibs started the 1950–51 League Cup campaign with six straight wins in a group comprising Dundee, Falkirk and St Mirren, scoring 19 goals in five of the games without reply. The other was a quite remarkable game against Falkirk at Brockville that older supporters still talk about. With only 15 minutes of the game played, the 'Bairns', led by the recently transferred former Hib Angus Plumb, were three goals ahead, but two first-half strikes by the visitors reduced the leeway. After the break the game seesawed from end to end, with the home side increasing their lead early in the half, but showing immense character as they attempted to save the game. Hibs eventually capped a magnificent fightback with a hat-trick goal from Gordon Smith in the dying minutes to win 5–4. One newspaper report of the match stated that 'for thrills, excitement and goals, this was probably the finest game seen at Brockville for many years.'

There was to be no repeat of the excitement in the return game at Easter Road, where Hibs goalkeeper Younger was a virtual spectator in a game that was as good as over at half-time, the home side eventually scoring four times without a reply as they marched on to the quarter-finals. An earlier section match against Dundee at Dens Park had been abandoned 20 minutes from the end with Hibs leading 2–0. Torrential rain made play on the slippery surface extremely dangerous, leaving the referee with no alternative other than to call a halt to the action. As the Edinburgh side had already won the section with 10 points, five ahead of their nearest rivals, it was thought to be unnecessary for the match to be replayed.

As a sign of Hibs' superiority over Falkirk at this time, four goals by Reilly and two from Turnbull, against his home-town side, saw them win 6–0 in the opening League game of the season in Edinburgh. Bobby Johnstone celebrated his 21st birthday by inspiring his side to the emphatic victory, and although he failed to get on the score sheet himself, his intelligent prompting from midfield helped set up several of the goals. Gordon Smith was forced to miss the game after picking up an injury in the 4–0 victory over Falkirk the previous week, when he had finished the game as a virtual passenger, and with both Tommy McDonald and Jim Souness unavailable, Jimmy Gunning made his first and only first-team appearance for the Edinburgh side before his move to Manchester City later in the year. Smith's usual understudy Tommy McDonald had a unique excuse for missing the game. On National Service with the Highland Light Infantry at the time, his Battalion Sergeant Major had refused McDonald leave, and he was one of the regimental dancers who entertained an appreciative crowd in Princes Street Gardens during that year's Edinburgh Festival as his teammates were running riot at Easter Road.

Still the controversy over Lawrie Reilly's best position continued. Many supporters remained convinced that the player's most effective position was on the left wing, but his four goals against Falkirk leading the attack capped a particularly productive spell for the player, who had now scored 10 goals in seven games wearing the number-nine shirt. This surely confirmed once and for all that the Scottish international's true position was leading the front line, leaving the newspapers to ask whether there was a consistently better centre-forward in the country.

In mid-September Pittodrie was the setting for the start of a remarkable League Cup quarter-final marathon that has gone down in Hibs folklore. Free-scoring Hibs, who had already scored an amazing 30 goals in just seven games, were again without the services of the injured Gordon Smith. Jim Souness, who would shortly win a League Cup-winners' medal with Hearts, was drafted into the side as his replacement. Aberdeen were captained by ex-Easter Road stalwart Davie Shaw, who was facing his former side for the first time.

In a punishing game packed full of thrills and excitement, Bobby Johnstone gave Hibs an undeserved first-half lead, but Aberdeen were by far the better side, scoring four times in the second half to seemingly put the tie beyond the visitors, and it could have been worse. With only two minutes remaining Hather missed an open goal, and almost certainly a four-goal deficit would have been too much even for a Hibs side playing to the top of their form in the return leg at Easter Road. The early strike by Johnstone had given Hibs some semblance of hope for the return game, but as far as the realists were concerned, the tie was as good as over.

The second leg took place at Easter Road on the following Wednesday evening. To accommodate the prospect of extra-time in those pre-floodlit days the Easter Road gates were opened just before 4pm for the 5.30 start. Fifteen minutes before the kick-off manager McCartney, much to the surprise of the other players in the home dressing room, ordered the obviously still unfit Gordon Smith to get stripped. The loudspeaker announcement that Smith would play was greeted by ecstatic cheers from the majority of the Hibs fans among the 35,000 crowd, an ovation that could be heard in the dressing rooms, and as the heavily bandaged Hibs captain took the toss, clearly far from full fitness, it was obvious from the look on the faces of Davie Shaw and his teammates that the away side had been dealt a major psychological blow.

If the home side were to have any real chance of overhauling the visitors' lead an early goal was desperately needed, and their prayers were answered when right-half Anderson put the ball past his own 'keeper after just three minutes. With an hour of a thrilling and pulsating game gone, Aberdeen still retained their two-goal advantage, but late strikes from both Johnstone and Ormond were enough to send the tie into extra-time. Reilly took advantage of an overhead-kick by Smith to score a fourth only two minutes into the extra period to give Hibs an overall lead that looked like being enough. But with the Hibs fans desperately pleading for referee Jackson to blow the final whistle, and the Aberdeen fans starting to drift away, Yorston levelled the aggregate score with the last kick of the game when he pounced on a loose ball in Hibs' penalty area to fire past Younger to force a replay.

A third game took place at Ibrox in front of 52,000, the largest attendance of the three games so far, but despite the advantage of yet another 30 minutes of extra-time the teams could not be separated, the tie finishing all square at one goal apiece. In the closing stages of regulation time both Reilly and Smith had chances to send Hibs into the semi-final, particularly in the dying seconds, when with the Aberdeen goal gaping Gordon Smith somehow managed to blast the ball high over the bar from close range when it seemed easier to score. In later years Smith would remember the miss as the worst of his entire career.

With the semi-finals of the competition scheduled for the following Saturday, it was imperative that the tie be settled quickly, and the second replay went ahead the following evening at the National Stadium. This game was also originally scheduled to take place at Ibrox, but the heavy rain the previous night had meant the closing stages of the tie being played on a pitch resembling a mud bath, so the fixture was quickly switched to Hampden. This time there would be no mistake. Striking top form immediately, Hibs ran their opponents ragged, scoring three times in a nine-minute spell of a pulsating first half, and although Aberdeen mustered a brief fightback, when in truth they could well have scored more, Hibs ran out emphatic 5–1 winners in the end. Although, considering the scoreline, Hibs would probably still have won well in any case, Eddie Turnbull was in no doubt that the fact that the Hibs players had spent the night in their own beds while the Aberdeen players had stayed overnight in a Glasgow hotel had been a contributing factor in the Edinburgh side's impressive victory. In the days before players were 'exhausted' after playing two games in the same week, Hibs had played six games in the space of 18 days. Five of them, including a League encounter at Pittodrie, had been against Aberdeen, watched by just under 200,000 spectators in total.

In the semi-final at Tynecastle on the Saturday, a game ruined in many respects by the blustery conditions, Hibs overcame a sticky opening spell after Second Division promotion candidates Queen of the South had taken an early lead. With memories of another Cup upset by lower League opponents at the semi-final stage of the competition at the same venue still fresh in everyone's mind, a 30-yard thunderbolt from three-goal Man of the Match Eddie Turnbull eased their fears and put the capital side well on their way to a 3–1 win and a meeting with Motherwell in the Final.

Two weeks before the Final, the teams met in a League game at Fir Park. Despite an injury to Smith in the opening 15 minutes that saw him a virtual passenger on the right wing and Hibs effectively reduced to 10 men, the east coast side ran out easy 6–2 winners and red-hot favourites to win the League Cup.

Because of international commitments Hibs had no League game on the Saturday preceding the Final. Smith missed a Scotland call-up because of the injury sustained at Fir Park, but Reilly was in fine form, scoring twice from the centre-forward position in Scotland's 3–1 victory over Wales in Cardiff. Turnbull, called-up to the squad, sat out the game after being injured during training at the team's headquarters.

In the days leading up to the Cup Final, Harry Swan made one of his rare errors of judgement. Turnbull, still suffering the effects of the injury picked up with Scotland, had no chance of playing in the game. Swan, who was in the habit of visiting the ground on a daily basis, watched the players in what was little more than an eight-a-side bounce game in midweek, with Willie Ormond playing in what could loosely be termed the inside-left position in impressive form. Instead of drafting in the obvious and ready-made replacement for Turnbull in Mick Gallagher, the chairman was insistent that Ormond should play in the inside position on the Saturday at Hampden, and after arguments to the contrary, manager Shaw reluctantly agreed.

Ormond's usual place on the left wing was filled by reserve outside-left Jimmy Bradley, signed from Port Glasgow Rovers in 1948, giving the youngster his first-ever first-team start. The experiment was a dismal failure, and Hampden, thought one watching reporter: 'once again became a burial ground for Hibs' Cup aspirations'. Watched by a crowd in the region of 60,000, Ormond was not a success as an inside-forward and Bradley found himself overawed by the occasion, leaving Hibs to play a Cup Final with nine effective men. Although the better side for the majority of the game, a Hibs forward line that had found goals so easy to come by just two weeks before encountered a Motherwell defence in a much more uncompromising and resolute mood, the Lanarkshire side deservedly taking the trophy in the end, winning 3–0, all three goals coming during the last 15 minutes. Goalkeeper Younger, who had been badly at fault for at least two of the goals, one when he miskicked a clearance straight to a Motherwell forward, who promptly took advantage of the gift to score, had to be consoled by his teammates at the final whistle as he broke down in tears. Turnbull's strength and forcefulness in the middle of the park had been badly missed, as had the ingenuity of Ormond on the flank. Jimmy Bradley never played for the first team again and would soon be on his way to Third Lanark. It was revealed only after the game that in the week leading up to the Final six Hibs players had been fighting a fitness battle to play on the Saturday, but unlike Turnbull, Paterson, Ogilvie, Johnstone, Smith and Reilly had all played, the last two obviously far from 100 per cent fit.

Before the game rumours had been rife that Smith and Turnbull had deliberately opted out of the Scotland side against Wales to save themselves for the Cup Final, but with Turnbull's omission from the Hampden showpiece and Smith's level of fitness questionable, that notion was quickly dispelled.

Hibernian: Younger, Govan, Ogilvie, Buchanan, Paterson, Combe, Smith, Johnstone, Reilly, Ormond, Bradley.
Motherwell: Hamilton, Kilmarnock, Shaw, McLeod, Paton, Redpath, Watters, Forrest, Kelly, Watson, Aitkenhead.
Referee: J. Mowat.

There was a slightly humorous postscript to the Final. In the early days of the competition there were no medals for those involved in the League Cup Final. Instead the winners received £10 and the runners-up £5. On entering the dressing room after the game, an obviously bitterly disappointed Gordon Smith crumpled up the envelope containing a white five-pound note, a substantial sum then, before angrily throwing it into the corner of the room. Reminded several times before leaving the changing room to collect his money, the outside-right ignored his teammates' pleas, and half a dozen Hibs players drowned their sorrows that evening in a Portobello hostelry courtesy of Smith's Cup Final reward.

With the disappointment of the League Cup Final behind them, the following Saturday the first encounter of the season between the likely title contenders ended in stalemate at Ibrox in front of 70,000 spectators. Rangers had the better of the first half, but only a Paterson own-goal separated the sides after an attempted pass back to Younger only succeeded in beating the goalkeeper. The renowned fighting qualities of Hibs came to the fore, however, and a vigorous second-half fightback was rewarded when Reilly scored a deserved equaliser.

By this time, Smith, Johnstone, Reilly, Turnbull and Ormond had long been the accepted front line, although they were yet to gain the 'Famous Five' *nom de plume*, credited to Rex Kingsley of the *Sunday Mail*. Fifty-two goals had been scored in just 17 games, including the League Cup ties, and the five had accounted for 51 of them, the other being an own-goal. Perhaps somewhat surprisingly, Turnbull was the leading scorer at that time with 16, including one treble and four doubles. Of the 16 League points possible between then and the usual defeat at Tynecastle on New Year's Day, none were dropped as Hibs scored 22 goals while conceding just four.

At Cathkin in mid-December, Eddie Turnbull was sent off for the first time in his senior career after he was involved in an incident with Third Lanark outside-left Staroscik, who had been giving Smith a hard time with some particularly harsh treatment. In the second half, the robust Turnbull tackled Staroscik out near the far touchline, taking man, ball and turf, leaving the referee no option but to send him off, and the inside-forward was forced to endure a barrage of jeers as he made the long walk around the trackside to the changing rooms.

Just four days after his dismissal at Cathkin, Turnbull won his fourth full cap in the unfamiliar position of inside-right, the sole Hibs player in a Scotland side beaten 1–0 by Austria at Hampden, the country's first-ever defeat on home soil by a foreign side. Coincidentally, Austria had been the first continental side to play in Scotland when they drew 2–2 at Hampden in 1933. Although unimpressive in the first half, Turnbull improved after the break, almost scoring with his side trailing, before hitting the post near the end. It would be almost eight years before he would again represent his country at full level.

An injured toe received during the match forced the player to miss Hibs' next League game against St Mirren in Edinburgh, and Bob Wood, a part-timer signed from Haddington Athletic two years before, made a scoring first-team debut deputising for the injured international. A few days before Christmas, Turnbull would receive an early festive present at Park Gardens when he was suspended for 14 days for his indiscretion at Cathkin. He made his farewell for the next fortnight against his home-town team at Brockville, and how Falkirk must have hated Hibs at that time. Having already conceded a five, a four and a six against the Edinburgh side in the three matches that season, Turnbull scored twice in yet another emphatic 5–1 victory as the home side were completely out-thought, outplayed and outclassed in every department. That same afternoon, at Easter Road, Hibs' reserves overwhelmed Falkirk's second string 10–0, centre-forward Jimmy Mulkerrin notching a hat-trick. As some indication of the tremendous reserve strength at Easter Road at that time, 10 of the side that faced Falkirk reserves either had, or would, figure in the first team while at Easter Road, and two, Howie and Gallacher, with international recognition.

Hibernian Reserves: Kerr, Howie, Cairns, Gallacher, Aird, Mackie, Souness, Ward, Mulkerrin, Wood, Allan.

Bob Wood would make another four appearances for the first team, scoring once, while again deputising in Turnbull's absence, but he would not be considered a long-term replacement. He would sign for English club Barnsley at the end of the season, remaining at the Oakwell Ground for 14 years.

Incredibly, if a player was suspended by the disciplinary committee in those days, SFA and Scottish League rules prohibited the offender from attending the ground during the length of the ban, even for training, and worse still, he was not supposed to be paid. Whether this indeed happened at other clubs is unclear, but Turnbull, like any other Hibs player in a similar position, trained as usual with his teammates and collected his brown pay packet on a Tuesday afternoon as normal.

Not always universally popular – and there are numerous stories of him falling out with certain individuals – Harry Swan believed in paying the players and paying them well. As well as a top class wage, unexpected 'illicit' bonuses were regularly to be found in the pay packet after a particularly important win. Occasionally these were as much as £100, which was more than eight times the average Easter Road first-team wage at the time, and it was fairly common for Hibs to receive a larger 'bonus' after losing a game than had been received by the victors. A famous instance is the now well-recorded tale of Willie Woodburn trying to wind up Lawrie Reilly during a game at Ibrox by telling him that Rangers were on £20 to beat Hibs. 'That's nothing,' replied Reilly, 'we're on £100 a man to beat you.'

Hearts continued their good form against their near neighbours in the 1951 New Year's Day fixture at Tynecastle with a 2–1 victory. It was their fifth successive League win and second consecutive double over their deadly rivals. It was also Hibs' first League defeat since September. Twenty-four hours later the Easter Road title challenge was back on the rails when well over 30,000 packed inside Easter Road to see top-of-the-table Aberdeen twice take the lead, before eventually being overwhelmed 6–2 in a second half display of devastating and scintillating football that rocked the visitors to the core. Gordon Smith in particular was in magnificent form as he inspired his teammates to the comprehensive victory. In the six games between the sides already that season Hibs had scored 18 times while conceding just 11, Bobby Johnstone the top individual marksman of the series with six.

A 3–1 defeat of Raith Rovers at Starks Park on the Saturday, thanks to a goal from Bobby Johnstone and two from Gordon Smith, meant that Hibs were now only one point behind new League leaders Dundee, who had played four games more. Only the recent defeat by Hearts had denied them the chance to go top for the first time that season, but they did not have too long to wait. In the middle of the month a 3–1 victory over Motherwell at Easter Road saw Hibs sitting proudly at the top of the table on goal average from Aberdeen. Both teams shared the same number of points, but in Hibs' case it had taken them

Harry Swan. Along with manager Willie McCartney he was the architect of Hibs' great post-war teams.

Manager Willie McCartney.

The Hibs party during their 1938 tour of Ireland. Harry Swan is extreme left in the back row, Willie McCartney is sixth from right in the same row.

The Hibs team before a match in Ireland in 1938. McCartney is second from the right, back row, trainer Shaw is third from left. Willie Finnigan, who would win the Championship in 1948, is third from left in the front row.

Sammy Kean and Willie Finnigan.

Elegance personified. The great Gordon Smith.

England v Scotland at Wembley, 1944. Hibs captain Baxter introduces Gordon Smith on his Scotland debut. On Smith's left are Walker (Hearts), Milne (Hibs), Black (Hearts) and Caskie (Hibs). It was an all Edinburgh front line.

Prime Minister Clem Attlee is introduced to Gordon Smith before the Victory Cup game Hibs v Partick Thistle, 25 May 1946.

Hibs 1944–45. Back row, from left: Finnigan, Hall, Kean, Downie, Baxter, Shaw and Bogan. Front row: Smith, Milne, Willie McCartney, Nutley and Caskie.

Davie Shaw: Hibs and Scotland.

Lawrie Reilly and Archie Buchanan wearing a Hibs strip for the very first time, c.1944.

The Hibs party prepare to leave on the first leg of their trip to Czechoslovakia in the summer of 1946. Front, from left: McCartney, Kerr, McIntyre (secretary), Smith, Fraser, Howie, Nutley, Peat and Swan. On the steps from front: Finnigan, Aird, Davie Shaw, Kean, Milne, Weir and Hugh Shaw.

Hibs line up before a game against Sparta in Prague, 1946. From left: Finnigan, Kean, Kerr, Shaw, Weir, Howie, Milne, Nutley, Aird, Smith and Aitkenhead.

Captain Willie Finnigan leads Hibs onto the field for a match during the Czechoslovakian tour, closely followed by Sammy Kean and goalkeeper Jimmy Kerr.

Jock Govan: Hibs and Scotland.

Queen of the South score against Hibs at Dumfries, August 1945. The Hibs players are Shaw (left) goalkeeper Downie and Govan. Note the absence of numbers on the shirts.

Gordon Smith, Archie Buchanan, Jock Weir, Johnny Cuthbertson and Johnny Aitkenhead, *c.*1946.

Eddie Turnbull scoring against Motherwell in the famous 1947 Scottish Cup semi-final at Hampden.

Jock Weir: Hibs, Blackburn Rovers, Celtic and Falkirk.

The official programme for the 1947 Scottish Cup Final.

The Hibs party before travelling through to Glasgow for the 1947 Scottish Cup Final. Centre front is teenager Lawrie Reilly, who would not be selected for the game.

The side that faced Aberdeen in the 1947 Scottish Cup Final. Back row, from left: Shaw, Govan, Kerr, Howie, Aird and Kean. Front: Smith, Finnigan, Cuthbertson, Turnbull and Ormond.

The legendary Easter Road groundsman Harry Reading tending to his beloved turf.

1948 Scottish League Champions. Back row, from left: Aird, Kean, Govan, Kerr, Farm, Howie, Buchanan and Reilly. Front: Linwood, Smith, Finnigan, Captain Shaw, Turnbull, Ormond and Combe.

Five Hibs for Scotland v Belgium, 1948. From left: Davie Shaw, Jock Govan, Bobby Combe, Gordon Smith and Eddie Turnbull. Hugh Howie was selected as travelling reserve.

The immortal 'Famous Five': Gordon Smith, Bobby Johnstone, Lawrie Reilly, Eddie Turnbull and Willie Ormond.

Gordon Smith.

Bobby Johnstone.

Lawrie Reilly.

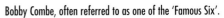

Eddie Turnbull.

Willie Ormond.

Bobby Combe, often referred to as one of the 'Famous Six'.

Turnbull scoring one of his four goals, three from the penalty spot, against Celtic, February 1950.

Gordon Smith evades Rangers Cox and Shaw.

The dejected Rangers players after Bobby Johnstone (at extreme right of picture) scores the winner in Hibs' famous Scottish Cup victory at Ibrox, February 1951.

1950–51 Scottish League Champions. Back row, from left: Paterson, McColl (trainer), Buchanan, Younger, Shaw (manager), Govan, Ogilvie, Souness, Kean (trainer) and Gallagher. Front: Terris (director), Reilly, Combe, Swan (chairman), Smith, Ormond, Hartland (director). In front: Johnstone and Turnbull.

John Paterson, a Scottish League cap.

Gordon Smith, Scottish Footballer of the Year, 1951.

Gordon Smith lies injured in a game against Raith Rovers at Easter Road. Reilly and Ormond are in attendance.

three games fewer to achieve parity. The Edinburgh side also had a far superior goal difference, scoring 45 goals while conceding just 16 compared to the Dons' 45 for and 33 against. With the exception of one week, it was a lead they would hold until the last game of the season.

At that time the country was in the grip of a spell of severe weather, and before the match with Motherwell could proceed, braziers were needed to soften the far top corner of the Easter Road pitch, which was rock hard with frost. The continuing inclemental conditions prompted renewed calls for a mid-season break, some even advocating a six-week lay-off during the 'traditional' bad weather period. Chairman Swan, a vociferous opponent of the idea, expressed the opinion that 'It was neither possible to regulate the weather for football, nor the football for the weather', adding that 'many more players suffer injuries on the hard baked summer pitches, than on the ice bound ones'. It would also be difficult, thought Swan, to 'keep players fit during this period. It went further than mere physical fitness, the mental aspect also had to be considered'. The mid-season break would eventually be tried, but not for almost another 50 years.

Meanwhile, in the Scottish League side to face the League of Ireland at Parkhead the selectors had chosen an all-Edinburgh inside trio. As well as obvious choice Lawrie Reilly at centre-forward, the committee had selected Bobby Johnstone at inside-right and Jimmy Wardhaugh of Hearts at inside-left, both of these players gaining their first representative honours. As it would turn out, the prolific Reilly would score twice in a one sided 7–0 victory, with Johnstone and Wardhaugh collecting one apiece. There was a further Hibs influence on the scoreline with former Easter Road star Johnny Aitkenhead also scoring twice. Unlike full internationals, no caps were awarded for inter-League games, the participants having to be satisfied with a medal and £10 for their efforts.

The now seemingly endless quest for Scottish Cup glory started that year at Love Street, but St Mirren were found to be a tougher nut to crack than in the previous three games against them that season, which had seen Hibs score 14 times. This time a goal for each side within a 60 second period midway through the second half meant that a second game was needed to separate the sides. With the incentive of a game against Rangers for the winners of the replay at Easter Road on the Wednesday, four goals in the first 26 minutes by a 'brilliant and bewildering' Hibs, left St Mirren requiring a miracle that failed to materialise. One of the highlights of the 5–0 win was the magical interchanging of the five home forwards, who bamboozled the St Mirren defenders while delighting the partisan support among the 30,000 crowd throughout the entire 90 minutes by rarely being found in the same position for long.

A 1–0 victory over Celtic in Glasgow at the beginning of February, after Eddie Turnbull had scored with the visitors' only real chance of the game, put Hibs clear at the top of the League table, one point ahead of now nearest challengers Rangers with three games in hand. Before any thoughts of the Championship could be entertained, however, there was the little matter of a second-round Scottish Cup meeting against the Light Blues at Ibrox.

The football special trains that collected supporters at North Leith and Abbeyhill stations before departing Waverley for Glasgow Queen Street were packed solid with fans who had stumped up the required 5s 3d return fare. Such was the incredible interest in the game that the Ibrox gates were closed well before the kick-off with over 100,000 people crammed inside. Twice behind, Hibs' famous resolve came to the fore as they refused to concede defeat. Level at one goal each at the interval, after Smith had cancelled out an early opener by Rangers centre-forward Simpson, the Hibs 'magical five' ultimately struck up an understanding that the home side failed to match, and they were rewarded with two second-half goals inside the space of two minutes to give the Edinburgh side a famous victory. Turnbull scored in the 75th minute with a thunderous drive to equalise for a second time, and only two minutes later Hibs were awarded a direct free-kick 20 yards from the Rangers goal after centre-half

Woodburn had fouled Smith. From the free-kick Turnbull feigned to unleash one of his trademark thunderbolt shots as expected, but instead he rolled the ball to Johnstone, who was standing just in front of the Rangers defensive wall. The slightly-built inside man cheekily flicked the ball into the air before chipping it over his shoulder and past the bewildered defenders for the winning goal, much to the surprise of Rangers' 'keeper Bobby Brown and the 106,000 spectators. The defeat denied Rangers the opportunity to become the first-ever side to win four consecutive Scottish Cups, and for only the second season since 1926 the Glasgow giants were now in real danger of failing to collect even one trophy. After the game, the *Evening News* columnist 'Tron Kirk' questioned the realism of some of the Glasgow-based newspaper reporters, who, obviously stunned that 'their' team had been beaten in the Cup, incredibly claimed the victory over Rangers as 'the finest thing that the Easter Road side had ever done'. This outrageous statement prompted a huge mailbag response from readers suggesting numerous other victories over the years that had been equally good if not better, and telling 'Tron Kirk' to urge his press colleagues to be 'lyrical without the hysterics'.

In the next round Hibs were drawn against Airdrie at Broomfield, but in a Scottish Cup rehearsal at the same ground at the beginning of March the Greens tasted League defeat for the first time since the New Year's Day reverse at Tynecastle. The 3–1 victory did not flatter the Lanarkshire side, who were well worth their win, and the victory suggested that the Cup tie seven days later would be no mere formality for the Edinburgh side.

There was a novel arrangement in place for fans wishing to attend the Cup game at Broomfield. As well as being able to purchase a rail ticket at Waverley for the trip to Airdrie, they could now also buy a match ticket for the game at the station. On the day of the sale a long queue had quickly gathered, and the British Rail allocation of match tickets was sold out within the hour. In a brilliant piece of enterprise, Airdrie had also distributed tickets via the SMT coach company, as well as supplying Easter Road with their usual allocation.

A sell-out 24,000 capacity crowd packed into Broomfield for the fourth-round Scottish Cup tie on 10 March 1951. There was an initial concern for manager Shaw that Younger, then on National Service duty at Dreghorn Camp in Edinburgh, might be refused permission to play, but the fair-haired custodian was in his usual place at the kick-off. Once the game started, a gritty and resolute home defence succeeded in holding out until half-time against a slick, fast-moving Hibs front line, but any hopes of consecutive wins over the visitors were dispelled in the second half when the quicksilver Reilly bagged all three Hibs goals, the sixth hat-trick of his senior career. All 11 who wore the famous green and white that afternoon performed well, but at the final whistle centre-forward Lawrie Reilly was carried shoulder high from the pitch by a group of enthusiastic supporters, many of them utterly convinced that this would at last be the year that the Scottish Cup hoodoo would be banished forever.

Jimmy Bradley, who had not featured in Hibs' first team since making his ill-fated debut against Motherwell in the League Cup Final five months before, had been transferred to Third Lanark at the beginning of the month, but neither he nor former Easter Road favourite Johnny Cuthbertson, who scored his side's goal in Hibs' 3–1 victory, was able to stem the tide of Hibs' determined march towards the title when the teams met in Edinburgh. Seven days later a solitary Bobby Johnstone goal on a treacherous snow-covered Love Street pitch gave Hibs the victory that almost certainly assured them their second League title in four years. Left-half Pat Ward made his debut in place of the injured Bobby Combe and performed well in a defence that had now conceded just two goals against St Mirren in the six games between the sides that season, while their colleagues in the forward line had now scored 21 times in the corresponding fixtures. With only six games remaining Hibs were three points ahead of second-placed Aberdeen, but with the added safety net of three games in hand over the Grampian side.

That same afternoon, the East of Scotland third-team fixture against Hearts at Easter Road drew a gate of almost 11,000 spectators, an attendance that would be the envy of most League clubs at the time. Many had been attracted by the promise of a ticket for the forthcoming Scottish Cup semi-final tie against Motherwell at Tynecastle, which could be purchased at the ground that afternoon. Not for the first time controversy surrounded the sale, with hundreds left bitterly disappointed when the allocation ran out prematurely, leaving 'Sucker' to complain to the *Evening News* that after queuing for nearly an hour he had been forced to leave empty-handed. Somewhat cynically he continued, 'Roll on the Speedway season where at least they try to cater for their regular supporters'.

In the Scottish Cup semi-final at Tynecastle, both Hibs and Motherwell took the field to encounter the worst surface that many of them had ever experienced. After an overnight frost, the Hearts ground staff had spread a liberal covering of peat over the bone-hard pitch underneath, resulting in a treacherous morass that deteriorated further as the game progressed.

Wilson Humphries, a future Hibs coach under Eddie Turnbull during the 1970s, and home on leave from the forces, was a surprise inclusion in the Motherwell side, his first start of the season. With thousands of fans still packing the streets outside the ground and the start delayed by several minutes, Hibs' hopes of gaining revenge for the earlier League Cup Final defeat suffered a severe setback when they found themselves a goal down inside the opening 40 seconds when Kelly finished off a move started on the left by former Hibs player Johnny Aitkenhead. Worse was to follow for Hibs 15 minutes later. A bad bounce on the uneven surface just outside the Hibs penalty area completely deceived centre-half Paterson, leaving the retreating John Ogilvie to challenge inside-left Watson. Although saving a certain goal, the Hibs defender was stretchered from the field with his right leg shattered in two places. In a pulsating match, 10-man Hibs showed all their renowned fighting qualities, but a further injury to Ormond, which effectively left them with nine men, was too much, and although Reilly pulled back a late goal at 3–1, and Gordon Smith had another disallowed for offside shortly after he had struck the bar with a thunderbolt shot, Motherwell went through to their second Cup Final of the season, where they would eventually lose 1–0 to Celtic.

Hibernian: Younger, Govan, Ogilvie, Buchanan, Paterson, Combe, Smith, Johnstone, Reilly, Turnbull, Ormond.

Ogilvie's unfortunate leg break was a tragic blow for the youngster, at that time playing the best football of his career. Since replacing Cairns for the return fixture against Aberdeen in the League Cup at Easter Road seven months before, he had been an ever present in the side and made the left-back position his own. The horrendous injury would keep the player out of football for over a year, but typical of the club, in a generous gesture designed to ease the player's concerns over his future, manager Hugh Shaw visited Ogilvie in the Western General Hospital the following day with a new contract in his pocket, and left after making him his first signing for the forthcoming season. The injury to Ormond that had resulted in the player finishing the match at Tynecastle as a virtual passenger on the left wing was later diagnosed as damaged ligaments, severe enough to require surgery. The news was yet another setback for the unlucky player, who had already had more than his fair share of injuries.

The horrific injury list continued to take its toll and it was perhaps just as well that Hibs had such a commanding lead in the League. Smith had missed the previous game, a 1–1 draw with nearest challengers Dundee, because of injuries received during the semi-final, and during the week Reilly had also called off, leaving Turnbull as the only one of the 'Five' to feature in what was virtually a League decider against Clyde at Easter Road. Fielding a side containing reserves Souness, Higgins, Cairns and Mulkerrin, who was making his first-team debut, Hibs' second League Championship title in four years was secured on 11 April 1951 when a 4–0 victory was enough to give them the flag, 10 points clear of their nearest rivals with four games to spare.

The Hibs team that secured the League Championship was: Younger, Govan, Cairns, Howie, Paterson, Buchanan, Souness, Combe, Mulkerrin, Turnbull, Higgins.

It was a week of double celebration at Easter Road. The impressive title-winning form of Bobby Johnstone had not gone unnoticed by the selectors, and he made his full international debut at inside-right on 14 April 1951, replacing colleague Eddie Turnbull in the side from Scotland's previous game, when both he and teammate Lawrie Reilly made scoring contributions in the 3–2 defeat of England at Wembley in front of just under 100,000 spectators. In truth Scotland's victory should have been far more emphatic. Hassall opened the scoring for the home side after 26 minutes, but Scotland equalised seven minutes later with a real 'Hibs inspired' move. With both players in their normal positions, Reilly started the move out wide on the left. He quickly found his clubmate with an inch-perfect pass, leaving Johnstone to round centre-half Froggatt before placing an accurate shot behind Williams in the England goal for a marvellous equaliser. Within three minutes of the restart Scotland took the lead, and again it was a move right out of the Hibs training ground. Reilly found Johnstone with a clever chip. Johnstone, who had been a thorn in the side of the England defence all afternoon, was quickly closed down by centre-half Froggatt, but managed to pass the ball inside to the waiting Reilly, who wasted no time in crashing home from nine yards. Liverpool's Billy Liddell added a third for Scotland a few minutes later, and although the legendary Tom Finney scored again for the home side, the goal proved to be a mere consolation, Scotland finishing the game as worthy winners.

With the League won, reserve goalkeeper Bill Bruce and outside-right John Munro were both given a run in the first team in a 3–0 victory over Raith Rovers, and a successful season ended in style with home victories over both halves of the Old Firm. Against Rangers, Gordon Smith's reappearance after an absence of several weeks delighted the crowd and inspired his teammates to a Championship display that ended in a comprehensive 4–1 victory. Three days later, the curtain was drawn over a fabulous season with a fine 3–1 win against Scottish Cup-winners Celtic.

For the first time, Lawrie Reilly had finished the season as top League goalscorer, claiming 22 of Hibs' 78 goals, ending Gordon Smith's near monopoly as top marksman in seven of the previous eight years. In all competitions Reilly had claimed 37 of the 129 goals secured, a new record under the 16-team set-up, all except 12 being scored by the Famous Five.

Twenty-three players had been used in securing the Championship, John Paterson the only ever present, playing in all 30 games. Younger, Reilly and Johnstone had all made one appearance less. Buchanan, Smith, Turnbull, Govan, Ormond, Ogilvie, Combe and Howie were the other regulars, with occasional outings for Cairns, Gallacher, Wood, Mulkerrin, Souness, Bruce, Ward, Gunning, Munro, Allan and Lawrie Higgins.

During the season just ended Hibs had bade farewell to yet another familiar face when centre-half Peter Aird, finding first-team appearances at Easter Road scarce, elected to join East Fife.

In what had been a quite phenomenal season, Hibs had come within touching distance of capturing the treble, and had done it playing incredible and scintillating attacking football in the best traditions of the game. Gaining a reputation as masters of near-guaranteed entertainment, they had bewitched soccer starved post-war crowds in their thousands throughout the land.

The season was not quite over, however. At the beginning of May, accompanied by the backroom staff, directors and Rex Kingsley of the *Sunday Mail*, the first-team squad (which consisted of 14 players) made a short, two-game trip to France where they secured a highly credible 1–1 draw against Racing Club de Paris and a 1–0 victory in Nice. Back home again they fared much worse, going down 5–3 to Rapid Vienna at Easter Road, and only then could most of the players turn their minds to a mid-season break.

It was business as usual, however, for Bobby Johnstone and Lawrie Reilly, who had both been selected for a series of four friendly international matches against Belgium, Austria, Denmark and France. Johnstone played against Denmark and France in Glasgow, while Reilly featured in all four, two in his favoured centre-forward position, the others at outside-left. It was during Scotland's 5–0 defeat of Belgium at the Heysel Stadium on 20 May 1951 that Reilly made his 12th full appearance for the international side to break goalkeeper Harry Rennie's 43-year record, which had stood since March 1908, when he became Hibernian's most-capped player.

An Experiment Under Lights and Another League Title

Writing in the official club handbook released at the start of the 1951–52 season, Harry Swan wrote that: 'although winning the Championship was a great achievement, the real test of greatness was the ability to keep a prominent position in the League year after year'. Although Hibs had now won the title twice in four seasons, he still wondered just what his players were capable of. He was soon to find out.

Because of the St Mungo Cup competition that was to be held as a forerunner to the season, training had started four weeks earlier than usual. Among the several promising youngsters who had been called-up that year was Ian Crawford, the son of a former Hibs and Leith Athletic player. Crawford was destined to make a name for himself in the game before too long, but it would not be at Easter Road.

One familiar face missing from the pack on the first day of training was that of goalkeeper Tommy Younger. Driving down Liberton Brae on his way to the ground that morning, Swan had been passed by a lorry containing soldiers from the Royal Scots Regiment, all waving furiously in his direction. He had been completely unaware, however, that the big goalkeeper was among them, on his way to a posting in Germany. The experienced Jimmy Kerr was a more than reliable stand-in for Younger, but as it would turn out 'Big Tam' would be home more often than not.

The Festival Trophy, or St Mungo's Cup, was an SFA-inspired tournament timed to coincide with the Festival of Britain exhibition then taking place in Glasgow, and the competition was used as a precursor to the season by all 16 First Division clubs. There had been initial concern in some quarters that a shortened summer break might be responsible for severe injuries during the season, but these fears would prove to be groundless. Although overcoming Motherwell and Third Lanark in the opening rounds, Hibs exited the tournament at the semi-final stage, losing to Aberdeen after a replay. Continuing a long-standing habit of winning one-off tournaments where the trophy was retained by the victors, Celtic beat Aberdeen 3–2 in the Final. The St Mungo Cup was not considered an important or attractive tournament by the spectators or players, although it helped boost Hibs' bank balance by the not inconsiderable sum of £2,970, a figure based on the number of games played. Hearts had been knocked out in the first round and received £742. The players themselves received £10 per game, the Easter Road players exiting the tournament £40 better off.

There was a comical footnote to the affair. While in Celtic's possession one of the handles accidentally came off the trophy, revealing that it had originally been produced in the mid-1890s and had first been awarded to a local gasworks side after they had defeated a Glasgow Police team in 1912. A demand by Celtic that they be presented with a new trophy was politely but firmly refused, and the trophy can still be seen at Parkhead today.

A close Edinburgh Charities game, the 11th in the series since Hearts started the ball rolling against Arsenal at Tynecastle in 1941, was won by Liverpool by the odd goal in three at Easter Road. The 'Galloping' right-back Jock Govan, who had moved to outside-right after an injury to Gordon Smith, twice came near to scoring and treated the crowd to a rare display of attacking football. Although the game was played in a friendly fashion and enjoyed by the large crowd, it was now on to the important business of competitive competition.

In the first League Cup encounter of the season, away to Partick Thistle, the Hibs supporters who had made their way to Glasgow were surprised to see Willie Ormond make an unexpected reappearance on the left wing, his first start since injuring a knee in the Tynecastle semi-final against Motherwell several months before. His return meant the forward line was once again along the now familiar lines of Gordon Smith, Bobby Johnstone, Lawrie Reilly, Eddie Turnbull and Willie Ormond. Living up to its famous reputation of Firhill for thrills, most of the excitement was enjoyed by the home fans as Thistle scored four times against Hibs' two goals, both scored by Eddie Turnbull, one from the penalty spot. Unfortunately, Hibs only managed to win two of the five remaining games in a section comprising Partick Thistle, Motherwell and Stirling Albion, one of them a comprehensive 5–1 revenge for the opening day defeat at Partick. Two were lost and the other drawn as the Easter Road side made an earlier than anticipated exit from the competition.

In a Championship made harder to win, according to Harry Swan, by its reduced size of 16 teams instead of the 20 favoured during and before the war, the Easter Road side embarked on a nine-game unbeaten run, although four of these ended level, including a 1–1 draw against Hearts at Tynecastle, Hibs' first League point in Gorgie for five seasons. Over the piece a draw was perhaps a fair result, with Smith again unable to get the better of left-back Tam McKenzie, and Reilly and Ormond successfully managing to escape the attentions of full-back Parker or centre-half Dougan. Bill Bruce, making only his second first-team start, replaced Jimmy Kerr, who had been in the unaccustomed position for a Hibs goalkeeper of conceding 17 goals in the eight games played so far.

Meanwhile, Swan had secured permission from the army to fly Tommy Younger back from his base in Germany whenever he was not required for the battalion team. It would cost the club the then substantial sum of £40 every time Younger made the trip home, a figure Hibs obviously considered worthwhile, and the former 'Hutchie Vale' 'keeper missed only two games between the beginning of October and the end of the season. All in all, Younger had an easy National Service. If required for the Hibs match on a Saturday, the PT Instructor would normally leave his base in Berlin on the Thursday, arriving in Edinburgh the following day, usually reporting back to Germany late the following Tuesday, shortly before the exercise began all over again.

Although it was still too early in the season to get carried away, seven days after the draw at Tynecastle a 5–2 victory against Third Lanark at Easter Road, in which Reilly and Johnstone both scored twice, saw Hibs lead the table for the first time on goal difference, ahead of nearest challengers Morton and East Fife. Despite the fact that they were yet to lose a game in the League, there had been early signs that this was not the Hibs of recent years, particularly in a game against Aberdeen in September. Ahead 4–1 at the interval, a side featuring youngster Pat Ward, recently introduced into the team at right-half, allowed the fighting Dons to equalise in injury time when former player Tommy Bogan, now plying his trade in the Granite City after his move from Celtic, made the score 4–4. The result was even more of an anticlimax for the home fans, considering that Lord Provost Millar had unfurled the League flag at the Albion Road end of the ground before the kick-off.

It was around this time that Hibs received a somewhat unusual and uniquely remarkable gift in the shape of a beautiful mural featuring scenes of Edinburgh, painted in full colour on the boardroom wall by artist W. Cuthill. One of the features of the mural was the way the artist had cleverly incorporated the boardroom clock into the painting of the clock tower of the North British Hotel. A token of appreciation for the Championship win the previous season, the gift had been organised and presented by the managing director of the well-known city firm of Morrison and Gibb, who was a fervent supporter of the club.

On 7 November 1951, the Easter Road side were involved in an historic friendly match against Stenhousemuir at Ochilview, when they defeated the home side 5–3 with goals from Johnstone, Souness, Turnbull and Mulkerrin (2), in what was Scotland's first modern floodlit game. The clash attracted great interest. Despite the fans being warned beforehand not to expect the lighting to be of a very high quality, normally suitable only for training but with several more lamps added behind both goals, all 7,000 tickets had been sold out early for a ground estimated to hold over 11,000, with more paying at the gate. There had been an initial scare that the fixture would have to be cancelled because of fog, but this had lifted by kick-off time, and with former Stenhousemuir player Willie Ormond made captain of the visiting side for the evening, the match went ahead as planned. Later, many of the players complained that it had not always been possible to follow the path of the ball, but nontheless the experiment was deemed a great success. The fixture had originally been arranged after a request from Stenhousemuir to play a second team Penman Cup tie under lights had been refused. It would appear that SFA rules prohibited a competitive fixture under lights and a friendly match was arranged instead. Interestingly, when the proposed Penman Cup tie was eventually played in April, this time without lights, both Mulkerrin and Souness, who had scored in the floodlit friendly, again figured on the score sheet in Hibs' 2–1 victory. But more of floodlights later.

With Hibs once again sitting proudly in their familiar position at the top of the table as the only undefeated side in Britain, their successful run was brought to an end by Morton just days after the Stenhousemuir experiment when they went down 2–1 at Cappielow. The better side throughout, Hibs undoubtedly missed the influence of the injured Gordon Smith, who was replaced by teenager Jim Souness on the right wing. Despite the absence of the international outside-right, Hibs more than did enough to win the game, but came up against Scottish international goalkeeper Jimmy Cowan at his very best. Throughout the 90 minutes, apart from an opening counter by Reilly, the goalkeeper proved in unbeatable form as he thwarted Hibs time and time again, even saving a thunderbolt penalty from Turnbull. In the closing stages the visitors stepped up their frantic efforts to take something from the game but were denied on half a dozen occasions by Cowan, whose sparkling performance ensured that the points remained in Greenock.

The defeat at Cappielow had allowed East Fife to leapfrog Hibs into pole position in the Championship race, but seven days later the capital side won the top-of-the-table clash 4–2 at Easter Road despite the valiant efforts of former Hibs centre-half Peter Aird, who had the beating of Reilly throughout the 90 minutes.

The title of unluckiest footballer in Scotland at this time would surely have belonged to Willie Ormond. Forced to limp from the field five minutes before half-time in a match against Airdrie at Broomfield, his injury left his teammates to play the entire second half with 10 men, in what was to prove a costly 2–0 victory for the visitors. The euphoria of the win was overshadowed by the news that Ormond had cracked a fibula. It was the third leg-break of the unfortunate player's senior career. He had also had the misfortune to suffer a severe knee injury, which had kept him out of the game for a considerable period.

At the beginning of December Gordon Smith was Hibs' sole representative in the Rest of Britain representative side that faced Wales in Cardiff in a match to commemorate the 75th anniversary of the Welsh FA. Smith chose the match to make the critics who claimed he never played well in representative or international matches eat their words. Described in one local newspaper as 'a forward of unusually high calibre', the Hibs outside-right tormented Cardiff City's left-back Sherwood throughout the game. After the match the Welsh player claimed to have been greatly impressed, not only with Smith's overall display, but also by his technique of suddenly changing to cross to the other wing with his left foot. He also thought that the Hibs man was: 'a most unorthodox and dangerous opponent, and I simply could not get near him'. The Welsh team manager was more succinct, simply stating that 'Smith was a great footballer'. Tommy Docherty, captain of the Rest of Britain side who were beaten 3–1 on the night, and well used to playing behind the great Tom Finney at Preston, felt that it had been a distinct pleasure to play behind the Hibs man. Interviewed after the game, Smith himself thought that his performance had been the best he had displayed in a representative game. Just a few weeks earlier George Young of Rangers, in his recently released book *Captain of Scotland*, had given the Hibs outside-right the following tribute: 'If any footballer could be said to have it all, then Gordon Smith of Hibernian is the man'.

Back at Easter Road, not withstanding the loss of Ormond, it was goals all the way until the festive break. With Combe deputising on the left wing, 18 were scored in a four-match spell with only one conceded. Three days before Christmas, in a comprehensive 5–0 defeat of Raith Rovers in Edinburgh, Bobby Johnstone, described in the press as a 'veritable Will o' the Wisp' was the best player afield by far and the architect behind most of Hibs' moves in this Scottish Cup tie rehearsal, the Selkirk man scoring two goals for the fourth game in a row.

A lone strike by Johnstone, however, was not enough to prevent Motherwell, who included recent signings Cox and Sloan from Hearts in their side, bringing Hibs' six-game winning streak to an end four days after Christmas. Despite this defeat and the by now almost expected New Year's Day failure against their deadly rivals Hearts, the Greens began 1952 at the top of the table, a lead they would hold until mid-March. Against Hearts at Easter Road on the opening day of the year, heavy snow had initially threatened the postponement of the fixture. The game was eventually allowed to go ahead, but the terrible conditions helped reduce the attendance to fewer than 40,000, and made good football extremely difficult for both teams on the treacherous surface. The home side trailed Hearts at the interval, but a tremendous second-half assault on the Maroons' goalmouth as they desperately tried to make up the leeway proved fruitless. Turnbull missed from the penalty spot five minutes from time after Milne was adjudged to have pushed Reilly inside the box, to keep Hearts' 3–2 lead intact, but few would have argued that an equaliser would have been just reward. By now both Edinburgh clubs were neck and neck at the top of the table, Hibs just ahead with 30 points from 20 games, Hearts with two points fewer from the same number played.

The successive defeats only reinforced Hibs' determination to retain their League title, and over the next two games against the luckless Third Lanark and Stirling Albion, 13 goals were scored without reply. Against the Albion Hibs served up a 'Championship display with the stamp of craftsmen, playing some classic football despite the treacherous underfoot conditions' in a convincing 8–0 rout. Bobby Combe, deputizing for Ormond, scored a hat-trick against Stirling and Reilly scored a hat-trick in both games.

Former players Willie Finnigan, Davie Shaw, Johnny Cuthbertson and Jimmy Cairns, who had been transferred to Third Lanark only the week before for a modest fee, mingled with other guests at the club's annual Dinner Dance, held as usual in the North British Hotel in Princes Street. Lord Provost James Miller presented the players with Zulu shield-shaped gold and enamel League Championship medals. In his speech, the first citizen relayed the appreciation of the people of Edinburgh towards

Hibernian on the splendid achievement of again winning the title. A special cheer was reserved for the injured Ormond as he stepped forward to collect his winners' medal, but the loudest roar of the evening by far was reserved for John Ogilvie, now well on the way to recovery after his horrific double leg break.

A 2–1 win over Partick Thistle at Firhill in the middle of the month should have set Hibs up nicely for the forthcoming Scottish Cup fixture with Raith Rovers. Played under a blanket of fog that at times prevented the fans from following play, a great first-half display by Gordon Smith, described in one newspaper as 'Gordon at his Gayest', should have seen the tie finished by half-time. The difficult underfoot conditions, however, allied to poor finishing by the away side, gave the determined Thistle the opportunity to get back into the game and Hibs were left hanging on to their slender lead until the final whistle.

Continuing bad weather seemed certain to cause the postponement of Hibs' first-round Scottish Cup tie against Raith Rovers at Starks Park seven days later, but excellent work by hundreds of local volunteers who had worked tirelessly throughout the morning to clear the pitch of several inches of snow allowed the match to proceed. Once the game started Raith quickly settled into their stride and were the better side, surprising even their own supporters with a spirited display against the League Champions. On a treacherous surface that was far from playable, a brilliant display, by Tommy Younger, particularly in the first half, kept the game goalless to earn his side a second chance in Edinburgh.

The Wednesday afternoon replay at Easter Road, with a 2.20pm kick-off time in those pre-floodlight days, attracted a huge crowd for a midweek game of 32,259, many of them presumably using the time-honoured excuse of attending a relative's funeral as an excuse for missing work. Even with the assistance of an extra 30 minutes, a thrilling game again ended goalless, and it was on to Tynecastle for a second replay.

Talk in the city of a potential all-Edinburgh clash against Hearts in the next round was again found to be seriously flawed when Raith somewhat surprisingly, but deservedly, defeated the champions elect 4–1. Despite Willie Ormond's return from injury, the defeat meant that the Hibs supporters' dream of Cup glory was on hold for at least another 12 months. Unbelievably, it was now exactly 50 years since their last Scottish Cup success, and during this time teams such as Motherwell, Aberdeen, Hearts, Clyde, Kilmarnock, St Mirren, Airdrie, Morton, Partick Thistle, Falkirk, Dundee and Third Lanark, as well as Celtic and Rangers, had all won the famous trophy, some of them more than once.

At the beginning of February Hibs increased their lead at the top of the table to five points with a 3–1 home win over a Celtic side containing such names as Jock Stein, Bobby Collins and Charlie Tully. The victory was easier than the scoreline would suggest, with all three of the inside trio of Johnstone, Reilly and Turnbull managing to get their names on the score sheet, but the real architect of the victory was Gordon Smith. At his sublime best, Smith taunted and teased the Parkhead defenders throughout the entire proceedings to earn what today would be considered dubious acclaim, the newspaper headlines again declaring 'Gordon in a gay mood today'.

As the country was coming to terms with the death of King George VI earlier in the week, a 2–2 draw against old adversaries Rangers at Ibrox on 13 February kept Hibs out in front in the Championship race, and near certainties, according to many, to retain the title, although there was still some way to go. During the game, a rumpus ensued when referee Hugh Phillips adjudged Woodburn to have handled inside the penalty area during a Hibs raid, and not outside as claimed by the angry pack of furious Rangers players who had immediately surrounded the official. Scotland captain George Young was booked for protesting too vehemently and future Scotland manager Ian McColl was fortunate to escape further trouble, before Turnbull placed the ball on the spot. Attempting to unnerve the Hibs player, goalkeeper Brown, a schoolboy teammate of Turnbull's, left his area to ask that he be given a feel of the ball, a request that was met with the curt reply that he would get a touch of it in two seconds when he picked it out of the net. It was a promise duly kept!

With Younger unavailable because of army commitments, Jimmy Kerr made a rare appearance when he was recalled for a 3–1 defeat by East Fife in Methil, but the Championship challenge was back on track seven days later with a comprehensive 4–0 home win against Airdrie. In a scintillating display of breathtaking attacking football by all of the home forwards, which the visitors just could not match, only a great performance by goalkeeper Fraser prevented a much heavier defeat. It seemed Hibs were now almost certain to retain the Championship.

Because of their early Scottish Cup exit at the hands of Raith Rovers, most of Hibs' Championship fixtures had already been completed, and they played only two competitive games during the month of March. The void was filled by a series of friendly matches, and in a welcome respite from the rigours of League football, 18,000 saw Hibs beat Doncaster Rovers 3–0 at Belle Vue at the beginning of the month in the first modern floodlit football game to take place in the north of England. At the post-match reception, the Doncaster chairman extolled the virtues of floodlit football, reminding all present that a few more games against such attractive opposition as the Edinburgh side and the lighting system would soon be paid off. Several days later Jim Souness again deputised for the injured Gordon Smith and earned the plaudits by scoring all Hibs' goals in a 4–1 defeat of Manchester City at Maine Road. The performance of Souness drew admiring glances from a host of English clubs, with Hibs asked to name their price for the goalscoring winger, but he would remain at Easter Road as understudy to Smith, at least for the moment.

Back on League duty against Queen of the South at Palmerston on 15 March, Hibs were in arrears after only 30 seconds when Brown opened the scoring for Queens, and the visitors' chances of retaining the Championship were seriously endangered when four goals by centre-forward Patterson enabled the Doonhamers to run out worthy 5–2 winners. The result left Rangers trailing by only three points, but with two games in hand. Hibs' next competitive game was nearly three weeks later, but by that time the Ibrox side had done the Edinburgh men an almighty favour by surprisingly drawing away to Queen of the South and dropping both points at Motherwell, leaving Hibs only needing to beat Dundee at Easter Road to retain the Championship.

Before then, the right-wing pairing of Gordon Smith and Bobby Johnstone had been selected, along with teammate Lawrie Reilly, for the match against England at Hampden. Watched by the newly elected SFA President Harry Swan, the disappointment of a 2–1 defeat was tempered slightly when Reilly, who overall had an impressive outing, scored Scotland's goal, his third against the Auld Enemy in as many appearances. Swan was also disappointed to learn that an injury to Bobby Johnstone would mean the inside-right missing Hibs' remaining two League fixtures.

At a ceremony held during the 'Festival of Sport' exhibition at the Waverley Market in Edinburgh on 18 March, the unique talent of Gordon Smith was recognised when he became the first recipient of the *Sunday Mail*-sponsored Scottish Player of the Year trophy, which was presented to the player by Lord Provost Miller. At the presentation journalist Rex Kingsley described Smith as 'a player of exquisite ball control, club spirit and uncanny skill, who was a popular winner'. In reply, Smith acknowledged the award as 'the greatest honour to come his way in football', but modestly and somewhat predictably he dedicated the success to his teammates who had made it all possible.

Wednesday 9 April 1952 was an evening of mixed emotions in Scotland's capital city. As Hearts were losing 3–1 to Motherwell in a Scottish Cup semi-final second replay at Hampden, two goals by Ormond and one from Combe cancelled out an early Dundee lead at Easter Road to give Hibs two crucial points and the League Championship. While again not at their best, the victory was enough to secure successive titles, something only Celtic and Rangers had achieved in modern times, and there was no doubt that the Easter Road side were worthy champions.

While it still remained mathematically possible for Rangers to overcome Hibs on goal average, the astronomical number of goals required made it not worth thinking about, even for a side with the renowned fighting abilities of Rangers.

The Hibs team that momentous evening was: Younger, Govan, Howie, Buchanan, Paterson, Gallacher, Smith, Combe, Reilly, Turnbull, Ormond.

In the final competitive game of the season, played on a Spring Holiday Monday evening and watched by over 35,000, the League champions confirmed their superiority by handing newly crowned Scottish Cup-winners Motherwell a lesson in irresistible scintillating football, with a 3–1 defeat in Edinburgh. Hibs even managed to miss two penalties, the first after only two minutes when Turnbull's powerful drive was brilliantly saved, and the second just over an hour later when Ormond shot straight at the 'keeper.

Two days later, the newly crowned champions made their way to London to play Spurs in a glamour friendly, winning 2–1. After a 2–2 draw against Bolton Wanderers in Edinburgh on the Saturday, a near-perfect season ended perfectly with a 3–0 win over Hearts in the East of Scotland Shield at Tynecastle. Hibs were reduced to 10 men for most of the game when Gordon Smith was forced to leave the field suffering from concussion after a clash of heads with Hearts full-back McKenzie, but the full strength Maroons had no answer to Hibs' dominance, and goals by Combe (2) and Reilly emphasised the Greens' undoubted supremacy as the top team in the City.

Incredibly, the coveted Championship trophy had been retained using just 17 players, only 12 of them on a regular basis. The others featured mainly in the case of injury, most of them making just one or two appearances, or in goalkeeper Kerr's case, when Tommy Younger had been unavoidably detained overseas. The players who had taken part in the historic League win were: Younger, Govan, Paterson, Howie, Buchanan, Combe, Gallagher, Smith, Johnstone, Reilly, Turnbull, Ormond, Kerr, Ward, Bruce, Souness and Mulkerrin.

Hibs had ended the season as the highest scoring side in the country with 92 goals, Lawrie Reilly once again coming top of the goalscoring charts with 36 in all games, 27 of them in the League. With the exception of two counters from Buchanan and a highly credible 12 scored by Combe while Ormond's understudy, once again all the Championship goals had been scored by the Famous Five.

Overall, although they had perhaps not displayed the form of the previous League Championship victories, Hibs had still on occasion played some superb football and were worthy titleholders. Amid the euphoria, there was no way that the supporters could be blamed for predicting that even greater successes lay ahead, but although they were not to know it at that moment, the best days were already behind them.

At the end of May Lawrie Reilly was Hibs' sole representative to take part in Scotland's 3–1 defeat by Sweden in Stockholm. He was now the only player from the 20 or so who had pulled on the dark blue jersey that season to have featured in all six Scotland games, and the 10 consecutive games since the defeat by Austria at Hampden 16 months before. Reilly also had the personal satisfaction of scoring his first hat-trick for the national side in a 6–0 win against the USA in April 1952.

A Testimonial for Gordon Smith, Murder at Highbury, Coronation Cup Disappointment and the Road to Rio

Back-to-back Championship wins had instilled a hunger for continued success among Hibs' players and supporters, and not unnaturally an air of expectancy surrounded Easter Road at the start of the new season. Confidence was high that an unprecedented third consecutive title could be captured, but, perhaps more importantly, that the interminable wait for Scottish Cup glory could be brought to an overdue and welcome end.

As always, several promising young players had joined the club in the summer, including wing-half Doug Moran, goalkeeper Tommy McQueen and the highly-acclaimed juvenile inside-forward Frank Donlevy, who had been signed in the face of stiff opposition from Wolverhampton Wanderers. Although he failed to make the grade at Easter Road, Donlevy started his brief career with the club in spectacular fashion by scoring seven goals in his first appearance in a Hibs jersey as the third team trounced Kelso United 9–1, and he scored another five in a 13–0 demolition of Murrayfield Amateurs the following week.

By this time goalkeeper Jimmy Kerr had joined Queen of the South after an Easter Road career spanning 15 years, and a farewell gathering was held in his honour in Tranent, attended by many of his former teammates. At the ceremony, Kerr was presented with a gift from the chairman of the local branch of the Hibs supporters' association, John Hart, brother of future Hibs owner and chairman Tom. For Kerr it was a sad parting of the ways, but although he was not to know it at the time, he would return to Easter Road as a director almost 20 years later.

The players of the Edinburgh Select took the field at Tynecastle for the annual charities match against Portsmouth sporting a natty new look, Hibs-style maroon jerseys with white sleeves. Never particularly popular with the Hearts fans, the white-sleeved shirts would be worn only intermittently during the next few years. The game itself was considered by many of the 30,000 crowd to have been the best of the series so far, the home side just edging it 3–2. Howie, Paterson, Smith, Turnbull and Ormond were the Easter Road representatives, and a brilliant hat-trick by inside-left Eddie Turnbull gave Edinburgh its first outright win since the Allison Cup was presented in 1944. All three goals were in the spectacular category. Turnbull's first was a trademark thunderbolt from all of 35 yards that the goalkeeper got a hand to but could not stop, and the second was an all-Hibs affair that ended with Turnbull crashing the ball into the net without breaking stride after Ormond had sent over an inch-perfect cross. Turnbull's third was from a retaken free-kick from 25 yards.

On the first day of the season proper, thousands of Hibs fans made the journey to Firhill for the opening League Cup tie against Partick Thistle, and at kick-off there were nearly 35,000 packed inside the stadium. Gaining sweet revenge for the previous season's opening-day defeat, the visitors demolished Thistle 5–1 to top the section. Bobby Johnstone, still not fully recovered from the injury received near the end of the previous season, was in the reserve side that defeated East Fife's second team 3–0 at Easter Road that same afternoon. Johnstone proved that he was well on the way to full fitness by scoring one of the Hibs goals, but the main talking point of the afternoon was the late arrival of the Fife players and the subsequent delayed kick-off. The Methil side had an extraordinary and almost unique reason for their late arrival. In those pre-Forth Road Bridge days, part of the journey from Fife to Edinburgh was made by ferry. While crossing the River Forth the ferry was diverted to rescue a canoeist who was in danger of drowning after his craft had capsized near North Queensferry harbour, the consequent delay resulting in the team's late arrival in Edinburgh.

Shortly before the 6.50pm kick-off against St Mirren at Easter Road on Wednesday 13 August, Lord Mathers unfurled the League Championship flag in front of the invited dignitaries and enthusiastic Hibs supporters, who then enjoyed a Championship-style performance that ended in a convincing 5–2 win for the home side.

Although they won three of the four League Cup section games against both Partick Thistle and St Mirren, an earlier 1–0 defeat at Parkhead made it imperative that Hibs took both points from Celtic in the final group game at Easter Road if they were to harbour any hopes of progressing into the next round. By this time Bobby Johnstone had returned to the side with Combe again dropping into midfield, and the forward line again assumed its familiar shape. Straight from the kick-off and before the Glasgow side had time to settle, Hibs took the game by the scruff of the neck and the contest was over by half-time. Encouraged by the vociferous Hibs support among the 52,000 crowd that had managed to gain admission before the gates were closed with thousands locked out, the home side turned on an exhibition of brilliant football not witnessed at Easter Road for many a day. Totally outplayed, the visitors were unable to match the determination of the home side. Two goals from Reilly and a solitary strike by Turnbull gave Hibs a comfortable 3–0 victory, but it was the elusive Johnstone who pulled all the strings as his side marched into the quarter-finals of the competition on goal average.

At Windsor Park in midweek, Turnbull failed to get his name on the score sheet after missing a penalty. Teammates Reilly and Ormond both notched two in the Scottish League's five-goal demolition of the Irish League, but there was to be no happy ending to the week as Hibs' first defence of the title ended in humiliating fashion. Gordon Smith received a rousing reception from the fans as he led his team out against Queen of the South at Easter Road in his 500th appearance in a green-and-white jersey. The captain celebrated the occasion with a goal, but Hibs looked a mere shadow of the title-winning side of only a few months before, and the game ended in a surprise 3–1 home defeat, an early warning that perhaps things were not as they had once been. Congratulating Smith on his momentous accomplishment, the match programme highlighted the feat by reminding fans that, 'his was a record of consistent service equalled by few in the Scottish game'.

Hibs recovered well from the unexpected opening-day defeat to overcome Morton over two legs in the League Cup quarter-finals by an overall 12–3 aggregate. Sandwiched between the Cup ties, on Monday 15 September 1952, League champions Manchester United, now managed by former Hibs wartime signing Matt Busby, and widely recognised as the most outstanding team in England since the war, travelled to Edinburgh to take part in the now famous Gordon Smith testimonial match and were soundly thrashed 7–3. In the build-up to the match an English correspondent praised both sides when relating that: 'Just as Hibs have built up a reputation for fast bewildering attacking football based on quickness and interchanging of positions, Manchester United have exploited much of the same kind of technique on their march to success'. One local reporter described Hibs at that time as 'undoubtedly the number one attraction in the land'.

In a thrilling game that has often been described as perhaps the finest exhibition of football artistry ever witnessed, United had actually been leading 3–2 at the interval. However, second-half goals from Ormond, Reilly, Smith himself and two more from Turnbull, added to the two that the inside-forward had scored in the first half, gave the Scottish champions an emphatic victory.

The result told only half the story. As well as the 10 goals scored, another three had been disallowed, a penalty for Manchester United had been missed and countless near things at both ends had kept the fans of both sides enthralled right to the end. In the second half, the home side, according to the *Evening News,* had 'proceeded to reach the heights of football perfection and pugnacity', and such was the quality of entertainment on display that hardly a soul dared leave before the final whistle. At the end both teams received a rousing and well-deserved standing ovation from the fans.

Even now the game is still regarded by those fortunate enough to have been present as the most fantastic advert for attacking football. Interviewed after the game, the renowned referee Jack Mowat even reckoned that 'the wonderful match', was the fastest he had ever officiated at.

Gordon Smith, who in the opinion of newspaper columnist 'Tron Kirk' of the *Evening News* was 'without peer in the modern game as an artist and entertainer', collected an estimated £3,000 from the 28,000 turnout, although it was believed that tax and expenses would account for more half that figure. There had been rumours of resentment among some of Smith's teammates at what was perhaps seen as 'preferential' treatment at his being granted a testimonial match, but if official sources are to be believed, the match had been organised by the player himself and not the club.

One innovation during the game was the use for the first time at Easter Road of the new laceless white ball with the then revolutionary small aperture that allowed for easy inflation. This did away with the usual mundane and laborious task of undoing and retying the lacing after inflation, and this, no doubt, was much appreciated by the groundsman.

Hibernian: McCracken, Govan, Howie, Gallacher, Paterson, Combe, Smith, Johnstone, Reilly, Turnbull, Ormond.

Continuing where they had left off in midweek, on the Saturday at Easter Road a hat-trick by Lawrie Reilly, his first ever against Hearts, gave the Greens a 3–1 win over their Gorgie rivals in a game that was no contest from the start. The result brought to an end Hibs' miserable run without a win against their local rivals that had lasted almost four years. A powerful exhibition of strength, pace and skill placed the Greens, who were still buoyant after the Manchester United result, in a different class to an admittedly weakened Hearts side who totally failed to contain a rampant Famous Five. The result meant that Hibs had now scored 22 in their last four games, with all five forwards among the goals, leaving one newspaper reporter to wonder 'if this was a record in Scottish, if not British football'.

The game was the first to be transmitted live to patients in the Royal Infirmary and Leith Hospitals by the newly formed Hospital Broadcast Organisation. Originally an experiment by Stirling Albion, who had relayed their home games to a hospital in the central area, the idea had been quickly adopted by Joe Gubbins, secretary of the Hibs supporters' association, who sponsored the voluntary organisation by helping to raise the initial £80 to set the scheme in operation by holding fundraising events, match-day collections and private donations. The historic first 100-minute broadcast was performed by volunteer

Wemyss Craigie from a booth resembling a telephone box, which was situated at the north end of the Easter Road enclosure, and over the coming years he would be ably assisted by Jim Bourhill and Tom Millar. The broadcasts proved so successful that they were soon extended to cover Hearts' home matches at Tynecastle. With regular pre-match collections at both grounds helping to subsidise the running costs, the popular service would eventually be received by 14 hospitals in the Edinburgh area. Gordon Smith, who would on more than one occasion in the future tune in to transmissions from Easter Road while in hospital recovering from injury, donated a percentage of the proceeds from the belated sale of programmes from his testimonial game to the hospital fund.

A week after the victory against Hearts there was an even more impressive 7–3 win at Fir Park. Hibs had actually been leading 4–0 at one point before the home side staged a tremendous fightback to trail 4–3. With Motherwell threatening to continue their revival, Reilly changed the course of the game by scoring what he himself acknowledges as perhaps the best goal of his career. Collecting a long kick out from goalkeeper Younger, the Scotland centre-forward beat off the challenge of two opponents by first back-heading the ball over the centre-half and then neatly deceiving the other. As he made his way towards goal, he successfully managed to evade the challenge of several other defenders before calmly walking the ball round the stranded goalkeeper and passing it into the net. The goal, one of four Reilly was to score that day, was received by the euphoric congratulations of his teammates and the deserved applause of both sets of supporters. Somewhat confusing for the supporters, and perhaps demonstrating the contradictory nature of the game, just five days before a strong Hibs side had been beaten 5–1 by Motherwell at Firhill in Glasgow in a benefit match for the dependants of a Glasgow policeman killed in the line of duty.

Irrespective of the heavy defeat at Firhill, the recent run of results had raised the expectations of the Hibs support. Unfortunately, any anticipation of silverware arriving at Easter Road in the very near future was soon to evaporate as Dundee ran out convincing 2–1 winners at Tynecastle in the League Cup semi-final. Once again, Tynecastle had been the burial ground for Hibs' Cup expectations, even after a typical strike by Reilly had given the Edinburgh side an interval lead, although in truth Reilly's goal had been scored against the run of play and Hibs were well beaten in the end.

At the end of September the Scottish selectors once again disregarded the wishes of the supporters when they failed to select the entire Hibs forward line for Scotland's game against the Irish League at Parkhead. Smith, Johnstone, Reilly and Ormond had all been chosen in the forward line, but to the disappointment of a large proportion of the general public, Dundee's Billy Steele was selected at inside-left in place of Eddie Turnbull.

It had long been thought that the perfect Scotland line up would consist of the entire Rangers defence and all five Hibs forwards, but the inclusion of Dundee's Billy Steel at the expense of Turnbull disregarded the wishes of the fans to test the popular theory and deny the entire Famous Five the opportunity of representing the country *en bloc* in an international match.

As for the game itself, many neutral observers thought that Gordon Smith had his best game yet in a dark blue jersey in Scotland's 5–1 victory, but the undoubted star of the show was four-goal Lawrie Reilly, who provided proof, if any were needed, that he was still the best centre-forward in the country. All Reilly's goals were gems, the first three from headers, although it has to be said that the victory was against very poor opposition. Steele in truth combined well with the Hibs forwards, scoring Scotland's other goal.

If thought surplus to requirements by his country, it was vastly different for Turnbull at club level. Warned that the player was unhappy at Easter Road and had requested a transfer, Newcastle United immediately opened negotiations with Hibs in a bid to secure the services of the inside-forward. Despite extended talks between the player and officials of the Tyneside club, Turnbull once again turned down the chance to move to the north-east of England, having previously rejected an offer from Middlesborough.

That was far from the end of the transfer drama, however. On hearing that talks regarding Turnbull's future had broken down, Matt Busby immediately caught the next train to Edinburgh in an attempt to secure the services of the player at Old Trafford. With a figure of over £30,000 mentioned, any deal would undoubtedly have broken the existing transfer records between Scottish and English clubs. Protracted talks between both clubs collapsed when Turnbull abruptly called a halt to the proceedings in order to catch the last train home to Falkirk, a clear indication to Busby that the player would be staying at Easter Road. Talks resumed in the morning but, to the relief of the Hibs support, Turnbull was going nowhere.

The rising costs of running a successful football club became worryingly obvious when a huge drop in profits was announced at the AGM in October. According to the accounts, the early exit from both Cup competitions during the 1951–52 season had resulted in a profit of only £318 being declared, as opposed to the £18,741 of 12 months before. With the drop in revenue, friendly matches were usually a lucrative and welcome respite from competitive football, and the players of Arsenal and Hibs were introduced to the Duke of Edinburgh before a floodlit challenge match at Highbury on 22 October 1952 to raise funds for the National Playing Fields Association. It was the Easter Road side's fifth game under lights. Billed as an unofficial 'Champions of Britain' match, Arsenal, who would win the English League that season, murdered a full-strength Hibs side 7–1 in front of over 53,000 fans to restore English pride after the recent heavy defeat of Manchester United in Edinburgh.

Before the game there was a surprise appearance in the visitors' dressing room by goalkeeper Tommy Younger, who had travelled directly from his base in Germany to take part in the match, resplendent in his full army uniform. The game itself was evenly matched in the early stages, but a second strike by five-goal Don Roper direct from a corner-kick seemed to unsettle the visitors, whose scant reward for their perseverance was a solitary strike by Reilly with the score at 5–0.

The entire second half was broadcast on television, one of the first games outside of an international or Cup Final to go out live. The Hibs contingent would no doubt have been pleased that in the days of television's infancy not many could afford a receiver, although it is estimated that over a million people throughout the country watched the proceedings, many viewing the medium for the first time. Pubs throughout the city, such as the Bellevue Bar in Broughton Street, reputed to be the first bar in Edinburgh to have a television set, were crammed to the rafters with hundreds of customers eager to view the action. Previously, the only opportunity most supporters had had of watching moving pictures of their favourite side would be on the *Pathé* or *Movietone News* programmes at their local cinema. A first-class floodlighting system and the use of a white ball had made it easy for viewers to follow play at Highbury, although the black-and-white pictures sometimes made it difficult to differentiate between the teams, with both sides wearing similar-looking strips with white sleeves.

At a banquet after the game, the respective chairmen received signed diplomas from Prince Philip. The players of both teams received commemorative plaques bearing the crests of the respective clubs.

Hibernian: Younger, Govan, Howie, Gallacher, Paterson, Combe, Smith, Johnstone, Reilly, Turnbull, Ormond.

As they trudged from the field at the final whistle the players had been painfully aware that they had let Scotland down. It was a view shared by a correspondent writing to the *Evening News* identifying himself only as 'Tee Vee'. He was furious that 'Hibs had deprived the supporters of the class of football they were entitled to expect and had paid good money to see. Moreover, they had let the club down and brought Scottish football to ridicule before an English crowd'.

In a letter of a different kind, Arsenal were later taken to task for contravening the Football League regulations prohibiting the screening on TV of any club game outside of the Cup Final. It was made clear that although there was no question of disciplinary action being taken, it was a reminder that a committee resolution had been broken. For some time now there had been concern regarding the live televising of matches, and even the official FA yearbook for 1951–52 had questioned whether televised football was a boon or a menace. A questionnaire sent to all 92 English League clubs had revealed that the consensus of opinion was that TV was detrimental to the game, and that there had been a significant drop in attendances at most matches when the Cup Final had been broadcast, the Final at that time being played on the same afternoon as a full League programme. Regardless of the poll, with well over 400,000 TV licence holders at the time and several new transmitters planned for the north of England, Scotland and Wales, it was clear that televised football was here to stay, whether the football authorities liked it or not.

From then until the turn of the year, Hibs played nine games, collecting only 11 points from a total of 18. Although they remained very much in the running for honours, and were still being described by the media as undoubtedly the number-one attraction in the country, this was clearly not the form of a team with genuine Championship aspirations.

In a 3–1 defeat of Airdrie at Easter Road at the beginning of November, there was the unusual occurrence of the referee and one of his linesmen missing the kick-off. The match started with the remaining linesman taking charge and a player from each side, Mick Gallacher from Hibs and Black from Airdrie, running the line until the belated appearance of the missing officials.

With Younger unavailable, goalkeeper Tommy McQueen, father of future Scotland centre-half Gordon McQueen, made his first-team debut in an easy 3–0 home win over Dundee on 15 November 1952. The official programme for the game contained an article taken from the *Dundee Sporting Post*, printed the previous week, which listed a table of all the results of the Division 'A' teams since the war. While Motherwell rather surprisingly came bottom of the 22 sides that had contested the division since 1945, it was no surprise to learn that Hibs were out on their own at the top, 10 points ahead of Rangers, who had played one game less. Although conceding 33 more goals than the men from Govan, Hibs had scored a highly impressive 106 more in the same period.

	P	W	L	D	F	A	Pts	Pts per Game
Hibernian	187	127	31	29	506	224	283	1.529
Rangers	186	120	33	33	400	191	273	1.468
Hearts (5th)	189	92	62	35	394	291	219	1.158
Celtic (10th)	189	76	72	41	311	313	193	1.021

At that time East Fife led the League table, but seven days after the victory over Dundee, a 5–3 win at Methil, the Fife side's first home defeat of the season, moved Hibs into second place and within one point of the leaders with two games in hand. According to the *Pink News*, Bayview 'was not a place for the faint hearted' as the game swung from end to end with good defending at a premium. In a display of power football allied to the now customary skill of both sides, Hibs had the legendary goalscoring talents of three-goal Lawrie Reilly to thank for the victory.

The unfashionable East Fife had done particularly well under the guidance of future Rangers manager Scott Symon since winning the Second Division Championship and the League Cup during the 1947–48 season. Since then they had won the League Cup twice, becoming the first side to win the trophy three times, also reaching the Scottish Cup Final in 1950. They had since consolidated their position as one of the leading sides in the country, finishing in third place twice in the four years since their promotion from the lower League.

With centre-half John Paterson down with flu, reserve John Brown made his first-team debut in the match against Partick Thistle at Firhill in mid-December. Although Hibs scored four times themselves, the young 'Pivot' had a poor game against centre-forward Stott, whose clever distribution helped outside-left Walker to score four goals in Thistle's 5–4 win. It would be one of only three first-team appearances by Brown in a Hibs jersey.

The Firhill defeat was the latest in a run of poor results that had seen Hibs drop five points from the last three games, which was anything but Championship form. In an attempt to rectify the situation, Scottish international full-back Jock Govan was dropped and replaced by the long-serving Willie Clark for the game against Queen of the South in Dumfries a few days before Christmas. Gordon Smith chose the game to score his first hat-trick for nearly two and a half years in a 7–2 rout of the Doonhamers, but by this time Lawrie Reilly had become by far the biggest contributor in the goalscoring stakes, having registered three goals or more on eight occasions in the intervening months. Smith's treble, however, left him only one goal short of the magical 300 for the club in all matches, a situation that was remedied on 27 December 1952 in a 3–0 home victory over Aberdeen. Kicking up the famous slope, only seven minutes remained of the first half when Smith collected the ball on the right-hand edge of the penalty box. Steadying himself briefly, he hesitated only long enough to blast a thunderous drive past the despairing arms of Aberdeen goalkeeper Fred Martin and into the top right-hand corner of the net. Acclaimed by rapturous applause from the Hibs support, it was a goal well worthy of the occasion, and one that was preserved for posterity by Wemyss Craigie, who had been experimentally recording several of the hospital broadcasts on his personal tape recorder. It was later transferred onto an 8in disc and presented to the player.

1953 got off to a bright start. On New Year's Day goals by Reilly and Turnbull ended a barren run of defeats at Tynecastle to give Hibs a 2–1 victory over the Maroons, their first competitive League double over their great rivals since 1939. Watched by a crowd of nearly 40,000 a typical thunderbolt strike by Turnbull from the penalty spot gave Hibs both points in direct contrast to exactly 12 months before when a miss from the spot by the same player had cost Hibs victory at Easter Road.

Hearts had been struggling in the lower reaches of the table for some time, and following approaches by the Tynecastle club, Hibs came to their ailing neighbours' aid by transferring Jim Souness for a nominal fee, believed to be in the region of £3,000. Souness, who would win a League Cup medal with the Gorgie club in 1954, their first silverware for 48 years, had earlier been on loan at Falkirk, who had wanted to make the deal permanent, but the Bairns' valuation of the player fell far short of that of the Easter Road side with Hibs refusing to negotiate further.

Reilly notched yet another hat-trick, his fifth of the season so far, in a 7–2 defeat of Motherwell at the beginning of the year, and by the middle of January Hibs were still just one point behind leaders East Fife. A dense fog that was responsible for all flights to and from Scotland being cancelled prevented goalkeeper Younger from travelling back from his base in Germany, and McQueen made his second appearance of the season in a 4–2 defeat at Starks Park. The result was a severe setback to Hibs' title hopes, but a 3–1 victory at Brockville at the end of the month saw the Easter Road side sitting proudly at the top of the table for the first time that season, two points ahead of second-placed Rangers, who still had two games in hand.

Meanwhile, an East versus West Select game, featuring mainly players from the smaller clubs, took place at Meadowbank Stadium on 14 January 1953. The match, won 8–2 by the East Select, was used to inaugurate the ground's brand-new lighting system and was the first modern game in the city to be played under floodlights.

In the Scottish Cup, the fans wondered if this was at last to be Hibs' year when their favourites hammered Stenhousemuir 8–1 at home in the opening round. Before the second round game against Queen's Park at Easter Road on 7 February 1953, Tommy Younger, by then completing the final few weeks of his National Service at Dreghorn Barracks, was presented with an engraved plaque by representatives of British European Airways in recognition of the many hours and the 150,000 miles the goalkeeper had flown with the company during his 76 journeys back to Edinburgh from his base in Germany. During the game a goal by Combe and yet another hat-trick by Reilly knocked the stuffing out of the spirited amateurs to set up a third-round meeting with Aberdeen at Easter Road.

It was at around this time that sporting cartoons and caricatures drawn by a young man recently released from the RAF were beginning to appear in local newspapers and match programmes at both Tynecastle and Easter Road. A young Harry Gilzean, who aspired to become a full-time artist, was following in the footsteps of another well-known caricaturist, Tom Curr, whose drawings depicting Hibs and Hearts, and many other subjects, had been a popular feature in local newspapers for many years. Gilzean's drawings would eventually become an integral part of Monday evening match reports in the *Evening News* and were immensely popular with the readers.

At a meeting of club representatives at the beginning of March, attended by the forward-thinking Harry Swan, a proposal backed by the League Management Committee was put forward that a 'Super League' of four divisions be formed. Three Leagues of 10 teams and one containing eight, each playing each other four times in a season extended to May was thought to be the best option, but although it was taken no further at the time, it would not be the last that was heard on the subject. A counter-proposal by East Stirlingshire a few days later that there should be a return to a First Division of 18 teams and a Second Division of 20 was also rejected.

Back-to-back wins over Airdrie at Broomfield, 4–0 in the Cup and 7–3 in the League, put Hibs strongly in the running for a Cup and League double. In the League game Bobby Combe, playing at centre-forward for the first time in his career, was Hibs' star man, scoring four of the Greens' goals, the others coming from a double by Johnstone and a solitary strike by Smith.

Normal service was resumed, however, in the quarter-final of the Scottish Cup against Aberdeen at Easter Road. A rail ticket at the time from Waverley Station directly to the ground would cost the supporter 4p, while fans travelling from Musselburgh, and stopping at the now mostly defunct stations at Duddingston, Newington, Blackford Hill, Morningside, Craiglockhart, Gorgie East, Haymarket and Waverley, before terminating at Easter Road Park Halt, could expect to pay the princely sum of 10p.

With Hearts facing Queen of the South at Tynecastle the same afternoon, Hibs easily won the 'battle of the crowds' when well over 47,000 packed into Easter Road for the Cup match with Aberdeen, testimony to the attraction of both teams. Over at Tynecastle, Hearts could 'only' attract 30,000, although admittedly against poorer opposition with a much smaller travelling support.

An Archie Buchanan headed goal with 12 minutes remaining in the second half of an evenly contested game cancelled out a Dons first-half strike, but in the replay at the tightly-packed Pittodrie on the Wednesday afternoon, an Aberdeen goal shortly after the interval doubled the home side's lead and put paid to the Greens' Cup hopes for yet another year. The disappointment of the Pittodrie defeat was eased somewhat with the news that Rangers had unexpectedly dropped both points at Starks Park that same evening. The title was now in Hibs' own hands, but with seven games left to play there was still considerable work to be done.

Injuries since the turn of the year had begun to take a heavy toll, and Ormond became the latest casualty when he received an injury at Love Street in March that would keep him out of action for almost a month. At Parkhead, Reilly and Johnstone gave the Edinburgh Greens a two-goal interval lead, but a second-half goal by Collins from the spot left Hibs hanging on, and it was only after a third goal, Johnstone's second, a couple of minutes from time, that Hibs could afford to relax. The Celtic programme for the game had paid Hibs generous praise, claiming that: 'In recent years there has been no more glamorous team than Hibernian, and it says a great deal for their consistency that they are in pursuit of their third consecutive Championship'.

For the forthcoming match against the English League in March, once again the selectors had resisted the temptation to yield to the desires of the man in the street by picking the entire Hibs front line. Again naming Smith, Johnstone, Reilly and Ormond in the Scottish line up, once again there was no place for Eddie Turnbull, whose place at inside-left this time round was taken by Jimmy Bonthrone of East Fife. In those days a complete reserve side was also selected, which in theory would be ready to step into the side in their respective positions in the case of injury. Turnbull was named at inside-left in this second team. Just a few days before the match it was revealed that Bonthrone had withdrawn from the side, leaving the way clear for Turnbull to take his place, and consequently the fielding of an entire forward line from the same side in a Scottish representative match for the first time since the early 1870s. The reason for Bonthrone's withdrawal is intriguing. It turned out that the East Fife player had arranged to be married only two days before the inter-League match. This cut no ice with the selectors, who insisted that the squad travel to the match together, leaving Bonthrone to choose between getting married or playing in the game. With the wedding arrangements too far advanced to cancel, Bonthrone had no option but to withdraw from the side. All was not plain sailing for Turnbull, however. Despite being chosen at inside-left in the reserve side, the Hibs man was again overlooked by the selectors when the position was filled by Willie Fernie of Celtic, who had originally been named as inside-right for the reserves. One can only imagine what Turnbull had done wrong. As it would turn out, however, injury would prevent Gordon Smith and Willie Ormond from taking part, leaving only Reilly, who would score the only goal of the match in Scotland's 1–0 victory, and Bobby Johnstone as Hibs' representatives.

Both Lawrie Reilly and Bobby Johnstone were selected for the full Scotland side to face England at Wembley in April. It was Reilly's fourth appearance against the Auld Enemy and his third consecutive game at London's biggest arena. The Hibs centre had already scored in each of his outings against England, and there was no doubting his claim to be Scotland's hero this time around as he scored both Scotland goals in the 2–2 draw, his second and equalising goal coming in the time added on for injuries at the end of the game. Both goals were laid on by Easter Road teammate Bobby Johnstone, and the legend of 'Last-minute Reilly' was born. It was the second time that season that the Hibs man had scored in the last minute of a Scotland match, the other instance coming against the Irish League a few months earlier.

Although a fine win had been achieved at Parkhead, both Rangers and East Fife kept up the relentless pressure on the League leaders, and three draws from the six remaining games saw the Edinburgh side go into the final game of the season still at the top of the League, but only one point ahead of Rangers, who still had the benefit of a game in hand. Despite winning 4–1 in their final game against Raith Rovers at Easter Road, with goals from Reilly, Turnbull and Johnstone (2), a Rangers 2–2 draw at Dumfries denied Hibs three consecutive League Championship wins to give the Ibrox side the title on goal average.

The victory over Raith Rovers had boosted Hibs' goals tally to an all-time record for the 'A' Division of 93, one better than the previous year's record, which had also been set by the Edinburgh side, and 13 more than had been scored by the Light Blues. The main difference between the sides was in defence, Hibs conceding 12 more than the champions. This statistic allowed Rangers to win the title by .23 of a goal, their average of 2.05 goals per game bettering Hibs' 1.82. If the modern method of goal difference instead of goal average had been in operation then, Hibs would have won their third consecutive League Championship by the grand total of one goal.

In the seven seasons since the restart of the official League programme after the war, Hibs had been champions three times, second three times and third once, altogether a quite incredible feat. Of the 14 League games played against Rangers, their nearest challengers during this period, Hibs had won six and drawn six, suffering only two defeats while scoring 21 against the loss of 14. Rangers had fared better during this period against Celtic and Hearts. Of the 14 games played against their city rivals Rangers had won nine, drawn three and lost twice, winning nine and drawing twice against the Maroons.

For a third consecutive year Lawrie Reilly had ended the season as not only Hibs' top goalscorer, but also as the top marksman in the entire country with 50 in all games, 30 of them in the League. In those more conventional days, forwards were expected to score the goals and the defenders prevent them, as illustrated by the case of John Ogilvie, who had scored all three of his side's goals in a reserve League Cup tie against Aberdeen earlier in the season from the left-back position, two of them penalties. In congratulating the player, manager Shaw also made it clear to the player that 'defenders scoring goals was not a practice encouraged at Easter Road'. Yet again the 'Five' had been responsible for all but eight of the Championship strikes. Combe had scored six, mostly as a forward, including a foursome against Airdrie from the centre-forward position in Reilly's absence, the others coming from Souness on understudy duty to Smith, and right-back Willie Clark from the penalty spot while regular penalty-taker Turnbull was injured.

To celebrate the forthcoming coronation of Queen Elizabeth II, the top four sides in England and League Champions Rangers from Scotland, plus Celtic, who had finished the season in eighth place, were invited by the SFA to take part in the Coronation Cup Competition. Aberdeen gained entry courtesy of finishing as losing finalists to Rangers in the Scottish Cup and Hibs as League runners-up.

The tournament would be staged in its entirety in Glasgow. Based on a straight knock-out formula, each Scottish club would meet English opposition in the opening round.

A 4–2 win over Hearts in the Final of the East of Scotland Shield at Easter Road on the Thursday evening, with goals from Reilly (2) Turnbull and Smith, set Hibs up nicely for the following Monday's opening Coronation Cup tie against Tottenham Hotspur. After disposing of Spurs by a 2–1 scoreline after a replay at Ibrox, Newcastle were swept aside 4–0 in the semi-final at the same venue, to line up a meeting at Hampden against Celtic, who had beaten Arsenal and Manchester United on their way to the Final.

In a game that must still rank as one of the finest ever seen at the stadium, watched by a crowd of over 108,000, magnificent football by Celtic saw the Glasgow side take a deserved one-goal lead into the interval, but after the break it was a different story. The famous Hibs attack moved into top gear, and for 45 minutes it was them against the 'keeper as they relentlessly bore down on the Celtic goal, where charmed Johnny Bonnar was having the game of his life. For the entire second half it was Hibs against Bonnar, who time and again saved his side, and latterly it was a question of how long the beleaguered Celts could hold out. With just minutes remaining, a tremendous Bobby Johnstone header seemed certain to give Hibs the goal that would force extra-time, but somehow Bonnar got a fingertip to the ball before it was swept down field for Mochan to score, totally against the run of play, and put the game beyond Hibs.

Celtic: Bonnar, Haughney, Rollo, Evans, Stein, McPhail, Collins, Walsh, Mochan, Peacock, Fernie.
The same 11 **Hibs** players who contested all four Coronation Cup games were: Younger, Govan, Paterson, Buchanan, Howie, Combe, Smith, Johnstone, Reilly, Turnbull, Ormond.
Referee: H. Phillips (Motherwell)

No sooner had the players arrived home from Hampden than they were off on their travels again. In the seven years since their groundbreaking tour of war-torn Czechoslovakia in 1946, Hibs had made many trips overseas, most notably to Norway, Belgium, Germany, Switzerland and France, but in the summer of 1953 they were destined to travel much further afield. By now Hibs' reputation had spread far and wide, and the previous year there had been fierce competition between the Argentine and Brazilian Football Associations to lure the Scots to tour South America. Despite an extremely tempting offer from the Argentines to play four games in that country, Hibs could not at that time be enticed to cross the Atlantic, choosing instead to tour Germany and Holland. Now, in an innovative move for the club, an offer to play at least three games in an eight-team tournament involving clubs from Brazil, Uruguay, Portugal and

Scotland was accepted, and Hibs became the first Scottish club to travel to South America since Third Lanark had toured Argentina and Uruguay in 1923, with Motherwell making a similar visit in 1928.

In June 1953, Hibs became first Scottish side to visit Brazil. Initially booked for a two-week stay in Rio, provisional plans had been made to extend the visit for a third week if they managed to qualify for the later stages of the tournament.

At a reception for the players, officials, family and friends in the Easter Road boardroom prior to their departure from Waverley Station on the first leg of their marathon 5,000-mile journey to South America, Harry Swan wished the team well. Swan, who had recently been elected as president of the SFA, was unable to make the trip himself because of Association business. The official party who would make the trip to South America consisted of manager Hugh Shaw, trainers McColl and Kean, directors Wilson Terris and Tom Hartland plus 15 players: Younger, Paterson, McFarlane, Combe, Johnstone, Reilly, Turnbull, Ormond, Ward, Smith, Govan, Anderson, Buchanan, Howie and teenager Jimmy Shields, who had been a late addition to the squad.

On arriving in London the following morning the Hibs players found the capital swarming with countless thousands of visitors of all nationalities who had made their way to the city for the coronation of Queen Elizabeth II at Westminster Abbey that same day, 2 June 1953, a day made even more magical by the breaking news that Mount Everest had been conquered for the first time by a British-led expedition only a few days before. After several delays caused by the abnormal demand for air travel to and from the capital, the Hibs touring party eventually left from London Airport on the next leg of their journey at 9pm after watching the coronation live on television. One leg of what was to prove a long and exhausting 28-hour journey to Brazil via Paris, Lisbon, Dakar and finally Recife was completed in a converted World War Two bomber. On eventually arriving at their hotel in Rio at 11.45pm the following evening, the travel-weary players were asked if they wanted anything, an enquiry that brought the immediate response from Willie Ormond: 'Aye, ah want to go ******* hame'.

Based in the Hotel Paissandra in the Flamengo area of soccer-mad Rio, and close to the world famous Copacabana beach, Hibs were introduced to the crowd in the giant Maracana Stadium before a local League game between Bangu and Flamengo. It is reported that the Brazilians were extremely disappointed to see that the Scottish players were not wearing kilts and that there was no sign of even a single set of bagpipes between them.

The 'Octagonal International Championship', or the 'Copa Rivadavia Correia Meyer Tournament' to give it its proper name, featured eight teams from Brazil, Uruguay, Portugal and Scotland, split into two groups of four, each playing the other once in a mini-league format, the top two sides from each section going into the semi-finals. Hibs were drawn in a section which included the Brazilian clubs Vasco da Gama, Fluminense and Botafogo, all the games to be played in the Maracana Stadium in Rio. The other section games between Corinthians and São Paulo from Brazil, Sporting Lisbon from Portugal and National from Uruguay, were all played at the Pacaembu Stadium in São Paulo.

Although failing to win a game in the tournament, Hibs gave a good account of themselves in drawing 3–3 with eventual winners Vasco da Gama in the opening match. In front of a 30,000 crowd, which was lost in the vastness of the Maracana Stadium, the Scots turned on what they thought was their best display of the tournament, although their performance in going down 3–1 to Botafogo six days later, a game shown live on television, earned the visitors the compliment of their play being described in the local newspapers as the best display a visiting team had ever given in that country.

Before the game against Vasco da Gama, manager Hugh Shaw had broadcast to the crowd over the loudspeaker system how pleased he and his players had been by the friendly reception they had received from the locals, an announcement that was received with generous applause from the spectators inside the cavernous stadium. The Hibs players took the field wearing new-look, lightweight, short-sleeved jerseys that had been specially designed to help the players combat the oppressive heat that they were expected to encounter during the games. Straight from the kick-off the tourists took the game to their opponents and halfway through the half Eddie Turnbull opened Hibs' account on the tour when he smashed home a trademark thunderbolt from a free-kick by Ormond, but an equaliser by the home side in the 35th minute saw the teams change over at the interval all square. Reilly restored Hibs' lead early in the second half but a second equaliser by Vasco da Gama, and another scored from what appeared to be a position at least five yards offside, gave the Brazilians the lead. Although they had been the better side during the second half, it required all of Hibs' fighting tenacity and skill to earn them a draw when Reilly, living up to his 'last minute' tag, scored his own second and Hibs' third goal in the dying seconds to give the visitors an encouraging start to their tour.

Hibernian: Younger, Govan, Howie, Buchanan, Paterson, Combe, Smith, Johnstone, Reilly, Turnbull, Ormond.

With a week between games, there had been plenty of time for the players to indulge in leisurely pursuits including swimming, and golf on courses inhabited by the occasional poisonous snake. It was while swimming in the sea that Lawrie Reilly had the misfortune to swallow a mouthful of what can only be described as putrid water, which resulted in the Scotland centre-forward being confined to a hospital bed for a few days, going straight from his sick bed to line up against Botafogo in the second game of the tour. The players had even been invited to the British Embassy in Rio to celebrate the Queen's birthday. During the reception, there was a dignified silence when one guest asked if the footballers were the famous Irish team from Glasgow. During their stay in Brazil, Tommy Younger had befriended a well-known local professional tennis player who owned an ice cream factory in the city, and in the raging heat of drought-ravaged Rio, the players took good advantage of the offer to sample the free and plentiful wares.

Hibs were not at their best against the Argentinian side Botafogo in the second game of the tour. Watched by over 18,000 and played in a stifling heat which proved a substantial disadvantage for the visitors, the Scots might well have taken the lead in the first half when full-back Govan, after one of his characteristic overlaps up the right wing, elected to shoot instead of passing to an unmarked Reilly. A good passing move by Botafogo after 27 minutes gave the South Americans a half-time lead, a lead that was further increased not long after the restart, but Reilly reduced the leeway five minutes later when he held off the attentions of two defenders to score from close range. Hibs were now the more dominant side, and Smith had the ball in the net only to see it disallowed for a dubious infringement. With 10 minutes remaining Botafogo capitalised on a mistake by Howie, who misheaded the ball straight to the opposing centre-forward, who had the simplest of tasks to net, and despite another fiery finish by Hibs there was to be no more scoring. It was obvious throughout that Reilly had not been at his best, understandably so, having taken his place at the kick-off straight from his sick bed.

Hibernian: Younger, Govan, Howie, Buchanan, Paterson, Combe, Smith, Johnstone, Reilly, Turnbull, Ormond.

Another defeat, this time by the Brazilian side Fluminense, ended any hopes of qualifying for the semi-finals; although if truth be told, the players by this time were all keen to return home. Ward replaced Turnbull who had injured his ankle against Botafogo in the Hibs line up. The Scots were first on the attack, but it was clear from the start that the visitors were not at the top of their form and their poor passing soon allowed Fluminense to take full command of the game, although it took them all of 43 minutes to open the scoring. Soon after the restart a mistake by Younger allowed the home side to increase their lead, Howie just failing to clear the ball as it crossed the line. Despite the prompting of Combe, who was Hibs' best player by far, the game was put beyond doubt when Fluminense scored a third on the hour mark. The nearest the Easter Road side came to scoring was an Anderson shot which was tipped over the bar by the 'keeper, and a late effort from Reilly, which was again well saved by the custodian. Bill Anderson, who had previously played for the famous English non-League side Bishop Auckland, alongside former wartime Hibs player Bob Hardisty in the Amateur Cup Final at Wembley, and had been bought out of the army to join Hibs, replaced Ward at half-time. He was so keen to impress that he collapsed with exhaustion at the end of a game in which the visiting players had again been severely handicapped by the stifling heat.

Hibernian: Younger, Govan, Paterson, Buchanan, Howie, Ward (Anderson), Smith, Johnstone, Reilly, Combe, Ormond.

During their stay in Brazil the visitors could not fail to be impressed by the wonderful ball control and amazing stamina displayed by even the youngest kids on the Copacabana beach. Several players, fortified by a couple of beers, fancied a game against the youngsters, but trainer Jimmy McColl – with only a little humour – retorted that the kids would probably be far too good for them. In direct contrast to the skilful and exciting play to be found on the beaches, most Hibs players found the performances of the professional teams boringly predictable. According to one, 'each team was far too stereotyped, with the average British fan likely to soon lose patience with his local team if they played like the Brazilians'. The observer went as far as to state that 'The attacking play of the South Americans is all on the deck, and there was none of the good old-fashioned lob into the goal mouth which typifies the British game'. Considering that this was only a few years before the fantastically skilful and exciting play of the Brazilian national team would thrill the soccer-mad public at the 1958 World Cup Finals in Sweden, and since, this could be considered something of a miraculous understatement.

Of the fact that the Brazilians were even then obsessed with their football there is no doubt. After each game the newspapers were full of diagrams and descriptions of the moves and goals from the previous day's games, including those involving Hibs, who as a team had impressed the vast majority of the fans. It was reported that Vasco da Gama had made a bid for both Gordon Smith and Bobby Johnstone, and according to the legend, Hibs played a major part in the advancement of the game in South America that would eventually lead to the winning of World Cups. A Brazilian football encyclopedia printed in the late 1960s devoted a whole chapter to the exploits of the Scottish side and their influence on the Latin game during the tour of 1953. Hibs, according to the book, 'played an interchanging positional game that bamboozled their opponents and delighted the watching aficionados, and were included because at the time they were at the forefront of the British game and brought to it a style that was original for those times'.

As already mentioned, the Maracana Stadium in Rio de Janeiro had been built to host some of the games for the 1950 World Cup, but for the only time, before or since, there was to be no Final in that year's competition. The top side from each of the four sections of four teams went forward into another League section playing each other once, the side with most points at the end to be crowned champions. As it happened, Brazil and Uruguay emerged as the top two at the penultimate stage and were due to play each other anyway in the final section game, which in effect became the World Cup Final. In front of the 199,854 supporters who had packed inside the Maracana, the much fancied and hot favourites Brazil, playing at home, were surprisingly beaten 2–1 by their South American counterparts, who won the trophy for a second time.

Reilly Goes on Strike and the End of an Era?

On the eve of the new season the Hibs supporters were stunned to learn that centre-forward Lawrie Reilly had refused to sign a new contract. The main reason for the dispute was the player's insistence that he receive a testimonial match, as had been awarded to Gordon Smith in 1952. Refusing to capitulate to Reilly's demands, the club claimed that the present management was not in favour of testimonials, and that Smith's benefit game had been arranged during a previous administration. This failed to placate Reilly, and with both sides stubbornly refusing to compromise, several more meetings between the parties failed to reach any kind of settlement, a stalemate that eventually led to a demand from the player to be placed on the transfer list, a desire reluctantly agreed by the club.

As well as demanding a benefit match, Reilly also wished to revert to part-time football and continue his trade as a painter. To demonstrate his resolve, as his teammates prepared for the first day of pre-season training, Hibs' most capped player went on holiday. As one would expect, the announcement that the Scotland centre-forward was available for transfer provoked widespread interest on both sides of the border despite a reputed £30,000 price tag, with Stoke, Manchester City, Burnley and Arsenal said to be leading the chase for his signature.

With an established club policy of rearing young talent rather than acquiring ready-made players via the cheque book, it was vital that the scouting system, under the supervision of chief scout Davie Wyper, or 'Wingy' as he was affectionately known, continued to spot the best teenagers available, and, as in previous years, another batch of promising young hopefuls had been called into the senior ranks during the summer. Ultimately, as at most other clubs, only a few would eventually 'make it', but there were always plenty prepared to take the chance. That year John Higgins, Tommy D'Arcy and George Boyle joined goalkeeper Donald Hamilton at Easter Road. All would play for the first team in the coming season, but although Boyle would remain at the club for several years, none of the four would become regulars in the League side.

Chief scout Davie Wyper ended up at Easter Road almost by accident. Several years before, while Wyper was secretary at Wishaw Juniors, he and Swan had had a bitter disagreement regarding the signing terms offered by Hibs to one of the Wishaw players. Wyper's resolve in standing up to Swan so vehemently impressed the chairman and he was invited through to Easter Road to be offered the position of chief scout. Hibs were fortunate to have yet another means of acquiring aspiring young talent close at hand. Demobbed from the RAF on account of invalidity at the beginning of the war, groundsman Harry Reading had joined the club as assistant to Paddy Cannon, eventually taking over as head groundsman a few years later. Reading was the secretary and a founder member of the well-known crack juvenile side Edinburgh Thistle, and it was through this connection that Hibs had secured, among others, the services of Reilly, Archie Buchanan and Jim Souness.

In the absence of Reilly, Bauld was the obvious candidate to lead the Edinburgh attack against Wolverhampton Wanderers in the annual charities game, and the Hearts player scored twice in a 3–2 win for the local side, his decisive second goal scored with just five minutes of the match remaining.

On the competitive front, even without the services of Reilly, who had by now posted a written transfer request, the League Cup challenge was successfully overcome with only a 2–2 draw at Love Street interrupting a sequence of five straight wins in the section games featuring St Mirren, Queen of the South and Falkirk. Jimmy Mulkerrin, on leave from National Service, had started the new season as leader of the attack, before young reserve centre-forward Tommy D'Arcy was given a run, making a scoring debut in a 4–1 win against Falkirk. Four-nil victories in both legs of the quarter-finals against Third Lanark, with hat-tricks by Bobby Johnstone at Cathkin and D'Arcy in the return leg in Edinburgh, saw Hibs progress comfortably to the semi-final stage of the competition for the fourth time in five years.

An item had appeared in the Third Lanark programme for the game against Hibs that suggested that these were more innocent days. In the article, the Third's directors were scathing in their comments regarding the behaviour of both sets of fans during the previous week's match against St Johnstone. During an admittedly uninspiring game, both sets of fans had apparently 'instigated that most modern of all football curses – the slow hand clap'. The fans of the Glasgow side were further warned: 'if they could not come and cheer on the lads, then stay away. Slow handclapping and good sportsmanship are not synonymous with each other and this type of behaviour at Cathkin will not be tolerated'.

It was in the League, however, that Lawrie Reilly was missed the most. In the opening game Hibs were crushed 4–0 by Raith Rovers at Kirkcaldy, all the goals coming in the first half, three inside a four-minute spell. Worse still, Eddie Turnbull was sent off for the second time in his senior career for punching outside-right McEwan after being kicked by the Raith player. Turnbull's offence was committed not far from the main stand touchline, and, well aware that a dismissal was inevitable, the player continued running towards the tunnel with referee Jackson frantically chasing after him to officially administer the caution. By coincidence, Turnbull's only other ordering off had been administered by the same referee at Cathkin the previous year. With the Easter Road side now propping up the table, admittedly after only one game, it was ironic that Reilly, one of their most influential players, was watching from the stand as he covered the match for a local newspaper.

A second consecutive League defeat proved even more concerning for the Hibs fans. Although the scoreline was no worse than that at Starks Park, the fact that another 4–0 drubbing was this time inflicted by city rivals Hearts at Tynecastle made it seem even more so. Again Reilly's absence was noticeable, particularly with the experiment of playing Bobby Combe at centre-forward quite obviously a failure. More of a worry for the Hibs fans was that as well as Reilly's strike action, it was also common knowledge that Bobby Johnstone was unhappy at Easter Road and had recently handed in a transfer demand.

Although it appeared that Hibs could do little wrong in the League Cup, they were now firmly anchored at the bottom of the League table without a solitary point. Perhaps even more worrying was the fact that they had not even managed to score a goal, even in a 1–0 defeat by old rivals Tottenham Hotspur in a friendly at Easter Road just a few days before.

Finally, at the end of the month, with Tommy D'Arcy reinstated at centre-forward at the expense of Bobby Combe, and future manager Willie McFarlane making his debut at right-back in place of the long-serving Jock Govan, Hibs finally managed to break their League duck with a comfortable 4–1 home win against Hamilton. Coincidentally, of the 11 competitive games played since the start of the season, including the League Cup, no fewer than seven had ended with the winning side scoring four times, five of the results ending in Hibs' favour.

As Hibs were defeating Hamilton, that same afternoon at Pittodrie, Bobby Collins of Celtic was emulating Eddie Turnbull's penalty feat of a little over three years before, when he scored all his side's goals in a 3–0 win against Aberdeen from the spot.

By now it was patently obvious that the Reilly situation was of benefit to neither side. League champions Arsenal, who incredibly had lost five of their opening seven games of the new season, the most recent a humiliating 7–1 defeat by Sunderland, saw Reilly as the answer to their goalscoring problems and stepped up their efforts to sign the Scotland centre-forward. Now stating a preference to stay in Scotland even if it meant quitting football altogether, Reilly incurred the wrath of the Hibs management by refusing to even speak to Arsenal or any of the other English clubs that were keen to secure the player's services. Asked if he would sign for Hearts, Reilly confessed that he would sign for any Scottish club prepared to pay the price. There was a brief flutter of interest from Dundee, and even a bizarre but highly ambitious £17,000 bid from Stirling Albion, who were then languishing in the lower reaches of the First Division. An announcement by Swan that Albion's offer would be seriously considered can be discounted, but still neither side was prepared to compromise their position. A request from a group of Hearts supporters that the *Evening News* start an appeal to raise money to buy the striking footballer for the Tynecastle club was rejected, whether genuine or not, on the grounds of partiality.

Still the Reilly saga continued, filling literally hundreds of column inches in the newspapers. The player himself had kept fit training with local juvenile side Alexander's Sports Club, who humorously announced that they had £50 in the bank and were having a whip round to raise the other £29,950 to buy him, but the dispute was finally settled to the relief of all concerned when SFA secretary Sir George Graham suggested that an International Select could be arranged to play in a testimonial match for the player. Graham's intervention was not philanthropic in nature, but inspired solely by the fact that the Scottish international side was missing the input of Hibs' most capped player, who, of course, was not eligible for selection while on strike. A benefit match between Hibs and an International Select did eventually take place at Easter Road, but not for several years, by which time the player had retired from the game. The gesture, however, ensured that the deadlock could be broken without loss of face on either side.

After an absence of 11 first-team games, Reilly hurriedly motored south to join his teammates at their Southport headquarters, where they were preparing to face Manchester United in a benefit match for United's long-serving trainer Tom Currie. Lining up in his regular position at Old Trafford on Wednesday 30 September 1953, Reilly scored both Hibs' goals in a 2–2 draw. Showing no reaction after his weeks of inactivity, he lived up to his 'last minute' *nom de plume* by scoring Hibs' equalising goal in injury-time with a brilliant header.

Making his competitive comeback at Palmerston on the Saturday, Reilly was again on target as Hibs went down 3–2, a result that saw them plummet once again to the foot of the table. Seven days later he scored twice more in a depressing but not totally unexpected League Cup semi-final defeat against East Fife at Tynecastle. With Turnbull midway through a three-match suspension after his dismissal at Starks Park, debutant Eddie Gray was brought in at inside-right with Johnstone moving to the left. After a poor first half, the Greens hit top form after the restart, and two wonderful pieces of Reilly opportunism gave them the lead. Victory, however, was snatched from their grasp late in the game when centre-half Hugh Howie, who otherwise had been in magnificent form, conceded two penalties that allowed the Fifers to snatch a victory that seemed beyond them at one point. The first, when he was penalised for handling the ball inside the penalty area, led to the player acquiring the nickname thereafter of 'Hands Howie'.

Eddie Turnbull returned to the side for Hibs' first away win of the season against Falkirk at Brockville in mid-October. The Bairns took an early lead after just 90 seconds, but a thunderbolt penalty by local boy Turnbull and a hat-trick, by the in-form Reilly, his first treble of the season and his eighth goal in four games since his return, turned the game in favour of the visitors. Alex Duchart made his debut in place of the injured Ormond, one of only three appearances he would make for the club before his transfer to Southend United in 1956.

Despite the opposition in certain quarters, the clamour for floodlit football was gaining in momentum, and three days after Hibs' visit to Brockville, Falkirk played Newcastle United at the same venue in what was Scotland's first-ever televised floodlit game. The home side won the friendly fixture 2–1, but most of the interest centred around the new lighting system and the television coverage, obvious and exciting indications that football was entering a new age.

With the return of Turnbull from suspension and Ormond from injury, the forward line was once again along the usual lines for the game against Clyde at the end of October. It was Lawrie Reilly's first game in front of his own fans since the previous season. As East Fife were defeating Partick Thistle that same afternoon in the League Cup Final at Hampden, to become the first side to win the trophy three times, semi-final losers Hibs were left to ponder what might have been, as they eventually struggled to overcome a stuffy opposition 4–0 thanks to two goals inside a minute by Gordon Smith. The game was Harry Swan's first as substitute manager. Hugh Shaw had complained of feeling unwell not long after returning from the summer break and he was eventually diagnosed as suffering from a duodenal ulcer, an illness that was serious enough to require attention on the operating table. By the end of the month he was allowed home from hospital, but it would be some time before he could contemplate a return to business, and he missed a considerable part of the season. Shaw's absence left Harry Swan to look after team matters at Easter Road.

An international regular for several years now, Reilly was immediately reinstated in the Scotland side to face Wales at Hampden at the beginning of November, replacing McPhail of Celtic, who had led the team to victory in the previous game against Northern Ireland in Belfast during the Hibs player's enforced absence. Winning his 24th cap, Reilly was joined in the side by teammate Bobby Johnstone, who was winning his eighth. Both players were on target in a 3–3 draw, but Reilly's goal would undoubtedly have been the sweeter after his two-month absence. Only a trip by centre-half Ray Daniels, when the Scotland centre seemed certain to score, robbed the home side of a win and Reilly of yet another last-minute goal to add to his growing reputation of scoring in the later stages of a game.

A 2–2 draw at Parkhead at the beginning of November, during which centre-half Jock Stein scored his only League goal for Celtic, was defender Hugh Howie's last-ever game for the club. After a playing career spanning 10 years since signing in 1943, the former Newton Juniors player was forced to retire from the game on medical advice after a reoccurrence of the illness that had ruled him out of the game for a period in 1949. Howie became a reporter for a Glasgow-based newspaper, often covering Hibs matches, but unfortunately he died prematurely as a result of a tragic car accident.

Regardless of their poor season so far, judged by their own high standards, Hibs were still a huge draw in England, and the following Monday evening they were invited to open the Elland Road floodlights. A crowd of 32,000 spectators saw Leeds United win a thrilling game 4–1, the great John Charles scoring twice for the home side, but despite the result, over embellished or not, a letter was received at Easter Road in midweek from a Leeds supporter, thanking Hibs for providing 'one of the greatest, if not THE greatest, displays of classical football ever seen at the ground'.

On a misty Wednesday afternoon at Wembley at the end of November 1953, the British game was changed forever when England were comprehensively thrashed 6–3 by Hungary, their first-ever defeat on home soil by a foreign side. Although the initial impact would be sorely felt south of the border, the result also cast a giant shadow the length and breadth of the entire country that has remained to this day. The performance of the ultra-talented Hungarians had exposed the shortcomings of the British game, and was described by one scribe as 'a warning that will have done the country a favour if it means a change in our approach to the game'. It was an alert that would be ignored, however, and it can be argued that we have now been left far behind, even by several third-world countries that have improved out of all recognition while we in this country have stubbornly rested on our laurels, smug in the confidence of the masters who gave football to the world.

By now Donald Hamilton had replaced Tommy Younger in the Hibs goal, making his debut in a 2–1 victory over East Fife. Once again Hibs owed the victory to the predatory instincts of Lawrie Reilly, who scored both goals. Young Hamilton was at fault for East Fife's goal, but otherwise played well and looked a real prospect. Younger, unhappy at losing his first-team place, immediately posted a transfer request.

The fascination for floodlit football was gaining momentum. At the beginning of December Rangers played Arsenal at the official opening of the new Ibrox lights, the first floodlit game in Glasgow. A huge crowd watched the English champions win 2–1, but amazingly there were still some, including many in the media, who were convinced that football under lights was only a phase that would soon pass. At the end of the month Hibs played Rangers in Glasgow, but although Ibrox now housed an excellent floodlighting system, first-class competitive games were still not allowed under artificial light. As a result the game finished in virtual darkness, with spectators finding great difficulty in following the play. Worse still, although both teams had used the then fairly new white balls for the pre-match warm-up, the game kicked-off with the familiar dark brown ball. Because the rules at the time insisted that the game should finish with the same ball that had started, the white ball could not be introduced late in the game when vision was at a premium. Even more ridiculous was the fact that just days before, the East of Scotland Junior side Newtongrange Star had played Dalkeith Thistle under the new Newtongrange lights in what was Scotland's first-ever Cup tie under artificial light.

A few days before Christmas, Hibs were back to their scintillating best with a comprehensive 5–0 win over Raith Rovers at Easter Road, but the impressive victory came at a heavy cost, with the home side finishing the game with only nine men. Gordon Smith collided with goalkeeper Drummond shortly after scoring the fifth goal and was taken to the Western General Hospital with a fractured right shinbone. Soon afterwards, Archie Buchanan was forced to limp from the field after a reoccurrence of his old cartilage trouble, an injury that would require another operation and yet another lengthy absence from the side. The players spent the weekend side by side in the same hospital ward.

By now Hibs were in the unfamiliar position of 11th in the table, one place below 10th-placed Rangers, who as usual still had several games in hand, and it was now very apparent that much of the sparkle and lustre of the immediate post-war years had gone. It was also apparent, even this early in the season, that Hibs were well out of the running in the League Championship race. Worse still, rivals Hearts were occupying second place in the table, just three points behind leaders Queen of the South. Apart from the recent injuries to Smith and Buchanan and the retirement of Howie, manager Hugh Shaw, now back to full fitness, found consistency of selection difficult. With Younger still in the reserves and Jock Govan missing long periods of the season due to injury, Mick Gallacher, Tommy McDonald, Willie McFarlane and Pat Ward had all played several games for the first team. There would also be occasional outings by Moran, Campbell, Duchart, Boyle, Brown and former Celtic and Scotland goalkeeper Willie Millar, who had been signed on a free transfer from Clyde at the turn of the year.

On New Year's Day a second-half equaliser by Jim Souness against his former teammates helped second-placed Hearts to a slender 2–1 win in the derby match at Easter Road, the 100th League meeting between the sides. The Maroons now held a commanding lead in the series with 51 victories compared to Hibs' 26. Twenty-three had ended level. The win also allowed the Tynecastle side to leapfrog Queen of the South to the top of the table as Hibs dropped to 12th. But just 24 hours later, with right-back George Boyle making his debut in place of Govan, Hibs secured their biggest win of the season with a 6–2 away victory against Hamilton. Tommy McDonald, deputising for the injured Gordon Smith, scored twice.

In the words of a famous member of the Royal Family many years later, 1953 had been an '*annus horribilis*' as far as the Easter Road side were concerned and one that they would not be sorry to see behind them. Not only had they surrendered their League Championship crown and lost in the Final of the Coronation Cup, there had also been the loss for a period of the best centre-forward in the country. General poor form, combined with the manager's illness and severe injuries to several key personnel had not helped, but there was no denying that Hibs were now far too often a pale shadow of the great side of recent years.

After the turn of the year League form improved, but with an average of less than a point per game Hibs had lost far too much ground to be considered serious challengers, and their best option now lay with the by now almost mythical Scottish Cup. In the first round proper, St Johnstone were beaten 2–1 at Muirton to set up a home game against Clyde in the second round. A Cup tie rehearsal the previous week saw Hibs win a thrilling game at Shawfield 6–3, Bobby Johnstone scoring his second hat-trick of the season, but seven days later, in the Cup tie at Easter Road, Hibs went one better by winning 7–0. Johnstone only scored two this time, as did Smith's right-wing deputy Tommy McDonald. Turnbull, Ormond and who else but Reilly were Hibs' other scorers to set up yet another meeting with old Cup adversaries Aberdeen.

Determined to make the best of the opportunity, outside-right McDonald had been in sparkling form in Smith's enforced absence and many were of the opinion that the veteran player just might find it difficult replacing the youngster when fully fit. The rave notices regarding McDonald's recent good form did not go unnoticed and he found himself a surprise inclusion in the Scotland B side to face England B at Roker Park. The game, a 1–1 draw under the Sunderland lights, played in very poor conditions, was watched by a crowd of just under 20,000, but this was not enough to convince even FA Secretary Sir Stanley Rous of the advantages of playing under artificial light. Rous thought the experiment was not a fair test because of the weather, but he stated that: 'when 20,000 turn up to watch on such a poor night there must surely be some possibilities for floodlighting. Clearly the conditions must be right but I don't think this time of the year is ideal. Frankly I do not think we will ever have full internationals by floodlight, except perhaps against visiting Continental sides or similar opposition later in the year'. The *Edinburgh Evening News* also joined in the debate. An article in the *Pink News* that weekend reported that 'The novelty of floodlit football has faded'. Citing as an example the size of crowd that had watched the recent B international, the writer was of the opinion that 'if the game had been played on a midweek afternoon then the attendance would have at least doubled'.

Meanwhile, the third-round draw for the Scottish Cup had thrown old Cup adversaries Aberdeen and Hibs together. In front of a massive 48,000 Easter Road crowd, two goals by Aberdeen in the first few minutes proved too much for a poor Hibs side. Another goal for the visitors just after the restart dashed any hopes of a comeback, and although Bobby Johnstone managed to pull one back late in the game there was no doubt that the better side had won. During the game the unfortunate Lawrie Reilly complained of feeling unwell and was later diagnosed as suffering from pleurisy and pneumonia. A lengthy spell in hospital meant that he missed the remaining eight games of the season, and the hunt was on again for a short-term replacement.

Again Mulkerrin and D'Arcy were tried, with a debut for Doug Moran against St Mirren, one of only three games the youngster would play for Hibs before to moving to Falkirk. In mid-March, with Combe again taking over at centre-forward, East Fife lost their unbeaten home record when goals by Johnstone,

Turnbull and Ormond helped Hibs into fifth place, seven points behind leaders Hearts but with three games in hand. The late title surge continued when Mulkerrin scored his only competitive hat-trick for the club in a 8–1 win over Airdrie at Easter Road, Hibs' biggest win of the season, but the Championship chase was derailed seven days later when third-from-bottom Stirling Albion deservedly won 2–1 at Annfield, a day that saw Celtic leapfrog Hearts to the top of the table.

At the beginning of the season Bobby Combe had replaced Gordon Smith as team captain at Easter Road, but it was still something of a surprise when he was selected to captain the Scottish League side to face the League of Ireland in Dublin later in the month. Combe was joined in the representative side by teammates Reilly and Johnstone, but as it turned out Reilly would play no part in the game because of his illness.

With Gordon Smith still injured, Reilly ill and both Jock Govan and Eddie Turnbull out of favour with the selectors, there was an unexpected announcement that after almost eight years at Easter Road, inside-forward Mick Gallacher had at last joined the Easter Road international brigade when he was selected to play for the Republic of Ireland against Luxembourg at the beginning of March. It would be Gallacher's first and only appearance for his country. The consistently brilliant form of Willie Ormond was also finally recognised at full international level when he was selected to play against England at Hampden in April. In an otherwise disappointing Scottish performance, Ormond was his side's top performer as they went down 4–2 to the Auld Enemy. In Reilly's absence, John Henderson of Portsmouth had been selected at centre-forward, and in the inter-League game against Ireland a few weeks before, Buckley of Aberdeen had been chosen to lead the attack, leaving not only the Hearts fans, but also many neutrals, bemused at the exclusion of Willie Bauld, at that time among the most prolific goalscorers in the country.

With the season all but over, youngsters Jimmy Thomson and Tommy Preston made their first-team debuts against Celtic, but they could do little to prevent the Glasgow side from winning their first League title for 16 years after defeating Hibs 3–0 in front of over 40,000 spectators at Easter Road. The Celts would go on to beat Aberdeen in the Scottish Cup Final to collect their first double since 1914, when, ironically, Hibs trainer Jimmy McColl had made a goalscoring appearance in the replayed Final against his current side.

Both youngsters retained their place for the final two League games, the first, a 3–0 victory over Aberdeen, with Thomson scoring his first goal for the club after only two minutes, and a 2–2 draw with Rangers a few days later, both games played in Edinburgh.

Over the previous 12 months there had been much criticism of Hibs' reluctance to use the cheque book during the injury crisis, but Hugh Shaw blasted the critics by declaring that 'Although plenty of money had been spent, it had mostly gone on upgrading the ground. Hibs prefer to nurture young players and this policy will continue'. He went on to complain about 'the advent of National Service that did little to help clubs intent on grooming young boys by taking them away halfway through their football apprenticeship'.

The outburst by the manager, however, cut no ice with many of the supporters. 'Disgruntled', wrote: 'Mr Shaw does not state any better policy for the future. A club that sells so many players is surely expected to buy as well. Players such as Leslie Johnston, Linwood, Ormond and Gallagher were added to the splendid reserve strength, which helped put Hibernian on top. The art of rearing players appears to be lost, and the present method of playing Preston, Thomson and Campbell three times in five days is not the best way to rear young players. Finally, one wonders if these promising youngsters will mature into great players for Hibs, or be transferred for big sums?'

'Fed Up' wondered why 'Hibs could not cut their cloth accordingly? Other teams can pay good money to keep their star men and still buy players when necessary'. He ended by 'wondering what state the club would be in if Turnbull, Paterson and Reilly had all been transferred as they very nearly had been'.

Trainer McColl with Ward, D'Arcy, Younger and McFarlane, *c*.1950s.

A game against Dundee at Easter Road *c*.1952. The referee lies injured after being struck by the ball. Note the old half-time scoreboard at bottom right of picture.

Lawrie Reilly challenges the St Mirren goalkeeper. 1950s. Saints Cunningham and Telfer look on. Gordon Smith is in middle distance.

Scottish League champions, 1951–52. Back row, from left: McColl, Combe, Howie, Paterson, Younger, Shaw, Govan, Gallagher, Buchanan, Kean. Front: Terris, Johnstone, Smith, Swan, Reilly, Turnbull, Ormond, Hartland.

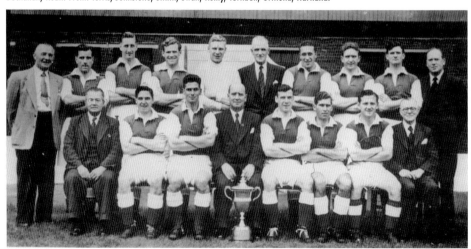

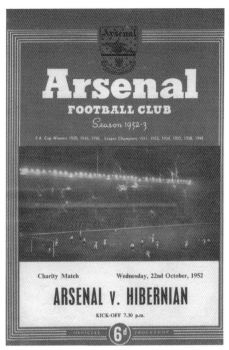

Lawrie Reilly, Hibs' most-capped player, wearing the colours of Scotland.

The official programme for the ill-fated game against Arsenal in 1952.

Gordon Smith introduces the Duke of Edinburgh to, from left, Gallagher, Paterson, Combe and Johnstone before the game against Arsenal.

The Hibs party about to embark on tour *c.*1950s. From left: McColl, Reilly, Paterson, Smith, Younger, Johnstone, Buchanan, Ormond, Howie, Turnbull and Gallagher.

In the Maracana Stadium during the trip to Brazil in 1953. From Left: Smith, Younger, Govan, Paterson, Buchanan, Howie, Combe, Johnstone, Ormond, Turnbull and Reilly.

Bobby Combe in action against Raith Rovers at Easter Road. Reilly is on the ground.

John Paterson watches goalkeeper Tommy Younger clear from former Hibs player Alec Linwood of Clyde.

Hibernian 1953–54. Back row, from left: Ward, Kean (trainer), Paterson, Howie, Younger, Govan, McFarlane, Gallagher and Archie Buchanan. Front: McColl (trainer), Smith, Johnstone, D'Arcy, Combe, Turnbull, Ormond and Hugh Shaw (manager).

Eddie Turnbull beats Dundee goalkeeper Bill Brown from the penalty spot, *c*.1952–53.

Tommy Younger: Hibs, Liverpool, Falkirk, Stoke City, Leeds and Scotland.

Tommy Preston.

Jock Buchanan, the scorer of the first-ever European Cup goal on British soil in 1955.

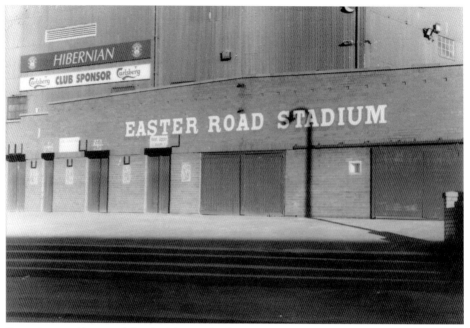

The new Easter Road frontage, which replaced the original wall containing the harp in 1955.

Hibs players on their way to training, c.1956. From left: Laing, Combe, Reilly, Buchanan, Kean (trainer), McFarlane, Grant and Plenderleith. Turnbull, Harrower, Frye and Ormond are at the back.

Archie Buchanan challenges Hearts goalkeeper Duff in a match at Easter Road, September 1956. Kirk of Hearts stands ready with Eddie Turnbull in the middle distance. Dave Mackay is partly hidden by the goalkeeper.

Jackie Plenderleith: Hibs, Manchester City, Queen of the South and Scotland.

John Grant: Hibs and Scotland.

The first and reserve sides that contested the public trial at the start of the 1957–58 season. Back row, from left: Combe (trainer), McClelland, McLeod, Anderson, Hughes, Baxter, Higgins, McFarlane, Grant, Paterson, Proudfoot, Muir, Leslie, Boyle, Wren, Plenderleith, Nicol, Preston, Kane, Bogie and Hunter (trainer). Front: Frye, Gibson, Baker, Slavin, Aitkin, Smith, Marshall, Fraser, Harrower and Ormond.

Hibs goalkeeper Lawrie Leslie punches clear from Alex Young of Hearts in a match at Easter Road, *c.*1957–58.

The dynamic Joe Baker.

Lawrie Reilly in action against Rangers at Easter Road. The picture is probably from Reilly's last-ever game, in April 1958. From left: Baxter (Hibs), Telfer (Rangers), Reilly, Fraser (both Hibs), goalkeeper Ritchie and Shearer (both Rangers).

Joe Baker, second from left in the front row, poses for a school team photograph.

Lawrie Reilly, Joe McClelland, Tommy Preston, Bobby Nicol and Eddie Turnbull.

The Hibs 1958 Scottish Cup final squad v Clyde. Back row, from left: Hunter (trainer), Mcleod, Grant, McClelland, Leslie, Paterson, Turnbull, Plenderleith and Baxter. Front: Fraser, Aitken, Baker, Reilly, Preston and Ormond.

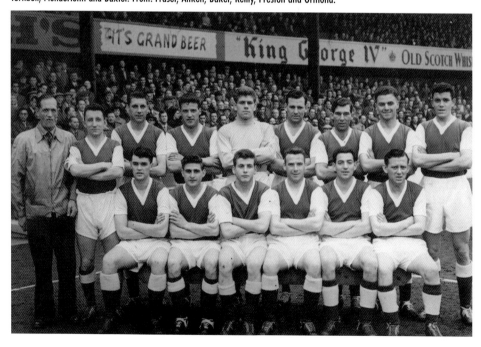

Joe Baker: Hibs, Torino, Arsenal, Nottingham Forest, Sunderland, Hibs again, Raith Rovers and England.

Joe Baker climbs above centre-half Bobby Evans to score in a match against Celtic.

Joe Baker puts the ball in the back of the net with his hand before it is chalked off during the 1958 Scottish Cup Final.

Johnny Mcleod: Hibs, Arsenal, Aston Villa, Mechelen, Raith Rovers and Scotland.

The great Gordon Smith, shortly before his move to Hearts in the summer of 1959.

Eddie Turnbull on his first day as Hibs trainer in 1959. From left: Turnbull, Jock Buchanan, Baxter, McClelland, Frye, Falconer.

Hearts goalkeeper Gordon Marshall clears a Newcastle United attack as Hibs right-back John Grant looks on. Edinburgh Select v Newcastle United, Easter Road, August 1959.

England's Joe Baker challenges Scotland's Frank Haffey during the international match at Hampden in 1960.

Hibernian 1959–60. Back row, from left: Falconer, Grant, Wilson, McClelland, Baxter and Hughes. Front: McLeod, Johnstone, Baker, Preston and Ormond.

Sammy Baird clears a Barcelona attack during the Fairs Cup game in Spain as right-back John Fraser looks on, 27 December 1960.

Gordon Smith presents Jimmy McColl with a watch on behalf of the club to commemorate 50 years' service at Easter Road before the friendly match with Shalke in August 1971. From left: Ormond, Turnbull, Reilly, Smith, Johnstone, Johnny Halligan (an ex-1920s teammate of McColl's) and McColl. It was Eddie Turnbull's first home game as manager of Hibs.

It was not all complaints, however. Many supporters wrote to congratulate the club on being able to replace players such as Smith, Reilly, Govan, Buchanan, Younger and Howie, who for one reason or another had missed large parts of the season, the team doing remarkably well in the circumstances to come through the bad spell.

Hibs ended the season in fifth place, a reasonable position considering the injury situation, nine points behind champions Celtic, who were winning their first League Championship since 1938, and four points behind Edinburgh rivals Hearts, who finished second. For the first time since the war the Easter Road side had failed to finish in the top three, and perhaps final proof that a dynasty had ended was the fact that their old adversaries Rangers had ended the season in fourth place, one above Hibs, but again only on goal average after collecting the same number of points. It was only the second time since 1928 that Rangers had finished outside the top two, the other occasion being in 1938 when they finished third.

For various reasons, either through injury, ill health or, initially in Reilly's case, a retraction of labour, the Famous Five had played just seven games as a unit that season. In contrast to previous years, by the end of the season Hibs had used a colossal 28 players throughout the League campaign, with only Bobby Johnstone an ever present featuring in all 30 games. The number of goals scored had also dropped alarmingly from previous years, and, somewhat surprisingly, Lawrie Reilly, who had taken part in only 18 League games, still finished top scorer for a fourth consecutive season with 15 goals.

At the start of that season, with the post-war crowd boom now largely a thing of the past, it had been decided, as a cost-cutting measure, to disband the highly-successful third team that had won the East of Scotland League Championship four times in five years, producing along the way several players who had made the first-team breakthrough, including Bobby Johnstone. Although not reported in the newspapers, it was said that as many as 40 youngsters were released at the end of the season, an indication of the tremendous number of signings made by the club at around this time. With hindsight, one may well wonder just what part this decision might have played in the club's barren mid-table struggle during the lean years that followed.

For the retained first-team players, no sooner had the season ended than they were off on their travels again. A four-game tour of Germany and Czechoslovakia, however, ended without a win, a match against old 1946 adversaries Spartak ending all square, but the players found it to be a most enjoyable experience nevertheless. On arriving at Prague Airport, the touring party was much humbled to receive an impressive reception from what appeared to be the entire Czech Army and Air Force, complete with bands, but unfortunately this proved only to be a dress rehearsal for the Independence Day Parade later in the week.

A Ray of Light, Yet Another Reilly Comeback and the Breaking up of the Five

The 1954–55 season was chairman Harry Swan's 20th at the helm at Easter Road. During this time he had more than confirmed his pre-war promise of leading Hibs to greatness, but although still more than capable of raising their game to great heights, the players of the glorious Championship years were mostly past their best, and it was now a period of transition for the club. During the summer several youngsters who would stand the club in good stead in the future had been called-up to Easter Road. Left-back Joe McClelland and centre-half Jackie Plenderleith had both been signed from Armadale Thistle, outside-right John Fraser from Edinburgh Thistle and centre-forward Jock Buchanan from Edinburgh Waverley. This fresh crop of talent, added to the young players already at the club, such as Thomson, Nicol, Preston, Grant, Mulkerrin, Boyle and Moran, gave the supporters great hope for the future. It was thought that the newcomers were the best group of youngsters to arrive at the club for many a year, particularly Plenderleith, who was rated by an Aberdeen scout at the time as the best prospect he had seen during the past 25 years, and, coupled with the vastly experienced older heads such as Smith, Reilly, Turnbull, Combe, Paterson and Ormond, once again the start of a new season was awaited with great anticipation.

Apart from SFA president Swan, Willie Ormond had been Hibs' lone representative in the World Cup Finals in Switzerland during the summer. Both he and teammate Johnstone had played in the qualifying match against Norway at Hampden, but a self-confessed mix-up over fixture dates by Harry Swan meant both players turned out for Hibs against Bochum in the final game of the tour of Germany instead of returning to take part in a Scotland training session. Consequently both players were dropped for the important return fixture in Oslo. They made a scoring return in the 2–1 victory over Finland in Helsinki that guaranteed Scotland's inclusion in the Finals, but for an ill-prepared squad the trip to Switzerland during the summer was to end in disaster. Reilly's illness ruled him out of Scotland's shambolic trip to Zurich and Basle, while teammate Bobby Johnstone was forced to withdraw from the squad after being injured in a warm-up match at Somerset Park, to be replaced by veteran Aberdeen player George Hamilton. The official SFA party that made its way to Zurich was 41 strong including the selectors, back room staff and the wives of the principal office bearers. There were just 13 players, Fred Martin of Aberdeen the only goalkeeper. Outside-left Ormond lined up on the left wing in Scotland's 1–0 defeat by Austria in Zurich and the humiliating 7–0 reverse at the hands of world champions Uruguay in Basle, results that highlighted the fact that Scotland were now falling well behind the rest of the world. To compound Scotland's lack of organisation, there were no training strips for the players, each having to supply their own from their club. Captain Willie Cunningham of Preston related later that before the start of the first match against Austria, he had been embarrassed to be presented with a pennant by his opposite number and be unable to reciprocate the gesture. As if aware of what was to come, manager Dick Beattie had resigned on the eve of the Uruguay game, and the heavy defeat gave Scotland the result that their preparation – or lack of it – deserved.

Fresh from the shock of England's recent humiliating defeats by Hungary, the World Cup had vividly exposed further, this time via the medium of television, the shortcomings of the British game, and it was now well recognised that a vastly improved standard of play was urgently required, a fact not lost on the management and directors at Easter Road. In changes to the backroom set-up, Sammy Kean, who had attended numerous coaching courses in both Scotland and England during the close season, studying modern training methods, took over as first-team trainer, with Jim McColl swapping places to look after the reserves. Considering the importance given by Hibs to the nurturing of young players instead of big-money signings, McColl had been handed a position of responsibility and of no little importance.

In an early-season match programme, Hugh Shaw reminded the supporters of the 'necessity to improve the standard of football on offer in Scotland'. The Cup tie atmosphere prevalent in most games north of the border was not, he thought, 'conducive to the introduction of new ideas and playing styles'.

Lawrie Reilly, now out of hospital after his recent illness but still far from a full recovery, visited his colleagues at the first day of pre-season training. Taking his usual place among the seasoned players and new starts was the superbly tanned Gordon Smith, now fully recovered from his leg break and fresh from 18 days on the French Riviera, a rare destination for most ordinary people in those days.

All was not well, however, on the contract front. In what was seen as possibly a display of petulance by the club, Jock Govan, who had recently opened a small grocer's shop in the Prestonfield area of the city, had been offered only part-time terms, a proposal instantly rejected by the rugged defender, who refused to put pen to paper. Govan's request for a free transfer was refused, but the club revealed that they were prepared to listen to any reasonable offer, and both he and Mick Gallacher, who had also refused terms, started the season on the sidelines. At that time several other players had business interests outside of the club, and many wondered why Govan appeared to have been singled out. An enquiry elicited a curt reply from manager Shaw, who reminded the fans that 'every case is judged on its own individual merits when new contracts are handed out', leaving the supporters still very much in the dark. In those pre-Bosman days, the retain and transfer system then in operation allowed clubs to retain a player's services indefinitely, as long as he was offered the minimal possible contract every year. The system would ultimately be found to be legally unsound when challenged in the early 1960s and replaced with option contracts, but this, of course, offered no comfort to either Govan or Gallacher.

Gordon Smith preserved his proud record of being the only player to feature in all Edinburgh Select charity matches since the inception of the series, when he helped the home side to a 3–2 win over a Bolton Wanderers side that included the famous English international centre-forward Nat Lofthouse. The visitors were only denied a well-deserved victory by a particularly outstanding display of goalkeeping by Tommy Younger. Younger, who had lost his place after several under par performances before Christmas, to be replaced by first Donald Hamilton, and then Willie Millar, for the last two games of the season, had been reinstated as the regular goalkeeper for the new campaign. Eddie Turnbull, in keeping with the new policy of switching the captaincy around the senior players, replaced the previous year's club skipper Bobby Combe. The game was Gordon Smith's first since breaking a leg against Raith Rovers in December but he showed that he was now back to full fitness when he scored the winner in front of almost 37,000 fans a few minutes before the end.

For the first time since the war, and in line with what was now common practice at most other clubs, Hibs broke with recent precedent by reinstating the public trial match. Neither Govan nor Gallacher, who were still refusing terms, featured in the game between the first and second teams, a fixture that raised £227 for a local charity.

On the morning of the match, reserve forward Ian Crawford, who had earlier been farmed out on loan to Hamilton Academicals, but found his services unrequired at either Douglas Park or Easter Road for the coming season, moved across the city to sign for Hearts on a free transfer. Crawford would have a major influence in the resurgence of the Gorgie side in the mid to late 1950s.

In the League Cup, Tommy Preston took over at centre-forward in Reilly's continued absence, scoring eight goals in six starts against East Fife, Aberdeen and Queen of the South; however, home and away defeats by the holders East Fife and a draw at Pittodrie resulted in a failure to qualify for the quarter-finals, the final game of the section, an impressive 5–3 away victory against Queen of the South meaning little.

The League campaign opened with a 1–1 draw at Ibrox. The official match programme paid tribute to their opponents. In it, the editor praised the 'rise of Hibs after years of misfortune as one of the true romances of the game. Only ill luck and injuries had prevented them winning one of the major awards last season, yet they still produced a brand of soccer unsurpassed by any'. Tommy Preston, in direct opposition to Rangers' giant international defender Willie Woodburn, scored Hibs' second-half leveller in a 1–1 draw. It would be Woodburn's last-ever game as a player. A few days later, after a meeting of the disciplinary committee, the entire country was stunned to learn that the international centre-half had been suspended *sine die*, banned from the game in any capacity for life. Woodburn had been sent off two weeks earlier after an incident involving Stirling Albion inside-left Paterson, but had already been warned, after three previous visits to the panel, which had resulted in severe censure and bans of three and six weeks respectively, for other infractions, that an extremely serious view would be taken if he appeared before them again. The 34-year-old Scotland pivot appealed unsuccessfully against the decision, which was only lifted several years later, by which time he was too old to play an active part on the field.

As during the previous season, Hibs would find early League victories scarce, and a 3–2 reverse against city rivals Hearts at Easter Road, when Younger allowed a weak shot to slip past him for the winner, and a 3–1 setback against Aberdeen at Pittodrie, a game that saw Archie Buchanan carried off with a broken leg, meant the Greens were once again languishing at the foot of the League table.

As a release from competitive concerns, old adversaries Spartak Praha Sokolovo, previously known as Sparta Prague, were defeated 6–2 on a visit to Edinburgh at the end of September. Plans to introduce floodlights to Easter Road had been announced at the start of the season, and before the game the supporters got their first glimpse of the four towering pylons set in each corner of the ground, which as yet were without the platform of lamps. Doubles from Smith, Ormond and Preston helped heap the misery on the Czech side, whose players were drawn from over 10,000 workers in a factory making motor cars in the communist-controlled country. The visiting side contained eight internationals and, friendly fixture or not, the victory went some small way to restoring Scotland's battered prestige on the Continent after the recent World Cup catastrophe.

As the first team was in action in a 3–1 floodlit victory over Leeds at Elland Road on the evening of 29 September, Lawrie Reilly, who had returned to light training at the end of August and had been included in the squad for the match against the Czech champions but was not risked at the last minute, made his comeback in a 2–0 Supplementary League defeat by Hearts at Tynecastle. He was only a few days behind his personal target of a making a comeback to first-team action against the Maroons at Easter Road.

At the beginning of October, both Jock Govan and Mick Gallacher, who had taken no active part in the season so far and had still not accepted the reduced signing terms at Easter Road, were involved in a double deal when they were transferred to Ayr United for a fee described as 'substantial'. In Govan's case, this ended a 12-year association with the Easter Road club.

In the middle of the month Jock Buchanan made a scoring first-team debut against Raith Rovers, and the youngster kept his place two days later when another important milestone in the history of Hibernian Football Club occurred, the official opening of the Easter Road floodlights. Oldest rivals Hearts accepted the invitation to inaugurate the system, the game taking place on 16 October 1954. The match would serve as a perfect and successful dress rehearsal for the visitors, who beat Motherwell 4–2 in the League Cup Final at Hampden the following Saturday. Bad weather limited the crowd to just over 18,000, with the Maroons winning an otherwise disappointing game 2–0 thanks to second-half goals from Tulloch and Whittle, but Lawrie Reilly had earlier laid claim to the distinction of scoring the first goal under the Easter Road lights when he netted from the spot during a full-scale practice match behind closed doors a few days before. Referee Jack Mowat, who had already officiated at many floodlit games, was of the opinion that the Easter Road system was without question the best that he personally had experienced. The quality of the lights had impressed not only the referee and fans, but also both sets of directors, and after the match the Hibs chairman offered Hearts the use of the Easter Road lights for a few games until they had installed their own system at Tynecastle.

Floodlights were not a new phenomenon, but their widespread introduction was to play a vitally important part in the growth of European competition, something accurately predicted by the far-seeing Hibs chairman. Swan had realised that if European football was to prosper, then the use of lights was imperative as it allowed clubs to play during the evening, making it easier to arrange fixtures that could be seen by a larger audience than the midweek afternoon matches often allowed.

The world's first-ever floodlit football match had taken place at Bramall Lane, home of Sheffield United FC, on 14 October 1878 between two Sheffield representative sides. The event organisers had made the great mistake of forgetting, or being unable, to light the approaches to the ground and it is reckoned that as many as 6,000 were able to enter the ground free of charge under the cover of darkness. The experiment, however, proved a great success. Over 14,000 paid to witness the event, a crowd several times larger than had attended that year's FA Cup Final between the Wanderers and Royal Engineers at Kennington Oval. The dynamo-driven light source was housed in four wooden towers with the lamps raised 30ft off the ground. Each lamp, it is said, was as bright as 8,000 candles. If there was one criticism it was that the light was too bright at the start, tending to dazzle the players if they faced directly towards the source. The match created tremendous interest in floodlit football and several other games were quickly arranged throughout the country.

A few weeks later, on 11 November 1878, a game between Hibs and an Edinburgh select took place at the Powderhall playing fields, on the site of what is now the Council Refuse Department. This was one of the first-ever football games to be played under lights in Scotland. A little over two weeks before, Third Lanark had played a friendly against Vale of Leithen at the first Cathkin Park in Glasgow, in what is thought to be the first floodlit game played in Scotland.

At Powderhall, arc lamps were mounted on columns very close to the pitch, but this experiment was not as successful as the one in Sheffield. One generator was found to be totally unreliable, breaking down midway through the game, and the remaining two, situated at the other end of the ground, produced light insufficient to illuminate the pitch, the match finishing in virtual darkness. Neither was it a financial success. A crowd of only a few hundred watched the match, due no doubt to the heavily falling snow before and during the proceedings.

Many other clubs took part in floodlit trials, including a short-lived experimental period at Parkhead in the 1890s with lights strung out over the pitch, but generally the lighting of games was found to be unsatisfactory.

As already mentioned, the first modern floodlit game to be played in Scotland took place on 7 November 1951 at Ochilview Park, with Hibs again participants. Under lights initially installed for training purposes, but with several extra lamps installed behind the goals, Second Division Stenhousemuir took on champions elect Hibernian in a friendly fixture. The usual brown leather balls were painted white to enable both players and fans to follow the play, and in the murky gloom, with the spectators occasionally failing to observe the action, the visitors successfully overcame a plucky home side 5–3.

The Hibs team that evening was: Younger, Higgins, McFarlane, Ward, Paterson, Combe, Smith, Turnbull, (J) Buchanan, Preston, Ormond. Hibs scorers were: Mulkerrin (2), Johnstone, Souness, Turnbull.

It was not the first time that Hibs had performed under artificial light in recent years. They had previously played under floodlights in Switzerland and Belgium, but the most notable occasion was the match against Racing Club de Paris in May 1951 when a Gordon Smith goal had earned them a share of the spoils. This was before the best-forgotten experience at Highbury. It was in Berne, however, on 23 May 1950, during the club's pre-season tour of Germany, Austria and Switzerland, that Hibs had first encountered the new medium. Neither Swan nor the players had been aware that part of the game was to be played under lights, and the chairman later admitted a sense of annoyance at the fact. But it was only as the evening grew darker and the lights brighter that the astute Swan recognised the enormous potential for floodlit football. Moreover, he had been immensely impressed with the pylon system in use in Berne and had already decided that if lights were ever installed at Easter Road then they would be of the same type and no other. The players themselves confessed to requiring time to get used to both the artificial light and the use of the white ball, but eventually went on to defeat the local side rather more easily than the 1–0 scoreline would suggest.

Arsenal had been the trailblazers of 'proper' floodlighting in this country. First used against Hapoel Tel Aviv in September 1951, the official opening of the Highbury lights took place against Rangers in October that same year, watched by a crowd of almost 60,000 including acting SFA President Harry Swan, who was reported to have been highly impressed with the Highbury setup. The ambitious London club had even installed floodlights at their training pitch as far back as 1932.

Although the visibility at the Stenhousemuir versus Hibs match at Ochilview had been far from perfect, it had alerted other enterprising clubs to the advantages of playing under lights, and by the end of 1953, Kilmarnock, Rangers and Falkirk had all installed their own systems. These lights were all roof-mounted on the main stands and covered enclosures. By 1954, East Fife, then a prominent First Division side, had also installed lights situated on low columns at each corner of the pitch.

As already mentioned, the first recognised floodlit games in Scotland in modern times took place in 1953, when Falkirk played Newcastle United, and Kilmarnock faced Manchester United, both in October of that year. Arsenal had returned Rangers' earlier gesture by travelling up to Glasgow in December to officially open the Ibrox lights.

There was not wholesale acceptance of the practicalities of floodlights, however, and as late as 1957 Aberdeen had refused to play a Scottish Cup tie against Hibs at Easter Road under the lights, with a similar refusal occurring before a League fixture between the sides the following year, the Dons being of the opinion that it gave Hibs an unfair advantage. Celtic, notoriously slow to accept many progressions within the game, did not install their own lights until 1959, the same year as Dunfermline, St Mirren and Aberdeen. The National Stadium at Hampden was not converted until 1961, and the last club in Britain to switch on, excluding the newer members who have joined the Leagues since, or sides that have relocated to new grounds, was Stranraer in 1981.

Harry Swan and the Hibs directors had travelled extensively, seeking advice on lighting systems, and after very careful deliberation work started in September 1954 on the installation of the Easter Road floodlights, or 'Drenchlighting' as the manufacturers, a well-known Edinburgh firm of electrical and civil engineers, had labelled them.

Only the best system of lighting available was considered good enough for Hibs, with particular consideration being given to even diffusion of light. Plans for the erection of four steel latticed towers were approved by the Dean of Guilds, with the rather quaint proviso that the towers must not be used to carry advertising material. On completion, the club were described as being the pioneers of real floodlighting. The ambitious project took six weeks to complete, and when finished the floodlights were described as being the brightest and best seen anywhere in Britain. The specially designed 100ft-high pylons required foundations in some places 32ft deep, and at the top the towers had inclined heads, each housing 30 lamps, with provision to increase the number if necessary after experimentation. The pylons were among the first such structures to be built anywhere in the world and were designed to last at least 50 years. In case of a power failure, a reserve generator was installed inside the main stand. A major benefit of the pylon system, as opposed to roof-mounted or corner-tower lights, was the reduction of glare. Being higher, there was obviously less chance of the players being dazzled by the brilliance of the lamps.

For a game played under artificial light, it was not only the pitch that required lighting, and for the Hearts match great care had been taken to illuminate the otherwise darkened stand, enclosures and terracing, with lighting also installed at the turnstiles and exterior approaches to the stadium. Typical of Swan and his directors, nothing had been left to chance, and Jimmy Wardhaugh, writing in his weekly column in the *Evening News,* had particularly admired the use of the white goal nets, not a common feature at floodlit games at the time.

Just days after the opening of the Easter Road lights, Scotland centre-forward Lawrie Reilly made his return to first-team action in a game against Clyde. As Hearts and former Easter Road player Jim Souness were winning the League Cup at Hampden just over a mile away, Hibs were struggling at Shawfield. It had been many years since Hibs had last been 5–1 behind at the interval, and it is reported that even the Hearts fans at nearby Hampden could not believe the half-time score. Two goals by Johnstone in the final few minutes made the 6–3 scoreline more respectable, but it was not enough to brighten a miserable day all round for the Easter Road support.

Seven days later, 17-year-old centre-half Jackie Plenderleith made his first outing for the League side, and Eddie Turnbull, who would hold the position with distinction during the later years of his career, made his first appearance for the club at right-half alongside the youngster in a 3–2 victory over Kilmarnock. Once again Donald Hamilton replaced Tommy Younger in goal, and, believing that he had once again been made the scapegoat for the heavy defeat at Shawfield the previous week, Younger wasted no time in posting a transfer demand.

Other floodlit friendly games quickly followed. Visitors Newcastle United, with future Hibs goalkeeper Ronnie Simpson making an appearance for the English side, drew 1–1, and Hibs were left still seeking their first win under their own lights when Manchester United gained revenge for the 7–3 drubbing in Gordon Smith's benefit match by defeating the Easter Road side 3–1. Several of the United side playing that evening, including Foulkes, Byrne, Berry, Blanchflower, Taylor, Violet and Scanlon, would perish or suffer serious injury in the Munich Air Disaster in 1958.

League form still continued to be unpredictable. Since losing so heavily at Shawfield several weeks before, the Greens had embarked on a run of six straight wins that culminated in a 2–1 home victory against St Mirren at the beginning of December. The result propelled Hibs into fourth place and rekindled Championship aspirations that had looked well beyond the club just a few weeks earlier. Future club captain John Fraser, deputising for the injured Smith, had made his debut in a fine 5–1 win against East Fife on 24 November. Bobby Johnstone, who scored yet another hat-trick, was among the marksmen. It was his fourth treble for the club and his third of the season, all achieved inside an eight-month period.

On 8 December Reilly made his return to the Scotland side after his recent illness for the friendly against Hungary, taking over from the most recent incumbent, Paddy Buckley of Aberdeen. In his absence he had missed eight full internationals including the ill-fated World Cup campaign in Switzerland. It was no surprise when the home side were defeated 4–2 by the World Cup runners-up, who included Puskas, Kocsis and Hidegkuti in their line up. Inside-right Bobby Johnstone scored Scotland's second goal immediately after the interval. It was his 13th appearance for his country at full international level and his last as a Hibs player.

Just three days later there was a 5–0 drubbing by champions Celtic at Easter Road, a goal by the visitors coming after only three minutes, and three in a nine-minute spell after the break was far too much for the home side, who were second best throughout. The defeat saw Hibs drop to sixth place and realistically out of the running as Championship challengers.

Tommy Younger, now reinstated to the first team after withdrawing his transfer request, was back to his brilliant best in an impressive 2–1 home victory against Rangers. It was only the fantastic display of the custodian, particularly in the later stages of the game, that allowed the home side to retain both points. The result saw Hibs climb to fifth in the table, one place ahead of rivals Hearts, who still had three games in hand on the Easter Road side, and this set up an intriguing New Year's Day encounter at Tynecastle. On the day, however, a goal by the in-form Bobby Johnstone was not nearly enough against the five scored by Hearts in a dress rehearsal for the forthcoming Scottish Cup tie between the sides, the result the first of three consecutive defeats for the Easter Road side.

In his weekly column in the *Pink News*, Bobby Combe came up with a radical suggestion regarding penalty-kicks. Although not often required to take spot-kicks with Hibs, the player was of the opinion that far too much pressure was placed on the taker, particularly when the award was at a crucial stage of an important game. Combe's revolutionary idea was to do away with the award altogether, replacing it with a free-kick from the exact spot of any offence. It was, he thought, ridiculous that a penalty-kick, an award that usually ended in a goal, should be given if a foul was committed on the bye-line, for instance, with very little chance of a goal being scored. It is not thought likely that Turnbull, a prolific scorer from the spot with his thunderbolt delivery, would have approved of the suggestion.

On 15 January, the match against Queen of the South at Easter Road was the only senior game in Scotland to escape cancellation owing to the heavy snow that was then sweeping the country. Watched by just under 6,000 hardy souls who had been brave enough to face the elements, Hibs were leading 3–0 thanks to another Bobby Johnstone hat-trick when, with just 20 minutes remaining, the referee was left with no option but to call a halt to proceedings when the falling snow started to obliterate the lines. It was the first match at Easter Road to be called off for seven years due to ground conditions, a tremendous tribute to the hard work and devoted care of head groundsman Harry Reading and his assistant Tommy Cannon.

Although he was not to know it at the time, when the match was eventually replayed, three-goal Bobby Johnstone would no longer be a Hibs player.

On Saturday 29 January 1955, Smith, Johnstone, Reilly, Turnbull and Ormond lined up as a complete unit for the first time since the 6–3 defeat by Clyde at Shawfield on 23 October. By coincidence, Clyde were again to be the opponents for what was to be the last-ever appearance of the legendary Famous Five forward line that had terrorised defences throughout the land during the past six years. One ahead at the interval, 14 minutes of the second half had been played when Bobby Johnstone provided Reilly with a chance the centre-forward just could not miss to go two in front. At no point did Hibs look in any real danger until the visitors scored midway through the half, and from then on there was only one team in it, and it was no surprise when Clyde scored twice more against a demoralised home side to take both points.

By now Hibs had adopted a so-called new style of play, which concentrated on a defensive strategy, interposed with a continental-style attack, a description that would no doubt bewilder the average fan. The system generally proved to be an out-and-out failure, and was heavily criticised because it appeared to rely on too many players, such as Grant, Paterson, Preston and Turnbull, operating out of position. But whatever the reason, it was not deemed a success.

In the first round of the Scottish Cup there was the eagerly awaited encounter against Hearts at Tynecastle, and an opportunity to gain revenge for the two earlier defeats at the hands of their local rivals. Watched by another huge crowd of just under 48,000, former Celtic and Scotland goalkeeper Willie Miller made his first start of the season when he replaced Younger after several below-par performances by the fair-haired custodian. For the first 10 minutes of the match Hibs totally dominated proceedings and were in absolute command; then the roof caved in. Wholesale defensive changes had proved ineffective. John Grant in particular, playing at centre-half, completely failed to curtail two-goal Willie Bauld, and the Maroons eventually ran out easy 5–0 winners. There was a moment of light relief for the Hearts fans leaving the ground at the end of the game, when, just as the referee was about to retrieve the ball, which was still lying forlornly in one of the goalmouths, a fan ran on to the pitch, seized the ball and, escaping the attentions of the police, was last seen making for the exits into Gorgie Road. The devastated Hibs supporters would no doubt have wished that the ball had been stolen earlier in the game. Rumours that a visiting player might have stolen the ball were unfounded, as in truth not one of them had got near enough to it during the previous 80 minutes to steal it. It was to be goalkeeper Miller's last game for the first team, and he would shortly announce his retirement. It was the 15th meeting between the sides in the competition since its inception, most of the clashes coming in the early days. To date the Tynecastle side was ahead with 10 wins to Hibs' four, with one match abandoned.

After the game, the management moved quickly to emphatically deny the rumours that were rife in the city that a bid for Eddie Turnbull had been received from a Manchester City deputation which had watched the game from the stand. Turnbull, who had missed the match in any case because of injury, was not the target. The following week, with Turnbull still an absentee, a Reilly hat-trick gave Hibs a comfortable 3–0 win at Kilmarnock, their first victory of the year, but it turned out to be the very end for Hibs' majestic all-international forward line. After 164 League appearances, in which time he scored 83 goals, plus another 36 goals in 53 games in Cup competitions, Bobby Johnstone had played his last game for the club, at least for the time being, before being transferred to Manchester City on 2 March for a fee reputed to be in the region of £22,000. The Kilmarnock game was also Gordon Smith's 600th appearance for the club, 366 of them in League games, scoring 331 goals, 214 in the Championship.

Like Turnbull before him, the dissatisfied Johnstone had also asked to be placed on the transfer list, and the player would recall many years later that one of the reasons for his move to England was an intense dislike of Harry Swan. The £22,000 paid for the Hibs man, however, was not a club record for Manchester City. That particular millstone belonged to Welsh international defender Roy Paul, who had joined the club from Swansea Town in 1950 for a reputed fee of £25,000.

In a paradoxical statement likened to a chairman's classical and dreaded vote of confidence for an under-threat manager, just days before Johnstone's move Swan had stated publicly that 'There was no financial necessity to transfer any player, and the club wished to keep the squad intact. If anyone were to be transferred it would not be for money but in pursuance of club policy and that Hibs had at their disposal the material to put them back quickly into the reckoning again, maybe even next season'. It later transpired that talks had been ongoing between the clubs since before the turn of the year, and regardless of the chairman's optimism for the future, the supporters were deeply concerned about how a player of Johnstone's undoubted ability could easily be replaced.

As would be expected, the sale of the player resulted in outright condemnation. Both the club and the newspapers were inundated by a mountain of mail, all voicing dissatisfaction over of the transfer of the player. 'Sure stay away' complained that 'It was a ridiculous state of affairs to contemplate selling a star player when there is not even the semblance of a fairly good substitute for his position. This is just the latest bitter pill, and the last surely that the long-suffering fans will take without complaint. Not enough light has been thrown on Hibs policy. What is it? The selling of Johnstone is poor reward for the fans who have paid hard-earned cash for years to see players go through an apprenticeship on the field, only to be sold when the time is ripe'. The incensed writer ended by reiterating that he would not be back, and reckoned that Hibs would have lost at least £1 that season through his absence, adding: 'If another 10,000 think like me, then Johnstone will have gone cheaply'.

Perhaps surprisingly, during the five and a half years of the partnership, the Famous Five had featured as an entire front line on only 80 occasions in League games, mainly due to the several serious injuries suffered by both Smith and Ormond, and the strike action and consequent illness of Reilly, and they had lined up as a complete unit only twice in 1954–55, coincidentally both times against Clyde. Of these games, 51 had been won and just 14 lost. In total, including League, League Cup, Scottish Cup and Coronation Cup, the five had formed a complete partnership 109 times, winning 69, losing 21. A total of 285 goals had been scored by the magical quintet during this time.

With Bobby Combe reintroduced into the forward line, an impressive 5–1 victory over Motherwell at Fir Park was secured without the services of Johnstone. Out of the Cup, and with a mid-table finish all but certain, there was nothing left to play for but pride, and a 4–1 victory over already-relegated Stirling Albion was said to have been watched by less than 1,000 supporters, probably the lowest attendance at Easter Road for decades.

In between there had been a 1–1 draw with Tottenham Hotspur in a floodlit friendly at Easter Road, Hibs' goal again scored, rather predictably, by Reilly. Seven days later Hibs were presented with an opportunity to avenge the humiliating 7–1 defeat by Arsenal at Highbury a little over two years before. It was Arsenal's first visit to Easter Road, and prior to the clash between the sides in 1952, both manager Hugh Shaw and trainer Jimmy McColl had played in the previous game between the teams, which took place in London in April 1926 as part of the deal which saw goalkeeper Willie Harper move south. At Easter Road the home side came within minutes of victory over the side described in one newspaper as 'the most glamorous club in football'. Two ahead with just seven minutes remaining, after strikes by Reilly and Turnbull, two late goals by the London club denied Hibs a deserved victory and the chance to record their first win under their own lights in floodlit friendlies after seven attempts.

On Saturday 2 April a spectacular strike by Gordon Smith and a brilliant piece of opportunism by John Fraser after a mix-up in the Celtic penalty area gave Hibs a 2–1 win at Parkhead and Celtic their first home defeat for nearly two seasons. That same afternoon in Paris Gabriel Hanot was hosting a meeting to discuss the setting up of a European, or Super Cup, as it was described at the time.

Hibs' victory at Parkhead had been achieved without the services of Lawrie Reilly, who was joined in the Scotland side by the recently-transferred Bobby Johnstone as England went on the rampage at Wembley, eventually running out easy 7–2 winners. Watched by acting SFA president Harry Swan, Lawrie Reilly managed to score one of Scotland's consolation goals after 15 minutes, his sixth in five appearances against the Auld Enemy.

A season that had started badly limped out unspectacularly with a 2–1 defeat at Starks Park, the only plus point being the debut at left-back of youngster Joe McClelland, who would go on to give the club several years of sterling service.

During the season several promising youngsters had been 'blooded'. As well as Jackie Plenderleith and John Grant, John Fraser had made his debut in a 5–1 win at Methil in November, and there had been the odd appearance by Jock Buchanan, but overall it had proved yet another bitterly disappointing season, with Hibs again finishing in fifth place, five points behind fourth-placed Hearts. Aberdeen had become League champions for the first time in their history, ending the season an enormous 15 points ahead of Hibs. Once again Reilly had finished the season as top scorer, but this time with only 15 goals, all of them in League games.

The European Cup

Always a man ahead of his time, it is said that the far-seeing Harry Swan had three main visions for the future. European competition, competitive floodlit football and the emergence of sponsorship within the game. Although it was 20 years coming, sponsorship would eventually play a prominent part in the game, with Hibs playing a major part in its advancement. European competition and floodlit football, however, would have a significant role to play in the coming season, 1955–56.

The Easter Road side had now been officially notified that they were to represent Scotland in the forthcoming inaugural European Cup competition. Although Aberdeen were the reigning League champions, there are differing opinions of the Dons' failure to be included in the new tournament. Some thought the club was highly sceptical of the new European competition, as were second-placed Rangers, neither wishing to be involved, a view shared by Harry Swan, while others thought that Aberdeen were angry at being snubbed in favour of Hibs. Several were of the opinion that a vested interest by SFA president Swan had influenced the selection process, but what most critics of the involvement of Hibs seem to forget is that at the time of the initial meeting in Paris, the League Championship race in Scotland was far from settled. Also, as far as Aberdeen were concerned, the lack of floodlights at Pittodrie and the club's cynical attitude towards the innovation would undoubtedly have proved a major obstacle to their taking part. The choice of Hibs was not unanimous in certain sections of the media, however, who thought that if not the current champions, then perhaps Scottish Cup winners Clyde or even League Cup holders Hearts should have been selected. Paying scant heed to the critics, the official Hibs handbook at the time stated that: 'It was a tribute to the prestige enjoyed by the Hibernians in Continental football that they should be invited to represent Scotland'. There were, it agreed, 'perhaps other teams based on last season's performance that may have had equal or stronger claims, but based over the past few seasons no Scottish side has undertaken so many testing games against the crack continentals, or fared so well against them all over Europe, than Hibs'.

Whatever, there were few dissenting voices from within the SFA that Hibs should carry Scotland's hopes in the new competition. Ultimately the governing body duly endorsed the invitation and Hibs became one of the nine sides contesting the inaugural competition not to enter as champions. All had been chosen on the basis of their entertainment appeal and crowd-drawing ability.

It is not common knowledge that the European Cup, or the European Champions League as it is now known, and probably the most important club tournament in the world, owes much of its conception to English arrogance. Late in 1954 the then English League champions, Wolverhampton Wanderers, a side not readily acknowledged for their skilful ball-playing approach to the beautiful game, preferring instead the route one long-ball game, reinforced with a rugged physical approach, played a couple of friendly matches against Continental opposition at their home ground Molineux. The first was against Moscow Spartak, with Wolves running out worthy 4–0 winners, three of the goals coming in the final four minutes of the game. But it was the second of these games, against the Hungarian side Honved, who were then generally regarded as one of the best club sides in the world, which really caught the imagination of the public. The English were still reeling from the humiliation of the 6–3 mauling inflicted on their national side by Hungary at Wembley the previous year, a side containing such household names as Matthews, Wright, Mortenson and Ramsey. This was closely followed by an even bigger embarrassment when they went down 7–1 in the return match in Budapest the following year. The fact that Hungary had gone on to reach the 1954 World Cup Final, losing only narrowly to West Germany, and that the Magyar side contained such players as Puskas, Hidegkuti and Kocsis, cut no ice with the English football community. They were badly wounded, and the Wolves versus Honved match was an opportunity to exact revenge, particularly as the Honved team contained no fewer than six of the side that had faced England at Wembley, including Kocsis and Puskas. The Wolverhampton players themselves were under no illusions that this was just another club game, being well aware that, as far as the public were concerned, it was an international match, England versus Hungary. Played under the recently installed Molineux floodlights on 13 December 1954, and shown live on television, the Hungarians, inspired by the brilliance of Koscis and Puskas, swept into an early two-goal lead and threatened to add to this tally. The balance of play changed in the second half when heavy rain started to fall. This, allied to the fact that the pitch had been heavily watered beforehand, allowed the rugged stamina of the home team to take control as the foreigners tired. Wolves scored from the penalty spot soon after the restart and the writing was on the wall. Honved somehow managed to hang on in the face of relentless pressure until near the end, but two late goals by the Midlands club gave them victory and sent their fans into ecstasy. English pride had not only been salvaged, but completely restored.

In the dressing room after the game, the Wolves manager Stan Cullis, himself a former England international centre-half of the no-nonsense variety, who had once been heard to remark that 'our forwards are not encouraged to parade their ability in an ostentatious fashion', surveyed his happy but exhausted players, and declared to the invited press reporters 'There they are', pointing to the players, 'the champions of the world'. Exaggerated or not, England awoke the next morning to sycophantic headlines in the newspapers such as 'Hail Wolves, champions of the world' and 'Wolves can now rightly declare themselves champions of the world'.

Meanwhile in Paris, Gabriel Hanot, the editor of the influential and widely-read French daily sports paper L'Equipe, on hearing of the newspaper headlines and the euphoria sweeping England, wondered how any team could possibly consider themselves world champions after playing only two games and both of them at home. There and then he decided to attempt to remedy the situation.

Gabriel Hanot had an illustrious background in the game. He was a former French international player and carried much influence within the sport. The idea of a European League was not new to him. Before the war he had tried to instigate such a tournament, but at that time there were too many difficulties to overcome, not least the gathering political problems that would eventually lead to the ultimate global conflict, and he was forced to shelve his plans.

Inter-country club tournaments were nothing new and had taken place as early as the opening years of the century, but the idea had not really caught on. In the late 1920s, teams from Austria, Hungary, Czechoslovakia, Italy and other mid-European countries had taken part in a competition called the Mitropa Cup, which was replaced in 1949 by the Latin Cup as the top club competition in Europe. This tournament was contested between the champions of France, Spain, Italy and Portugal, but because it involved sides from only one area of the Continent, it had not proved universally popular.

Times were different now. An air of post-war optimism was sweeping the Continent; an atmosphere of change, and the time was right, thought Hanot, to reinvent the idea of a European League. With the help of his associate Jacques Ferran and backed financially by the *L'Equipe* newspaper and its managing director Jacques Goddett, who were also co-organisers and sponsors of the immensely popular Tour de France, a committee was formed and representatives of selected teams were invited to an all-expenses-paid meeting in Paris. On learning of the proposal to form a European League competition, FIFA, the world ruling body, insisted that such a tournament would have to be organised through an official body. They themselves were not keen on becoming involved, but suggested that perhaps the newly formed UEFA, founded only the previous year, would take them under their wing. The response from UEFA was also lukewarm, and it was only when Hanot and his committee demonstrated their resolve by insisting that their meeting would still go ahead, that UEFA relented and decided that they would after all take the newly proposed competition under their umbrella. This move, however, would eventually mean exclusion for the enterprising Hanot and his committee, but a place for Scottish League secretary Sir George Graham, who took over as chairman of the new organising council. Instead of the League format favoured by Hanot and his colleagues, UEFA insisted that the tournament should be on a straight home and away knock-out basis. Entry in the first year would be by invitation only, but the following season and thereafter it would be played only between the champions of each country and named the European Champion Clubs' Cup.

In a newspaper article many years later Swan would recall that the idea of a European tournament had been broached during the 1954 World Cup Finals in Switzerland. During the competition he had been asked if he thought that SFA secretary Sir George Graham would be in favour helping to form a European Association to combat what was seen as the rising influence of the Eastern Bloc on FIFA. Although assuring the questioner that he had no doubts that Graham would be extremely enthusiastic about the suggestion, no more would be heard about the subject until Swan was contacted by Hanot the following year.

An invitation to attend the inaugural meeting in Paris on 2 April 1955 was sent out to 18 teams. Hibernian of Edinburgh were invited to represent Scotland, and although they were one of only three sides not to attend the meeting, they did agree by letter that they would be prepared to take part in the tournament. All 15 clubs who attended the meeting were accepted for the first-round draw, and of the three who agreed their interest by letter, Hibs were duly accepted and became one of the 16 sides that would contest the first competition. In the draw made that day Hibs had initially been paired against a West German side, but it was unclear at the time whether they would face current champions Rot-Weiss of Essen or some other side nominated by the German FA. Football League champions Chelsea were drawn against Swedish side Djurgården, but they later withdrew from the competition on the advice of the Football League, who felt it would perhaps be unwise to play too many games in a season. Many thought, however, that English pride had already suffered enough on the European stage in recent years without risking further embarrassment, and that this was the real reason behind the request for Chelsea's withdrawal.

For only the second time since the war, Hibs had not embarked on a foreign pre-season tour during the summer. Tommy Younger had made the first of his 24 appearances for Scotland alongside teammates Gordon Smith and Lawrie Reilly in the friendly against Portugal at Hampden in May, Gordon Smith's first appearance at full international level since playing against the USA a little over three years before. All three had been included in the Scotland party that had toured Yugoslavia, Austria and Hungary during the close season, and in the absence of the international threesome it had been decided that the rest of the playing staff would stay at home to recharge their batteries. This did not mean, however, that they could take it easy, and as early as 2 June manager Shaw called all the remaining players to the ground for initial training in an effort to reinforce Hibs' reputation of being the fittest team in the country.

That same day it had been announced that a new frontage was soon to be built at the players' entrance of the ground and other improvements made to the perimeter that would enhance the appearance of the stadium and further improve the safety and comfort of the large number of fans who were then attending home matches. Prior to the renovations, admission to the centre stand, south stand and enclosure had been through turnstiles built directly into the outside wall of the grandstand. Now a new 15ft-high red brick wall was to be built at the main entrance in Albion Road. The existing wall and ornamental club crest of a harp set into a three-foot circular design painted green, white and gold, was to be demolished and replaced by a new players' entrance and turnstiles for the fans. As a matter of interest, the harp was not situated above the players' entrance, as some say, but several yards to the right, on top of a row of turnstiles that led directly into the south terracing. The original 1924 turnstiles from the grandstand would be resited in a new construction at the south-west corner of the ground.

The club crest was never replaced, and to this day there are some who look upon this development as having sinister overtones regarding Harry Swan's religious allegiance. In his book *The History of Celtic* Gerry McNee questions the reasons why a wall was demolished and a similar one built on the same spot, but minus the harp. However, the new wall was built approximately 10ft forward of the old one and was constructed to house more up-to-date turnstiles than the aging 1924 mechanisms and give divided access into the grandstand and enclosure.

This was not the first time that Swan had been involved in a controversy over a symbol of Hibernian's Irish heritage. On New Year's Day 1952, crowd trouble had erupted during 10-man Rangers' 4–1 defeat of Celtic at Parkhead, and several arrests were made. The matter had been brought to the attention of the Glasgow Magistrates' committee, who made several recommendations to the SFA, one being that neither of the two Glasgow giants should display any banner that was likely to provoke unrest among the supporters. At the time Celtic flew the Irish tricolour over the covered enclosure opposite the main stand, and the club's board of directors took the view that the magistrates' recommendation was a veiled attempt at the removal of the symbol of the team's long-established connection with Ireland. Despite requests that the flag be lowered, Celtic refused to do so and even threatened to take the matter to court. For a time it seemed as if Celtic would even be suspended from the League, but the club stood firm, claiming that no law or SFA rule had been broken. In the face of the determination shown by the Parkhead side it was agreed to suspend any decision for a few weeks, and the matter was eventually allowed to drop. Many felt that Rangers had been the main instigators of the dispute, but they in fact were in favour of the stance taken by Celtic. The prime movers in the incident had been the Scottish Football Association. Accusations of anti-Catholic bias had been levelled in some quarters towards the then acting SFA president Harry Swan, who at one stage had recommended that Celtic be given just three days to remove the offending item or face suspension, and secretary George Graham, allegedly a well-known Freemason and anti-Catholic. Some even thought that, rather than a religious bias, Swan's involvement was more from a business standpoint, with Hibs standing to gain many of the Celtic 'traditional' support in the event of the Parkhead side's expulsion from the League. Swan would reveal in later years that although he had taken no part in the original decision and had attended the magistrates' meeting strictly as an observer, although duty bound to act on the committee's recommendations, the incident had resulted in numerous abusive and threatening letters of complaint being forwarded to him, one from as far afield as America, and for some time afterwards his wife, concerned about his safety, had begged him not to attend matches at Parkhead.

In his book McNee also recollects a humorous story regarding the incident. Harry Swan decided to seek a bit of free advice on the issue from a lawyer who was a regular visitor to the Easter Road boardroom. Harry was stunned, and silenced for once, when notified that the lawyer was unable to discuss the subject as he had already been engaged to act on behalf of Celtic regarding the matter.

It was not only at the stadium that ambitious changes were being made. A Hibs supporters' association had first been formed on 1 May 1946, mainly at the instigation of a Mr Robert Cowan, when several dozen supporters had met at a club in Royal Terrace. Since then individual branches had met regularly at various venues throughout the city and surrounding areas with delegates attending monthly meetings in places such as the Liberal rooms at the foot of Leith Walk and other locations. It had long been thought that premises should be acquired on behalf of the various supporters' clubs, and the official opening of the Hibernian Supporters' Clubrooms at 7 Carlton Terrace, Edinburgh, took place on 29 June 1955. It was the first operation of its kind in the whole of Great Britain, beating a similar venture by Hearts supporters in the west end of the town by several weeks on account of a building strike delaying its completion. The acquisition of the Carlton Terrace property for the then princely sum of £2,600 and its decoration proved an expensive business, but one that was felt by an enterprising committee to be well worthwhile. As well as a public bar, function room and games room, overnight accommodation for travelling Hibs fans was planned for the near future. A special dinner accompanied the official opening, which was performed by chairman Harry Swan, to which the players and directors of the football club were invited. During the evening a presentation gift of a radiogram was made to the recently retired Hugh Howie.

In a break from pre-season training, fine summer weather encouraged a crowd of just under 5,000 to watch the latest in the series of annual charity cricket matches against Leith Franklin on Leith Links. Thirty-one runs by Ormond, and 18 not out by Tommy Preston, helped Hibs win the match by five wickets, giving the footballers a 3–2 lead in the fixture. There were also the usual five-a-side pre-season football tournaments and the annual sports meeting at Old Meadowbank. Hibs beat Hearts 5–2 after extra-time in the Final to lift the trophy. A huge crowd of over 12,000 had watched the game.

As usual, the now familiar Edinburgh charities match heralded the start of the new season. FA Cup-holders Newcastle United, led by the irrepressible England centre-forward Jackie Milburn, who had defeated a Manchester City side that included former Hibs favourite Bobby Johnstone 3–1 in the Final just a few months before, were that year's visitors to the capital.

In those days the Scottish League allowed only a limited number of season tickets to be sold by each club, and the coveted briefs were always in demand. Regular season-ticket holders that had not already done so were advised by manager Shaw to purchase their tickets for the coming season within the next few days or the precious briefs would be allocated to others waiting in the queue.

The new season kicked-off in earnest with a League Cup tie against champions Aberdeen at Easter Road. Former Hibs captain Davie Shaw, making his competitive debut in the Pittodrie managerial hot seat, saw his side get off to an excellent start with a 1–0 victory. The Greens were denied the draw that most felt their play deserved when Eddie Turnbull fired wide from the penalty spot, and later the same player could only watch in disbelief as goalkeeper Fred Martin made a spectacular save from his net-bound bullet-like header to preserve the Dons' lead.

A draw at Shawfield and a home victory over Dunfermline would ultimately mean little after another defeat by Aberdeen, this time at Pittodrie, secured the Grampian side an early place in the quarter-finals of the competition. With the remaining games against both Clyde and Dunfermline meaningless, manager Shaw gave the highly promising 19-year-old inside-left Desmond Fox his debut in Hibs' 2–1 home win against the Shawfield side.

Now called the Scottish League 'A', the division had been expanded from 16 to 18 teams at the beginning of the season, a move that saved both Motherwell and Stirling Albion, who had finished bottom the previous season, from the embarrassment of relegation. Hibs' title challenge opened with yet another defeat at the hands of Aberdeen, the third in a little over three weeks. Despite a scintillating performance by outside-right Gordon Smith, the Dons went on a goal rampage, and the embarrassing 6–2 final scoreline was not an ideal preparation for the encounter with West German side Rot Weiss in the first round of the European Cup in Essen four days later.

Well before the advent of the convenient charter flight direct to the destination, the Hibs party made their way to Germany for the first leg via an early morning flight from Turnhouse Airport to London. From there they caught a connection to Dusseldorf, finally arriving in Essen at teatime after a long and exhausting journey. Thirteen players, plus manager Hugh Shaw, trainer Sammy Kean and director Tom Hartland, made the trip. Harry Swan had remained behind in Edinburgh to meet representatives from Partick Thistle, Hearts, Newcastle United, Manchester City and Tottenham Hotspur at a meeting to discuss the setting up of a floodlit football League. Although not at the meeting, Arsenal and Rangers had also intimated an interest in a tournament that would feature only games between clubs of the two opposing countries. Celtic, who had no lights anyway, completely cold-shouldered the idea, declaring that club policy was to install better amenities for the public as their primary consideration. At the meeting the clubs had gone as far as drawing up a provisional constitution for the proposed tournament, but there was an immediate drawback to their plans when they were informed that at an earlier meeting of the executive committee, the SFA had discussed the proposal of a Floodlight League, and in line with a similar judgment by the FA, were totally opposed to the idea. The possibility remained that some League and Cup games could be permitted under floodlights in the near future, but the matter was not due to be discussed until the next meeting of the SFA.

That same evening at Easter Road, a young Hibs colts side beat Armadale Thistle 10–1 in a friendly match. Provisional signing Malcolm Bogie lined up alongside a 16-year-old Joe Baker, who scored four goals while wearing the famous green-and-white shirt for the very first time.

Back in Essen, there was an early scare for Hibs when full-back John Higgins and wing-half Tommy Preston, who had travelled together on the outward journey, awoke next morning covered in spots, and in Preston's case with heavily swollen eyes, but after treatment in the forenoon, both players were passed fit to play. Arriving at the Stadion Georg Melches, the Scottish players were surprised to find that although the pitch was excellent and not far behind Wembley in standard, the stadium was rather ramshackle, with only a small grandstand capable of seating fewer than 2,000 fans. The dressing rooms were described as being no bigger than a broom cupboard. The incessant rain that had not stopped all day made the playing surface extremely heavy and treacherous, and had also helped to dissuade the local fans from turning out in numbers. At kick-off there were barely 5,000 inside the ground, nearly 1,000 of them soldiers from the British Army on the Rhine, but regardless of any home-town allegiance they were determined to provide loud vocal backing for the Scottish team, and this they did, out-roaring the home crowd throughout the game.

Tommy Preston recalls that in the small dressing room before the kick-off, manager Hugh Shaw urged caution, advising his players to take it easy for the first 20 minutes or so and not take unnecessary risks against the unknown continental side. It was the first time in his experience that he could remember the normally cavalier Hibs players ever being told to take it easy before the start of a match, but in fairness to Shaw, the two-legged home and away games were a new experience at that time.

The following players were entrusted with the task of preserving the dignity and reputation, not only of Hibs, Edinburgh and Scotland, but also of being the British ambassadors in the country's first-ever competitive European game.

Tommy Younger: Since taking over from Jimmy Kerr several years before, Younger had made the goalkeeping position his own and was now also the established Scottish custodian. An agile man despite his large frame, he was incredibly, some say foolishly, brave in the pursuit of the prevention of a goal.

John Higgins: The right-back from Dalry Thistle had been called-up to Easter Road only the previous season and had made the first-team breakthrough almost immediately. Already he had shown a wonderful temperament for the big time. **John Paterson:** An outstandingly reliable defender, Paterson demonstrated his versatility by moving to full-back from his more favoured centre-half position. Signed during the war, and a Scotsman in all but birth, he had first seen the light of day in Aldershot, where his Scottish father was serving with the army. Not eligible to play for the full Scotland side, he had since been selected for the Scottish League. **Jimmy Thomson:** Initially a centre-forward, the tenacious 'Tiger' had made his debut only at the end of the previous season. He now seemed to have found his best position since moving to half-back, but still retained an eye for goal. **Jackie Plenderleith:** At the time one of the most promising centre-halves in the game. He had made his first start at the beginning of the 1954–55 season and became first choice almost immediately. Good in the air, he had a quick eye and was a clever distributor of the ball on the ground. **Tommy Preston:** Like Thomson, Preston had also made his debut at the end of the previous campaign. An extremely skilful player, he had a good football brain and was a prolific goalscorer. Initially an inside man, he took over from Reilly during the centre-forward's enforced absence owing to illness, and such was his impact that a place had to be found for him on Reilly's return to the side. **Gordon Smith:** At that time, Smith was captain of Scotland after several years in the international wilderness. Now fully recovered from his leg break in 1953–54, he had made his 600th appearance for the club at the end of the previous season and had scored over 300 goals wearing the green and white. Started his career as a centre-forward, but it was as an outside-right that he achieved legendary status. **Eddie Turnbull:** The acknowledged engine room of the team, but Turnbull had much more to offer than that. Allied to his non-stop running and encouragement, he had a brilliant football brain and was a tremendous passer of the ball. The possessor of a thunderbolt shot which he put to good use, he was the acknowledged penalty-kick expert of the team, and as previously reported had once scored three from the spot in a match against Celtic. **Lawrie Reilly:** Hibs' most capped player ever, Reilly had made his return to the international scene the previous year after recovering from the serious illness that had threatened his career. Although still only 26, he was in his ninth season as a first-team player. Spearhead of the magical Famous Five, Reilly had been top League goalscorer at Easter Road for the past five consecutive seasons, and overall top scorer in all but one. **Bobby Combe:** Making his debut for Hibs on the same day as Gordon Smith, Mr 'versatility' Combe had featured in every one of the front positions as well as both wing-half slots, and had returned to the forward line after Johnstone's transfer to England earlier in the year. A full and League international, the clever and skilful two-footed player was regarded as a mainstay of the side. **Willie Ormond:** The directness of Ormond on the left wing gave the team the perfect balance to the artistry of Smith on the right. An unbelievably fast and tricky ball player, it was said that at times he only had one trick, but regardless of the full-back knowing what he was about to do, there was no way that the defender could prevent it happening. Despite several serious mishaps due to injury in the past, Ormond had been chosen to represent Scotland in the 1954 World Cup in Switzerland.

European Cup first round (first leg), Wednesday 14 September 1955, Stadion Georg Melches, Essen.

Rot Weiss: Herkenrath, Jaenisch, Sastrau, Hoechling, Wewers, Roettger, Roemtig, Vorderbaumen, Abromeit, Sauer, Steffens.

Hibernian: Younger, Higgins, Paterson, Thomson, Plenderleith, Preston, Smith, Turnbull, Reilly, Combe, Ormond.

Referee: Mr Bronkhorst (Holland).

With Hibs now sporting new-look continental-style white V-neck jerseys with white sleeves, and the home side their famous red shirts with the distinctive Airdrie-style white V in front, the game kicked-off under the Rot Weiss lights on Wednesday 14 September 1955. The heavy rain that had continued to fall made the already heavy playing surface even more precarious, but within a few minutes of the start it was evident that the Scottish team were handling the atrocious conditions better, and even more evident that there was no need to adhere to manager Shaw's pre-match warning to display caution. The players soon realised that the Germans held no threat for them and they turned on the style, much to the delight of the British 'Tommys' soaked to the skin on the terracing. The weak home defence was breached time and time again, and only poor finishing and some fine goalkeeping by Herkenrath prevented Hibs from taking the lead. In the 30th minute a piledriver from Ormond was tipped over by the 'keeper, but he was only delaying the inevitable.

In the 35th minute, Eddie Turnbull made history by becoming the first British player to score in a European competitive match. Ormond took a corner from the left. His cross found Turnbull completely unmarked inside the box and, completely unaware of the significance of the event, the inside-right's resulting drive made its way past the despairing dive of Herkenrath and into the far corner of the net. Repeatedly prompted by wing-half Thomson, Hibs renewed their attack but were yet again thwarted by inept finishing and some efficient goalkeeping at the home end as they cut through the German defence at will. Two minutes from the interval, Reilly collected the ball near the halfway line and a wonderful solo run ended with the forward slipping the ball past the home 'keeper for goal number two, having beaten several defenders on the way. Right on the stroke of half-time there was a scare for the Scottish team when Younger was injured making a save in one of the rare German attacks, but the goalkeeper recovered after treatment from trainer Kean.

Half-time: Rot Weiss 0 Hibernian 2

After the restart, Rot Weiss, as expected, went into concerted attack for a short spell, but the Hibs defence stood firm, coping well with all that was thrown their way. The aggression and exuberance of Reilly was causing the Germans all kinds of problems, and it was no surprise when the visitors increased their lead in the 56th minute. Good work between Ormond and Preston saw the ball land at Turnbull's feet and the inside-right wasted absolutely no time in crashing the ball into the net from an acute angle to put the game, and perhaps the tie, beyond doubt.

The play from Hibs understandably slackened somewhat midway through the second half as the visiting side tired after their exhausting efforts in the extremely heavy conditions. The German team redoubled their efforts to take something from the game, but on the rare occasions that they managed to penetrate the midfield, they encountered Hibs' rearguard in fine form. In 68 minutes Reilly found the ball at his feet right in front of goal, but the centre-forward uncharacteristically shot high over the crossbar when he knew that he should have increased his side's lead. Eight minutes from the end, Thomson broke down the right wing before squaring a wonderful ball inside to Ormond, and from 20 yards the outside-left crashed a left-foot drive into the net off the underside of the crossbar.

In the dying seconds of the match, Gordon Smith had the ball in the German net again just as the final whistle blew, and the Edinburgh men left the field unaware whether they had scored a fifth goal or not. Only later, after consulting the Dutch referee, did they learn that the whistle had been blown just before the ball had crossed the goal line and consequently the goal had been disallowed.

Full-time: Rot Weiss 0 Hibernian 4

The Edinburgh side had recorded an important victory over European opposition, and they left the field to wild celebration by both sets of supporters. They had delivered as good a performance as they ever had done and, apart from rare spells of pressure by the home side, they had totally dominated the match from start to finish. After the game, Dutch referee Bronkhorst, who only a few weeks before had officiated at the Great Britain versus the Rest of Europe match in Belfast, was of the opinion that on this performance Hibs would have beaten both international sides, although presumably not both at the same time.

Although they had been beset by injury problems, there should be no doubt that Rot Weiss were an extremely good side. The glamour side of West Germany, like Hibs they were also much travelled, having visited South America in recent years, beating the famous Penarol. Since the end of the war the German side had met foreign teams on no fewer than 85 occasions, losing only a dozen times; indeed, Hibs were one of the few sides to emerge victorious in Essen. It is also worth remembering that Rot Weiss were both West German and unification champions and that at the time Germany were the current World Cup holders.

The German press was ecstatic about the Scottish performance. Headlines such as 'Hibernian from Scotland give the finest display of any British team in Germany since the war', 'Hibs demonstrate pure Scottish short pass', and 'Wonderful performance of miracle forwards', were splashed across the German newspapers the next morning. Back home in Scotland there was a much cooler reception. Precious few newspapers gave more than a passing mention of the result; indeed, it has been said that not one home-based journalist made the trip to the Continent to cover the game, leaving Rex Kingsley of the *Sunday Mail* to wonder why the score should create a bigger fuss abroad than here? Why an achievement that was such a boost for Scottish football, coming when it did, on the back of Scotland's successful close season tour of Yugoslavia, Austria and Hungary should receive only limited coverage back home? Bobby Combe in his *Evening News* column, wondered if it was the power of the national press exercising their disagreement at the choice of Hibs as the country's representative, that had resulted in the tournament receiving less coverage than it deserved.

Always a great attraction in Glasgow, Hibs were given a rousing reception by the fans of both teams in recognition of their midweek victory in Germany when they took the field at Shawfield the following Saturday to face Clyde. The midweek exertions had perhaps taken their toll, however, and in the end they had to be content with a 2–2 draw, after goals by Reilly and Ormond had given them a two-goal interval lead.

On the Monday evening, Hibs faced Manchester United in a floodlit friendly match, their first game of the season under the Easter Road lights. A crowd of 23,000 saw the Edinburgh side bring the local September holiday to a fitting end by beating United 5–0. There were four survivors in the Manchester team from the Gordon Smith testimonial game, including goalkeeper Ray Wood, who had now conceded 12 goals in two visits to the capital. The victory over Manchester United was Hibs' first under their own lights. Since the beginning of the season, they had opposed the reigning Scottish champions, the previous year's League Cup winners, the Scottish Cup holders, the Champions of Germany and now one of the top sides in England, losing only once, which was not bad going in anyone's book. A week after thrashing United, a Mulkerrin goal five minutes from the end gave Hibs both points against Hearts in a fairly drab game at Tynecastle in front of 35,000 fans, and an odd goal in three home win over Kilmarnock a week later saw them in fine form to face the second leg of the European tournament.

Gordon Smith and Tommy Younger had been selected to represent Scotland in the forthcoming game against Denmark in Copenhagen on Tuesday 11 October, only 24 hours before Hibs were due to play the return fixture against Rot Weiss at Easter Road. To complicate things even further, Lawrie Reilly had been called into the squad as a late replacement for Paddy Buckley of Aberdeen, who had withdrawn because of injury. The Scots were victorious against a Danish combination XI in Copenhagen, the first-ever game to be played under floodlights in that country. Both Younger and Smith had featured in the match, but Reilly had been forced to withdraw shortly before the game after picking up a niggling injury in training. Chairman Swan had earlier made careful calculations and had determined that if everything went as planned the trio would arrive back from the Continent in time to face Rot Weiss at Easter Road. The Hibs players would fly from Copenhagen to

London with the Scotland party and catch an immediate flight to Prestwick, where a fast car would be waiting to transport them to Edinburgh in time, it was hoped, for the game. Swan could only pray that there would be no hitches, but he was out of luck. Heavy fog had lain over parts of northern Europe for the best part of the previous 24 hours, causing a four-hour delay in the departure of the Rot Weiss party from Germany the day before. Unluckily for Hibs it had also delayed the return of the Scotland flight from Copenhagen by an hour, by which time the London connection to Prestwick had gone. By the time the Hibs players arrived back in Scotland, play at Easter Road would be midway through the second half. Frustrated at missing the game at Easter Road, Gordon Smith had even suggested chartering a plane direct to Edinburgh. One can only imagine Harry Swan's reaction on receiving the bill…

Jock Buchanan was the most surprised man at Easter Road when he was informed by programme editor Magnus Williamson, as he entered the stadium, that he would be playing in place of Gordon Smith that evening. He had just eaten what he himself described as a 'plate of mince and tatties that would have killed a store horse'. Buchanan, a tireless worker with a keen eye for goal, had been on Hibs' books for just over a year and his only first-team experience had been a couple of outings the previous season. Reilly's replacement was centre-forward Jimmy Mulkerrin. Like Buchanan, Mulkerrin was a bundle of energy who never stopped running and was well capable of 'rumbling up' opposing defences. He had already made numerous first-team appearances, scoring several goals. Reserve goalkeeper Bill Adams took Younger's place. Signed at the beginning of the season from Jimmy Kerr's former club Ormiston Primrose, he had only limited second-team experience.

Rot Weiss had brought a much stronger team to Edinburgh than the side which took the field in Essen, including Islacker, then regarded as the best inside-forward in West Germany, and Helmuth Rahn, generally accepted as the country's finest outside-right. Eighteen times capped, Rahn had made a goalscoring appearance in the recent World Cup Final, and the Hibs management were well aware that Rot Weiss would be very formidable opponents and an entirely different proposition from the side faced in Germany. As it happened, the experienced Rahn, who had failed to shake off the injury that had prevented him taking part in the first leg, did not feature in the match, disappointing many of the crowd who had looked forward to directly comparing the German's intricate dribbling skills with Gordon Smith.

European Cup first round (second leg), Wednesday 12 October 1955, Easter Road.

Hibernian: Adams, McFarlane, Paterson, Thomson, Plenderleith, Preston, Buchanan, Turnbull, Mulkerrin, Combe, Ormond.
Rot Weiss: Herkenrath, Grewer, Kochling, Vorderbaumen, Wewers, Jahnel, Abromeit, Sauer, Seeman, Islacker, Rochrie.
Referee: Arthur Ellis (England).

As was their habit, in European fixtures or otherwise, Hibs went on the attack straight from the kick-off, and following hectic action inside the German penalty area in the opening minute Abromeit required treatment following a heavy tackle. He soon recovered, however, and the home side were surprised in the first few minutes when the inside-forward tested the inexperienced Adams with the first shot of the match, which went narrowly past the post, much to the relief of the goalkeeper. Any hopes of a German comeback were dashed as early as the fifth minute when a ball from Mulkerrin found Ormond on the left. The speedy winger literally left several defenders standing before dispatching an inch-perfect cross to Buchanan, who crashed a first-time volley into the net to score the first-ever goal on British soil in serious European competition.

The goal inspired the Edinburgh side, and they stepped up the pressure with some direct play, only brilliant goalkeeping by West German international Herkenrath preventing Hibs from adding to their lead. Midway through the half, the visitors attempted to play some neat dainty football interspersed with typically 'continental-style short passing', which was met with disapproving jeers by the Hibs support, but some decisive tackling from the Hibs defenders soon upset the foreigners' rhythm.

Hibs' determination to be first to the ball prevented Rot Weiss from settling, with only Islacker looking likely to trouble the home side on rare occasions, but this danger faded the longer the game progressed. In the 23rd minute Preston sent Ormond off on another run, but this time his cross was headed against the post with the 'keeper completely beaten.

Young Adams in the Hibs goal was dealing competently with all he was asked to do, and only an Abromeit shot midway through the half, which again sailed inches past the post, caused him any kind of trouble.

By now Ormond was causing all kinds of problems for the visitors, and right on the interval yet another deceiving run up the left wing left a string of defenders stranded in his wake. His pass found Buchanan, whose shot this time was magnificently parried by Herkenrath. Ormond following up drove the rebound against the post and out for a goal-kick. Based on this first-half performance Hibs were quite clearly coping well without the absent international trio.

Half-time: Hibernian 1 Rot Weiss 0

Directly on the restart, and before a Hibs player had even touched the ball, Abromeit had the best move of the game when he embarked on a mazy run, beating several defenders. His first shot at goal hit centre-half Plenderleith, but he made no mistake with the rebound, crashing the ball past Adams to level the match.

The goal gave the visitors new-found confidence, and they started to play some solid constructive football, which troubled the Hibs defence on several occasions, only to let themselves down in front of goal.

Spurred on by the mostly partisan 30,000 crowd, Hibs soon recovered their composure, but there was to be no more scoring. As in Germany, the young Hibs half-back line of Thomson, Plenderleith and Preston, the youngest midfield line at that time in the country, had played superbly throughout. Up front the speed and trickery of Willie Ormond had been a constant thorn in the side of the Germans. Ever on the lookout for a goal, this was his best game for some time. The industrious Turnbull had covered every blade of grass in his efforts to inspire his team's entry into the next round. Best for Rot Weiss were goalkeeper Herkenrath, centre-half Wewers, who kept Mulkerrin quiet for most of the 90 minutes, and Abromeit, who had been dangerous throughout. However, the Germans had had far too much to do right from the start.

Some of the typically continental-style midfield play, with neat passing to no evident purpose, had bored the home crowd, and they had not been slow to let the visitors know that they were unimpressed.

Full-time: Hibernian 1 Rot Weiss 1

On Monday 1 November 1955, yet another unofficial floodlight match took place at Easter Road. Although Harry Swan had repeatedly warned that football under floodlights without an end product would surely wither and die, over 18,000 fans still turned up to watch Hibs beat a Manchester City side that included former fans' favourite Bobby Johnstone 2–1. The big talking point was the fact that the last 30 minutes of the match were shown on TV, the first-ever game to be beamed live from Easter Road. It is believed that the first Scottish club to appear in a live televised football match was Queen's Park, when the cameras covered their game against Walthamstow in 1950, while the Arsenal versus Hibs game at Highbury in October 1952, and the University International between Scotland and

England in November of the same year had also been broadcast on the small screen, as had the 1955 Scottish Cup Final between Celtic and Clyde only months before. As already mentioned, the first floodlit game to be televised north of the border was the match between Falkirk and Newcastle United at Brockville two years earlier.

The relatively few people who owned a television set in those days had no great difficulty in deciding which channel to view: there was only one, the BBC, Scottish Television still being more than a year in the future. A temporary 20ft-high gantry to house the cameras had been built at the north end of the enclosure, and many of the inquisitive spectators spent more time studying the off-field proceedings than concentrating on what was happening on the pitch. Because it was broadcast in black and white it was often difficult for the viewer at home to distinguish between the teams, something that would become easier in future years, with the advent of second, and more likely third or even fourth-choice jerseys. At half-time the crowd were entertained by a five-a-side game between, or so it was hoped, Hibs stars of the future. With the great side of recent years quite clearly deteriorating, there were still regular calls for the manager to splash out and buy experienced established players, but the board was insistent that the way forward lay in the development of the youth players already at the club. Some of the young players taking part in the half-time entertainment that evening, such as provisional signings Malcolm Bogie, Joe Baker, Bobby Nicol, Andy Aitken, George Muir, John Frye and Pat Hughes, would break through to the first team in the near future.

Further developments were taking place at the stadium at that time. Work was started on a new modern half-time scoreboard at the south-east corner of the ground, which replaced the obsolete pre-war structure at the north-east corner. The designers, Millers and Stables, who had recently overseen the construction of the Easter Road floodlights, had included features such as a gantry for television cameras, and accommodation for match commentators. With space for advertisements that could be lit during evening games it also had the potential to raise much-needed revenue.

By this time Hibs had been informed that their next European opponents would be Djurgården from Sweden, who had disposed of the Polish side Gnearoia in the earlier round, winning 4–1 away after a 0–0 draw in Stockholm. The credentials of the experienced Swedish team were impeccable. Since the end of the war they had toured 33 countries, beating teams of the calibre of Wolverhampton Wanderers, Brazilian champions São Paulo and Spanish title-winners Real Madrid. During a recent visit to Bucharest, they had also defeated that country's full and B international teams. Their current squad consisted of six internationals and still contained four of the side that had beaten Hearts 5–1 in a friendly in Stockholm 18 months before.

The first leg was due to have been played in Sweden, but the pitches in that country were now icebound, and the tremendously popular ice hockey season well under way. By coincidence the local ice hockey team had beaten Paisley Pirates in a friendly in Stockholm only the week before. It was agreed that Djurgården's home leg would be played at Firhill, home of Partick Thistle, under the recently installed floodlights. The visitors would stay over at the Carlton Hotel in Edinburgh before the return fixture at Easter Road five days later.

The first leg was played in Glasgow on 24 November 1955. Special trains were laid on for supporters from the capital, leaving Waverley Station at five o'clock, arriving back in Edinburgh at 11.03pm. A cheap day return cost 5s.

Djurgården would be without two of their star players for the match. Outside-right Johansson was unable to travel because of his university studies, and Tvilling because of injury. Currently lying a modest seventh in the Swedish League table, the visitors' team selection had suffered badly lately, with 11 first-team players being absent from the side at one time or another since the start of the season owing to injury. Hibs' only selection worry was Reilly, who would miss the game because of a chill.

European Cup second round (first leg), Wednesday 23 November 1955, Firhill.

Djurgården: Arvidsson, Forsberg, Gustafsson, Holmstrom, Olsson, Parling, Andersson, Grybb, Eriksson, Eklund, Sandberg.

Hibernian: Younger, McFarlane, Paterson, Thomson, Plenderleith, Preston, Smith, Combe, Mulkerrin, Turnbull, Ormond.

Referee: A. Ellis (England).

The tie had created incredible interest. More than 22,000 packed into Firhill, a quite exceptional figure considering that most had travelled more than 50 miles to see the game. The official Celtic programme a short time before had cast doubt on the future, not only of floodlit football, but also of European competition, stating that football fans were already losing interest in the subject. As further proof that this was indeed the case, the article went on to say that Hibs had been forced to travel to the other side of the country in the hope of attracting a big crowd, failing completely to realise that this was Hibs' away fixture. The statement is doubly ironic considering that, apart from the fact that Celtic were the first British team to win the European Cup, their primary aim nowadays would appear to be in the direction of a European League, this even taking precedence over their domestic circumstances.

Perhaps surprisingly, the Swedish team took the game to their opponents from the start, and within 90 seconds they had shocked Hibs by taking the lead with a quite magnificent goal that was straight out of the training manual. Collecting the ball just inside Hibs' half, Parling sent a perfect pass into open space on the right-hand side of the penalty area. Before the Hibs defenders could react, Eklund pounced, and in a flash had crashed an unstoppable thunderbolt past the startled Younger and into the far corner of the net.

Shortly after, Andersson smashed a screamer off the underside of the crossbar, and it looked like Hibs were in for a torrid evening. Gradually, the Easter Road men started to take a firm grip on the proceedings, with Bobby Combe immense in helping to turn the tide in Hibs' favour. Dominating the midfield, he was involved in nearly every Hibs move and had a tremendous game. Fetching and carrying from his own defence, Combe still had time to send in several shots, which fortunately for Djurgården were wide of the target.

With 19 minutes gone Hibs at last got the goal their play had been threatening. Collecting the ball out wide on the right wing, Gordon Smith sent over a precision cross. Combe fastened on to it, and in an instant he had sent a thunderous drive into the net from 20 yards before the 'keeper could even move.

Although they were now mainly well on top, Hibs' finishing was generally disappointing. Even Eddie Turnbull, who had joined Combe in shooting on sight of the Djurgården goal, was sending his efforts either high or wide. The Swedes were still dangerous opponents, however, and clever interpassing midfield play as the half came to an end determined that a close watch be kept on them.

Half-time: Djurgården 1 Hibernian 1

Five minutes after the restart, the bustling Mulkerrin gave his side the lead. A long through ball from deep in the Hibs half was chased by the ever-industrious centre. Anticipating the move, he chased a short attempted headed pass-back to the 'keeper. Arvidsson and Mulkerrin collided and the ball bounced free, but the Hibs man was the quicker to react and was on his feet in a flash to prod the loose ball over the goalline. Mulkerrin, who required treatment after the incident, had come in for some rough treatment throughout by the Swedish rearguard, who were unsettled by his wholehearted and robust play.

Although it had taken some time, by now Preston and Thomson had the measure of the game and, assisted by the redoubtable Bobby Combe, Hibs took total control of the midfield.

In the 62nd minute, centre-forward Mulkerrin was sandwiched in the box by two defenders, leaving referee Ellis with no option but to award a penalty. Somewhat uncharacteristically, however, penalty-kick expert Turnbull, who had already converted four goals from the spot that season, blasted wide.

Turnbull made amends for the penalty miss five minutes from the end when his screaming thunderbolt was deflected past the helpless 'keeper by centre-half Olsson to give Hibs a two-goal cushion for the second leg in Edinburgh.

Djurgården had at times demonstrated their brilliant footballing abilities, but it was Hibs' own skilful play, allied to their pace and determination, that had counted in the end.

Full-time: Djurgården 1 Hibernian 3

Three days after their European exercise at Firhill, a clinical 5–1 demolition of Partick Thistle at the same venue gave Hibs two valuable League points to sustain the East of Scotland challenge to leaders Celtic, who even this early were chasing a League and League Cup double.

Meanwhile, Djurgården had sent an urgent telegram to Johansson and Tvilling back home in Sweden, outlining the importance of them both making their way to Edinburgh for the return leg on the Monday evening. The urgency would indicate that the Scandinavians thought the tie was far from over, and it was a perhaps a view shared by the powers that be, as a statement was issued that in the event of the tie being level at the end of the second 90 minutes, a third game would take place, possibly in Brussels.

Johansson was still unable to get leave from his studies, but Tvilling, fully aware of the seriousness of the situation, departed for Scotland immediately after playing in the semi-finals of the Stockholm ice hockey championships.

European Cup second round (second leg), Monday 28 November 1955, Easter Road.
Hibernian: Younger, McFarlane, Paterson, Thomson, Plenderleith, Preston, Smith, Combe, Mulkerrin, Turnbull, Ormond.
Djurgården: Arvidsson, Forsberg, Gustafsson, Edlud, Olsson, Parling, Andersson, Tvilling, Eriksson, Eklund, Sandberg.
Referee: A. Ellis (England)

The opening period of the match was played at full stretch as the sides tested each other out, probing for any possible weaknesses that might result in the goal that would either let the Swedes back into the match or, in Hibs' case, probably end the game as a contest.

Djurgården started brightly, but they soon faded as the home side stepped up a gear, adding powerful play to their delicate footwork. Hibs' first chance came early in the game when a Smith free-kick from the right allowed Turnbull to power in a great header that was magnificently held by Arvidsson at the left-hand post. After 20 minutes Smith started to turn on the style, consistently tormenting his marker. A tremendous cross-field pass from the winger found Ormond in the clear in the inside-left position, and the outside-left should have done much better than balloon the ball wildly over the top. Just moments later, Hibs came near to opening the scoring when another devastating Smith cross found Mulkerrin, whose powerful header hit the crossbar before bouncing to safety.

Next it was Smith himself who attempted to break the deadlock. Just after the 'keeper had produced another brilliant save to defy Mulkerrin, the winger smashed a tremendous volley from the centre-forward position. The ball barely left the ground and looked a goal all the way, but somehow the goalkeeper, who must have seen it only at the last second, tipped the ball round the post. It was by all accounts a stupendous save.

It was now mostly Hibs, but as in the first leg, the visitors occasionally showed that they could still be dangerous opponents, and a great run by Andersson produced a corner, which fortunately for the home side came to nothing.

Hibs were still prepared to shoot on sight, and shortly before the first half was brought to an end, Bobby Combe produced the best attempt of the night when the stretching Arvidsson brilliantly held his low, first-time shot from 20 yards.

Half-time: Hibernian 0 Djurgården 0

Kicking down the slope in the second half, the home side took up where they had left off in the first half. Combe was everywhere, prodding and passing from midfield as he tried to encourage his team to end the deadlock, and the 31,500 spectators showed their appreciation for one particularly wonderful piece of skill by the inside-right. On a run toward the Djurgården goal, Combe completely bamboozled three defenders when he stopped dead in his tracks, before cleverly back-heeling the ball to Smith who cracked a first-time drive against the bar with the 'keeper stranded.

The Swedes still had a part to play in the game, but in reality they were now rarely of any threat to the Hibs goal. The momentous efforts exerted to get Tvilling to Edinburgh had so far been in vain. The inside man had made absolutely no impact on the game, and one newspaper reporter at the time thought that 'he might as well have stayed at home and went to the pictures for all the use he had been to his colleagues'. Only once did he show any signs of creating danger, but his final shot soared as high as the new floodlight pylons.

A goal just had to come, and with half an hour remaining the home side broke the deadlock. Ormond, on a dangerous run through the middle of the park, was brought crashing down in the penalty area by a combined tackle by Olsson and Edlud. As in the first game at Firhill the referee had absolutely no option but to award a penalty, but this time Eddie Turnbull made no mistake from the spot when he blasted a trademark thunderbolt past the despairing Arvidsson and into the net for the only goal of the game.

From then until the final whistle it was mainly one-way traffic down the slope towards the Swedish goal at the Albion Road end of the ground. Djurgården were by now rarely seen as an attacking force, but although there were a few close things, there was no more scoring.

Full-time: Hibernian 1 Djurgården 0

With the semi-finals of the European Cup still four months away, it was back to League business on the Saturday, and only a Mulkerrin strike five minutes from the end gave Hibs a rather fortuitous two points at Love Street against a fighting St Mirren outfit. Seven days later Dundee, who were on a seven-game unbeaten run, were given a comprehensive 6–3 drubbing at Easter Road. The game, which was watched by under 6,000 hardy souls who braved the sleet and driving rain, saw the home side produce a Championship performance to go top of the table and set them themselves up to face both Rangers and Celtic in consecutive weeks.

Controversy and the Old Firm are never far away, and both these encounters were no exception. The first game was against Rangers at Ibrox on 18 December 1955, and although the home side deservedly earned their 4–1 victory, the big talking point was the incredible performance of referee W. Liston of Larbert, described by Rex of the *Sunday Mail*, a well-known Rangers 'sympathiser', as 'the most amazing performance he had ever witnessed by a referee in all his years covering the game'. Hibs had taken a somewhat fortuitous lead in the 17th minute, when an Ormond free-kick had deflected off McColl and into the net with the goalkeeper stranded. Four minutes later the fun started. In a Rangers attack the ball was deflected off a Hibs defender high into the air. As goalkeeper Tommy Younger steadied himself to catch the ball, which was now still about 12ft in the air, centre-forward Simpson shoulder-charged the 'keeper into the net, leaving the flabbergasted custodian lying helplessly on the ground as the ball dropped where he had earlier been standing before trickling over the line. The referee was immediately surrounded by a mêlée of irate Hibs players, but when the dust had settled Reilly had been booked for protesting too vehemently and the goal was allowed to stand.

Rangers now settled down to playing some attractive football, but their next goal also fell into the controversial category. Shortly before the interval Gordon Smith, according to many neutral observers, was quite clearly fouled in the centre circle. Instead of awarding a free-kick to Hibs, however, referee Liston waved play on and Rangers swept downfield to take the lead. Worse was to come. In the second half, as Hibs struggled to make any impact against a determined Ibrox defence, Rangers scored a third, and again it was shrouded in controversy, with even the most partisan 'Gers fan bewildered by the outcome. Younger, bending to collect a loose ball in his penalty area, was suddenly aware of an impending shoulder-charge by the rugged Don Kitchenbrand. The 'keeper braced himself for the challenge as the two players collided, and the Hibs contingent were incensed when the whistle-happy referee awarded a penalty-kick against Younger, a decision described by Rex as 'a truly amazing decision by the man from Larbert'. Hubbard scored from the spot and another Simpson goal 10 minutes from the end finally killed a game that was already in the death throes due to an overzealous referee's whistle.

Immediately after the match a still-incensed Swan sent an official letter of protest to the authorities complaining about the referee's handling of the game, but as perhaps should be expected, no more was heard of the incident.

One interesting statistic concerning the foul count compared to that of the modern game, was the award of 15 fouls given against the rugged Rangers, who had persisted with a 'rumble them up' policy all afternoon, to just three conceded by Hibs.

Seven days later Celtic were the visitors to Easter Road, and although not in the same category as the previous week's refereeing débâcle, the Hibs fans were once again outraged by the performance of the man in the middle. In an otherwise thrilling and engrossing encounter Celtic were leading 3–2, with Hibs staging a late effort to save the game, when referee Youngston of Aberdeen blew the final whistle four minutes early. The home fans roared their disapproval, pointing to their watches, but to no avail and the narrow victory allowed the Celts to go two points clear at the top of the table.

By this time Gordon Smith had become one of the few footballers at Easter Road to enter the licensed trade when he took ownership of a brand-new roadhouse located at the junction of Willowbrae Road and Northfield Broadway in the Duddingston area of the city. Named 'The Right Wing' in honour of the landlord's celebrated position in the Hibs attack, it was officially opened on Monday 5 December 1955, and it became a favourite haunt of Hibs supporters on that side of town for many years.

It was also at about this time that Harry Swan was ordered by his doctor to stay away from Easter Road for a while. Swan had been guilty of overdoing things and was diagnosed as suffering from a 'tired heart'. The enforced few weeks' rest would see the chairman return to the helm completely refreshed and ready for challenges new.

Christmas 1955 saw the very first publication of a book which was to become compulsive reading for the discerning football fan for many years to come. The *Scottish Football Book*, edited by the well-known *Glasgow Evening News* sports columnist Hugh Taylor, covered all the big games and incidents of the previous 12 months, including the Cup Final and the 7–2 England versus Scotland match at Wembley. Unfortunately for the green half of Edinburgh, but possibly unsurprisingly considering the lack of interest shown by the media in covering the opening games, there was no mention at all of Hibs' European Cup exploits to be found anywhere inside the pages.

As usual, Hearts were the traditional first-footers to Easter Road on the first day of the New Year, and a 2–2 draw allowed both sets of supporters to leave the ground in a reasonably happy mood. All the goals had been scored in an eight-minute burst during the second half, and although Hearts could possibly claim to have been slightly the better side, no one, including the player himself, would be able to explain just how Bobby Combe managed to miss what would have been the winner late in the game. With the goal gaping wide and the ball seemingly going in anyway, Combe somehow managed to blast it high over the bar.

On 25 January the first competitive floodlit game between two Scottish sides took place at Easter Road when a Hibs second XI defeated a Falkirk reserve side 2–1 in a Penman Cup tie. European goal hero Jock Buchanan scored both Hibs' goals. Another first for the young Edinburgh-born forward!

Although briefly sharing top spot in the table with Celtic in the opening weeks of the year, several indifferent results, excluding a 7–0 home win over Motherwell, meant that by the time the Scottish Cup came round in February Hibs had dropped to third place. The opening tie of the Cup campaign was a 1–1 home draw against Raith Rovers, whose obvious tactics seemed to be to stop Smith at any cost. In this game Reilly was played in his original position of outside-left in place of Ormond, who had broken a wrist in a friendly match against the Scottish Under-23 side in mid-January, with Mulkerrin taking Reilly's place at centre-forward. In the replay, Raith took a 3–0 lead, and although Reilly pulled one back and Hibs staged a spirited effort to save the game, it was all in vain. Although winning Cup ties in Europe seemed no problem, they could not do the same in Kirkcaldy and Hibs' Scottish Cup dream was over for yet another year.

By now Hibs' League challenge was faltering badly. There had been some decent results, including a 7–1 victory over Dunfermline at Easter Road, with Eddie Turnbull scoring a hat-trick, his second in recent weeks, but again a lack of consistency was proving expensive. By the time the semi-final of the European Cup came round the League Championship race looked all but over. Although they flitted between third and fourth place in the table, there were never any real doubts that the title would rest elsewhere.

After a 2–0 midweek defeat by Airdrie at the beginning of March, Tommy Younger and the current Scotland leader Lawrie Reilly were both dropped for the home game against Raith Rovers, a decision that was promptly followed by yet another swift transfer request from the giant goalkeeper. After a hastily called board meeting it was agreed to listen to offers for the player, but because the English transfer deadline was only a few days away it was not anticipated that any business would be done in the meantime. As it happened Younger was back in the side the following week to face East Fife, and a week later he took part in the 4–1 win over Queen of the South, the first League game to be played under floodlights in the capital.

It had now been confirmed that Hibs' European Cup semi-final opponents would be Stade de Reims, the reigning French champions, who had secured their place in the last four with victories over Saarbrucken in the first round and Hungarian champions Voros Lobogo in the quarter-finals. The away leg would be played at either the Parc des Princes in Paris, or in the brand new stadium at Nice, and although little was known of them in this country, it was anticipated that they would be worthy adversaries. Formed only in 1934, like Hibs Reims had started their recent run to prominence during the war. With the assistance of locally-based soldiers guesting for the side they had become Professional Champions of France (Occupied Zone) in 1942. Winners of the French Championship in 1949, 1953 and 1955, they had recently reached the Final of the Mitropa Cup, a tournament contested by the champions of France, Spain, Portugal and Italy, beating Milan on the way before losing narrowly to the Spanish side Real Madrid, who incidentally had now been installed as the favourites to win this inaugural European Cup.

On the eve of the semi-final there was an injury scare for Hibs. John Grant, now a regular in the side, had injured his knee in a tackle the previous Saturday at Firhill and it was only after a late thorough fitness test by trainer Kean that he was considered fit enough to play.

As in the journey to Essen in the first round, what would now be considered a short routine journey was a fairly involved affair in those days, with the party travelling to London by rail from the Waverley station, before catching a plane to the French capital.

Archie Buchanan, only recently recalled to the side for the first time since breaking his leg 18 months before, took his place in the Hibs line up replacing the injured Tommy Preston. The veteran defender, who had joined the club in 1943 and was the proud holder of three League Championship medals, was playing in his first-ever competitive European tie. Like Buchanan, John Grant was also making his competitive Continental debut. Although making 14 League appearances the previous season, it was only since his inclusion in the first team for the 6–1 win against Stirling Albion on Hogmanay afternoon that Grant had been considered a regular, first at wing-half and now at centre-half in place of the injured Jackie Plenderleith.

European Cup semi-final (first leg), Wednesday 4 April 1956, Parc des Princes, Paris.
Reims: Jacquet, Zimny, Giraudo, Siatka, Jonquet, Cicci, Hidalgo, Glovakie, Kopa, Leblond, Bliard.
Hibernian: Younger, McFarlane, Paterson, Thomson, Grant, Buchanan, Smith, Turnbull, Reilly, Combe, Ormond.
Referee: Mr M. Asensi (Spain)

Before an all-ticket capacity 36,000 crowd, Reims went into attack from the first whistle, and within minutes of the start Raymond Kopa, who was leading the French front line, began to display his extraordinary talents as he demonstrated just why he was then regarded as the best centre-forward in Europe. After surviving a hectic opening period, Hibs fought their way back into the game and Thomson broke through to rifle in a shot that went narrowly over the bar, before a good bit of combined play involving Reilly, Thomson and Turnbull ended with the inside man forcing a good save from the French 'keeper. The neat ball control and understanding of the French half-back line was taking the eye, and their clever constructive back-up play to their forwards created several dangerous moves which allowed Younger in the Hibs goal to show his worth on more than one occasion. It was far from one-way traffic, however, and the Edinburgh men brought out the best in French Army international René Jacquet in the home goal as play raged from end to end until the referee's whistle brought the first half to a close. Despite the valiant efforts of both sides, the game remained goalless at the interval.

Half-time: Reims 0 Hibernian 0
Hibs restarted the second half in confident style, and they were clearly well on top during the opening period. Ormond and Reilly both had shots that were well saved by the 'keeper, and a Smith effort caused all kinds of bother in the Reims penalty area before it was eventually cleared to the immense relief of the home defence. Almost immediately afterwards, a dangerous Turnbull shot was well saved by Jacquet, although the goalkeeper required two attempts to gather the ball.

The Hibs defence was standing up well to the sporadic pressure from the Reims front men, and there seemed little danger when the Frenchmen were awarded a corner on the left in the 69th minute. As the corner was swung over by Kopa, inside-left Leblond, who had found himself completely unmarked, came from nowhere to put a header past the helpless Younger for the opening goal of the game to send the Parisian crowd into a frenzy.

The Edinburgh men reinforced their efforts to secure an equalising goal, and for the remainder of the match they were well on top with several near chances in front of Jacquet's goal.

Despite sustained pressure, during which they looked the more likely to score, the visitors were stunned when, with only one minute of the game remaining, Reims took advantage of a mistake by a Hibs defender which allowed another Kopa cross from the left to be turned into the net by outside-left Bliard to give the French side a somewhat undeserved 2–0 victory.

The Hibs players left the field aggrieved at the final scoreline. Reims might just have been worth a one-goal lead, but considering the all-round resolute performance by the Easter Road side it was felt that a two-goal advantage had greatly flattered the Frenchmen.

Full-time: Reims 2 Hibernian 0

After the game the French newspaper *The Parisian* was of the opinion that on this performance 'Reims could go to Edinburgh with a full degree of confidence', while understandably the Scottish press saw it differently. The *Edinburgh Evening News* was in no doubt that the tragedy was that: 'when the goals came late in the game, it was the Edinburgh side who looked the likelier to score them'. According to *The Scotsman*, 'Hibs have a hard task in front of them in the replay, but the players are confident that they can overcome the two goal deficit'.

The Scots had put up a spirited and skilful display, but all were agreed that the difference between the sides had been Raymond Kopa. Kopa, whose every touch had been greeted with roars of expectancy from the crowd, was a centre-forward in the old-fashioned Scottish mould, not unlike the great Hughie Gallacher of Newcastle and Scotland fame in the 1920s. He spent more time on the ball than any other two players combined, taking throw-ins, free-kicks and corners, and frequently coming back deep into his own half to collect the ball before setting up moves for others. Perhaps surprisingly, one of the few things Kopa did not expend energy on was the customary centre-forward's task of taking the kick-off, which he left to a colleague. Allied to his industry, his incredible ball control and trickery, his great vision made him a quite exceptional player, and it was well known that many of the top continental sides were watching his progress with great interest.

Replying to a speech by the president of the French club at the after-match reception for the players and officials, chairman Swan, as was his usual habit on Hibs' frequent trips abroad, forwarded the best wishes of the Lord Provost of Edinburgh to the hosts, before proceeding to relate that Kopa had made the biggest impression of all on the Hibs party. 'Although he had not scored himself, he had generally lived up to his reputation as the best centre-forward in Europe, and was a footballer with all the craft of a master'.

On the Saturday, two goals by Willie Ormond saw the same 11 players who had faced Reims secure a victory against St Mirren at Easter Road. The game marked the official opening of the new half-time scoreboard at the south-east corner of the ground, which replaced the flimsy structure that had stood at the north-east corner for as long as anyone could remember. In yet another step to further improve Easter Road, it had recently been announced that plans were in hand to construct two brick 'dug outs' at the entrance to the tunnel, designed to protect the trainers from the elements.

The annual international match against the Auld Enemy took place at Hampden Park, sandwiched between both legs of the European Cup semi-finals. Tommy Younger, by now Scotland's regular goalkeeper, was facing England for the first time in a full international. Scotland, featuring Gordon Smith, Lawrie Reilly and former Famous Five member Bobby Johnstone, were held to a 1–1 draw. The big 'keeper Younger was one of the top performers on the day, denying England on numerous occasions, twice bringing off spectacular saves that amazed even his teammates. Younger's brilliant all-round performance also alerted English predators to his agile and at times breathtaking ability between the posts.

The international game had forced the cancellation of the League programme on the Saturday, leaving Hibs to play the outstanding fixture against Motherwell at Easter Road on the Monday evening prior to the Reims match 48 hours later. It was not the ideal preparation for such an important game. In addition John Grant, who had been an injury doubt before the game in Paris, had had to leave the field during the first half with a suspected depressed fracture of the cheekbone, leaving his teammates to play with 10 men for nearly an hour. The injury proved not to be as serious as first feared and the defender was fit enough at kick-off to take his place in the Hibs line up against the French champions.

Harry Swan was at Turnhouse Airport to greet Stade de Reims when they arrived in Scotland on the eve of the return fixture. On touchdown it was discovered that the French visitors lacked the necessary landing permits, claiming ignorance of any such stipulation, and it required the intervention of the Hibs chairman and his legendary persuasive powers before the airport authorities would relent and allow the visitors to proceed.

In direct contrast to the first-round tie against Rot Weiss in Essen just a few months before, there was now an incredible interest in the European tournament and for several weeks the ticket office at Easter Road had been inundated with demands for tickets from all parts of the country. Fife had always been a well-known breeding ground for the Hibs support (including the legendary Jim Baxter, whose self-confessed all-time favourite player was Gordon Smith), and a special train had been laid on for supporters from the Kingdom leaving from Cardenden, picking up passengers at Lochgelly, Cowdenbeath and Dunfermline before arriving at Waverley station. The stand had been made all-ticket, with the precious briefs being priced at 10s, 7s 6d and 5s.

In the days leading up to the game hopes were high in the city for an Edinburgh double. Hearts had already booked a place in the Scottish Cup Final, where they would face Celtic the following Saturday at Hampden. Hibs reaching the European Cup Final would be a massive double boost for the city.

European Cup semi-final (second leg), Wednesday 18 April 1956, Easter Road.

Hibernian: Younger, McFarlane, Paterson, A. Buchanan, Grant, Combe, Smith, Turnbull, Reilly, Thomson, Ormond.

Reims: Jacquet, Zimny, Giraudo, Siatka, Jonquet, Leblond, Hidalgo, Glovakie, Kopa, Bliard, Templin.

Referee: A. Ellis (England)

Shortly before the game the Reims players, as was their usual custom, went to a local piece of waste ground adjacent to the stadium, probably Lochend Park, to perform a series of limbering-up exercises, only for the bewildered players to be moved on by some over-zealous members of the Edinburgh Constabulary.

Both teams took the field to a rapturous welcome from the 49,941 fans, a record crowd for a floodlit game at Easter Road at the time and also by far the biggest crowd of the entire tournament (including the subsequent Final in Paris, which was watched by only 38,329). Hibs were again wearing the new-look continental-style strip of green jerseys with short white sleeves and a white V-neck collar, Reims their customary red shirts with white sleeves and black shorts.

The French champions, with Kopa an early influence, impressed the large crowd in the early stages with some intricate play, but it did not take Hibs long to reassert themselves as an attacking force, and as early as the sixth minute goalkeeper Jacquet did well to hold a Reilly shot from inside the six-yard box. Next, Reilly was impeded by the 'keeper inside the area, and the subsequent indirect free-kick, taken by Ormond, was almost touched home by the centre-forward. The Easter Road side began to turn on the pressure and for several minutes the Reims defence were quite unable to get the ball clear as Hibs mounted attack after attack in an effort to secure the early goal which would be so important in their desire to reverse the scoreline. Smith and Turnbull were both in impressive form as they helped to set up several more chances in front of the away goal, none more so than when Reilly found himself with only Jacquet to beat, but to the disappointment of the centre-forward, the goalkeeper was alert to his snap shot.

There was a surprise for Hibs in the 25th minute. Nothing had been seen from the Reims front line for some time when Kopa suddenly switched play after picking up a loose ball, and his strong drive was parried by Younger. The rebound fell straight to Bliard, whose fierce shot struck the upright with Younger this time well beaten, and the Hibs defence was relieved to see the ball eventually cleared behind for a goal-kick.

From then until the break Hibs resumed the onslaught on the French goalmouth, but the French defence were in resolute mood, especially 'keeper Jacquet and centre-half Jonquet, and as the half-time whistle sounded, Hibs, with just a little luck, could quite easily have wiped out the French side's two-goal advantage.

Half-time: Hibernian 0 Reims 0

The home side resumed the second half in determined mood, gaining three corners in the opening two minutes, but despite this pressure they just could not manage to score the vital goal that their play so richly deserved. As so often happens, after a mesmerising 10-minute spell, which at times left the Reims defence in a state of bewilderment, Hibs conceded a goal. Kopa, picking up a stray ball in midfield, moved forward quickly, his pass finding Glovakie, who looked at least a couple of yards offside. Without hesitation, the French international tucked the ball past Younger, and although there were still 34 minutes remaining, Hibs were effectively out of the European Cup.

From then until the final whistle it was mostly all Hibs, and no one will ever explain how the French side failed to concede at least once during this period, with Ormond alone having at least half a dozen efforts which could quite easily have resulted in a goal. The incisive thrusts of the Reims attack, though rare, were still incredibly dangerous, and at times they created panic in the Hibs rearguard. With just a few minutes remaining, full-back Willie McFarlane came nearest to giving the Edinburgh men the draw they deserved, but his thundering drive went inches past.

Although saving the tie had been well beyond Hibs for at least half an hour, few of the enthralled spectators had left the ground, and at the final whistle both sides left the field to a resounding and appreciative applause.

Full-time: Hibernian 0 Reims 1

At the official reception in the North British Hotel, Harry Swan was generous in his praise for the performance of the French team, again particularly that of Kopa, and wished them well in the forthcoming Final. The Hibs party had all received a bottle of French champagne from Reims after the game in Paris, and in a reciprocal gesture all the visiting players and officials received a tartan travelling rug from the Easter Road side.

History records that Reims faced Real Madrid in the inaugural European Cup Final in Paris, eventually going down 4–3 only to a late winner by the Spanish giants that saw them embark on their famous run of five successive victories. The impressive form of Kopa did not escape the attention of Real Madrid, however, and the newly crowned European Champions signed the Frenchman at the end of the season. He would eventually win three European Cup medals with the Spanish side.

For Hibs, there was little left to play for. Rangers had won the League Championship on the very night that Hibs were losing to Reims at Easter Road. Of the final four League games, two were won, one was drawn and the other lost, including a 2–2 home draw against the champions and a 3–0 victory over Celtic at Parkhead to finish, in the circumstances, a respectable fourth in the table behind Rangers, Aberdeen and near neighbours Hearts on goal average.

However, to make matters worse for Hibs fans, just days after the disappointment against Reims at Easter Road, Hearts won the Scottish Cup with a 3–1 victory over Celtic, their first success in the competition for 50 years. Ian Crawford scored two of the Maroons' goals, and the Hibs fans could take a little comfort from the fact that a former Hibs player had helped to win the Cup for their greatest rivals.

Even for a supporter who had been blind to the team's recent failings, the fact could not now be disguised that the great days at Easter Road were well and truly over. Although they had been marvellous ambassadors for Scotland on the European stage, it was a great pity, as Gordon Smith himself would say in later years, that the European Cup had not come into being just a few years earlier. Had it done so, Smith was convinced that Hibs would have won the trophy.

A Transitional Period

League champions Rangers were not slow to realise the enormous potential for international prestige, not to mention financial gain, of Hibs' great European run, and they had now changed their opinion regarding the viability of the new tournament by agreeing to be Scotland's representatives in the 1956–57 European Cup. Though keenly anticipated by the fans, the Ibrox side's first venture into the competition ended at the preliminary stage against French side Nice after a third game play-off. In England, manager Matt Busby brushed aside the continuing opposition to the new tournament by the Football League, and Manchester United took the first steps on the road that would ultimately lead to disaster at Munich two years later by becoming England's first ambassadors in the competition. Like Hibs the previous year, United reached the semi-final stage before going down 3–2 to eventual winners Real Madrid in Spain after a 2–2 draw at Old Trafford.

Back in Edinburgh, Scotland's regular goalkeeper Tommy Younger, still at loggerheads with the club after being dropped earlier in the year, and keen to try his luck in England, had been transferred to English Second Division side Liverpool during the summer. The move created a goalkeeping crisis at Easter Road, with only three inexperienced and untried first-year youngsters on the books: Jim Rollo, Jackie Proudfoot and Jackie Wren.

Former Hearts wing-half Davie Laing became the club's first major purchase since the acquisition of Leslie Johnstone in 1947 when he was signed from Clyde in the summer for around £2,500. Laing had joined Hearts in 1946, quickly becoming a regular in the side. Transferred to Clyde in 1954, the wing-half had been part of the Shawfield side that won the Scottish Cup in 1955 when defeating Celtic 1–0 after a replay.

Laing made his debut as a signed Hibs player once again wearing the Maroon shirt of his former side in the Edinburgh Select's 2–1 victory over Birmingham City at Tynecastle, alongside Gordon Smith, who was preserving his fantastic record of having played in every Select game since 1944. Goals from Wardhaugh and Reilly were enough to give the local side a narrow victory. The FA Cup finalists, who included in their line up England goalkeeper Gil Merrick, who had played in the disastrous game against Hungary in 1953, were seemingly so impressed by the hospitality they received in the capital that they donated 100 guineas of their match fee to the charity fund.

An impressive performance in the Public Trial match at Easter Road, watched by well over 5,000 fans, earned former Bo'ness United 'keeper Jackie Wren, signed only that summer, a quick promotion to the first team, and both the goalkeeper and Laing made a competitive debut for the club in the opening League Cup fixture against Hearts.

For Hibs, the abysmal Tynecastle performance was to be a portent of the miserable season to come. Although opening the scoring as early as the sixth minute, when a flashing header from Turnbull easily beat Brown, the goal was one of the few highlights for the visitors in an otherwise dismal afternoon. Looking completely disjointed at the end, the 6–1 final scoreline failed to flatter the Gorgie side as Hibs surrendered ignominiously, and it could well have been worse. Twice scoring from the spot, full-back Kirk missed the opportunity to emulate Eddie Turnbull by scoring a rare hat-trick of penalties when Wren saved a third. Laing, a Scottish Cup-winner with Clyde in 1955, was not a success and only featured in a handful of matches before being transferred to Gillingham before the start of the following season.

The Edinburgh sides at that time were:

Hearts: Brown, Kirk, McKenzie, MacKay, Glidden, Cumming, Young, Conn, Bauld, Wardhaugh, Crawford.
Hibs: Wren, Higgins, Paterson, Laing, Grant, Thomson, Smith, Turnbull, Reilly, Combe, Ormond.
Referee: Tiny Wharton (Glasgow)

With the future of Hibs still dependant on signing the best youngsters available, Andy Aitken, Des Anderson, Johnny McLeod, Alex Marshall and Davie Gibson had all been called-up from the juvenile and junior ranks during the close season. There was to be quick promotion for Gibson. After only a few weeks at the club, the intelligent ball play and positional sense of the Winchburgh youngster had impressed the manager enough to hand the 17-year-old a first-team debut against Falkirk at Easter Road in place of the veteran Bobby Combe. A bright and intelligent first start by Gibson, however, could do little to prevent his side suffering a second successive League Cup defeat. In a disastrous Cup campaign, the Easter Road side's worst ever up until then, five of the six opening games ended in defeat and the other was drawn, leaving Hibs anchored firmly at the foot of the section. Somewhat surprisingly, Partick Thistle qualified for the later stages of the competition at the expense of second-placed Hearts.

During the game against Partick at Firhill, Gordon Smith fell foul of the referee because of his honesty. After a soft penalty had been awarded to Partick late in the game, the Hibs outside-right remonstrated that it was the worst decision he had ever seen. Asked by referee Mitchell of Falkirk to repeat his remarks, the player did and was promptly booked. It was one of only three bookings he would receive in his long and illustrious career.

Hibs' recent European run had not gone unnoticed on the Continent and an invitation was received from Real Madrid to play a friendly in the Spanish capital. Commitments made it impossible for the Scottish club to fit the friendly into their busy schedule at that time, but as part of Hibs' policy of bringing glamour sides to Easter Road, Swan invited the European Cup holders to play a prestigious friendly in Edinburgh in the near future. Several months later Real took Swan up on his offer, but the required financial guarantee was far more than Hibs, or any other Scottish club for that matter, could afford, and the game did not take place for several years.

In the Championship, now officially called the Scottish First Division, things looked brighter when Falkirk, who had taken four points and five goals from Hibs in the League Cup, were walloped 6–1 in the opening match. The result appeared to justify the confidence of the management in playing a number of the younger players such as Wren, McFarlane, Muir, Plenderleith, Fraser and Harrower, alongside the experienced Turnbull, Combe, Ormond and Reilly, who was back to his best in scoring a hat-trick. It was to be a false dawn, however, and four defeats and four draws from the next eight games made it compellingly obvious that time had finally caught up with the great side of only a few seasons before.

Tommy Younger made an early return to Easter Road at the beginning of September, when Liverpool defeated Hibs 2–1 in a friendly. Twenty-year-old goalkeeper Lawrie Leslie, signed only two days before from junior side Newtongrange Star, was handed a first-team debut. The youngster made an impressive start to his senior career, and a bright future was predicted for a player who would go on to win international honours for Scotland.

Proudfoot replaced Leslie in goal for a nightmare 5–1 defeat by Tottenham Hotspur at Easter Road in the first match of that season's unofficial Floodlit League. The League, which had stumbled the previous season because of opposition from the authorities on both sides of the border, had been revived, with Hearts again playing their home matches under the Easter Road lights.

A 2–0 defeat at Palmerston led to Rollo replacing Wren between the posts for the game against Hearts at Easter Road, making him Hibs' fourth 'keeper in as many games. In one of the most exciting encounters between the sides for many a year, the Greens had the better of the thrilling duel, with Reilly in immense form, but again poor finishing let the home side down in a 3–2 defeat. Hearts' winning goal came from an unlikely source when injured full-back Tam McKenzie, a passenger on the right wing, prodded the ball past Hibs' young goalkeeper in injury time.

Pat Ward, who had signed for Hibs on Christmas Day 1948, had been unable to secure a regular first-team place recently, and at the beginning of October he was transferred to Leicester City, teaming up again with former Easter Road colleagues John Ogilvie and Tommy McDonald. Ogilvie, now fully fit after his horrendous leg break at Tynecastle, was now at City after a short spell in Sheffield following a free transfer from Easter Road two years before.

Proving that nothing is completely new in football, in the middle of the month the Scottish League turned down a request from the Professional Players' Union for a meeting to discuss the general standard of refereeing in the country. Although he did not specify any particular incident or name any individual official, according to the union secretary the players had lost confidence in the entire refereeing set-up. It was a subject that was to crop up several times throughout the coming years.

Swan had long been confident that floodlit football's doubters would, in his own words, 'emerge from the darkness sooner or later'. Press reports revealed that a new chapter had opened for Scottish football on Saturday 3 November 1956, when the Rangers versus Hibs match at Ibrox, and the Kilmarnock versus Falkirk game at Rugby Park that same afternoon, became the first official League matches in the country to take place under artificial light when the systems were switched on 15 minutes from the end, but that honour had already fallen to Hibs when they defeated Queen of the South in a League match under the Easter Road lights the previous March. The improved visibility at Ibrox was of little benefit to the Edinburgh side, however, as the title-holders won a thrilling match, packed with goalmouth incidents and brilliant football, 5–3.

The defeat at Ibrox had brought a sequence of four consecutive draws to an end, and still Hibs had failed to taste victory since overcoming Falkirk on the opening day of the season nine games before. In a vain attempt to bolster results, Bobby Nicol and Pat Hughes were drafted into the side alongside centre-half Plenderleith, making the half-back line the youngest in the country at the time, but only four wins out of 17 starts meant that Hibs were still languishing in the lower reaches of the table with half the season completed. Perhaps predictably, the year ended with a 3–3 draw against Celtic in Edinburgh, leaving Hibs in 11th place in the table. Only four of the 25 games played since the start of the season, including the friendlies against Liverpool and Spurs, had been won, and although eight had ended even, official statements released to the press at that time made it clear that the board were concerned about the poor showing of the team.

In November Lawrie Reilly had briefly escaped the pressures of Hibs' uncertain League form when he became the solitary Easter Road player to represent Scotland against Northern Ireland and Yugoslavia, both games being played at Hampden. Winning his 36th and 37th caps respectively, he was not to know it at the time, but at only 28 years of age his international career was fast drawing to an end.

At Tynecastle on New Year's Day, a blistering Turnbull thunderbolt from well outside the box, after only 20 seconds, set the visitors well on their way to a 2–0 victory and gave the Hibs support something to smile about for the first time in quite a while. It was the first time that season that Hearts had failed to score, and it was also the visitors' first victory over their city rivals in four starts. Under the cosh for most of the game, Hearts had goalkeeper Brown to thank for preventing an even heavier defeat when he saved a powerful Turnbull penalty in the second half, which had been awarded after Reilly had been brought crashing down in the box. Before the game, the home side had introduced the controversial and unpopular 'no change given' ruling at the turnstiles, which required the handing over of the correct admission money or the surplus would be forfeited. Signs warning of the danger of pickpockets were also well displayed.

On 2 January, another miss from the spot by Turnbull, his second in 24 hours, cost his side a valuable point as yet another game, the third in the last five, ended all-square, this time against Queen of the South. In yet another change of personnel, three days later outside-right Andy Aitken, who had been earning rave reviews in the reserves, made his first-team debut in a 1–0 win against bottom-of-the-table Falkirk at Brockville.

In midweek the now traditional Annual Dinner Dance in the North British Hotel was its usual sparkling success. With numerous former players mingling with other dignitaries and invited guests, a thoroughly enjoyable evening ended with Mrs Harry Swan being presented with a bouquet of flowers by 16-year-old provisional signing Joe Baker, at that time the youngest member of the staff.

In mid-January an emphatic 4–1 win over Aberdeen at Easter Road saw Hibs climb to seventh place in the table. The sides met again in the first round of the Scottish Cup at the same venue a few weeks later, but this time it was the Grampian side who ran out 4–3 winners in a pulsating match, described in one newspaper as 'Cup football at its very best'. A magnificent first-half performance by Aberdeen allowed the visitors to change ends at the interval with a comfortable 4–0 advantage. However, in an immense second-half display of tenacity and skill, as the home side kicked down the famous slope, the brilliant Smith in particular displayed signs of the vintage 'Gay Gordon' of old as Hibs staged an incredible fightback and were only just denied the replay their fighting performance deserved when Ormond's left-foot shot flew inches past the 'keeper's far post in the dying seconds. With Hearts facing Rangers in the Cup at Tynecastle that same afternoon, and Scotland playing Wales at Murrayfield a few hundred yards away, Swan had requested that the game against Aberdeen be played in the evening under floodlights with a 7.15pm start. With the Welsh supporters in town, there was the possibly of the gate being swelled by neutrals, which would be of benefit to both sides. The request was turned down flat by Aberdeen, however, who felt that the home side's experience playing under lights would constitute an unfair advantage. The attitude of the Aberdeen directors provoked a great deal of criticism in some quarters, but in fairness to them, there was also the question of the travelling fans to be taken into consideration, most of them having to endure a journey home that took almost four hours in those pre-motorway days. The then firmly established Hospital Broadcast service, which normally beamed the action from both Edinburgh grounds, relayed the first half of the action at Tynecastle to the waiting patients before switching to the second half at Easter Road. Again it was to be Scottish Cup disappointment for both Edinburgh sides. Although Scotland defeated Wales 9–6 at Murrayfield, Hearts joined their Edinburgh neighbours on the sidelines after losing 4–0 to Rangers.

Willie Ormond was now due a second benefit payment, after almost 11 years' sterling service with the club, but after talks between the player and manager Shaw failed to reach an amicable settlement of the sum involved he asked to be placed on the transfer list, a request that was immediately, if reluctantly, agreed by the club. While not initially affecting Ormond's selection for the first team, negotiations dragged on for some time before both parties eventually agreed a satisfactory conclusion. At that time the veteran Archie Buchanan was also in dispute with the club for the same reason, and he too had asked for a transfer. As allowed by the authorities, a benefit could be paid to a player after six years' service, but this, and any payment, was completely at the discretion of the club. Buchanan, who had not featured in the first team since a 6–1 victory against East Fife at the end of November, was later given a free transfer as a reward for his years of loyal service to the club, and he soon signed for St Mirren. The personable wing-half was the latest of a dwindling band of players signed during the war years to leave the club. Now only Gordon Smith, Bobby Combe and John Paterson remained. By coincidence, at that time former Easter Road favourite Bobby Johnstone was also in dispute with Manchester City regarding the allocation of complimentary tickets for the recent derby between City and Manchester United. Like Ormond and Buchanan, Johnstone had also asked to be placed on the transfer list, but he later withdrew the request.

With a blank Saturday courtesy of their premature Scottish Cup exit, Hibs invited English Second Division runaway leaders Leicester City to Easter Road. Leicester, who included former Hibs players Tommy McDonald, Pat Ward and John Ogilvie in their line up, proved worthy winners in an otherwise disappointing game. Watched by a crowd of around 15,000, McDonald scored one of the Leicester goals against his former teammates in a 3–2 victory. That same afternoon, Hearts, also with a free Saturday after being knocked out of the Cup, suffered an even heavier defeat at Tynecastle when going down 6–3 to First Division Bolton Wanderers.

A 3–0 victory at Dens Park at the beginning of March brought a miserable run of seven straight defeats, including the Leicester friendly and the Cup game against Aberdeen, to an end. Not since defeating Aberdeen in the League almost two months before had the Easter Road players enjoyed the delights of a win bonus.

With the premature exit from the Cup, little was left to excite the fans for what was left of the season, and this transitional period – as the Easter Road board of directors were now officially calling it – saw Hibs flitting between seventh and ninth place in the table.

At that time Harry Swan was contributing to a regular column in the sports edition of the *Evening News*. Never afraid to court controversy, the Hibs chairman revealed his radical ideas on the subject of promotion and relegation when he stated that he 'personally was not in favour of the system being applied in Scotland. Put simply, there are clubs in this country who simply could not face the responsibilities of life in a higher League'. Citing as an example Edinburgh City, or the case of another Edinburgh side, St Bernards, whose directors had admitted that the club could not undertake the extra burden of life in the top League if they were promoted. Swan continued: 'Many years before, Leith Athletic won promotion to the top tier, but it ultimately proved the end for the club because they did not have the financial capabilities to survive'. At that time it was thought that at least 95 per cent of the clubs in Scotland were failing to make a profit. Always a man ahead of his time, one must look no further than the modern example of Gretna to realise that perhaps Swan was right.

In another issue Swan mentioned the work that had been done in improving the stadium during the past few years. His comments did not go too down well with many of the fans, however, who had grown accustomed to success but were now disillusioned and dissatisfied at what was happening at Easter Road. One, perhaps echoing the thoughts of many, complained that: 'other clubs such as Motherwell, Falkirk, Dunfermline and Kilmarnock had also provided floodlights and cover for the supporters, but had also managed to buy players as well.' 'Swan', he thought, 'offered nothing hopeful for the future. Do the Hibs fans have to wait until the club is sold into the Second Division? If we continue to sell without buying things will only get worse.' With the selective memory perhaps typical of the average football fan, forgetting what had been achieved under the chairman's tenure, the dissatisfied fan 'wondered if perhaps Swan needed a rest, but if nothing else new faces are desperately needed at board level'.

In another floodlight first, with Scotland's rugby side on international duty at Murrayfield that afternoon, the game against relegation-haunted East Fife at the end of March was the first-ever Saturday evening floodlit match in the country and Hibs' 21st match under their own lights. Two goals from the powerful Harrower, who was by this time beginning to form a productive left-wing pairing with Andy Aitken, and further strikes by Reilly and Jimmy Thomson, gave Hibs a third consecutive victory.

Yet another friendly match, this time against Irish club Distillery and, appropriately enough considering the scoreline, taking place on April Fools' Day, was played under the Belfast side's lights and watched by a derisory 3,000 crowd. The match, which was played in a thunderstorm of incessant rain, ended in a humiliating 2–1 defeat, Turnbull netting Hibs' lone strike from the penalty spot.

A few days later, at Wembley, Lawrie Reilly failed to score against England for the first time in five starts at the famous stadium. Sadly, it would also be Reilly's last-ever appearance in a dark blue jersey. After an illustrious international career spanning eight years and 38 games, scoring 22 goals, injury would soon force his early retirement from the game. He would finish his career as Hibs' most-capped player, a record he holds to this day, well ahead at the time of next-best Gordon Smith, who had made 15 full appearances for Scotland.

That same evening, at Easter Road, Airdrie became only the second side in the country to realise the sense of playing on a Saturday evening with nothing else to distract the supporters, and the 14,000 attendance was well above the average that could be expected for a match between the sides at the time. Gordon Smith chose this particular match to exhibit his fantastic skills with a virtuoso performance of wing trickery, and as well as creating goals for others, he scored two beauties himself in a somewhat one-sided 6–0 victory. Bobby Nicol scored his first goal for Hibs, the others coming from Turnbull, Aitken and the newly promoted Derek McWilliams, making the first of only two League appearances for the club.

In that year's budget, the Chancellor of the Exchequer had decided at long last to completely scrap the unpopular entertainment tax that had been responsible for the ongoing dispute between the Treasury and Scottish clubs dating as far back as 1946. The decision was a timely and much-needed boost for the game north of the border, particularly for the smaller clubs, many of whom were now in dire financial difficulties with the post-war crowd boom a fading memory.

Once again a dreadfully disappointing season ended as it had started for Hibs, with an away defeat. After a dismal 0–0 home draw the previous week against struggling Dunfermline, who had already been all but relegated, typical end-of-season fare at Parkhead was watched by a pitifully small crowd of under 8,000. It required a last-minute penalty to give the home side both points before the referee's final whistle brought welcome relief for the small number of Hibs fans who had bothered to travel to Glasgow.

Hibs ended the season in ninth place, a massive 22 points behind champions Rangers and 19 behind second-placed Hearts, who were showing definite signs of taking over Hibs' mantle as the top team, not only in the city, but also in the country. Nine of the 34 games had ended level and 13 in defeat, form far removed from the halcyon days of just a few years previously.

Lawrie Reilly had finished as the club's top goalscorer for a seventh consecutive season, but his total of 18 goals in all games was a lot smaller than the excellent standards set by the player not long before. The centre-forward missed the final four games of the season due to a niggling cartilage injury which would require surgery during the summer, and although he would return to the first team, complications from the injury would ultimately hasten the premature end of the playing career of one of the greatest Scottish centre-forwards of all time.

On the positive side, however, George Muir, Bobby Nicol, Pat Hughes and Andy Aitken had all acquitted themselves well since their introduction during the season, as had the forceful Jimmy Mulkerrin, and the year's experience would have done the youngsters a world of good. Twenty-five players, plus the provisional signings including teenagers Johnny McLeod and Joe Baker, were retained for the following season. John Higgins, Eddie Gray and Jim Rollo had featured in just two League games between them during the past 12 months and were given free transfers. Davie Laing had been offered part-time terms and refused to resign. He would soon sign for English Second Division side Gillingham.

Doug Moran, who had joined Falkirk on loan in the January, ended a more than satisfactory season on a personal high by scoring one of the Brockville side's goals in the Scottish Cup Final replay win against Kilmarnock. Although he would eventually sign for Falkirk at the end of the season, at the time of the Cup Final Moran was still on loan from Easter Road, and technically he can claim the distinction of being the last Hibs player to collect a winners' medal in the Scottish Cup. The former juvenile, who had joined Hibs from Musselburgh Union in 1952, would soon be on the move again to the all-conquering Ipswich side that would eventually sweep from the English Third Division (South) to First, in title-winning seasons under the guidance of former Tottenham player and future England World Cup winning manager Alf Ramsey.

A short while before the end of the season an invitation had been received at Easter Road for the club to tour Mexico during the summer, but for a second consecutive season it was decided that the players should stay at home to recharge their batteries for the coming campaign.

The End of the Road for Reilly, Baker Comes of Age and Another Scottish Cup Failure

In a surprise move that suggested all was not well behind the scenes, trainer Sammy Kean had been released from his Easter Road duties during the close season, severing a 20-year association with the club. The well-respected Kean immediately accepted an offer to join Dundee as first-team trainer, a position he would hold when the Dens Park side swept to League Championship success in 1962 under the guidance of future Hibs manager Bob Shankly and the on-field influence of Gordon Smith. It later emerged that a rift had developed between Kean and the chairman earlier in the year, and only the intervention of several senior players had prevented the trainer from leaving at that time. Kean was replaced at Easter Road by Raith Rovers trainer and physiotherapist Willie Hunter, who had overseen the Fifers' recent good run, their best for many years. Meanwhile, a new position had been specially created at the club for veteran Bobby Combe, who became assistant first-team trainer and coach. The 33-year-old Combe had spent most of the preceding year in the reserves, featuring in the first team set-up only rarely, and had ultimately decided to retire from the playing side. The evergreen Jimmy McColl remained in charge of the second XI.

Diminutive inside-forward Jimmy Shields, of whom so much had been expected when joining the club in 1950, had failed to make the anticipated impact and was transferred to Cowdenbeath for a nominal £500 fee before the start of the season. A surprise late inclusion in the party that had made its way to Brazil in 1953, Shields' Easter Road career had been hampered first by cartilage trouble and then by National Service, circumstances that made a first-team breakthrough very difficult for the youngster to achieve.

A £1,750 bid was received from Raith Rovers for part-time reserve centre-half John Grant, which was rejected. The Fifers immediately switched their attention to veteran John Paterson, who was then yet to sign a new contract. Turning down the chance of a move to Kirkcaldy, the Englishman soon put pen to paper for his 13th season in a green-and-white jersey.

In the usual start to the season, Gordon Smith again managed to keep his record of having featured in all 14 of the charity games intact, when he captained the Edinburgh Select against Preston North End at Easter Road. A Preston side containing such personalities as Willie Cunningham, Tommy Docherty and the illustrious Tom Finney eventually overcame the challenge of the capital side to secure a 3–1 victory and become only the second successful visitors since Liverpool's win in 1951.

As well as provisional signings Joe Baker and Johnny McLeod, several other promising youngsters had joined the club during the summer recess, including Des Anderson, Jimmy Kane, Tommy Kilbride, Tommy Slavin, Malcolm Bogie and John Young. Coach Bobby Combe described them as the 'best group of new recruits to join the club for a very long time', but as usual the number of youngsters who actually made an impact in professional football was low and only Baker, McLeod and, to a lesser extent, Young would make any real impact on the game.

Lawrie Reilly, still recovering from the effects of the cartilage operation on his right knee, missed the start of the season, but to make the absence of the Scotland centre-forward easier to bear for the frustrated Hibs supporters, 17-year-old Joe Baker was soon to explode onto the scene. First spotted by the club when playing for Lanarkshire Schools against Edinburgh at Tynecastle, Joe had been on Hibs' books since 1955. Called-up only during the summer, he had played just one game in the reserves, in which he surprisingly failed to score in a 8–1 drubbing of East Fife's second team, before being handed a first-team debut at Airdrie in the League Cup. Although having lived in Scotland for all but the first few weeks of his life, and as Scottish as the next man in spirit, Baker had been born in Liverpool. In those less enlightened days, even a Scottish parent, far less a grandparent, was not enough to entitle a player to represent any other home country than that of his birth, a state of affairs that would have unfortunate consequences as far as Baker and Scotland were concerned in the near future.

Called into the side as a late replacement for the injured John Fraser for the League Cup tie against Airdrie at Broomfield, on Wednesday 14 August it would be fantastic to describe Baker's debut as a fairytale start to his Hibs career, with the youngster scoring the winning goal in the dying seconds. In truth he was completely dominated by the far more experienced giant centre-half Doug Baillie, who would soon be transferred to Rangers. Although the youngster tried hard, Airdrie eventually ran out comfortable 4–1 winners, and it was back to the second team for Baker. But it would not be for long.

An impressive showing by inside-forward Alex Marshall in the public trial match at the beginning of the season suggested that Hibs had uncovered yet another 'gem', and he was given almost immediate promotion to the first team. Signed during the previous season from Royal and Douglas Amateurs, Marshall made his debut in a 3–1 home win against Celtic in the middle of August, replacing the injured Turnbull.

For a fourth consecutive season, Hibs failed to qualify for the later stages of the League Cup, this time from a section comprising Airdrie, East Fife and Celtic. Still well in the running for a place in the last eight with only one game to play, a 2–0 defeat at Parkhead relegated Hibs into second place, with the Glasgow side embarking on an historic run to the Final that would culminate in the famous 7–1 victory over deadly rivals Rangers, still a record score for a League Cup Final.

During an earlier League Cup encounter between Hibs and East Fife reserves, Joe Baker had revealed both sides of his character. After scoring both Hibs' goals in the 2–0 victory, Baker's fiery temperament was unveiled for all to see when both he and an opponent were sent off after a clash near the end of the game. He would later be severely censured for his part in the incident.

By this time Lawrie Leslie had taken over from Wren in goal, and in the opening League game of the season at Pittodrie, 21-year-old John Baxter, recently released from National Service, made an impressive first start to a Hibs career that would span almost a decade. The 1–0 victory over Aberdeen was followed by a 2–1 home win against Motherwell, the first time since the Championship-winning season of 1947–48 that Hibs had recorded consecutive wins at the start of a campaign.

Both Edinburgh sides had made a promising start to the League campaign, but once again Hearts were found to be a difficult hurdle to overcome, and two goals inside the opening seven minutes set the Gorgie men well on the way to a much easier home victory than the 3–1 scoreline would suggest. A lacklustre performance by Hearts that incurred the wrath of their supporters and later that of manager Tommy

Walker was still much too good for an extremely poor Hibs side, and the game was all but over at half-time. The more experienced Hearts team, which would win the Championship that season, was far too good for the Hibs youngsters, 'but where,' asked one reporter covering the game, 'was Hibs' once renowned fighting spirit?' Hearts had now won 14 of the last 25 League games between the sides since the war, with two drawn.

In an attempt to bring some fluency to the forward line, Fraser, Baker and Harrower had all been tried in the middle of the attack, but a week after the defeat at Tynecastle, Lawrie Reilly, displaying much of his old form, made a scoring return to the side in a 4–0 victory over Airdrie at Easter Road. Ten minutes before half-time, Baxter demonstrated the awesome shooting power that would become his trademark when he scored his first goal for the club from a direct free-kick fully 40 yards from goal.

The benefit of playing under floodlights had again been clearly demonstrated a few days earlier when a crowd of almost 10,000 turned out to watch the reserve Edinburgh derby at Easter Road, more than double the usual attendance for these matches. Although failing to register on the score sheet that evening, six goals in a handful of reserve-team starts meant Joe Baker could not be held back much longer, and he made a return to first-team action, scoring his first senior goal in Hibs' 4–2 win over city rivals Hearts in a match arranged to officially open the Tynecastle floodlights. Tommy Preston took the goalscoring honours when notching a hat-trick, but it was the lightning-fast Baker who caught the eye as he harassed the experienced Hearts centre-half Glidden for 90 minutes, looking every inch a star of the future.

Reciprocating a similar gesture made by Hibs at the opening of the Easter Road lights by their city rivals in 1954, the Hearts directors commemorated the occasion by presenting Hibs with a beautiful silver Loving Cup, which can still be seen in the Easter Road boardroom today. The players all received Parker pen writing sets, and silver tankards were presented to the Hibs officials to mark the occasion.

Joe Baker made his League debut five days later against Queen's Park at Easter Road, with Reilly moving to inside-forward. The youngster was again on target, scoring both his side's goals in a 2–0 win. He would rarely, barring injury, be out of the first team again.

Baker's double against Queen's Park was quickly followed, two days later, by his first top-team hat-trick, against Tottenham Hotspur in the opening game of that season's unofficial Floodlit League. It could well have been four for the teenage sensation when a long-range, last-minute effort hit the bar, but his goals in the 5–2 victory marked the beginning of a true 'Roy of the Rovers' story, and the birth of yet another Hibernian legend. Surrounded by a pack of adoring youngsters as he left the field after the final whistle, it was obvious even this early in his career that Hibs had unearthed a new hero.

By now matters had finally come to a head regarding the future of the proposed Floodlit League pursued so vigorously by Hibs, Hearts, Partick Thistle, Newcastle United, Manchester City and Spurs. Played as a series of friendly matches during the previous two years, now, at long last, permission had been received from the SFA that the tournament could proceed on a competitive basis with silverware the reward for the victors. This decision, however, outraged Scottish League president William Watters of St Mirren, who threatened expulsion from the League for any Scottish side continuing to defy their ruling prohibiting the competition. A ray of hope emerged for the exasperated pioneers when the SFA announced that the League was guilty of exceeding its powers, but the stalemate continued for some time. Swan and Hibs were adamant that no rule had been broken and failed to understand the reluctance of the Scottish League to sanction the competition, the fans proving its popularity by turning out in more than acceptable numbers. The post-war boom in attendances was now long gone and many clubs were struggling financially. At that time some were lucky if they drew enough at the gate to pay the visiting club's guarantee. Indeed, at the recent game against Airdrie at Broomfield, the home side had barely covered the Hibs fee, and that, thought Swan, 'was poor reward for a team chasing the Championship. If fans were not prepared to turn out in their numbers to see a team of Hibs' calibre then the future is bleak.' Something had to be done, and surely a Floodlit League was worth considering. Partick Thistle took matters further by demanding the withdrawal of Rangers from that year's European Cup competition, the Firhill side having great difficulty in understanding why it was permissible for one floodlit tournament to proceed and not the other. Hearts, meanwhile, had announced that they would only continue with the permission of both ruling bodies. At a further meeting of the SFA, the motion failed to gather the 13 votes necessary for the competition to proceed on a competitive basis, and the immediate withdrawal of Hearts effectively killed off the competition, much to the everlasting disgust of the Hibs chairman.

The unofficial floodlight series limped along for a short time under the guise of friendly games, with Hibs attempting to go it alone as Edinburgh's representatives, but with the Football League following the line of their Scottish counterparts, Manchester City and Newcastle United both claimed to find the proposed dates for their fixtures inconvenient and the matter was at an end. There is little doubt that the capitulation of Hearts had denied the participating clubs the rewards that their floodlight enterprise had deserved, and this left a sour taste in the mouth of Swan, who had always felt that the only way forward lay in solidarity. Even now, with the benefit of hindsight, it is still difficult to understand this lack of foresight and the reasons for such vehement opposition to a tournament that would in no way have affected the non-participants.

As well as Baxter and Baker, several other young hopefuls who had recently been signed on professional terms, such as Bogie, Frye, McClelland, McLeod and Slavin, were all knocking on the first-team door. Frye made a satisfactory debut against St Mirren at Love Street in November with Baker scoring all his side's goals in a 3–0 victory, but unfortunately for the tricky inside-right he was carried off 12 minutes from the end with an injury that would keep him out of the game for several weeks.

Now approaching the veteran stage, Gordon Smith was involved in a situation that was as odd as it was ludicrous. Selected for the Scottish side to face Switzerland at Hampden in November, the outside-right picked up a slight injury playing against Wolves in a friendly at Easter Road 10 days before. Hibs, as was required, immediately informed the SFA, reassuring them that the injury was only slight and would not mean the forward missing any games. Smith, however, was immediately replaced in the Scottish team by the rising Rangers star and future Hibs signing Alec Scott. Smith later admitted that the bizarre decision was one of the biggest disappointments of his entire career. He was not to know it at that moment, but his international days were over. He never represented his country again.

Four days before Christmas, outside-left Johnny McLeod made an immediate impact on his first-team debut. A former teammate of Baker's at Armadale Thistle, McLeod proved an instant success by scoring two and setting up the others in Hibs' 4–1 victory at Kilmarnock. Like Baker, McLeod would retain his place in the side, and with the return of a fully fit Ormond from injury in January, the former Scottish Youth international would be switched to the right wing to replace the injured Gordon Smith, who had damaged his ankle.

As late as Christmas 1957, Hibs held on grimly to second place in the League table, but a 3–1 defeat, ironically as it would turn out, by Clyde at Easter Road, Baker almost predictably scoring Hibs' goal, ended a reasonably consistent spell of just four defeats from 16 games.

In the run-up to the holiday derby, Bobby Combe, writing in his weekly column in the *Pink News*, could not recall when both Hibs and Hearts had been in a healthier League position at the turn of the year. His comments would prove the kiss of death for the Greens and Hearts won 2–0 at Easter Road. The defeat was the first of four consecutive reverses, and by the middle of the month Hibs had dropped to seventh place in the table. After a season that had started so well they were to win only two more Championship games between then and the end of the season.

Tommy Preston's three goals against Hearts in the game to mark the official opening of the Tynecastle lights at the beginning of October had alerted clubs south of the border to the potential of the left-half, but a bid from Newcastle United was immediately turned down. One move that did materialise, however, was that of 22-year-old centre-forward Jimmy Harrower, who joined Liverpool for a fee believed to be around £10,000. The transfer came just a few weeks after the player had rejected a move to Leeds United after both clubs had agreed terms.

In mid-January, news was received that former player Hugh Howie had been tragically killed in a traffic accident on the Hamilton road midway between Blantyre and Cambuslang. Test-driving a car for a friend, it had swerved off the road and hit a lamppost at a notorious black spot. Thirty-three-year-old Howie, then a sports journalist for the *Daily Express*, was trapped behind the wheel and died later in hospital with his wife at his bedside. Many of Howie's former Easter Road colleagues and officials attended the funeral in Glasgow several days later, and, on the Saturday, the players of both Hibs and Falkirk wore black armbands as a mark of respect for the long-serving popular former Hibs player who had manfully managed to overcome the debilitating illness that had forced his premature retirement from the game, only to meet an early death in such unfortunate circumstances.

At Brockville Gordon Smith scored direct from a corner, the first time in his career that he had achieved the feat. The strike was not enough to guarantee victory, however, and the visitors had to content themselves with a 3–3 draw, only one of a sequence of poor results that left Hibs still seeking their first win in six games. The situation resulted in Hugh Shaw dropping a bombshell with the news that both Gordon Smith and Lawrie Reilly had been excluded from the first team against Queen's Park the following Saturday. With Turnbull at wing-half and Ormond injured, it would be one of the very few occasions since October 1949 that the attack had not contained at least one of the legendary Famous Five. The decision by the manager proved to be an astute one, and goals from Baker and Frye gave Hibs a perfect pre-Scottish Cup tonic in a 2–1 victory over Queen's at Hampden.

Smith and Reilly had both been earmarked to play against Queen's Park reserves that same afternoon. For Smith it would have meant his first-ever appearance for the second team since signing for the club in 1941. Instead, the outside-right took the opportunity to have surgery on an ankle injury described as 'career threatening' that had been niggling him for some time. He would not play again that season.

It was during that year's Scottish Cup competition that Joe Baker's goalscoring reputation was finally established. After a bye in the preliminary stages, the first round proper had paired Hibs against Second Division Dundee United at Tannadice, whose players included future Liverpool and Scotland centre-half Ron Yeats and goalkeeper Willie Lucas, who would figure in a famous Hibs Cup victory in the near future.

Heavy falls of snow that had affected the whole of Europe wiped out the entire fixture list on the Saturday, postponing the Cup tie for seven days, but the inclement weather was to have even more tragic consequences for the Manchester United party travelling back from a European Cup game in Belgrade. Twenty-four hours earlier, after stopping to refuel in Munich, their plane had failed to clear the runway in a blinding blizzard. Colliding with a nearby house, eight of the players and numerous other passengers on board were killed, many of them pressmen, including former England goalkeeper Frank Swift. Manager Matt Busby was seriously injured and for several days hovered between life and death. The accident stunned the football world, and for a while called into question flying as a means of travel for football teams. Ironically, a Football League ruling prohibiting teams from flying to domestic games had been relaxed less than a year before. The incident encouraged Manchester City and several other sides to modify plans for end-of-season tours, and former Hibs player Bobby Johnstone and several others refused to take part in the club's projected six-week trip to Canada in May. Unfortunately, it had not been the first such incident in recent years. In May 1949 the aircraft carrying the all-conquering Italian League Champions Torino back from a match in Lisbon had crashed into a hillside on the outskirts of Turin, killing all on board.

In the Scottish Cup tie at Tannadice the Second Division side offered a plucky resistance, and it required goals from Baker and Frye, after a replay at Easter Road, to subdue United, who were playing their first-ever game under lights. Neither the glare of the lights nor the play of their First Division opponents dazzled United and the Second Division side had Hibs rocking on numerous occasions throughout the 90 minutes. In the end superior fitness and finishing told, and a much-relieved Hibs went through to face champions-elect Hearts in the next round.

Before the game with Hearts, there was a quite amazing 5–5 draw with St Mirren at Easter Road, a match described in the press as 'gallant but certainly not graceful'. Thrice in arrears, Hibs finally managed to get their heads 5–4 in front in the later stages thanks to two goals from the penalty spot by Eddie Turnbull, who by this time was a regular in the right-half position, only to concede an equaliser 10 minutes from time. Perhaps not the greatest of games for the purist, the supporters certainly got their money's worth with incidents and goals galore.

On Saturday 1 March 1958, a huge crowd of over 41,000 packed into Tynecastle to see overwhelming favourites Hearts, who were the bookies' choice to win the League and Cup double, face the still transitional no-hopers from Easter Road. An inspired tactical move by manager Hugh Shaw saw John Grant pushed into the inside-forward position to counter the midfield probing of Mackay and Milne. The move paid dividends by allowing Baker more space in the centre of the park, and the entire country was shocked at the news of Hibs' 4–3 victory.

In midfield, Turnbull and Baxter were immense, as was 'keeper Leslie, who performed exceptionally well when called upon, particularly in the later stages of the game, but the undoubted star of the show was 17-year-old Joe Baker, who scored all four Hibs goals.

Hearts took the lead against the run of play after 10 minutes, but they were ahead for only seconds before Baker fired past Marshall after an Ormond drive had come back off the crossbar. By that time the visitors could well have been further ahead had they taken their chances against an unusually shaky Maroons defence. The young centre-forward refused to give pivot Milne a second's peace as he ran the experienced player ragged, scoring twice more with tremendous drives from close range. With only a minute remaining on the clock and Hibs leading 4–2, Hearts pulled one back to ensure a barnstorming finish, but although having to survive a late spell of pressure in injury time as the home side went all out for the equaliser, there was no doubt that it was a merited, if surprising, victory for the visitors.

Goalkeeper Lawrie Leslie, who had been in brilliant form throughout the entire 90 minutes, performing miracles in the dying stages of the game to deny Hearts an equalising goal, was carried shoulder high from the pitch by the fans at the end, but the real hero of the hour was teenage goalscoring sensation Joe Baker.

Hearts: Marshall, Kirk, Thomson, MacKay, Milne, Bowman, Hamilton, Murray, Young, Wardhaugh, Crawford.
Hibernian: Leslie, Paterson, McClelland, Turnbull, Plenderleith, Baxter, Fraser, Grant, Baker, Preston, Ormond.

A few days after the Tynecastle triumph, Famous Five member Lawrie Reilly announced that he would be retiring from football at the end of the season. The Scotland centre-forward had not managed to fully recover from the cartilage operation the previous season, the knee swelling up after each game and often preventing him from training. In the circumstances, unable to perform to the impeccably high standards he had set himself during the previous 13 years, he had reluctantly decided to call it a day. Despite appeals by the management and even the offer of a pay rise, Reilly was adamant that he was making the correct decision and he could not be persuaded to change his mind.

Yet another two goals by the in-form Baker and one from Fraser gave Hibs a 3–2 advantage over a battling Third Lanark in the Cup quarter-final at Easter Road. Thirds were the better side for most of the game, but the result set up a place in the last four for the Edinburgh side and another meeting with old adversaries Rangers.

In the semi-final at Hampden on 5 April 1958, watched by a crowd of 76,727, Hibs conceded an early goal when Millar scored for Rangers after only three minutes. Undaunted, the Edinburgh side fought back well and they took the lead when both Preston and Aitken scored in a five-minute burst shortly before the interval. After the break, Hibs continued in rampant style and still deserved their slender lead. For long spells in the second 45 minutes they played stunning football that was vastly superior to anything Rangers had to offer, but with only 13 minutes remaining disaster struck when a Murray header was magnificently saved by goalkeeper Leslie, who could only watch in horror as the ball was deflected onto the post and over the line for an equaliser that agonisingly denied Hibs the Scottish Cup Final place their play had deserved.

Because the national stadium lacked floodlights the replay took place the following Wednesday afternoon. The absence of lights traditionally meant a lower attendance at afternoon games because of work commitments, one of the main reasons why the proponents of floodlit football all these years before had been instrumental in leading the fight to convert those who had been against their use.

Matches between Hibs and Rangers are seldom without their drama, and this one was no exception. In direct contrast to the first game, Rangers were the better side overall, but only rarely did the Hibs goal find itself under direct threat, thanks to some cool and resolute defending by the Edinburgh rearguard. In one of their rare attacks during the first 45 minutes, Hibs took a shock lead when Turnbull smashed home from the penalty spot after Baker had been brought crashing down in the box by 'keeper Ritchie. Within five minutes of the restart, the Edinburgh side somewhat surprisingly took a two-goal lead when Fraser headed home after Ritchie could only deflect an Aitken shot into his path. In desperation Rangers now adopted a powerful route one policy, and it paid dividends four minutes later when Baird scored with a penalty-kick, awarded after a Rangers player had been sandwiched in the box.

In a thrilling finale, with the Ibrox men giving their all in the search for an equaliser, the Light Blues believed they had levelled the tie three minutes from time when Leslie in the Hibs goal appeared to drop a cross at the feet of Murray, who wasted no time in smashing the ball into the net. Referee Davidson had no hesitation in awarding a goal, a decision that sent the Ibrox legions wild with delight, but the irate Hibs players immediately surrounded the official, insisting that he consult the linesman, who still had his flag raised. The tension was unbearable as Davidson spent agonising seconds talking with his linesman, each one seeming like minutes to the players and fans of both sides, before returning to award a free-kick to Hibs, much to the fury of the Rangers players and their supporters. The final few minutes were played out to a cacophony of jeering from the Ibrox faithful, directed solely in the direction of referee Davidson and his assistant. After the match one newspaper columnist bravely reported that 'many might have wondered how the linesman could have seen any more than the referee, but on the law of averages the Glasgow side can have no real grouse about losing on a disputed goal as they have trooped from the field many a time to a chorus of "Lucky Rangers".' After the game, newsreel and press pictures of the incident revealed the referee's final decision to have been correct. In photographs, the Rangers centre-forward Ralph Brand's hand can be clearly seen punching the ball from Leslie's grasp.

There was a sinister footnote to the affair. In the days following the semi-final the SFA received a request from Rangers that referee Davidson, who was due to take charge of the Ibrox side's next fixture against Falkirk, be replaced. According to the Glasgow club, this was on the advice of the police, who feared trouble from the fans. After investigation, the authorities discovered that the police knew nothing of the matter, and embarrassed Rangers were severely censured at the next meeting of the SFA committee.

Hibernian: Leslie, Grant, McClelland, Turnbull, Paterson, Baxter, Fraser, Aitken, Baker, Preston, Ormond.

Four days after the excitement of the Hampden semi-final, Hearts completed the first half of an Edinburgh League and Cup double when they clinched their first League Championship since 1897. It was now up to Hibs.

As stated earlier, Lawrie Reilly, unable to play or train properly without discomfort, had decided to retire from the game, and at Easter Road on Monday 22 April, just six days before Hibs faced Clyde in the 1958 Scottish Cup Final, the celebrated centre-forward bade a moving farewell to the fans with his last-ever appearance in the famous green-and-white jersey. At the age of just 29, 'Last Minute Reilly', Hibs' most-capped player and the proud holder of the record number of League goals for the club since making his debut as a 16-year-old against Kilmarnock in October 1945, was forced to retire prematurely. Reilly's final game was against Rangers, whom he had faced in numerous titanic battles throughout his career, and it seemed only fitting that he should score one of Hibs' goals in a 3–1 defeat of an old enemy. At the final whistle the players of both sides formed a ceremonial line as the clearly emotional Reilly was applauded from the field by over 25,000 cheering fans.

Veteran centre-half John Paterson, who had been dominant in the middle of the Hibs defence throughout their great Cup run, had been injured during a 1–1 draw with Dundee at Easter Road several weeks before, but he was considered to have a good chance of making the Final. On the morning of the game, however, Hibs were dealt an early blow when the experienced defender failed a late fitness test on his injured ankle and was replaced in the heart of the defence by Jackie Plenderleith. Another player who would miss the Final, perhaps his last chance to win the coveted trophy, was the inspirational Gordon Smith. Beset by troublesome injuries for most of the season, Smith had sustained a severe ankle injury against Falkirk in mid-January that had required two operations to remove bone fragments, and he had not featured since.

By three o'clock on the afternoon of 27 April 1958, 95,123 excited fans had packed into the vast slopes of Hampden, the strong chilly winds and intermittent rain doing little to dampen their enthusiasm. The supporters wearing the green and white of Hibs seemed to far outnumber those of Clyde, and the many thousands of fans who had travelled through from the capital and its surrounding areas were convinced that their favourites were at last about to bury the Scottish Cup hoodoo that had hung over Easter Road for 56 years. Not since defeating Celtic in the 1902 Final at Parkhead had a Hibs captain lifted that most coveted and prestigious silverware. The Finals of 1914, 1923, 1924 and 1947 had all ended in glorious failure, but this time expectations were high that the trophy would at last be making its way to the east side of Edinburgh at the end of the afternoon. Sadly, it was not to be.

An early injury to inside-right Andy Aitken, at that time playing the best football of his career, meant that his effectiveness was drastically reduced and Hibs were forced to battle manfully for almost three-quarters of the game against full-strength opponents. With 29 minutes played, a Coyle shot that looked to be well covered by 'keeper Leslie was deflected into the opposite corner of the net by the leg of the in-rushing John Baxter to give Clyde an interval lead. A few minutes before the break, Aitken was again cynically chopped down by wing-half Clinton, who had been very aware of the player's threat, and the crippled number eight became a virtual passenger for the remainder of the game.

Despite the misfortunes suffered by Hibs, there was no doubt that Clyde were the better side. In the first half, Tommy Ring alone had squandered enough chances to win two or three Cup Finals. After the break, the depleted Edinburgh side admirably fought themselves back into contention as they forced Clyde onto the defensive, and with just 14 minutes remaining they seemed to have succeeded in their quest for an equaliser. The brave Aitken, who had spent the second half shuffling up and down on the right wing with his right knee heavily bandaged, managed to send over a delightful cross that beat the Clyde defenders. At the far post Joe Baker, who had been fairly subdued all afternoon, rose to head the ball into the net from almost under the crossbar, but the joy of the Hibs players was short-lived when the referee, rightly, decided that Baker had used his hand to force the ball over the line. From then until the end it was nearly all Hibs, but try as they might, they could not force the vital counter, and at the final whistle the Cup made the short journey to Shawfield.

Over the years, many of the Hibs supporters who watched the game have remained convinced that Baker could quite easily have headed the ball into the net, but the player himself has consistently refuted this, borne out by television evidence, insisting that the ball was too high to reach with his head. The argument, however, is totally immaterial as the record books state, quite categorically, Clyde 1, Hibernian 0. It has also been suggested that perhaps the vastly experienced Reilly should have played instead of the raw youngster, who admitted himself that he was overawed on the day, but this argument is also irrelevant. Reilly was unwell with tonsillitis on the day of the match and was not even at the game.

Hibernian: Leslie, Grant, McClelland, Turnbull, Plenderleith, Baxter, Fraser, Aitken, Baker, Preston, Ormond.
Clyde: McCulloch, Murphy, Haddock, Walters, Finlay, Clinton, Herd, Currie, Coyle, Robertson, Ring.
Referee: J. Mowat.

There had been some signs during the previous 12 months that Hibs were slowly beginning to leave the transitional stage behind them, particularly during the first half of the season, but in the end it had been yet another season of dashed hopes and disappointment as they once again finished in ninth place, with exactly half the number of points of champions Hearts.

For only the second time in 15 years, neither Gordon Smith nor Lawrie Reilly had ended the season as Hibs top marksman. Seventeen-year-old scoring sensation Joe Baker took that particular honour in his very first season with 29 goals in all games, 14 of them in the League. Smith, whose appearances had been extremely limited owing to injury, had scored only three League goals, while the recently retired Reilly had only managed two for the same reason. Turnbull, who had had his best season for some time, culminating in an international recall, had scored 16 in all games, six of them from the penalty spot, an extremely credible total for a wing-half. His one time left-wing partner Willie Ormond ended the season with 20, the highest total of the four surviving members of the Famous Five.

In his efforts to unearth a successful blend, Hugh Shaw had selected 27 players during the League campaign. Although four fewer than the previous season, it was still a considerable total in those pre-substitute days, but several had been youngsters making sporadic appearances such as Slavin, Anderson, Nicol, Frye, Boyle, Gibson and Marshall. After a promising start, Alex Marshall had failed to make the expected impact on the first team, but had been playing well in the reserves when he suffered a broken leg against Clyde at Shawfield a few days after Christmas missing the remainder of the season.

At the beginning of April, Bobby Charlton made a goalscoring debut for England on the left wing as the Auld Enemy defeated Scotland 4–0 at Hampden, a result that more than suggested that changes were required in the home set-up. Mackay, Docherty, Fernie and McColl had all been tried in the wing-half position in the recent past and discarded. Now 35-year-old powerhouse Eddie Turnbull, by this time permanently back at right-half, made a return to the international arena after an absence of almost eight years, an interval that had more to do with politics than ability after he had fallen out with one of the SFA selectors years before. Recalled to the Scotland side for the World Cup qualifying matches against Hungary and Poland, Turnbull had not even been included in the original pool of 40 players that had been selected for both the England game and the World Cup qualifying matches, but a withdrawal from the squad because of injury by Denis Law, combined with the poor showing at Hampden, had forced the selectors' hand.

A 1–1 draw against Hungary in Glasgow and a 2–1 win against Poland in Warsaw was enough to guarantee the Scots a place in the World Cup Finals in Sweden, the first time all four home nations had qualified for the Finals, and as his Hibs teammates took part in a four-game round robin Festival Cup tournament in Holland, Eddie Turnbull travelled to Scandinavia with the Scotland squad. Taking part in all three group games against Yugoslavia, Paraguay and France, the Hibs player provided the pass for Jimmy Murray of Hearts to score Scotland's first-ever goal in a World Cup Finals in the 1–1 draw with Yugoslavia.

While not nearly as embarrassing as the 1954 tournament, in which they had been humiliated 7–0 by Uruguay in Berne, the results in Sweden were still a huge disappointment for the supporters, the team failing to win any of the three first-round matches. As often happens after a less than satisfactory outcome, recriminations were not slow in following. Several weeks later, at a meeting of the SFA committee, Tom Ferguson, the colourful and at times outspoken chairman of Stirling Albion, demanded that all the selectors be sacked. Many felt that a lack of coaching at grass roots level lay behind the country's poor showing on the international stage and that Scotland were now paying a heavy price for past recalcitrance. Several years before, both Hibs and Hearts had organised their own occasional basic coaching classes for local school kids, but these sessions had lacked encouragement from the football authorities. Now, even a suggestion that schoolteachers were perhaps best placed to recognise the 'right type of boy' to make advances into the professional game fell on deaf ears, the SFA showing a complete lack of vision by rejecting the idea out of hand, arrogantly declaring that 'any SFA work was entirely a matter for the committee'.

Although Scotland had failed to progress past the opening stages, such was Turnbull's influence on the competition that the Hibs captain was later selected by the organisers as the best right-half of the entire tournament, receiving an attractive commemorative plate to mark the occasion.

The otherwise highly successful World Cup competition ended, according to the legend, with a Hibs-inspired Brazilian side that included the 17-year-old Pelé lifting the trophy for the first time.

As in 1954, the tournament had been shown on television, the British public captivated by the skill shown by several of the continental and South American sides who had demonstrated so expressively that they were no longer the poor relations of the game.

Then There Was One

Back in Edinburgh, the fine Scottish Cup run of the previous season had created a mistaken perception of expectation among a section of the support who were convinced that a return to the glory days was imminent. For the realist, however, the relative inexperience of the playing staff suggested that the 1958–59 season would perhaps be another difficult one for Hibs, and so it would prove.

Club captain Gordon Smith, bitterly disappointed that the ankle injury received against Falkirk in January had failed to respond to treatment as expected, was forced to sit out the start of the season. Two operations on the ankle itself had been a complete success, but the prolonged lay-off had weakened the leg muscles, preventing the player from training properly despite Smith's self-diagnosed treatment of running daily through the knee-deep salty water of the River Forth near his North Berwick home. Yet to sign a new contract, the player was quick to reassure the concerned supporters that this was definitely not for financial reasons or a desire to leave the club, but merely a wish to satisfy himself of his complete fitness before putting pen to paper for his 18th season at Easter Road. Smith's absence from the side was a major blow to the development of the younger players at the club, who would undoubtedly have benefited greatly from the veteran's experience and influence. No fewer than three of the side that started the season had made their debuts only during the previous campaign, and with the exception of Turnbull, Preston, Plenderleith and Ormond, the majority of the rest had made only a handful of appearances during the 1956–57 season.

In the official handbook for the new campaign, the chairman again urged supporters to exercise patience in the team's rebuilding phase. Borrowing a pre-Munich quote from Manchester United manager Matt Busby, then well on the way to full recovery after the Munich disaster, Swan insisted that: 'It was impossible to unearth overnight a team of players of the calibre that Hibs have been used to during the past 10 years'.

In the by now accustomed opener to the new season, former Hibs players Tommy Younger and Jimmy Harrower received a warm welcome from the fans when they took the field at Tynecastle wearing the colours of Liverpool. The visitors were eventually held to a 2–2 draw by an Edinburgh Select who were without the services of Gordon Smith for the first time since the inauguration of the series. Although failing to attract the huge crowds of the immediate post-war years, the annual event was still relatively popular with the fans at this stage, this particular fixture drawing almost 35,000 paying customers.

In keeping with the now well-established club policy of grooming their own players, particular interest centred around the public trial match at the stadium in midweek. Recent provisional signing

Kenny Allison from West Calder United caught the eye as the reserves, or Whites, deservedly defeated the Greens 3–1, with Baker scoring for the first XI, but the star of the show was undoubtedly 19-year-old Davie Gibson, who showed a maturity well above his years, oozing class and quality with his every move. Gibson, a Hearts supporter from Winchburgh in West Lothian, birthplace of Hibs' legendary goalkeeper of the 1920s Willie Harper, had already featured in a handful of first-team games, but his slight frame had filled out considerably since his debut two years before, and it was felt that the youngster was now ready to make the breakthrough into the top side.

Just days before the start of the new season, Bobby Combe severed an Easter Road connection that spanned more that 17 years when he accepted the position of trainer at Dumbarton. Former Motherwell player Willie Redpath replaced Combe as assistant to Willie Hunter, but Redpath's tenure at Easter Road would be short. He resigned just a few months later as the travelling involved made it difficult to combine the Easter Road job with his other occupation as a publican in the Motherwell area.

As usual, the season proper began with the League Cup. Drawn in a section that included Falkirk, Aberdeen and Kilmarnock, the crowd were given full value for their money on the opening afternoon with an action packed and exciting 3–2 home win over the Bairns. Admission prices had been raised from 2s to 2s 6d at the start of the season, but there could have been few complaints as the teams served up a treat of attacking play that thrilled both sets of supporters. Somewhat predictably, Joe Baker scored Hibs' first goal of the new season after only five minutes, but as exciting as the victory turned out to be, by far the biggest cheer of the afternoon was reserved for the still far from fit Gordon Smith, who was watching from the sidelines, when he kicked a loose ball back into play. Only that morning Smith had put the supporters' fears to rest by signing a new contract that would keep him at Easter Road for an 18th consecutive season.

It was around this time that the club recorded another first, although hardly one of national importance. Fans attending the reserve League Cup tie against Aberdeen at Easter Road at the beginning of August would notice that the pitch markings were wider than usual. During Hibs' pre-season tour of Holland the directors had been impressed with the 4in-wide lines used in that country as opposed to the normal 2.5in lines then in use by British clubs. No machine existed in this country that was capable of laying the 4in lines and one had been specially imported from the Continent. The new measurements not only made it far easier for fans at the other end of the pitch to follow play, but were also a boon for the television cameras. To back up this claim, a programme at the time reminded us that when matches at Wimbledon's centre court were televised the lines were normally widened for the benefit of the viewer.

Quicksilver Joe Baker kept Hibs' hopes of qualifying from the section alive when he scored three of his side's four goals against Aberdeen in a midweek fixture at Easter Road. In what turned out to be yet another memorable game for the livewire youngster, he ran the Dons' defence into the ground, particularly centre-half Clunie, who had no answer to the antics of the 17-year-old soon-to-be England Under-23 star. Because of Aberdeen's continuing refusal to play under floodlights, the evening kick-off had been brought forward by 15 minutes, but even this did not prevent the latter stages of the game being played out in virtual darkness. As if in a gesture of defiance by an exasperated Harry Swan, who still failed to understand the reluctance of teams to play under illumination, the field was bathed in a warm glow of light as the floodlights were switched on as the teams left the field at the final whistle.

In the corresponding reserve game at Pittodrie that same evening, a horrific injury to part-timer Jimmy Kane, father of future Hibs player Paul, led to the youngster being stretchered from the field suffering from a broken left leg after a sickening collision with giant Aberdeen goalkeeper Tubby Ogston. Snatched in 1957 from under the noses of both Hearts and Raith Rovers, who had both been keen to sign the player, there was only ever going to be one destination for lifelong Hibs supporter Kane. Tipped by some as a juvenile to be a Scotland player of the future, the injury would retard Kane's progress at Easter

Road, and he would shortly leave without managing to break into the first team. It was the second time in consecutive seasons that Hibs had been denied the services of a promising youngster by a serious injury. Twelve months before, at Shawfield, the blossoming Alex Marshall had suffered an injury similar to Kane's. He too would fail to make the grade at Easter Road.

Even this early in the season, Baker was at his goalscoring best, notching five in six League Cup games including the hat-trick against Aberdeen, the third of his Easter Road career so far. The section ultimately depended on the results against bogey team Kilmarnock, who won both home and away games against Hibs to progress into the quarter-finals on goal average at the expense of the Easter Road side. The much-travelled Joe McBride, later to join Hibs after an extremely productive spell with Celtic, scored against his future side in both League Cup games.

At the beginning of September, Hearts visited Easter Road for the first League encounter between the sides of the season. Fresh from a humbling 5–1 midweek defeat by Standard Liège in Belgium, the Tynecastle side's first-ever venture into competitive Continental competition, an anticipated European Cup 'reaction' from the Maroons after their disastrous midweek setback failed to materialise, and once again Hearts were far too good for their city rivals, running out easy 4–0 winners. All the goals were scored in a first-half blitz, and although the home side refused to capitulate during the second half, it was always a lost cause, and after just two games Hibs were in 13th position in the table.

A poll released around this time in the popular sports magazine *France Football* listed Hibs in 11th place out of the 47 clubs who had participated in the European Cup competition up until then. Manchester United were in second place behind runaway leaders Real Madrid. Rangers, Scotland's only other representatives apart from Hearts, who were yet to win a game in the tournament, were listed in 22nd place.

The sparkling form of Baker had come to the attention of the England selectors and Joe made football history by becoming the first-ever Englishman playing for a Scottish side to represent his country when he was selected for the Under-23 side to face Poland at Hillsborough. Previously the English authorities had refused to even consider any player for selection if playing outside the Football League, but England's poor showing in the recent World Cup Finals in Sweden and Baker's goalscoring exploits had made it difficult to ignore the player. Although failing to score himself, Baker laid on one of the goals in England's victory, and only a late foul when he was about to shoot, resulting in a penalty-kick that was scored by Bobby Charlton, prevented the Hibs player from figuring on the score sheet. Watching from the stand against Poland were his proud mum and brother Gerry, who would soon replace Joe at Easter Road. Chairman Swan and manager Shaw had also travelled to Sheffield to lend moral support. Baker's selection for England meant that Hibs had now supplied players to all five home countries.

The recent impressive form of John Grant had also come to the attention of the Scottish selectors, and the speedy and constructive defender, who had already represented Scotland several times at Under-23 level, won his first full cap in a 3–0 victory over Wales at Wrexham. Converted from his original position of inside-forward or wing-half to full-back by manager Hugh Shaw, Grant had benefited greatly by playing directly behind the experienced Eddie Turnbull and had developed into a first-class defender. Also making their debuts against Wales were 18-year-old Denis Law of Huddersfield, at that time the youngest player to represent the full Scotland side, and Kilmarnock centre-half Willie Toner, who would sign briefly for Hibs a few years later.

The Scottish selectors had attracted the fury of the national press when they discarded the 'ageing' Turnbull from the full international set-up after the Hibs skipper's impressive World Cup campaign. He was chosen instead to captain the Scottish League side against the English League at Ibrox. The former Manchester United target found himself in direct opposition to United's recent record £45,000 acquisition from Sheffield Wednesday, Albert Quixall, and as if to show United what they had missed when they failed to land the Hibs captain a few years before, Turnbull was in immense form and hardly gave the fair-haired Englishman a kick of the ball, the game ending in a 1–1 draw.

Full-back Willie McFarlane, who had joined the club from Tranent Juniors in 1949 and had featured in Hibs' inaugural European Cup tie in 1955, was transferred to Raith Rovers in mid-September for a fee in the region of £1,500. Like Govan, Ormond and several others before him, McFarlane had been in dispute with the club over a benefit payment and had refused to sign a new contract, a stalemate that had resulted in the defender being placed on the transfer list. McFarlane would return to Easter Road as manager 11 years later after spells in charge at Hawick Royal Albert and Stirling Albion.

With the post-war crowd boom largely a thing of the past, that year's AGM revealed that a profit of £8,165 had been made during the 1957–58 season. This still represented a substantial return, although the Scottish Cup run had been responsible for much of this figure. By now the board of directors had been increased to four for the first time since the 1930s, with the earlier unanimous co-opting of Robert Powrie. After 12 years as a director at Easter Road, a period that included the halcyon days of the late 1940s and early 1950s, Wilson Terris, as the retiring in turn director, lost his seat to Kenny McIntyre in a vote taken that same evening. MacIntyre had been the club treasurer for more than 20 years. Rumours of a rift between Terris and Harry Swan had been rife for some months following a dispute involving the Scottish League's opposition to the ill-fated Floodlight League. Swan felt that Terris, as a Hibs director, should have toed the party line and voted in favour of the competition, but solicitor Terris, as vice president of the Scottish League, felt obliged to go along with his committee's recommendations and oppose the motion. Things had never been quite the same between the two men since. Terris, like Swan a legislator of considerable ability, immediately accepted an offer to join the board of directors at Cowdenbeath, a role that would allow him to continue as vice-president of the Scottish League.

As rivals Hearts were winning the League Cup at Hampden with a convincing 5–1 victory against Partick Thistle at the end of October, there was even more misery for the Hibs fans at Easter Road that afternoon when Airdrie won a dour game 3–2. Thrice in the lead, Kenny Allison, in only his third game for the first team, twice managed to pull one back for the home side, only narrowly failing to score a third that his industry would have deserved. For the first time in senior football all three Ormond brothers were playing in the same game. As well as older brother Willie of Hibs, the Airdrie side included inside-forward Robert and outside-left Gilbert, who scored his side's winning goal.

On the first day of November, Rangers easily won a one-sided encounter at Ibrox 4–0 against a lacklustre Hibs side that had been forced to play much of the second half with 10 men after Ormond had limped off injured. That same afternoon at Easter Road, after being told at one stage that he might never play again, at his own request Gordon Smith made his first-ever appearance for the reserve side after a remarkable career spanning 18 seasons. Pitched as a 16-year-old directly into first-team action during the war years, Smith had rarely been out of the team since, usually only because of injury, each time returning directly into the League side without the benefit of a run in the reserves. To be totally accurate, technically Smith had played several games for the second team during the war years, but although some reserve competitions had remained, the wartime shortage of players made fielding a reserve side almost impossible, and the same players usually turned out for both the first and second teams. On a miserable wet and windy winter afternoon, a crowd of over 6,000 were drawn to Easter Road, most of them to see Smith. The Hibs side also included Eddie Turnbull, who had been dropped after the defeat by Airdrie the previous week. Goals by McCalman and Thomson gave the home side a share of the spoils against a Rangers second team featuring future Hibs captain Sammy Baird, but the most important thing for the majority of the spectators was the fact that Smith's ankle held up well after his lengthy absence.

The 'Gay Gordon' made a fairytale return to first-team action seven days later in a 4–4 home draw with Third Lanark, Joe Baker scoring yet another hat-trick. By a curious twist of fate it was exactly 11 years to the day since Smith had equalled the record goal-scoring tally for a wide man when scoring five of Hibs' eight goals against the same opposition. The dropped point meant that Hibs were now 15th, or third bottom, almost the entire length of the table separating them from table-topping Hearts.

At Love Street a few weeks later, Joe Baker came face to face with brother Gerry for the first time in senior football. Gerry, who would replace his younger brother at Easter Road before too long, was making his first appearance for St Mirren after his recent transfer from Motherwell. Despite his broad Scottish accent Gerry was actually born in America, but unlike Joe, with the regulations then in place concerning national eligibility, he was entitled to represent Scotland. He never did manage to play for Scotland, but he was capped at full international level by the country of his birth. The afternoon ended in disappointment for the Englishman as the older brother made a goalscoring start to a St Mirren career that would culminate in his winning a Scottish Cup medal against Aberdeen in April.

Davie Gibson had been earning rave reviews in the reserves since the beginning of the season and he replaced Andy Aitken in the team to face Celtic at Easter Road to become a fixture in the side. Against the Hoops, the Winchburgh lad was an immediate success with his subtle prompting from midfield, but not for the first time Joe Baker was the star of the show with another brilliant hat-trick, his second in four games, as the Celts were defeated 3–2.

Before the start, only four of Hibs' 14 League games that season had ended in victory, seven in defeat, and the local press had been inundated with letters from concerned fans voicing anxiety over the poor form of the side. Chairman Swan felt the need to reply in print regarding the concerns of the supporters alarmed at the fall from grace of a side that only a few years before had been among the finest in the land. Denying rumours of dissension in the camp, Swan again pleaded with the fans to have patience, adding that: 'No excuses were needed'. 'The team', he said, 'were merely going through the bad spell that befalls most sides, but we have the foundation and potential to overcome the difficulties'. As if to prove the point, Hibs recovered from a disastrous start against Celtic, conceding two goals in the first six minutes, to win 3–2. Livewire Baker, playing his best game for weeks, was immense, with Scottish international centre-half Bobby Evans a helpless spectator as the fleet-footed 18-year-old ran him into the ground.

By this time Baker had become the hottest property in the Scottish game. An enquiry from Liverpool for the centre-forward was immediately rejected by Swan, and at Dens Park a few days later Wolves manager Stan Cullis arrived in the boardroom after the game claiming to have been in the area watching a junior player, when it was thought he had watched at least part of the game, and presumably Baker, from the terracing.

The Hibernian Supporters' Association held the first of what it was hoped would be an annual rally in the Usher Hall on Sunday 7 December 1958. All proceeds from the highly successful evening, which featured the well-known Hibs supporter Johnny Victory and his repertoire company, were donated to the Hospital Broadcast Fund, which continued to be run by Willie Fairgrieve despite the recent sudden death of co-presenter Jimmy Bourhill. During the proceedings, which were attended by past and present players from several prominent Scottish and English clubs, Lawrie Reilly was presented with a cine camera on behalf of the Association by Leith MP James Hoy in recognition of the player's services to club and country.

A few days after the Usher Hall rally, the long overdue Lawrie Reilly testimonial match took place at Easter Road. As promised by Sir George Graham, secretary of the SFA, a Scottish International Select lined up in opposition. The legendary Stanley Matthews had promised to play for the International XI, but injury prevented him from travelling to the capital and he was replaced in the side by Blackpool teammate Jackie Mudie. Like Matthews, the star of the evening found himself unable to take part in his own testimonial, but in Reilly's case it had nothing to do with injury. Shortly before the game, the bureaucratic SFA ludicrously decreed that because he was not registered with any official body, Reilly himself could not play in the match, and so he was forced to watch the proceedings from the stand. Even more bemusing was the fact that for insurance purposes, all the players in the International Select had to be temporarily transferred to Hibs for the evening, making the Easter Road squad worth an additional £150,000 overnight.

Apart from Mudie and former Hibs and Scotland teammate Bobby Johnstone, a number of other prominent personalities had willingly given their time to pay tribute to a former colleague, but unfortunately the cold biting wind and driving rain had kept the attendance under the 7,000 mark. Nevertheless, this could still be determined a reasonable turnout considering the atrocious conditions, and those who were brave enough to face the elements enjoyed a great night of high scoring and thrill-a-minute incident as the home side ran out 9–3 winners. All the remaining four members of the Famous Five managed to get their names on the score sheet, and it was deplorable that Reilly had been denied a final opportunity to join them. Although only a friendly, Scotland player Tommy Docherty, then with Arsenal, had been particularly impressed by the display of inside-left Davie Gibson, predicting a big future for the Winchburgh player.

Goalscorers for Hibs were Baker (2), Smith (2), Ormond (2), Turnbull, Fox and McClelland. Scorers for the Select were Johnstone (2) and Liddell.

Hibernian: Leslie, Young, McClelland, Turnbull, Paterson, Preston, Smith, Fox, Baker, Gibson, Ormond.
Scottish International Select: Farm, Grant, McNaught, Docherty, McColl, Peacock, McKenzie, Fernie, Mudie, Johnstone, Liddell.
Referee: J. Bissett (Edinburgh)

At the post-match banquet for the players in the North British Hotel, Harry Swan paid tribute to Reilly for his outstanding service to club and country. Praising the player's loyalty, the chairman confessed that even during the dark days of the dispute between the parties in 1953, he never really expected Hibs fan Reilly to leave Easter Road.

Just after Christmas Tommy Preston was sent off for the first time in his senior career after a clash with former Hibs player Gerry Mayes during a narrow 4–3 victory against Kilmarnock in Edinburgh. Goals from Desmond Fox, who by this time had become something of a regular in the side, Baker, who scored twice, and a Turnbull penalty gave Hibs their third win in a row, results that saw them climb from a precipitous basement position to end the year in the top half of the table for the first time that season.

There was a unexpected boost for the team and the supporters when the famous Continental football journalist Dr Willy Meisi, writing in *World Sports* magazine, proposed the young Joe Baker of Hibernian as a possible long-term replacement for the legendary Nat Lofthouse in the full England side. Already the goalscoring ability and exciting performances of Baker were drawing a rapidly increasing circle of admirers, and in Meisi's opinion the centre-forward, while not yet the finished article, certainly had the capability to develop his physique and technique further and blossom into a top-class player.

At Tynecastle on the opening day of 1959, veteran Willie Ormond was in international form. Both sides were handicapped by the strong winds and driving rain that made good football difficult, but Hibs managed to harness the conditions better, playing neat passing football on the ground while their opponents continually persisted in playing the ball in the air. Ormond headed a Baker cross past Marshall early in the first half to open the scoring, and although Hearts equalised against the run of play shortly after, Hibs never looked in any real danger of losing. As if to make a mockery of his years, this was the Ormond of old. Using all of his experience, trickery and speed, the outside-left tantalised the Hearts defence throughout the 90 minutes, particularly left-back George Thomson, scoring a second himself and laying on a third for Desmond Fox near the end in Hibs' 3–1 victory. The result, and more importantly the performance, encouraged 'Outlook' of the *Edinburgh Evening News* to report that: 'On the evidence offered at Tynecastle yesterday it begins to seem as if we shall have to look to Easter Road for the next attempt to bring the League flag back to Edinburgh. For this had all the appearance of a defeat over a team on the way out by a team on the way in.' While premature to say the least, and eventually proved to be well wide of the mark, 'Outlook's' comments were still well appreciated by the Hibs supporters, who had been forced to watch from the sidelines as their great rivals won not only the League Championship and two League Cups, but also the coveted Scottish Cup.

Although failing to figure on the score sheet at Tynecastle, Joe Baker continued to make goalscoring headlines as he taunted defenders the length and breadth of the country. The impressive victory at Tynecastle was followed 48 hours later by a 2–2 draw against Motherwell at Easter Road, Baker almost inevitably scoring both Hibs' goals. His second, emulating the great Lawrie Reilly, was scored with the last kick of the game. It is perhaps interesting to note that according to press reports at the time, over 36,000 watched the game. It was estimated that 'only' 6,000 of them were visiting supporters, a figure that nowadays would be the envy of most sides in Scotland for home games. Yet another hat-trick, his fourth of the season, in a fine 4–1 Hibs victory against Queen of the South in Dumfries, shot Baker to the top of the League goalscoring charts with 25, one ahead of second-placed Willie Bauld of Hearts.

The ongoing pursuit of Scottish Cup glory began that year at Starks Park. In a desperately disappointing 90 minutes, Raith's lead from the penalty spot appeared to be enough to send the Fifers through to the next round, but shortly before the end Gordon Smith saved the day when he struck a low shot into the net from a Baker cross to earn his side a replay at Easter Road. The goal would prove to be Gordon Smith's 364th in a green-and-white jersey, including wartime games, and although he was not to know it at the time it was to be the last he would ever score for Hibs. With the replay designated for the following Monday, it seemed at first that this would prevent Baker from making a piece of football history as the first Scottish League player to represent England against Scotland in an international match. Both he and teammate Jackie Plenderleith had been selected for their respective sides in direct opposition to each other in an Under-23 match, the game due to take place at Ibrox in midweek. Unfortunately, bad weather forced the postponement of both games, the Under-23 fixture indefinitely.

In the Scottish Cup replay at Easter Road a week later, a strike by Turnbull from the penalty spot after Smith had been somewhat fortunate in being judged to have been fouled in the box, and another by Fox, kept Hibs' Scottish Cup hopes alive with a 2–1 win that set up a meeting against Falkirk in the second round. Ten minutes before the end of the game, Joe Baker was stretchered off with a suspected broken leg after a particularly hefty challenge, giving Raith a real opportunity against 10 men, but the weakened home side just managed to hold on to their lead against a spirited Fife side who were then labouring in the lower regions of the League. Alfie Conn, signed earlier in the season from Hearts, scored Raith's goal, and both he and former Hibs player Willie McFarlane had been determined to put one over on Hibs for entirely different reasons.

An X-ray after the game revealed Baker's injury to be not as serious as first feared, and he was selected for the Scottish Cup meeting with Falkirk at Easter Road the following Saturday. Within minutes of the start, however, it was obvious that Baker had not recovered sufficiently to give his best. A 3–1 victory with all the Hibs goals coming in the first 45 minutes greatly flattered the home side, the unlucky Bairns striking the woodwork three times in the second period as they endeavored to force a replay. Regardless of merit, however, Hibs took their place in the draw for the third round. The decision to rush Baker back prematurely had rebounded on Hibs. Clearly still not fully fit, it had been a mistake to play the talented centre-forward, who had now exacerbated the injury and would be forced to miss the following five games.

Against Partick Thistle at Easter Road in the next round, Hibs again raced to a three-goal interval lead, but this time there was never any doubt about the final result. Two goals each from Aitken and

Ormond eventually gave the home side an emphatic 4–1 win and a place in the quarter-finals against Third Lanark at Cathkin Park.

A League rehearsal at Cathkin a week before the Cup tie at the same venue showed Third Lanark, then managed by future Hibs manager Bob Shankly, to be dangerous opponents as they came from behind to earn a 2–2 draw. It was anticipated, however, that the return of Baker, who had almost recovered from his Stark's Park injury nearly a month before, and Gordon Smith, who had also missed the League match after being injured in training, would enable the visitors to take another step on the road towards a second successive Scottish Cup Final seven days later. The game, which took place on Saturday 14 March 1959, was played in typically exciting Cup-tie spirit. Even boosted by the return from injury of both Smith and Baker, Hibs still found themselves two goals behind at the interval. Man of the Match Ormond gave the Edinburgh side a glimmer of hope when he pulled a goal back midway through the second half, but even with the home side reduced to 10 men after outside-left McInnes had been sent off midway through the second half, try as they might the Edinburgh side just could not snatch an equalizer. Scorning a string of chances to take the tie back to Easter Road, the Scottish Cup dream was over for yet another year. During the at times 'towsy' game, Gordon Smith picked up yet another niggling injury, and although the 25,000 spectators were not to know it at the time, the 'Gay Gordon' had played his last game for Hibs after 18, often illustrious, seasons. Near the end of the game Smith changed places with Baker, who moved to the right wing. Ironically, the move meant that Smith, who had established his reputation mainly as an outside-right, ended his Easter Road career as it had begun all those years before, as a centre-forward.

As would be expected, the Cathkin defeat brought letters of complaint by the sackful from irate Hibs fans. One complained of being repeatedly let down by a club who 'continually fielded obviously unfit players'. According to him Turnbull, Baker and Smith were in no way fit enough to play, and their selection in his eyes may have cost Hibs the Scottish Cup victory so craved by the supporters. One can only wonder whether, in the circumstances, the correspondent would have been prepared to suffer a half-fit Gordon Smith than not at all?

The defeat at Cathkin had also put paid to the Baker brothers' dreams of opposing each other at the concluding stage of the tournament. In the semi-final Third Lanark were beaten by Aberdeen, who in turn were defeated 3–1 by St Mirren in the Final, Gerry Baker scoring one the goals that took the Cup to Love Street for only the second time in the club's history. In roles reversed from 12 months before, this time it was the younger Baker's turn to watch from the stand.

Just a few weeks after the Cup defeat by Third Lanark, yet another of the legendary Famous Five made his last competitive appearance for the club when the inspirational captain Eddie Turnbull led the team onto the field before the 2–1 home defeat by Dundee on 4 April 1959. It was perhaps fitting that a poor game worthy of little comment should include an own-goal by either side. Newspaper columnist 'Tron Kirk' of the *Evening News* bemoaned the fact that the end-of-season games were with us again, wondering why players 'could not keep faith with the loyal fans who turned up, by giving them value for their money'. Both Jim Scott and John Young were given their first-team debuts, but it was asking too much of the youngsters to perform well when their more experienced colleagues appeared disinterested. Although he managed to finish the game, Turnbull picked up an injury after 20 minutes that would keep him out of the side for the final two League games.

With Turnbull and Preston injured, and Ormond on international duty, a weakened Hibs side could only manage a 2–2 draw with Partick Thistle at Firhill in the penultimate game of the season. That afternoon at Wembley, England captain Billy Wright of Wolves was making his 100th full international appearance, as Willie Ormond of Hibs was winning his sixth and final full Scotland cap in the 1–0 defeat by the Auld Enemy. All five of Ormond's other appearances had come in 1954, two of them in the World Cup Finals in Switzerland. The word 'cap' is actually a misnomer. At that time England players received one cap per game, but Scottish players were only physically awarded an actual cap when playing against either of the home countries. Only one per season was issued, which would list the games played during that time.

Bringing the curtain down on yet another disappointing domestic season, the final whistle came as welcome relief to the fewer than 5,000 fans who had suffered a dreadful afternoon that ended in a 1–0 home defeat by lowly Stirling Albion, a result that was perhaps indicative of the season the Hibs fans had endured. Regardless of the poor fare on offer at Easter Road, the attention of most Hibs fans inside the ground was focused via transistor radios towards Parkhead where, that same afternoon, Celtic were doing deadly rivals Rangers a huge favour by defeating Hearts 2–1 to deny the Tynecastle side their second consecutive League title. Although losing 2–1 to Aberdeen themselves, the defeat of Hearts gave the Light Blues the Championship by two clear points.

That same afternoon, relegation strugglers Dunfermline, who desperately needed both points from their final game to escape the drop, incredibly defeated mid-table Partick Thistle 10–1 to doom Falkirk to the Second Division. Outside-left Harry Melrose scored six of his side's goals to shatter Gordon Smith's First Division record score for a winger when he scored five against Third Lanark in 1947 from the outside-right position.

Once again, Baker ended the season as Hibs' top goalscorer with 25 League goals from 26 appearances as the Greens were forced to settle for a disappointing 10th place in the table, a massive 18 points behind the leaders. There had been plus points, however. During the year Davie Gibson had become a regular in the side, John Frye was used more and more, and youngsters Jim Scott, John Young and Malcolm Bogie had all made a breakthrough into the first team. True to policy, the directors had refused to satisfy the cravings of the supporters by signing big names and had again decided to follow the process of giving youth its chance.

Eight players were released at the end of the season, including the long-serving John Paterson, who had been a regular throughout the glory years, Jim Thomson, John Boyle, Kenny Allison and Alex Marshall, who had failed to recover from the horrific injury received in 1957. Although not initially listed among the frees, Gordon Smith was not on the retained list either, causing widespread anxiety and speculation among the supporters. These fears were realised a few days later when, after a meeting between the manager and player, Harry Swan having opted out of that particular responsibility, it was announced that the club were reluctantly freeing the veteran player with the 'keenest of regrets' after satisfying themselves that his injury would not respond to the rigours of another hard season. Smith would later confess that he felt as if he had received a sledgehammer blow when he was informed that the club he had grown to love had released him. Since first pulling on a green-and-white jersey nearly 20 years before, the former Hearts fan had become a devout Hibs supporter and found great difficulty in coming to terms with the fact that he had been discarded by the club, particularly as he still felt fit enough to play at the top level for several more years.

The news of Smith's departure from Easter Road was greeted with disbelief, not only in the capital but also throughout the entire country, and it brought the expected backlash of protest from supporters stunned at the lack of loyalty and sentiment shown by the club. Once again the newspapers were inundated with letters of protest, many from Hearts supporters. One Hibs fan, labelling himself 'A Gordon for me' went as far as to claim that 'Loyal Hibs fans will never forget this despicable treatment to one of Scotland's premier footballing artists'. But it was too late, the Maestro had gone.

An offer of a five-game end-of-season tour of Spain had been accepted, with the opening match to be played against Spanish champions and Fairs Cup-holders Barcelona, who would retain the European trophy the following year as well as representing Spain in the European Cup. Played in the recently opened 'Grande Stadia', which was soon to become the 'Nou Camp', and watched by over 50,000 spectators, Desmond Fox opened the scoring inside the first few minutes, and although the home side equalised before the interval, Hibs had been the better side during this time. Taking advantage of six second-half substitutes, a move denied the Scottish team under SFA regulations, the much fresher Barcelona went ahead when Grant put one past his own 'keeper, and after that it was no contest as the home side ran out worthy 5–1 winners.

Further defeats by Tarrasso and Second Division side Elche followed, and with the match against Murcia cancelled due to a waterlogged pitch, the tour ended without a win on 31 May 1959, when Gijon, who had recently beaten the mighty Real Madrid, recorded a slender 2–1 victory after Scott had equalised in the first half. It was during this match that Eddie Turnbull, now fully recovered from the injury that had ruled him out of Hibs' final two League games of the season, brought the curtain down on an illustrious playing career when he made what would turn out to be his final appearance in a green-and-white jersey.

Although disappointed at ending the tour without a victory, it was felt that the experience of playing in football-mad Spain would ultimately be of more use, particularly for the younger players, than playing against opponents of a lesser calibre.

Any Hibs fan wishing to follow his team's progress in Spain via the pages of the newspapers would have to look extremely closely for coverage in one local daily publication. Whilst Hearts tour of Australia, where they played mainly against inferior amateur opposition, was covered extensively in photographs, match reports and interviews with players and officials, even the 'Sporting Card' column in the *Pink News* listing all the sporting fixtures for the forthcoming week, including cricket, bowls and athletics, failed to mention most, if not all, of Hibs' Spanish fixtures.

Gordon Smith's Return and a Goalscoring Record

John Paterson and 'Tiger' Thomson, both released at the end of the season, had joined Ayr United during the summer. Gordon Smith, who had personally financed a third operation on his injured ankle, which was carried out by Sir John Bruce, was still far from full fitness but not short of offers from other clubs. Several were said to be actively seeking his signature, with Dundee thought to be favourites to sign the former Easter Road star, but as yet he was still to decide his future.

Shortly after arriving back in Scotland from the tour of Spain, trainer Bill Hunter announced that he had decided to return to his previous post at Raith Rovers. The club had originally decided to keep Eddie Turnbull, now obviously nearing the end of his playing career, for another year despite the player's stated preference for a free transfer to his home-town side Falkirk. Bill Hunter's vacant position was immediately offered to the veteran player. Turnbull had no hesitation in accepting the post, leaving Willie Ormond as the sole on-field survivor of the legendary 'Five'. Turnbull would end his playing career as the only member of the celebrated forward line not to gain financially from either a transfer or a benefit match. Smith would ultimately receive the proceeds from two transfers as well as his testimonial match, Reilly a testimonial, Johnstone several lucrative moves and Ormond a free transfer to Falkirk in 1961.

Determined that Hibs should remain one of the fittest sides in the country, the new first-team trainer sacrificed part of his summer holiday to attend a course on weight training, demonstrating even then an attention to detail that would help establish his reputation as one of the leading thinkers in the game.

As always, a fresh crop of young hopefuls had joined the club during the summer. Duncan Falconer, Morris Stevenson, Graham Pate, Alan Robertson and goalkeeper Willie Wilson lined up alongside their more experienced colleagues to be put through their paces by the new trainer and his assistant Jim Cumming on the first day of pre-season training. Jimmy McColl was still in charge of the reserve side. John Grant replaced Turnbull as club captain. Joe Baker, a part-timer since joining the club in 1955, had decided to sever his tenure as an apprentice engineer with a Motherwell firm and was now a full-time footballer.

There was an early meeting of the Edinburgh rivals, but this time not on the field of play. By a strange twist of fate, both the capital clubs had decided to relieve the monotony of pre-season training by hiring a coach to transport the players to a training session on the Gullane sands on the same day. With a 15-

minute start on their rivals, the Hearts players had been dropped off at Aberlady with instructions to run the rest of the way. Several minutes later the Hibs players unknowingly disembarked at the same location. On arriving at Gullane by coach, Jimmy McColl was astonished to find Hearts trainer John Harvey welcoming the first of the Gorgie players with a much-needed cup of tea. After the arrival of the Easter Road players a few minutes later, and the good-natured jocular taunts between the contestants, most of whom knew each other well, both sides settled down for their respective training sessions a few hundred yards apart.

The 1959–60 season was Harry Swan's 25th at the helm of the club and he was by now firmly established as one of the finest administrators in the history of the Scottish game. Since standing down as president of the SFA in 1956, he had remained within the corridors of power but in a deliberately lesser capacity, and he was now actively involved with the SFA Finance Committee.

At that year's AGM, Swan was elected a life director of the club in appreciation of his long, faithful and shrewd service. It was disclosed at this meeting that a loss of £4,000 had been made the previous year. This deficit had been mainly due to the considerable costs incurred in concreting the main and north terraces, a contract, incidentally, that had been won by a building company owned by Harry Swan's brother. This modernisation, the club was assured, would be much appreciated by the supporters. Gone were the archaic, weed-infested, ash-backed wooden sleepers that had been in place since 1924, and it was announced that the remainder of the ground would be completed in the near future.

By now the attraction of the annual charity game against English opposition was beginning to wear thin. Although an otherwise healthy 26,237 watched the Select side defeat Newcastle United 4–3 at Easter Road, in what one correspondent described as 'a marvellous advertisement for the game of football', the attendance fell well below that of previous years. Future Hibs goalkeeper Ronnie Simpson, then nearing the veteran stage even for a 'keeper and thought by many to be nearing the end of his career, was in the visitors' goal for the first half. Fate would intervene in spectacular fashion before he would play his last game.

Only that morning the inconceivable had happened. Mirroring a similar move by Peter Kerr, a Hibs legend of the 1920s, Gordon Smith had stunned the whole of Edinburgh, and the entire country for that matter, by signing for Hibs' greatest rivals Hearts, in spite, it was said, of stiff opposition from around 14 clubs. Almost 20 years too late, the Maroons had got their man at last. As with Smith in 1941, Hearts had dallied before making a move for Peter Kerr in 1910, allowing Hibs to step in to sign the player. After 16 years at Easter Road, during which time he had captained the great side of the 1920s, Kerr had also switched his allegiance to Tynecastle in a move that caused the same consternation among the Hibs fans then as Smith's move did 33 years later. The Gay Gordon's move to Gorgie, however, was not universally accepted by some in the Tynecastle boardroom, who still resented what they considered to be a snub by the player in 1941, but any fears that he would not be made welcome by the playing staff, after almost two decades wearing the green and white of Hibs, were soon dispelled. On entering the home dressing room for the first time, Smith was greeted by a standing ovation from his new colleagues who were fully aware that they had been joined by a genius who still had much to offer the game. In later years he would recall fondly the reception of the Hearts players, which had made him feel instantly at home, but confessed to a certain resentment during his time at Tynecastle at being cheered by the same Hearts fans who had mercilessly jeered him throughout his time as a Hibs player.

As if losing Smith to their nearest rivals was not bad enough, the League Cup campaign could only be described as disastrous. Failing to win even a single point in the six section games, it was the club's worst-ever performance in the tournament. In the opening game at Easter Road, the Scott brothers, Jim of Hibs and Alex of Rangers, opposed each other for the first time in senior football, emulating Davie and Jock Shaw in the 1940s.

During the summer goalkeeper Lawrie Leslie had received treatment on the operating table for an elbow injury received the previous season that would ultimately threaten his career, and he was replaced in goal on the opening day by Jackie Wren. In the blazing summer sunshine, a first-half goal by Willie Ormond at the Dunbar end of the ground was poor consolation against the six scored by the Ibrox side as Rangers, and in particular four-goal Edinburgh-born Ralph Brand, ran a makeshift Hibs team into the ground. Wren was made the scapegoat for the humiliating start to the season, and the following Wednesday Hibs gave 17-year-old goalkeeper Willie Wilson, only recently signed from Musselburgh Windsor, his first-team debut at Dens Park. The youngster, who had been on the Easter Road payroll less than a month, although badly at fault for one of the goals, made a satisfactory first start to his senior career as his side went down 4–3. Future Hibs player Alan Cousin scored the winning goal for Dundee just 15 seconds from the end.

The goalkeeper had performed well in the public trial match, and although on the wrong end of a 7–2 defeat with Joe Baker scoring four, the young custodian was blameless for any of the goals and his display suggested that the club, well known for unearthing brilliant young goalkeepers, had made yet another exciting capture. Taking over the mantle from Tommy Younger, albeit by only a few weeks, as the youngest Hibs goalkeeper since the war, Wilson was still well behind Ronnie Simpson as the youngest ever to play for a Scottish side. Future Hibs goalkeeper Simpson had been called from his school classroom to make his debut for Queen's Park against Clyde in the Summer Cup in the closing days of World War Two at the ripe old age of 14.

Wilson kept his place against Motherwell at Easter Road three days later, prompting the obviously dissatisfied Jackie Wren to table a transfer request, and the way was clear even this early for the youngster to make the position his own. With only 18 minutes remaining of a hard-fought Cup tie, Hibs were deservedly leading after a strike by Desmond Fox when Motherwell centre-forward Ian St John, playing up the slope, recorded his own piece of history by scoring three goals in only two and a half minutes. The previous fastest hat-trick by a Scottish player had been the three goals scored in three minutes by Celtic's Jimmy McGrory in 1936, ironically also against Motherwell. It was not the fastest treble in British football, however, as that record belonged to John Scarth of Gillingham, who was reckoned to have scored three in only two minutes against Leyton Orient in 1952.

Further defeats by all the teams in the section, including a 5–1 rout at Ibrox on the same day that Gordon Smith was making his debut for Hearts against Kilmarnock at Tynecastle, saw Hibs plunge to the bottom of the group, having failed to win even a solitary point, scoring only nine goals against the 25 conceded. Although in the circumstances not much of a consolation for the disconsolate fans, that afternoon at Easter Road the reserves had beaten the Rangers second team 7–0.

In view of the disastrous League Cup campaign this may not have been the correct time to announce the fact that more centre stand season tickets had been made available to the general public. Also, at the insistence of the current holders, there had been a change of policy and tickets could now be transferred within the same family.

In the League, a makeshift Hibs side put up a great fight in a 2–2 draw at Tynecastle, with the unusual sight of Gordon Smith in a Hearts jersey almost too painful for the large Easter Road support to contemplate. Once again it was Baker who proved a thorn in the side of the home defence, scoring both his side's goals, but in the latter stages of the game Gordon Smith missed a great chance to give his new side both points when he blasted high over the bar from close range after a Murray shot had rebounded from the post.

After repeated attempts to sign the player had failed, Andy Aitken finally joined English First Division side West Bromwich Albion in mid-September for a fee around the £8,000 mark. First spotted by Matt Busby playing for Irish side Cliftonville during his National Service days, Aitken had been recommended to Hibs by the Manchester United manager. His best spell for the club had been during the Scottish Cup run the previous season when his form had been inspirational, but since his injury in the Cup Final he had been unable to regain a regular place in the League side and welcomed the opportunity of first-team football in England. Albion, then one of the top sides in the country, would finish the season in fourth place.

After only four League games, consecutive defeats by Rangers and Third Lanark, the latter by a 5–3 scoreline, meant that even this early in the season Hibs were languishing a lowly 13th in the table and something clearly had to be done. An audacious attempt to sign Jimmy Wardhaugh of Hearts, who had recently asked to be placed on the transfer list at Tynecastle, was rejected out of hand by the Gorgie club, and instead Hibs turned their attention to a former player. The predatory skills of Baker had already accounted for half of the 16 goals scored by the Easter Road side in both competitions, and it was felt that an experienced old head was necessary to take the pressure off the youngster. With this in mind, Hugh Shaw motored to Manchester to sign former Famous Five stalwart Bobby Johnstone from Manchester City, in only Hibs' second major financial venture into the transfer market since the signing of Alec Linwood more than 10 years before. Unsettled for some time in Manchester, with the club usually struggling at the wrong end of the table despite reaching consecutive FA Cup Finals in 1955 and 1956, Johnstone had posted several transfer demands. Just recently he had rejected moves by Leicester City and several other top English sides and was keen to return to Scotland. Such was the excitement surrounding the player's return that just under 10,000 turned up to watch the reserve derby against Hearts at Easter Road on the Tuesday evening in anticipation of seeing him play. Sadly they were disappointed, as Johnstone was still in Manchester tidying up his affairs, but they did witness the Greens second string continuing their four-game unbeaten run by winning 5–2, with goals from Fraser, (2) Fox (2) and Baxter.

Although significantly more portly than when he left the club in 1955, Johnstone soon proved a valuable acquisition. Receiving a rousing and enthusiastic reception from an above average home crowd of 24,000 as he took the field, the player coincidentally resumed where he had left off in his first stint with the club in a League encounter against Kilmarnock. Although failing to score himself and looking short of match practice, which was only to be expected as it had been over a month since his last game, Johnstone showed that he had lost little of his flair, and it was obvious that the forward line, and Baker in particular, would benefit greatly from his presence and experience. John Baxter chose the 4–2 victory over the Ayrshire club to finally confirm that he had replaced Eddie Turnbull in the power shooting stakes by twice scoring from free-kicks well outside the box. A third effort went narrowly past the post with the 'keeper well beaten.

Even with Johnstone in the side, Hibs at first found victories hard to come by, particularly another 3–1 defeat by Motherwell, this time at Fir Park, the Lanarkshire side's third victory over the Greens in just under two months. In what would prove to be another rollercoaster of a season, however, among the lows there were some remarkable highs. A 7–4 victory over Dunfermline at Easter Road, Joe Baker scoring three, was followed seven days later on 24 October 1959 by an 11–1 victory over at Airdrie at Broomfield. Incredibly, Hibs' first away win of the season was the highest scoring League victory ever by a visiting side in British football, beating the previous best of 10–0 established by Sheffield United against Port Vale in 1892. The free-scoring Baker again scored a hat-trick, but on this occasion he was upstaged by Tommy Preston, who scored four. Hibs' other goalscorers were McLeod (2) and Ormond, with even full-back McClelland getting in on the act.

Hibernian: Wilson, Grant, McClelland, Young, Plenderleith, Baxter, McLeod, Johnstone, Baker, Preston, Ormond.

Amazingly, as the first team were running wild at Broomfield, the reserves were also going goal crazy at Easter Road, defeating Airdrie's second team 8–0. Unfortunately for the Hibs supporters, however, the ecstasy of the Broomfield result was tempered by the news that Hearts had defeated Third Lanark in the League Cup Final at Hampden, Gordon Smith collecting his first-ever Cup-winners' medal in senior football. Hibs' victory, however, supplied one newspaper with what was entitled 'the quote of the week', sent in by one optimistic Easter Road supporter, who stated: 'If we can afford to give Hearts two forwards [Smith and Crawford] to help them win the Cup, and still score 11 goals ourselves, then we are doing alright.'

A 3–3 home draw against Celtic in the League, Bobby Johnstone scoring his first goal for the club since his return from Manchester City, Baker predictably scoring both the others, was followed by a 5–2 victory over Bolton Wanderers and a quite incredible 6–6 draw against Middlesbrough, both of the latter being floodlit challenge matches. The high scoring meant that Hibs had now notched an amazing 32 goals in five games played over just 17 days, a feat unequalled even by the Famous Five or the Hearts Terrible Trio.

Before the match against Middlesbrough, the England selectors had announced that they would be travelling up to Edinburgh to run the rule over the two prospective centre-forward candidates for the forthcoming full international match against Ireland, Joe Baker and Brian Clough, both of whom had ended the previous season as top goalscorers for their clubs. This was in the days before international squads were used, with only the 11 players and a reserve selected for the game. There was simply no comparison on the night between three-goal Joe Baker and the Middlesbrough leader Brian Clough, who had been first choice for the previous two England games. Clough was good, but the fast, intelligent and always-dangerous Baker completely overshadowed the less mobile Boro man in an intensely exciting 6–6 draw, and there seemed no way that the selectors could ignore the claims of the Hibs player.

The home side opened the scoring in typical fashion after only two minutes when Baker smashed a tremendous volley into the net from a narrow angle without even breaking his stride, and from then on the goalscoring switched from end to end with nail-biting regularity. Keeping goal for Middlesbrough in the high-scoring friendly was Peter Taylor, who would later form half of the famous and immensely successful Clough and Taylor managerial team. Another familiar face in the visiting side was ex-Celt Willie Fernie. During the second half, goalkeeper Taylor looked particularly ill at ease to find himself confronted by some long-range bombardments from John Baxter, all of which excited the home crowd. Three times in as many second-half minutes Baxter's thunderbolt shots crashed only narrowly past the post with the 'keeper well beaten.

Ironically, the England selectors failed to make it to Edinburgh after their plane was delayed by fog in London.

By now Joe Baker was the hottest prospect in the country, and another two goals in a 3–2 defeat of St Mirren at Paisley enhanced his growing reputation. The result meant that Hibs had now moved up to sixth place in the table, but there was still plenty of light between themselves and League leaders Hearts.

Watched by an England selector at Love Street, Baker was chosen to lead the England Under-23 attack against France at Sunderland in midweek. On arriving at the squad's training camp at Wigan there was a surprise in store for the Hibs wonderkid when he was informed that he had also been selected for the full England side to face Northern Ireland at Wembley the following week. Scoring twice in England's Under-23 victory over the French at Roker Park, Baker was on the goalscoring trail again two nights later during Hibs' 4–3 win in the return friendly match with Middlesbrough at Ayresome Park. By now the home crowd were aware that Baker had replaced local idol Brian Clough in the England line up, and a small but vociferous section of the crowd, unhappy that their favourite had been overlooked, barracked the Hibs centre-forward incessantly. Soon to suffer a horrific injury that would bring a premature end to his playing career, Clough did not play for England again.

Baker had first come to the attention of the selectors when chosen to play for an England XI against the British Army at Ibrox the previous October, along with Hearts goalkeeper Gordon Marshall. Marshall had earlier been selected to represent the Scottish Under-23 side before it was realized that, like Baker, he too had been born in England. The game itself was disappointing, but Baker was one of the few successes on the night, hitting the post early on and scoring one of the goals in England's 3–1 victory.

And still the goals continued. On 18 November 1959, Joe Baker made a scoring debut in England's 2–1 victory over Northern Ireland, confirming the faith of Wolverhampton Wanderers and former England captain Billy Wright, who had recommended the Hibs player to manager Walter Winterbottom several months before. Wright had first encountered Baker during a friendly match with Wolves at Easter Road in 1957, and in his own words rated: 'Joe Baker as among the best centre-forwards in Europe at that time. What is more, he is going to get better and better. When I first played against him he made me work so hard and used his brain so quickly that I was convinced even then that he would reach the very top'. Coming from one of the most famous players in the world, this was praise indeed.

Baker's goal against Northern Ireland made him an instant hero with the home crowd. In typical fashion, well known to the Easter Road supporters, Baker had trapped a free-kick in the box, quickly rounding a defender before firing a wicked drive past the helpless Manchester United goalkeeper Harry Gregg. Cheered from the field at half- and full-time, the press was in raptures over the new cap. According to *The Times*: 'The England selectors can pat themselves on the back for at last having found a centre-forward of real quality'. The *Manchester Guardian* thought the player 'full of life, verve and speed, who brought a touch of real intelligence to the game. His was undoubtedly an outstanding performance'. Another thought Baker 'the best leader of the game since Tommy Lawton. At only 19 years of age he could become England's best football asset. The class of the boy is there for all to see'.

Still not even halfway through only his second full season in the game, it seemed impossible to prevent the young Baker from scoring as he netted nine times in the next five games, including two doubles and a treble, the Easter Road side collecting eight points from a possible 10.

It was far from the end of the excitement for free-scoring Hibs. Although failing to score himself, Bobby Johnstone gave another dazzling display of tantalising football, having a hand in almost all of his side's goals in a completely one-sided 10–2 victory over Partick Thistle at Firhill on Saturday 19 December 1959. The Hibs goalscorers were McLeod (3), Preston (2), Baker (2), Ormond (2) and Wright (og).

Hibernian: Wren, Grant, McClelland, Young, Plenderleith, Baxter, McLeod, Johnstone, Baker, Preston, Ormond.

Joe Baker now led the goalscoring charts with 29, well ahead of next-best Jimmy Millar of Rangers with 22. The exciting free-scoring centre-forward was undoubtedly benefiting from playing in a settled side. After the numerous permutations used by manager Shaw over the previous couple of seasons in trying to find the ideal blend, Hibs had now not made an enforced change to the side since the middle of October.

By this time goalkeeper Lawrie Leslie had fully recovered from the operation to cure his tennis elbow problems, but Hibs were convinced that the injury was beyond repair and he was allowed to join Airdrie for a fee believed to be around £8,000. At Broomfield he would replace the recently transferred Jock Wallace, who had joined Andy Aitken at West Bromwich Albion. Like Gordon Smith only months before, it would prove yet another terrible blunder by Hibs. Leslie had devised a splint to protect his vulnerable elbows while in action, and he would soon go on to make five full international appearances for Scotland before moving to West Ham for a fee much larger than that paid to Hibs. Leslie was to have an amazing escape from infamy in April 1961. Originally selected for the Scotland team to face England at Wembley, injury forced his withdrawal, leaving the luckless Frank Haffey of Celtic to take his place in the side, and history, as England defeated the Scots by a record 9–3 scoreline.

It was also around this time that Jimmy Kane, unable to force his way into the first team after his horrendous injury at Pittodrie some time before, joined Cowdenbeath for a nominal fee.

There was yet another accolade for Joe Baker just before the turn of the year. In a poll conducted by the *News Chronicle* newspaper, the young Hibs leader was named in second place to Dave MacKay, then with Spurs, in a list of the top five players in the country. The others were Jimmy McIllroy of Burnley, Cliff Jones of Spurs and Denis Violet of Manchester United. Exalted company indeed for a player not yet 20 years of age.

After the excitement of the earlier high-scoring matches, Hibs' next two games also featured a sackful of goals, but unfortunately most were conceded by the Easter Road side. After a 6–4 defeat at Pittodrie on Boxing Day, it was on to Easter Road for the New Year's Day meeting with Hearts, who had Gordon Smith making his first appearance at Easter Road as a player since moving across the city at the beginning of August. Just a few days before, Hibs reserves had scored a resounding 6–2 victory over Hearts' second team to go top of the reserve League and set up an exciting New Year's Day encounter between the sides, but on the day most of the excitement would be reserved for those wearing maroon jerseys. With Hibs looking for their first home League win against their local rivals since 1952, a hat-trick by Alec Young set Hearts well on the way to an easy 5–1 victory. The defeat was made even more difficult to accept for the home fans by the sight of their beloved Gordon Smith scoring against Hibs wearing the colours of their greatest rivals.

In a game marred by ruthless tackling, two soft first-half goals gave Hearts a somewhat fortuitous interval lead. Johnstone pulled one back after the break, but the earlier goals had shattered Hibs' confidence and the second period belonged almost entirely to the visiting side. At the time Hibs were the top scoring side in the country, but a newspaper report summed up the match perfectly by stating: 'Right from the start, Hearts were probing Hibs' weaknesses, and by full-time had found every one of them'.

At times the football on display had been secondary to tough tackling, and a correspondent from the *Toronto Mail and Globe*, covering the game for his readers back home in view of Hearts' impending end-of-season tour of Canada, was of the opinion that 'On this display Hearts may have wrested the claim from Rangers of being the roughest team in Scottish football'. The report, as expected, provoked outrage among the Hearts support, many sending letters of complaint to the local papers. The tackling had indeed been rash at times, but it had certainly not been confined to just one side.

Hibernian: Wren, Grant, McClelland, Young, Plenderleith, Baxter, McLeod, Johnstone, Baker, Preston, Ormond.

It was now a new decade. The 10 years just ended had been one of the most progressive in the history of the game. Not only had we witnessed the birth of floodlit football, the emergence of European competition and the spread of the World Cup into a truly global competition, but football was now more popular than ever thanks to television. In just a few years the suspicion over the use of floodlights had changed into an almost universal acceptance, although there were still some reservations, but these were now mainly concerned with the poor quality of the lighting rather than any conceived advantage to the home side. The European, Fairs and Cup-Winners' Cups had developed into extremely popular competitions in less than five years, and the World Cup had become a genuinely global competition, due mainly to television coverage of the two previous tournaments. Although it was yet to be generally accepted by the football authorities, and still had its many critics, including the Hibs chairman Harry Swan, who were concerned that it must be controlled or it would lead to the financial ruin of the professional game, televised football was here to stay.

Goalkeeper Jackie Wren had played the last half dozen games in place of Willie Wilson, who was suffering from a back injury made worse by attempting to play through the pain barrier, a complaint that would trouble him in later life. But, as after the Rangers game on the opening day of the season, Wren was again made the scapegoat for the defeat by Hearts and would not feature in the first team again. It would be unfair, however, to heap all the blame on Wren, the goalkeeper quite obviously failing to receive the assistance he would, and should, have expected from the experienced defenders in front of him.

Nineteen-year-old Willie Muirhead, who had started only a handful of reserve games since his call-up from Arniston Rangers in the summer, was seen as the answer to the goalkeeping crisis at Easter Road, and this faith seemed justified when the young custodian performed exceptionally well in a 1–1 draw at Ibrox 24 hours after the Hearts débâcle. The goalkeeper was in particularly impressive form during the second half when his teammates found themselves under almost incessant pressure from the home side. Pat Hughes had been recalled at centre-half in place of Plenderleith for the match, and both he and Muirhead retained their places during the coming weeks, joined in the side that faced Kilmarnock in the middle of the month by Duncan Falconer.

The first goal of the three scored by Joe Baker in Hibs' 6–0 demolition of Third Lanark at Easter Road on 9 January 1960 was a personal milestone for the player, his 100th for the first team in all competitions. Incredibly, it had taken the prolific Baker just 25 months to achieve the target.

Baker notched the by now almost obligatory hat-trick, his fifth of the season, and the 13th of his senior career so far, in an amazing 5–5 draw with Clyde in Edinburgh just two weeks later. In an incredibly thrilling encounter Hibs found themselves 4–2 behind at the interval, but eventually clawed themselves back to take the lead, only for the Shawfield side to earn a deserved share of the spoils in the very last minute.

In the space of just a few weeks Hibs reserves had beaten Hearts' second team 6–2, Rangers 6–4, Third Lanark 9–0 and Kilmarnock 3–2. At that time they were by far the highest scorers in the League, but their form was often inconsistent, and they were as likely to be well beaten by a high scoreline as secure victory. To illustrate the point, as the first team were engaged in the high-scoring game against Clyde at Easter Road, the reserves were losing 5–1 that same afternoon, only one of several high-scoring reverses during the campaign.

Hibs' reserve side at that time was along the lines of: Wren, Robertson, Muir, Falconer, Nicol, Davin, Fraser, Frye, Buchanan, Fox, Bogie.

In the Scottish Cup, Hibs received a bye in the opening round and were handed a home draw against Dundee at the second stage of the competition. Originally scheduled to be played on Saturday 13 February, a combination of frost and heavy snow that wiped out a large part of the programme for several weeks determined that it would be almost three weeks and seven postponements before the game finally went ahead. When it eventually did, Hibs' 3–0 win on a Monday evening in front of a 30,000 crowd set up a meeting with Second Division East Stirling in the next round.

Bad weather had proved an enduring problem for football from its earliest days, but around this time a revolutionary new device was unveiled by its inventors who claimed that it had the capability to prevent games being cancelled owing to frost-bound pitches. Now, using a newly invented material, it was possible to cover the entire playing surface with a plastic sheet that could be kept hovering a few inches above the ground by a steadily circulating current of hot air designed to keep the frost at bay. One of the advantages of the system, or so it was claimed, was that it could be removed in only 20 minutes, and another, that fans on the terracing could be kept warm by well directed powerful jets of hot air while the game was in progress. Despite these wondrous claims, the system, like many others before it, would fail to gain universal approval, and only the widespread adoption of the underground electric blanket many years later, similar to the one that had recently been installed at Murrayfield rugby stadium, would finally and satisfactorily solve the problem of ice-bound playing surfaces.

Although only officially receiving 3,000 of the allocation of 11,000 tickets for the sell-out Scottish Cup meeting with East Stirling at Firs Park, most of the spectators inside the ground at the start were from the Edinburgh area. A trip to Ibrox awaited the eventual winners, and two goals by Baker and another by Fox were enough to overcome stuffy lower League opponents in Hibs' first visit to the ground since 1932. Only director Tom Hartland from the current staff could remember the previous encounter with the Shire during Hibs' dark Second Division days, when the visitors had been soundly beaten 4–1 after a 1–1 draw in Edinburgh. That season East Stirling would win the first, and so far only League Championship in their history on goal average, returning immediately to the lower reaches the following year after finishing bottom of a 20-team First Division.

At Ibrox in the next round, Bobby Johnstone gave Hibs a sensational start when he scored from the penalty spot after only two minutes. Baker had been sent sprawling inside the box in Hibs' first attack of the game, only for the referee to wave aside the Greens' appeals for a penalty, but the award was merely delayed. Sixty seconds later, Rangers centre-half Paterson handled inside the area, leaving the official no option this time but to point to the spot. The Glasgow side, who had not beaten Hibs in a Scottish Cup tie at Ibrox since 1897, refused to buckle, however, and in the end well deserved their 3–2 victory. They would progress all the way to the Final, eventually defeating Kilmarnock 2–0 at Hampden.

At that time, as well as the four he had scored in both League and Scottish Cup ties, Joe Baker was well out in front of the rest in the list of top League goalscorers. With 10 games still to play, he had scored 37 and was well on target to overtake the Scottish record of 52 scored by Willie MacFadyen in Motherwell's League Championship-winning season of 1931–32.

For many years the football authorities, who considered anything remotely connected to gambling as 'tainted money', had politely declined the offer of payment from the Pools companies for the use of the fixture list. But now, the worrying financial fragility of the game, created in many cases by a massive drop in attendances, particularly among the smaller clubs who were finding week-to-week survival difficult, made the offer suddenly more attractive. Initial negotiations with the Pools organisations had dragged on for some time, but now there came the welcome news that each club was to receive an immediate first payment of £1,531.65 as part of the deal. A second smaller payment would be made later in the season. This figure, however, while welcome, was a pittance compared to the huge profits made by the likes of Littlewoods and Vernons, and paled into insignificance when measured against the money that could be earned by allowing the highlights of a single game to be shown on television, but at least it was a start.

At the second Annual Hibernian Supporters' Rally, again held in the Usher Hall, John Paterson, then with Ayr United, was presented with a tape recorder in appreciation of his loyal service in the Hibs colours. The presentation was made by Northern Ireland and Spurs captain Danny Blanchflower, just one of a host of celebrity guests including Willie Woodburn, Tommy Docherty and Willie Bauld of Hearts. Also present at the highly successful event were the brothers Ormond, Scott and Baker. During a short speech, Joe was on the receiving end of good-natured jeers from the fans when he cheerfully announced that his ambition was to score a hat-trick for England against Scotland in the forthcoming international at Hampden in April.

In a flurry of activity to beat the transfer deadline, an enquiry by First Division Luton Town for Johnny McLeod, their third in as many months, was rejected after the player refused to move south regardless of a threat by Harry Swan that he would never play for the club again if he resisted the advances of the English club. Talk was also rife throughout the city that Hearts were interested in signing Desmond Fox, who had recently failed to command a regular place in the first team, but the rumours came to nothing. At about the same time, Johnny Frye was transferred to St Mirren for a fee in the region of £3,000. Frye would make a winning first start for his new club by setting up the second goal for Gerry Baker in Saints' 3–1 victory over his former colleagues in a rearranged League game at Easter Road.

The passing of the transfer deadline came as a huge relief to manager Hugh Shaw, who had been almost driven to despair in recent months by a seemingly never-ending flood of enquiries and continual newspaper speculation regarding the availability of goalscoring sensation Baker. Hibs were to be congratulated in their efforts to keep the player at Easter Road, but it was clearly only a matter of time before the centre-forward would move on.

A 3–0 home reverse by Raith Rovers, Hibs' fourth consecutive defeat, saw Duncan Falconer, who had made his first-team debut at the beginning of November, recalled at the expense of John Young, but this failed to stop the rot as the Edinburgh side were humbled 6–3 by Dundee at Dens Park. The visitors had been reduced to nine men for most of the game after Baxter was sent off in the first half following an incident with Alan Gilzean. Shortly afterwards, John Grant was forced to leave the field due to injury.

The continual transfer speculation had clearly had an unsettling effect on Baker, who had not been at his best in recent weeks. Although still top goalscorer in the country at the time with 38 League goals, well ahead of brother Gerry of St Mirren and third-placed Jimmy Miller of Rangers, Joe had scored only three times in his last six outings and, with only five games remaining, it would now require a miracle to overtake MacFadyen's record of 52. Amazingly, eighth-placed Hibs had already scored 92 goals, the same number as League leaders Hearts, but the defence had let them down too often, conceding more than any other side in the division bar two.

Joe Baker achieved a unique double when he lined up in the number-nine shirt for England for their clash against the Auld Enemy at Hampden at the beginning of April 1960. Capped at Schoolboy level for Scotland against England in 1955, he now found himself in the unequalled position of having won a full England cap playing against Scotland. The game kicked-off with Baker finding himself in the unenviable position of man in the middle. A stranger to his teammates and regarded as a foreigner by the majority of the huge partisan home crowd, who were desperate to see the Scots beat England at Hampden for the first time since 1937, Joe failed to achieve his ambition of scoring a hat-trick against Scotland, but it was a challenge by the Hibs player on centre-half Evans that forced the Celtic player into conceding the penalty that allowed Charlton to score England's goal in a 1–1 draw after a twice-taken spot-kick. Carried off injured in the 77th minute after a collision with Frank Haffey, Baker soon returned to the fray, and the performance of the Hibs man, who had the ball in the net after a shoulder-charge on the goalkeeper that was ruled illegal by the referee, was one of the few bright spots in an otherwise drab game acknowledged as one of the worst ever between the sides.

Seven days later Hibs scored their 103rd League goal of the season in a 5–0 whitewash of Arbroath at Easter Road. That same afternoon, Hearts had also joined the century club with a last-minute equalising goal by Bauld at Love Street, which was enough to give them the League title for the second time in three years, Gordon Smith continuing his personal fairytale by winning his fourth League Championship medal.

In midweek there was some consolation for the long-suffering Hibs fans when their side defeated the new League Champions 3–2 at Tynecastle in front of 20,000 fans, although it required a magnificent performance by Hibs goalkeeper Muirhead to deny Hearts at least a draw. It seemed only fitting that the two oldest players in the side, Bobby Johnstone, who scored twice, and Willie Ormond, should score the Hibs goals. Honours were now equal between the sides, who had each won one and drawn the other.

The record books show Joe Baker as having scored 42 League goals during the season, an all-time Hibs record, but the official club programme at the time and the handbook edition the following season only credit the centre-forward with 41. In the final game of the season against Partick Thistle at Easter Road, which ended in a 2–2 draw, Bobby Nicol opened the scoring for Hibs, his first goal for the club, before John Baxter lobbed the ball over stranded goalkeeper Freebairn and Partick centre-half Harvey late in the game to earn Hibs a point. Neither the watching supporters nor the journalists in the stand had been entirely convinced who had touched the ball last, Baxter or defender Harvey, but most awarded the goal to Baxter.

The 'mystery' was cleared up in the home dressing room after the game when Baker claimed the goal, insisting that he had got the merest of touches on the ball as he stood on the goalline. Despite the assertion by a *Daily Record* reporter that if he was standing on the goalline then he should have been flagged offside, Baker has now been officially credited as having scored 42 times during the season. Interestingly, as late as August 1967, in reply to a query from Nottingham Forest, who wanted to produce a special feature programme devoted to the centre-forward and wished to know how many goals the player had scored during his time at Easter Road, Hibs said that he had scored 127 times in 139 games, including the 41 scored in the 1959–60 season.

At the end of the season goalkeeper Jackie Wren, earlier placed on the transfer list after the New Year's Day débâcle, was among those freed, as were Slavin, Rumbles and Pate. Reserve defender Alan Robertson was notified by letter that he had been released as he lay in a hospital bed recovering from an injury received while playing for the club.

The highlight of what had been another erratic season had been without doubt the form of the free-scoring Joe Baker. Although finishing only in seventh place in the table, Hibs had scored an amazing 106 League goals, four more than champions Hearts. Baker, who would be the first to admit to the invaluable contribution of the experienced Bobby Johnstone, had scored almost half of them plus another four in the Cup competitions; the best-ever tally by a Hibs player. Baker's 42 goals in a single season had been bettered by only six players in the First Division since 1918, all scored in the years between the wars when the 20-team League gave the added advantage of playing four more games, and not even Reilly or Bauld in the golden years had come anywhere near the youngster's total. Of the six players, two had played for Championship-winning sides, and fourth-placed Sam English of Rangers would undoubtedly have scored one more than his total of 44 had not the legendary Celtic goalkeeper John Thomson made his final and fatal save at Ibrox that disastrous day in 1931. On the downside, Hibs had conceded 85 goals, a figure only exceeded by St Mirren, who had conceded one more, and bottom-of-the-table Arbroath who had let in 106.

For the first season since the war no Hibs player had been chosen to represent the full Scotland side. John Grant had played twice for the Scottish League against the League of Ireland and the Irish League and Jackie Plenderleith against the Welsh Under-23 side, but perhaps this had been more than balanced by Baker's historic selection for England. During the season just passed Baker had won five full caps and represented the Under-23 side against both France and Holland.

At the end of the season Baker was allowed to join England's touring side, while, after watching Wolves defeat Blackburn Rovers in the FA Cup Final at Wembley, his teammates made their way to Germany and Yugoslavia, where they played three games. Defeating Bayern Munich 3–2 in Germany, they drew 1–1 with Dinamo Zagreb, winning 3–1 against Rejeka in Yugoslavia. Provisional agreement had been reached to play Fiorentina and possibly Roma in Italy, but only on the understanding that Joe Baker would be available for the games. When told that Baker would not be part of the Hibs touring party the arrangements had been hastily cancelled.

The Fairs Cup

The Inter-Cities Fairs Cup was inaugurated in 1955. Originally established to celebrate the 50th anniversary of the founding of the Swedish Football Federation, it was also seen as a means of fostering international relationships within the game. Contested in the early years by cities hosting Festivals or Fairs, as the name suggests, 12 sides, some of them composite selects, took part in the first competition, including select sides from both London and Birmingham. Teams were split into four groups of three, playing each other home and away, with the winners of each section progressing into the semi-finals. The first tournament dragged on interminably, taking almost three years to complete before eventually being won by Barcelona, who defeated London 6–0 in Spain after drawing 2–2 away. Expanded to 16 teams for the next competition, the tournament was by now determined on a straight home and away knock-out basis, and this time took only two years to complete, with holders Barcelona retaining the trophy, defeating Birmingham 4–1 at home after a 0–0 draw in England.

Sir Stanley Rous, a member of the Fairs Cup Organising Committee as well as secretary of the FA, had contacted Harry Swan as early as October 1957 asking whether either of the Edinburgh sides would be interested in taking part in the 1958 competition if invited, either in their own right or in a joint effort. Acknowledging Hibs' willingness to enter, Swan made it clear in his reply that he had lost none of his bitterness towards the Gorgie side, whom he blamed for the demise of the ill-fated floodlit friendly tournament, by refusing to contact the Tynecastle side until he had more information on the matter. Swan reminded Rous that: 'Hearts, as you know, were the culprits in preventing us carrying on with the Anglo-Scottish Floodlight Competition, and as such you will readily understand why I will not contact them in the meantime'. However, representatives from both Edinburgh clubs were eventually invited to attend a committee meeting in Barcelona the day after the second leg of the 1958 Final, but previous commitments had made it impossible for either to take up the offer, and consequently both were represented at this meeting by an agent from the Sheffield and Hallamshire County FA, arranged through Rous.

Nothing more was heard regarding participation in the 1958 competition, but an invitation was received more than a year later for both Edinburgh sides to enter the 1960 event, again either individually or as a select. Both clubs immediately indicated a willingness to enter in their own right as Scottish representatives, but somewhat surprisingly the Fairs Cup committee did not receive either application until after the closing date, and consequently neither were included in the first-round draw.

Chelsea had represented England when the tournament was expanded to 16 teams in 1958, reaching the quarter-finals, but after their late withdrawal from the 1960 competition, it was decided that another British side should take their place. Probably because Edinburgh hosted its famous International Festival, a joint invitation was sent out to both city clubs. Hearts chairman Nicol Kilgour was one of the few who still had reservations about the wisdom of European competition, but after initial hesitation the League champions somewhat reluctantly decided to take part in the European Cup instead, leaving the way clear for Hibs to become Scotland's first-ever representatives in the Cup, which was now to be played on an annual basis.

Just before the start of the new season centre-half Jackie Plenderleith was transferred to Manchester City for a fee in excess of £10,000. Although Plenderleith had been a member of the Hibs party that had toured the Continent during the close season, the highly-rated defender had failed to feature in any of the games and had been unsettled since losing his place to John Young for the last half-dozen games of the previous season. The move to Manchester would be of almost immediate benefit to the cultured Under-23 international, who had also attracted interest from several other English clubs including Arsenal, when he won his first, and as it would turn out his only, full Scotland cap in a 5–2 victory against Northern Ireland in November that year.

By now the idea of inter-continental competition had really caught on, and during the summer another French-inspired concept was born. The Friendship Cup competition was played between teams from France, England and Scotland, the games being played home and away in sections. Bizarrely, the country and not the side that finished with most points at the conclusion would be judged the winners. In Scotland, invitations had been sent to Rangers, Clyde, Motherwell and Dundee, but Rangers, who were involved in the newly-formed Cup-Winners' Cup, declined the invitation. Hibs were invited to replace the Ibrox club, but they too declined because of Fairs Cup commitments, leaving Celtic to make up the Scottish foursome. The tournament failed to live up to expectations, however, and the lack of interest by the public was evident from the start with a poor turnout for all the games, the four fixtures played in Scotland only attracting a total of 14,000 spectators between them. Motherwell's home game at Fir Park was watched by only 2,546 fans and it was obvious almost immediately that the tournament was doomed to failure. Although a draw was made for the following year's competition, none of the games would take place and the Friendship Cup was allowed to slip quietly into obscurity.

In the Greens vs Whites public trial match at Easter Road, four-goal Joe Baker gave notice that he was ready to take up where he had left off the previous season, as the first team ran out easy winners. Willie Wilson, in goal for the reserves, showed that he had fully recovered from the mysterious back injury that had plagued him for most of the previous campaign by bending to pick the ball out of the net seven times.

In the Edinburgh Select charity game at Tynecastle, bright summer sunshine had helped draw a big crowd for the visit of English First Division side Chelsea, who fielded several youngsters in their line up who were destined to soon become household names, including goalkeeper Peter Bonetti, teenage goalscoring sensation Jimmy Greaves and a recently signed 17-year-old Terry Venables. Also in the Chelsea line up and making a rapid return to Scotland was international centre-half Bobby Evans, a close-season signing from Celtic. Jim Cruickshank, signed by Hearts from Queen's Park during the summer, was in goal for the select. In what was thought to be one of the best games yet in the series, Edinburgh won a thrilling encounter played in heatwave conditions by five goals to four. The select goals were scored by George Thomson of Hearts, who notched two from the penalty spot, and the Hibs trio of Baker, Ormond and the recently appointed Easter Road club captain John Baxter.

By now Tommy Preston was in full training after his cartilage operation the previous season, but Desmond Fox was still refusing to accept new terms after posting a transfer demand at the end of May, a request that had been accepted by the club.

Although recent seasons had failed to live up to expectations, at least there was now tangible evidence of improvement. The highly successful partnership of Joe Baker and Bobby Johnstone offered fresh hope for the immediate future, as did the form of outside-right Johnny McLeod, although the leadership and firm tackling of the experienced Eddie Turnbull, who had retired more than a year before, was still badly lacking in midfield.

For a seventh consecutive season, qualification to the later stages of the League Cup eluded Hibs. Not since losing to East Fife in the semi-final at Tynecastle in 1953 had they progressed past the group stage, and it was to be no different this year, winning only two games in a section comprising Airdrie, Dunfermline and Kilmarnock. On the opening day, a 4–2 defeat by Kilmarnock was a severe setback for the supporters who made their way to Rugby Park, although once again the prolific partnership of Baker and Johnstone was responsible for both the visitors' goals. Bobby Kinloch, who would have a major part to play in a famous victory later in the season, made his first start in a green-and-white jersey at right-half. A 2–0 home win against Dunfermline a few days later was the Fifers' first defeat since Jock Stein had taken over at East End Park near the end of the previous season before leading his side to an almost impossible escape from relegation. With Bobby Kinloch scoring his first goal for the club, the win saw Hibs back on track.

Things looked even brighter on the Saturday against Airdrie. Former favourite Lawrie Leslie received a warm welcome from the Hibs fans on his first visit back to the capital since his transfer. It would not be a happy return to his first senior club for Leslie, who had since taken over the captaincy at Broomfield, with the former Newtongrange Star 'keeper beaten six times. Joe Baker scored four to impress the watching England selectors and could well have added to this tally had it not been for the impressive form of Leslie, who saved his side from a much heavier defeat.

Newly promoted Dundee United, managed by the astute Jerry Kerr, won the opening League exchange of the season at Tannadice, the Tayside club's first game in the top flight for 28 years. The 3–1 scoreline did little to flatter United, who were worthy winners, only Fraser and goalscorer Ormond a success for Hibs.

The following Saturday there was the surprise news that both Willie Ormond and Bobby Johnstone had been dropped for the home League Cup tie against Kilmarnock, meaning that for the first time in many years the Hibs forward line would not feature at least one of the Famous Five. Johnstone watched the start of the match from a seat on the trainers' bench, but within minutes was seen to storm from the ground before departing by taxi. When asked, he would only say that there had been an argument when he was told that he would not be playing. In midweek, a short statement was released by the club revealing that Johnstone had been sent from Easter Road on the Saturday and instructed not to report back until contacted. The statement explained little and the stalemate continued for several weeks. Rumours that Johnstone had been influencing Baker on the merits of English football remain unsubstantiated, and it would now appear that a blazing row with Harry Swan was the real reason for the dispute. Whatever the facts, Johnstone had played his last game for the club.

Goals by Baker and Fox against Kilmarnock meant there was still an outside chance of qualification to the last eight of the League Cup, but any lingering hopes were dashed in the final group game at Broomfield. Despite an impressive debut by centre-half Jim Easton, signed only in the close season from Drumchapel Amateurs, the Easter Road side surrendered meekly, going down to a 3–1 defeat to shatter any hopes of progress. The débâcle prompted manager Hugh Shaw to comment acidly in the editorial page of the next match programme that 'Seldom in his experience has any Hibs side shown such lack of spirit and determination, two factors essential in football irrespective of whether points mean anything or not'. Hibs' solitary goal against Airdrie had been scored by the former Forres inside-forward Bobby Kinloch, who had improved out of all recognition after a quiet start to the season. The player had been the surprise find of the pre-season Continental tour. In the middle of his National Service with the RAF at the time, Kinloch's impressive form had persuaded Hibs to buy out the remainder of his time in the service.

In the first capital derby of the season at Easter Road, a second-half goal by Preston was all that Hibs could muster against the four scored by arch-rivals Hearts. Although putting up a terrific show for 90 minutes, only a fourth goal late in the game allowed the Gorgie side to feel confident of both points, but already the warning signs were being posted for the Greens.

Later in the week Heart of Midlothian were fined £150 and their manager Tommy Walker £75 for an administration irregularity concerning the registration of Edina Hibs player Eric Stevenson, who had been training with Hearts since the age of 15. The incident would have far-reaching consequences, not only for Hibs but for Scottish football as a whole. Stevenson had just turned 17, the legal minimum age in Scotland to sign a professional contract at that time, and Hearts duly returned the signed contract to the football authorities confirming the player as a full professional at Tynecastle. The trouble was, this was news to Stevenson, who could not recall signing any contract. It later transpired that Stevenson had unwittingly signed the agreement two years earlier aged just 15, which was a clear breach of the rules, and the contract had been retained by Hearts until the time was right. While the authorities and the Tynecastle club dithered over whether Stevenson was still a registered Hearts player or not, Hibs, who had been keeping close tabs on the situation, immediately sprang into action to contract the player to Easter Road. The deal was to pay long-term dividends for both parties. Stevenson, a life-long fanatical Hibs supporter from a Hibs family, achieved his dream of playing for his boyhood heroes, while the club reaped the reward of over 10 years of sterling service from one of the best players ever to wear the famous green-and-white jersey. The situation also helped highlight an anomaly within the rules concerning the signing of young players. In England the introduction of an 'Apprentice Professional' scheme had meant that clubs south of the border could sign schoolboys at 15, while in Scotland the existing rules prohibited clubs from signing a boy on a full contract until he had turned 17. This obviously gave an unfair advantage to the English sides, which were allowed to cream off the best of the young talent north of the border, with the home clubs helpless to act. The Stevenson case underlined the injustice of the situation and the rules were eventually changed to bring the Scottish clubs more into line with their southern counterparts.

In England, the television companies had recently signed a contract with the Football League, said to be worth £150,000, which allowed the screening of 26 live matches during the coming season. The last 10 minutes of the first half and the whole of the second period of a selected game were to be shown at 7.30pm on Saturday evenings, but only south of the border. As far as Scotland was concerned the screens would remain football free. Although the transmission of the Blackpool verses Newcastle United game did take place, several sides, including Arsenal, refused to allow the cameras inside their grounds, leading to the eventual abandonment of the scheme. In Scotland, gates had risen by over 270,000 during the previous 12 months, but south of the border there was a major concern over the still steadily decreasing attendances at most games, and it was obvious that the screening of live matches would do little to arrest the trend. Harry Swan, to the forefront as usual, was vociferous in his opposition to the screening of live games, warning that if the threat of TV was not countered, or at least made to co-operate with the clubs, it could sound the death knell for football, particularly for those in the lower Leagues. Forty years later, and given the near stranglehold that television companies now have on the game, it perhaps goes to show that Swan and his fellow doubters were not too far wide of the mark.

Injuries are a common and expected occurrence in the world of professional sport, but in mid-September captain John Baxter was the unfortunate victim of a freak training-ground accident. The players were in the middle of an impromptu game of baseball on the Easter Road pitch, when the greasy bat slipped out of the hands of Joe McClelland, briefly clipping Tommy Preston on the shoulder as it flew through the air before striking Baxter full on the face. The Glaswegian defender received a broken nose and jaw in the incident; injuries that required a stay of several days in the Eastern Hospital in Edinburgh.

By now Hibs had been informed that their Inter-Cities Fairs Cup opponents were to be FC Lausanne of Switzerland. After protracted negotiations between the clubs it was finally agreed that the first leg would take place in Lausanne at the end of September with the return at Easter Road three weeks later.

Marcel Gigue, the French gendarme who had refereed the 1958 World Cup Final in Sweden, was earmarked to take charge of the second leg in Scotland.

Defeats by Kilmarnock at Rugby Park, Raith Rovers at Easter Road and Partick Thistle away meant that Hibs were now firmly anchored at the foot of the League table without a point after five games. This was hardly the ideal preparation for the forthcoming European game, which was scheduled for the following midweek, but as the Scottish party was preparing to depart on the journey to Switzerland on the Monday morning, notification was received that the tie had been postponed. The news at first was confusing. A message from an agency stated that the tie had been postponed indefinitely, while a telegram from the Swiss club indicated that they were now prepared to play in Edinburgh four weeks later with the return leg on 3 November. The game did not take place. According to the Swiss, international demands on their players and a series of injuries had made it impossible for them to honour the commitment. But the reality was different. Lausanne had been in turmoil for some time. Having gone through two managers the previous season, a third was now in place. Although they had beaten Basel 3–1 the previous Sunday, the result had been preceded by five straight defeats and the club was now in crisis with nearly every player handing in a transfer request. In the circumstances, Hibs were awarded a walkover and a passage into the next round.

The goalkeeping position at the club was again proving a major source of concern. Wilson was back in the reserves, Wren had moved on and the inexperienced Muirhead was proving unreliable. Ronnie Simpson, then with Newcastle United and who had featured in two FA Cup Finals with the Tyneside club in the early 1950s, had been the victim of a long-term injury that ruled him out of the game for almost two years. Although now fully recovered, he was considered to be past his best and available for transfer. Consequently the veteran 30-year-old goalkeeper, who had turned out for Queen's Park as a 15-year-old against Hibs in 1946 alongside future Hibs manager Walter Galbraith and a soon-to-be Hibs outside-left Johnny Aitkenhead, was signed by Hugh Shaw for a fee in the region of £12,000.

Three days after the acquisition of Simpson, the experienced wing-half Sammy Baird was signed from Rangers, and the three debutantes, Simpson, Baird and 17-year-old Eric Stevenson, lined up against St Johnstone at Muirton on 8 October 1960. Simpson, playing behind a poor defence, made a fairly impressive start, while the other newcomers also showed promise, but they could not prevent a 2–0 defeat, leaving the Edinburgh side still seeking their first League point six games into the season.

Worse was to follow seven days later at Easter Road. With Muirhead replacing the injured Simpson in goal, Celtic scored six with considerable ease. That same afternoon Bobby Johnstone was making his debut for Fourth Division Oldham in a 5–2 victory over Exeter City. Terms had earlier been agreed between Hibs and Port Vale, but the player had failed to turn up for a meeting with both clubs. Joining Oldham for a fee reported to be in the region of £4,000, the first appearance at Boundary Park of the 1956 FA Cup-winner had created tremendous interest in the town, and a crowd of over 18,000, which was four times Oldham's average gate at the time, turned out to see his debut. It is said that the increased attendances at Johnstone's first two home games more than allowed Oldham to recoup his entire transfer fee.

Almost a year to the day after Hibs' historic 11–1 victory at Broomfield, Airdrie gained a modicum of revenge with a 4–3 home win, the Diamonds' winning goal scored in the very last minute. The result caused the alarm bells that had been ringing in the east side of town to positively peal out loud and clear. So worrying was the situation that a panel of reporters from the *Edinburgh Evening News* were instructed to investigate the poor showing not only of Hibs, but also of Hearts, who while not playing as badly as their Edinburgh rivals were still displaying inconsistent form in the League Championship. The recent poor form of the Gorgie side was proving a great worry for their supporters considering that they had won the title less than five months before. From Joe Baker's personal point of view, Hibs' poor form was doing little for his cap prospects. Since the start of the season he had found the net only twice in eight games, compared with 11 at the corresponding stage 12 months earlier.

At the end of the month a hat-trick by Man of the Match Bobby Kinloch and another from Willie Ormond gave the Greens their first League points of the season in a close-run 4–3 win over St Mirren. Gerry Baker and former Hibs player Johnny Frye were among the St Mirren goalscorers.

John Baxter, now back in full training after his encounter with the baseball bat, but yet to return to first-team duty, unexpectedly found himself back in hospital. Accepting a lift from teammate Des Fox back to his home in Glasgow after training one day, Baxter required 12 stitches to a head wound after they were involved in a crash with a lorry not far from Bangour Hospital. The incident resulted in the wing-half acquiring the nickname 'Lucky' from his teammates.

At the end of October chairman Harry Swan travelled to Zurich for the Fairs Cup draw. Initially notified that Hibs were to play the German side Cologne, he was later informed that they had actually been drawn against Spanish champions Barcelona, the games to be played in January of the following year. This was exciting news for the Edinburgh fans, who would now have the opportunity to witness in the flesh some of the famous stars they had previously only read about in football magazines and newspapers or managed to catch a glimpse of on television, but for the Easter Road players it was a daunting task to face a team rated at the time as the best club side in the world. The Spanish giants were still in both the European and the Inter-Cities Fairs Cup competitions, a situation that was allowed at that time, and they had only recently knocked great rivals and World Club champions Real Madrid out of the European Cup, making them red-hot favourites to win both trophies.

Although it was not yet the end of October, Hibs had already made an incredible 59 positional changes in trying to find the blend that would lift them away from the foot of the table. Back-to-back wins over Dundee and Ayr United, and a draw against Aberdeen, saw them climb the table for the first time since the beginning of the season, but a 4–1 defeat at Motherwell saw a quick return to bottom place, and the outlook was now desperate.

The first leg of the Fairs Cup tie against Barcelona was initially to have been played at around the turn of the year, but a surprise appeal from the high-flying Spanish side to bring the fixture forward meant the Easter Road game being hastily rearranged for Wednesday 14 December 1960. Five days before the visit of Barcelona, Rangers travelled through to Edinburgh to take on rank outsiders Hibs. Although they lost 2–1 to the League champions, much-needed confidence was taken from the performance of the home side, particularly that of the much criticised defence, who were magnificently marshalled throughout by Baird, who was facing his former teammates for the first time since his move to the capital. Hibs' performance, while inspiring, came nowhere near that of Barcelona, who only days before had defeated Real Madrid 2–1 in the Nou Camp after a 2–2 draw in the Spanish capital to end Real's five-year dominance of the European Cup.

Barcelona arrived at Turnhouse Airport on the Tuesday afternoon before the game, training at Easter Road that evening. On inspecting the pitch the following day, the referee found the ground conditions to be perfect, but he decided to hold another inspection at 5.30pm that evening on account of the heavy fog that had lingered over the city throughout most of the day. A contingency plan had earlier been agreed that in the event of a postponement, Barcelona would delay their stay in the Scottish capital another 24 hours and attempt to play the game the following evening. At a pitch inspection at around 5pm, the dense fog still hung heavily over the area, making satisfactory visibility for the spectators a near impossibility, and, taking the expected huge number of travelling fans into consideration, the referee had no option but to abandon any thoughts of play that evening. After a brief consultation, Barcelona announced that they would not now be delaying their stay in the city 24 hours as previously agreed, but would be leaving as originally planned early the following morning. The news came as something of a surprise to Hibs, although the concerns of the Spanish side that preparations for the forthcoming League match on the

Sunday should not be disturbed, was grudgingly accepted. It was agreed that what was originally to have been the return leg in Spain would still go ahead on that date, with the return game at Easter Road rearranged for a later date. It was while he was in the Scottish capital that Brazilian Luis Suarez learned that he had just been voted European Footballer of the Year.

Third Lanark were early seasonal visitors to Easter Road on Christmas Eve 1960, and Joe Baker took full advantage of the Cathkin side's Yuletide hospitality by scoring five of Hibs' eight goals. It was the first-ever 'nap hand' of Baker's professional career as he ran riot, completely demoralising the Thirds defence throughout the 90 minutes. Hibs' other goalscorers were John Baxter (2) and Jim Scott, but the Hibs manager would not have been enamoured by the uncertainty shown by the home defence, who dithered and slithered from start to finish, finally conceding four goals.

On Boxing Day, the same 11 that had defeated Third Lanark, plus Willie Ormond and Eric Stevenson, the youngster's first trip abroad with Hibs, joined manager Shaw, trainer Turnbull and directors Powrie and McIntyre at Turnhouse Airport for the flight to Spain. On arriving at their destination in the early evening, an anticipated light training session on the Barcelona pitch was cancelled when they were informed that as it was the holiday period an electrician could not be found to operate the floodlights. Whether this was part of the Continental gamesmanship which was prevalent at the time is uncertain, but, nonetheless, the visitors had to be content with a short session in the gym to relieve their travel stiffness.

On the morning of the match there was a huge boost for Hibs with the news that the recently named European Player of the Year Luis Suarez would miss the game. Only just recovered from a serious injury, Suarez had been hurt again playing for the Rest of Spain against Real Madrid in a representative match only 24 hours before. There was further encouragement for Hibs with the news that 'Golden Head' Sandor Kocsis would also miss the game, but this later proved not to be the case.

Two days after Christmas, Hibernian, languishing four places from the bottom of the Scottish First Division, prepared to face arguably the greatest club side in the world at that time.

Fairs Cup second round (first leg), Wednesday 27 December 1960, Gran Estadio.

Barcelona: Ramallets, Segarra, Gracia, Verges, Garay, Gensana, Villaverde, Kocsis, Evaristo, Kubala, Bieta.

Hibernian: Simpson, Fraser, McClelland, Grant, Easton, Baird, Scott, Baxter, Baker, Preston, McLeod.

Referee: C. Tonni (Italy)

Over 50,000 fans greeted the teams as they took the field at the recently completed Gran Estadio in Barcelona. Originally named the Joan Gamper stadium after a former president, it would soon change its name to the more familiar Nou Camp. Constructed at a cost of over £1,750,000, raised almost entirely by the purchase of bonds and long-term season tickets by supporters, it had finally opened in September 1957. Originally designed to hold 90,000, it had since been increased to a 105,000 capacity, and plans were in place to increase this to 150,000 in the near future.

The Hibs players lined up nervously before the kick-off, but almost from the first whistle the Spanish champions were found to be strangely hesitant and uncertain, allowing the visitors to immediately find the pace of the game. Playing with a confidence which belied their home form, the Edinburgh side almost took a shock lead in the opening minutes when Baker just failed to get on the end of a beautiful through ball from Baird. Even this early in the game Baker's pace was causing all kinds of problems for the home defence, as he tormented the veteran Spanish international centre-half Garay.

As it was, the inevitable was only delayed, and in the 10th minute goalkeeper Ramallets, who had advanced to the very edge of his box, fumbled his catch. Like lightning the ever-alert Baker pounced to coolly round the crestfallen 'keeper with the ball before tapping it into the net.

The huge crowd immediately made their dissatisfaction known by aiming a barrage of jeers in the direction of the home team. This helped to settle Hibs even more and 11 minutes later they were two ahead. McLeod, who had drifted back into midfield, received a pass from Baird. Baker drew his marker wide, allowing the winger to drive deep through the heart of the unguarded defence, and the hastily retreating defenders were totally stunned when, after first feigning to pass, the outside-left suddenly let fly from all of 20 yards, the ball screaming past the helpless Ramallets to bulge the back of the net.

Again the supporters were not slow to make the home side aware of their displeasure, and a crescendo of derisive whistles rained down on the Spanish team. Barcelona now began to settle, playing the ball about with purpose, demonstrating the skill and control expected of a side with their reputation, and Baird, who was in inspirational form at the heart of Hibs' defence, was forced to come to Simpson's rescue by heading clear from under the bar with the 'keeper beaten.

The visitors missed a great chance to increase their lead when a Baker pass across an empty penalty area found no takers, but eight minutes from the interval Barcelona, who were now well on top, scored the goal that had been threatening for some time. Awarded a free-kick just outside the penalty area, Gensana sent over a beautiful cross, which was met by Kocsis, whose magnificent header evaded the despairing dive of Simpson to settle in the back of the net.

The spirited Hibs refused to capitulate and shortly before the break they almost increased their lead when a wonderful drive by Baker came crashing back off the upright.

Half-time: Barcelona 1 Hibernian 2

On the restart Barcelona upped the tempo, and with Hibs forced to endure a 10-minute period of intense backs-to-the-wall pressure, there were several near chances in front of Simpson's goal before the by-now anticipated equaliser arrived. Bieta, wide on the left, beat both Grant and Fraser with ease before his inch-perfect cross again found the head of the totally unmarked Kocsis, who once again had little difficulty in directing the ball past Simpson.

The partisan Spanish crowd now sat back eagerly to await the expected goal blitz by their favourites, but gradually Hibs began to claw themselves back into the game and were denied what appeared a certain penalty when McLeod was brought crashing down inside the box. Although not playing as well as they had in the first half, the Edinburgh side were far from out of it, and shortly after the home side had squandered a couple of decent chances, Hibs went ahead when Preston smashed home a great left-foot shot that went in off the post with 18 minutes of the match remaining.

Incredibly, three minutes later, Baker scored a fourth with a carbon copy of Preston's goal. Losing his marker in the middle of the park, the adopted Englishman cracked a terrific drive from all of 25 yards that flew past Ramallets and into the net off the same upright. In near desperation, and amid the slow hand clapping by their own supporters, Barcelona reduced the deficit when Kocsis scored his third goal of the night after a wild scramble in the Hibs goalmouth. There were now just six minutes remaining for Hibs to hold on to their lead and a famous victory, but, three minutes from the end, the visitors were cruelly denied the win their valiant efforts had so richly deserved when Evaristo fired home from a Kocsis cross.

Full-time: Barcelona 4 Hibernian 4

Not only had Hibs come within a few minutes of a fantastic victory, but it had been no fluke. There were times in the match that they had given Barcelona a lesson in football, and the scoreline sent shockwaves reverberating around Europe. According to one news reporter, 'Hibs didn't hold Barcelona to a draw, it was quite the reverse'. Every Hibs man was a hero, none more so than Simpson, whose brave performance inspired his outfield colleagues. Baird had been a shrewd tactician, and the teenager Easton, who was making his first European appearance, immense, but it was the livewire pairing of Baker and McLeod up front that had caused the Spanish side the most problems. In an interview before the game the Barcelona secretary had categorically denied that they were interested in signing Baker. Perhaps they had now changed their minds. One local newspaper was in no doubt, urging Barcelona to buy Baker, 'who had been so much ahead of our centre-forward'.

At the after-match banquet, a Barcelona official complimented the Scottish side: 'We knew we would have a hard game, but were very surprised at the standard of Hibs' play'.

The scoreline had also resounded throughout Scotland. The *Scottish Daily Mail*: 'Hibs struck a glorious blow for Scottish prestige…they put on a dazzling exhibition…the first hour was unbelievable. It was like watching the Hibs team of the 1948 era'. The *Daily Record*: 'Eleven Hibs heroes gave Scotland its greatest ever boost…the Easter Road miracle men were close to bringing off the football story of the century. Hibs were magnificent, every man of them'. The *Scotsman*: 'Barcelona were dealt a moral defeat'.

Bobby Kinloch was among a large group of well-wishers at Turnhouse to welcome the team back from Spain. Kinloch had been out injured since damaging his ligaments against Rangers at the beginning of December but was now back in full training. He would have a significant part to play in the return leg at Easter Road in February. Much was made in the press of two-goal hero Joe Baker, and it was reckoned that his performance in Spain had put him in the £100,000 category and on Real Madrid's shopping list as a possible successor for the aging Alfredo Di Stefano.

Back on League business against Dundee United at Easter Road on the last day of the year, the same XI that had faced Barcelona were given a rousing reception by the ecstatic home fans as they took to the field to the strains of the *Pasa Doble*, before going on win 2–0 with goals from Baxter and Scott. It was Hibs' fourth game without defeat, and it would be another seven before they would lose again in either the Championship or the Scottish Cup.

In a 2–1 win over Hearts at Tynecastle on New Year's Day, Ronnie Simpson, playing in his first Edinburgh derby, had his best game yet in Hibs colours, even saving a spot-kick, his sixth penalty save in a row. The 'keeper had yet to concede a goal from the penalty spot since joining Hibs. 'Penalty King' Simpson's trick was to stand slightly nearer one post than the other, leaving a larger space to one side, supposedly by accident. The gap usually enticed the kicker to aim for the bigger target, which the 'keeper had already anticipated. With Hibs deservedly 2–1 ahead at the interval thanks to goals from Scott and McLeod, Hearts stepped up the pressure in the late stages of the game in a bid to secure their first New Year's Day derby win at Tynecastle since 1957. Although forced to endure a few near things near the end, Hibs managed to hold out until the final whistle, the result all but banishing any remaining relegation fears.

A 2–0 victory against Clyde at Shawfield in the Scottish Cup in an otherwise unconvincing performance saw Hibs progress into the next round. The home side had played for more than an hour with only 10 men after losing goalkeeper McCulloch with a broken finger, but they still put up a spirited display, and it was only during the final four minutes of the game that Hibs could relax after Baker scored a second goal. The centre-forward had been kidnapped 24 hours before the Cup tie, along with his Clyde counterpart McLaughlin, but it was only a students' Charity Day stunt. Both players were released overnight, but the incident incurred the displeasure of Harry Swan, who was not amused at Hibs' Cup preparations being interrupted, saying: 'These things should not be allowed to happen, and Hibs will not be paying the ransom fee demanded by the Charities Committee'. Ormond was making his first appearance since losing 4–1 at Motherwell at the end of November. During his absence Hibs had won eight of the 10 games played; both the others had been drawn.

In the second round of the Cup Hibs were drawn against Peebles Rovers at Easter Road, the first meeting of the teams since 1923, when a Hibs side that had included manager Hugh Shaw and second-team trainer Jimmy McColl had won 3–0 after a 0–0 draw. That year Hibs had progressed all the way to the Final before eventually losing 1–0 to Celtic, the only goal conceded by the Edinburgh side in the entire competition. The supporters wondered if this could be an omen. Were they finally to see the almost mythical Scottish Cup back at Easter Road at last?

In a totally one-sided game Hibs ran up their biggest Scottish Cup score in living memory against the unfortunate non-League side, who were harassed into conceding 15 goals. One of the biggest cheers of the day, however, was reserved for former Hibs player Walter McWilliams when he scored Peebles' solitary counter with the score standing at 6–0. Goalkeeper Lucas, who had put up the shutters when Hibs faced Dundee United in the Scottish Cup in 1958, pulled off several fine saves to prevent his side from suffering an even more embarrassing defeat. Twelve months earlier, Joe Baker's brother Gerry had scored 10 goals against Glasgow University while playing for St Mirren in the same competition, and it soon became a contest to see if Joe could better this tally. Despite his teammates doing everything possible to lay on chances galore, the game finished with Baker having scored nine, one from the penalty spot. Hibs' other goalscorers were Ormond (2), Baxter (2), Baird and McLeod. Only Preston of the forwards failed to get his name on the score sheet.

After an 11-game unbeaten spell in which 47 goals had been scored, 21 of them by Joe Baker, Hibs' successful run finally came to an end at Parkhead, five days before they were due to face Barcelona in the return leg of the Inter-Cities Fairs Cup, when Celtic ran out comfortable 2–0 winners. In direct opposition to Baker that day was 19-year-old centre-half John McNamee, making his Celtic debut in place of the injured McNeill. McNamee would be manager Jock Stein's first signing for Hibs a few years later after joining the club from Dunfermline, and the defender would attract a cult following during his relatively short stay at Easter Road.

Interest in the Fairs Cup tie since the amazing 4–4 draw in Barcelona had been nothing short of phenomenal, with the ticket office handling enquiries from all over the country, including many from England. There had even been a request for a block booking of 100 tickets from a group of exiled Spanish resident in Scotland. The Spanish champions, now still clear favourites to progress into the semi-finals to face either Cologne or Roma, held a slight advantage regarding substitutions. The rules of the competition allowed the use of a substitute goalkeeper in the case of injury, and although Hibs would also be allowed the use of the extra man as far as UEFA were concerned, SFA regulations still prohibited the use of substitutes, and as such the Scottish team would be denied this if the need arose.

Since the 4–4 draw with Hibs in December, Barcelona had relegated manager Ljubisa Brocic to the role of assistant manager, replacing him with Enrique Orizaola Velazquez, their third managerial appointment inside a year. Since then, their form had been in decline. Of the seven games played since the game against Hibs, four had been lost and one drawn, a slump almost unprecedented in the illustrious history of the club, and they had now dropped to fourth place in the League table. The blame had been placed squarely on the shoulders of former manager Brocic, who had been accused of using incorrect training methods, his regular use of heavy medicine balls during the training sessions being blamed for the unprecedented number of muscle strains and other injuries sustained by the players during the season.

Wing-half John Grant, a regular all season in a defence that had almost selected itself, had picked up a slight injury at Parkhead and was replaced by inside-left John Baxter, who moved back into defence. Baxter's replacement, a fortuitous one as it would turn out for both player and club, was Bobby Kinloch, who had not featured in the side since a 2–1 defeat by Rangers in mid-December.

Fairs Cup second round (second leg), Wednesday 22 February 1961, Easter Road.
Hibernian: Simpson, Fraser, McClelland, Baxter, Easton, Baird, McLeod, Preston, Baker, Kinloch, Ormond.

Barcelona: Medrano, Foncho, Garay, Gensana, Verges, Segarra, Evaristo, Kocsis, Martinez, Suarez, Villaverdi.

Referee: J. Malka (Germany).

A huge crowd, including many neutrals, only just failing to beat the record attendance for a floodlit game in Edinburgh set by the visit of Reims, packed the terraces of Easter Road, eager to see the famous Barcelona players in the flesh. Most were hopeful of a Hibs victory and totally unaware that before the evening was out they would witness scenes almost unprecedented in the history of the British game, certainly in living memory.

The early part of the game was a disappointing affair. For the first 10 minutes or so, the ball spent most of the time in the air being frantically booted from one end of the pitch to the other by both sides, before play gradually settled down to a more composed tempo. Baird, in midfield for Hibs, was inspirational. Slowing the game down and passing confidently, his play brought out the best in his forward colleagues, as he set up most of the telling moves in the early stages of the game. Most of Hibs' play was directed toward Baker, who appeared in determined mood, and it was obvious that the Spanish defenders were showing the centre-forward the utmost respect as he became the victim of numerous heavy tackles. With 11 minutes gone good work between McLeod and Baker ended with the Englishman being fouled on the edge of the box by Gensana. McLeod took the free-kick and swept over a cross, which looked the 'keeper's ball all the way. But before Medrano could collect it, Baker, who had anticipated the flight of the ball, intercepted it to glide a delicate header into the net and sent the Easter Road crowd wild with delight. Hibs were now well on top, but stung into action, Barcelona settled into an ominous rhythm as Evaristo and Koscis stepped up the pace.

After winning several corners that had created danger in the home goalmouth, the visitors scored a well-deserved equaliser. With 29 minutes of the game played, Hibs were caught completely flat-footed as a throw-in on the right-hand side was taken quickly. The ball was passed to Martinez lurking on the edge of the six-yard box, and, before the Hibs defence could react, the Spanish centre-forward had pivoted to prod the ball past the helpless Simpson. It was a simple and sudden goal executed with an economy of movement.

With 35 minutes gone Hibs squandered a great chance to take the lead. A brilliant three-man move involving Baird, Baker and Kinloch saw the inside man shoot weakly past with only the 'keeper to beat.

From then on the home side were second best and eager to hear the half-time whistle, but with two minutes of the half left to play, an aimless low cross was sent over by Evaristo that looked likely to pass harmlessly behind Kocsis. The Hungarian international, however, screwed round to trap the ball, and almost in the same movement turned to fire it into the net past the sprawling 'keeper to give Barcelona the lead for the first time in the tie.

Half-time: Hibernian 1 Barcelona 2

On the half-time whistle, the Barcelona players had left the field looking confident and composed, but this composure soon evaporated at the start of the second half when fully 10 minutes of relentless Hibs pressure found the visitors unable to escape from their own penalty area.

The bewildered Spanish had no answer as they were tormented by the pace and aggression of Baker, and it took a succession of cynical fouls by both Gensana and Garay, who had each been warned by the referee in the first half for similar indiscretions, to stop the marauding centre-forward. Twice the England cap was barged off the ball in the box, but unbelievably the referee awarded an indirect free-kick on both occasions to the bewilderment of the near 49,000 spectators. Barcelona were now struggling as Kinloch just failed to get on the end of a Baker cross, and a goal just had to come.

Hibs won a corner on the left in the 74th minute. Ormond took the kick and found Baird lurking at the edge of the box. His header deep into the penalty area was met by Preston, who nipped in to head the equalising goal past Medrano. Barcelona, whose nerves had been fraying since the start of the second half, gradually getting worse as the game progressed, now went completely to pieces. They had no answer to Baker and his teammates other than force, and with five minutes remaining McLeod was blatantly hacked down in the box by Garay as he collected a defence-splitting pass from Baker. This time the referee was left with no option other than to point to the spot, and this was the spark that led to some of the most amazing and disgusting scenes ever witnessed at a football match in Scotland. For several minutes the game was delayed as mayhem ensued on the pitch. The referee was jostled and pushed by goalkeeper Medrano and his teammates in an attempt to persuade the official to change his decision. For a while some Hibs players looked as if they might also become embroiled in the mêleé, particularly Baker, but wisely they soon decided to stand back and watch the incredible scenes that were unfolding before them. Bobby Kinloch, who had been designated to take the penalty, was the calmest man on the pitch as he stood in amazement with the ball held securely in his hands watching the astounding scenes that were unfolding before him. Order was eventually restored, and the cool Kinloch calmly stepped forward to drive the ball past Medrano for the winning goal. This was merely the signal for the mayhem to resume, with the referee again being assaulted, this time with more ferocity. A group of players, led by European Player of the Year Suarez, again surrounded the official, who was brutally battered to the ground. The pursuers were about to pounce again, and only the intervention of dozens of police guaranteed the official's rescue. Incredibly, the visiting players then turned their aggression towards the police, punching and pushing before they were eventually jostled away. The few Hibs players who had tried to calm the situation had also been in danger of being assaulted, and on seeing this, a number of spectators had spilled onto the pitch, anxious to enter the fray. The situation was now seriously out of hand. Eventually the police succeeded in ushering the spectators back onto the terracing and order was restored, but it had taken more than seven minutes to get the game restarted.

The remaining minutes of the match were played out in almost farcical conditions, with the by now highly excitable referee blowing his whistle for even the most innocuous offence. Barcelona threw everyone forward in the dying seconds in an attempt to save the match, but Hibs held out comfortably to earn a deserved victory. During the final seconds the referee had been controlling the game from a position just a few yards from the tunnel, and immediately on signalling the end of the game he made his way to the safety of the tunnel and the protection of the waiting policemen. Even then it was not over, however. Followed from the pitch by a posse of Barcelona players who were intent on renewing their attack, it again required the intervention of the police to lead the referee to safety. Not so fortunate was the far side linesman, who was viciously attacked from behind and punched to the ground as he was leaving the field. Even in the dressing room the officials were not safe, with the Spanish players repeatedly trying to get at the referee, and until recently the impression of stud marks could still be plainly seen on the door of the referee's changing room. Unbelievably, there were no arrests and no formal complaint of assault made by the referee. Herr Malka did say, however, that his penalty award had been correct and that a full report of the incident would be forwarded to FIFA and it would be up to them to decide on any appropriate action. Never before, he confessed, in a career that had seen him officiate at several international matches, had he experienced a situation remotely similar to that witnessed at Easter Road.

Full-time: Hibernian 3 Barcelona 2

After the game a spokesman for Barcelona ludicrously claimed that: 'Even the Hibs players thought the penalty award unjust. The Referee knew the decision was wrong and ran away, and naturally our players chased after him. It can perhaps be put down to Latin temperament, but anyone would have rebelled in the situation. I have seen it happen in English football'. Perhaps predictably, the Spanish media also thought the result scandalous and that Barcelona had been unfairly eliminated from the competition, but in Scotland the press viewed it differently. The *Daily Express*: 'The deplorable incidents only pushed into the background what was a truly wonderful display by Hibs. There was no greater star than Joe Baker, who outshone by far every one of the high priced Barcelona forwards'.

The *Daily Mail* thought: 'Hibs can again take their stance in world football', and the *Evening Dispatch*: 'A glittering triumph. The Easter Road side fought with a fervour and spirit, which has seldom been equalled by any Scottish club or national side. Floodlight the castle, fire a 21 gun salute for the Hibs, never-say-die heroes who gave Scottish football its greatest boost for years'.

Amid the seriousness of the situation, there was also humour. When order had initially been restored and Kinloch was about to take the vital penalty, he was approached by captain Sammy Baird, who grasped the youngster by the shoulders before passing on some words of advice. The newspapers reported the incident the following morning, describing the experienced player as giving words of encouragement to the youngster. In truth, Baird had actually told Kinloch, 'If you miss this penalty, I'll break your f****** neck'.

Just days after the famous Fairs Cup victory, Desmond Fox and 1955 European Cup goal hero Jock Buchanan, both unable to claim a regular first-team spot at Easter Road, were transferred to Raith Rovers for a fee described by Hugh Shaw as 'substantial'. Only the week previously, former player Andy Aitken, who had found great difficulty in settling in England since his move from Hibs to West Bromwich Albion 17 months before, had joined Falkirk.

Joe Baker's goal against Barcelona was his 148th in all games since making his debut a little over four years before. He did not have to wait long for his 150th. Scoring once in a 4–0 Scottish Cup victory against Hamilton at Douglas Park, Kinloch (2) and McLeod notching the others, Baker achieved the magical milestone in the goalscoring charts when he scored Hibs' second goal in a 3–3 home draw with Airdrie on 27 February 1961.

As well as success in Europe, the Fairs Cup semi-finalists now also had one eye on a place in the last four of the Scottish Cup. Paired against Celtic at Parkhead in the quarter-final, only a goal four minutes from time had earned the Glasgow side a second chance in a replay at Easter Road. After a fairly ordinary first half, the game developed into a thriller after Barcelona goal hero Kinloch opened the scoring just after the interval. Hibs, full of spirit and confidence after their European victory, attacked in style, particularly Baker and McLeod, who caused all kinds of mayhem in the Celtic defence. Young Eric Stevenson on the left wing had the opportunity to finish the game near the end, but he somehow managed to miss the target from six yards with the 'keeper helpless. With the game seemingly well beyond Celtic, and many of the home fans making their way to the exits, a late harmless-looking lob from deep in the Celtic half allowed Chalmers to latch onto a knock-down by a Hibs defender, to steer the ball past Simpson and give his side an undeserved equaliser.

In their wisdom, the Easter Road directors had decided against making the replay the following Wednesday evening all-ticket. This turned out to be a major error of judgement on their part. Twenty minutes before kick-off, the Easter Road gates were locked with just under 40,000 inside. With the ground capable of holding over 60,000 it was obvious that a miscalculation had taken place, and such was the desperation for admission that several hundred fans gained entry to the ground by smashing their way through the exit doors in Albion Place. Scores of supporters attempted to watch the game from the roofs of the nearby tenements, and several more were arrested, later to appear in court, after climbing on to the roof of the Dunbar's lemonade factory behind the south end of the stadium. Thousands more, angry at being denied admission, particularly those who had made their way through from Glasgow, milled around the surrounding streets in restless mood, with hordes invading the local graveyard, damaging several headstones in an act of wanton vandalism.

As in the first game at Parkhead, the opening 45 minutes were pretty even, although the home side probably just shaded things. After the interval there was only one team in it, with Celtic forced to endure a Barcelona-style barrage as Hibs did everything but score as they mounted a series of sustained attacks. Stevenson again had a great chance to break the deadlock, but the inexperienced player held the ball just a second too long, allowing the relieved Celtic defence to clear. The home crowd were incensed when the Glasgow side survived a penalty scare after McLeod had been clearly barged off the ball in a carbon copy of the Barcelona incident, but this time amazingly the referee awarded an indirect free-kick inside the box which ultimately came to nothing. Only a brilliant display by goalkeeper Frank Haffey prevented Hibs from taking a merited lead, and Celtic, who had been reeling at times, were mightily relieved to hear the whistle end the regulation 90 minutes.

In the first half of extra-time, Hibs continued to relentlessly attack the Celtic goal in an effort to make the vital breakthrough, but were totally stunned with only 60 seconds of the period remaining. Following a short corner on the left the ball found young John Clark, playing one of his first games for Celtic and soon to find immortality as a Lisbon Lion, on the edge of the penalty area. Clark's diagonal shot/cross evaded the despairing lunges of several Hibs defenders before deflecting into the net off goalkeeper Simpson's leg for the only goal of the game. After a quite magnificent performance the goal totally deflated Hibs, and the second period of extra-time belonged almost entirely to Celtic, who should have scored more as they progressed towards the Final of the Cup, where, in a date with destiny, they would be beaten after a replay by a Dunfermline side managed by a young Jock Stein.

Wins over Ayr, Dundee, Aberdeen and Motherwell in the League saw Hibs climb to sixth place in the table, their highest position of the season, which was an amazing feat considering that as late as the end of October they had been rooted firmly at the bottom of the table and yet to win their first point. But two consecutive away defeats in four days at East End Park and Ibrox, the latter thanks to a freak goal by McMillan, scored after a Baird clearance had struck Easton on the back before falling kindly for the Rangers player, meant a drop to eighth.

Just a few days before facing AS Roma at Easter Road in the semi-final of the Fairs Cup, Johnny McLeod won his first full Scotland cap. In what turned out to be a day of extremely mixed emotions for the former Armadale player, McLeod took his place on the right wing as Scotland were massacred 9–3 by the Auld Enemy at Wembley, their heaviest-ever defeat by England in the history of the series. Although an inexperienced newcomer to the international scene, the Hibs man was one of the few relative successes on the day. As already mentioned, more fortunate than Johnny was former teammate Lawrie Leslie, then with Airdrie, who had originally been selected in goal for the game but had been forced to withdraw because of injury, leaving the hapless second-choice Frank Haffey of Celtic to carry the can and earn the unenviable reputation of being the man who conceded nine against England.

The Joe Baker situation was a proving a major headache for Hibs, and an impromptu board meeting was held to discuss the situation as the directors made their way by train to Wembley for the game. Although Baker insisted that he had not asked for a transfer, it was well known that several top clubs were keen to sign the England international. At an earlier meeting with manager Hugh Shaw, the player had expressed his concern at losing his England place to Bobby Smith of Spurs, and even a place in the Under-23 side. Although adamant that he would not ask for a transfer, he did, however, demand a wage rise, thought to be in the region of £5 per week. Ultimately, on the Monday after the heavy Scottish defeat in London, a statement was released by Hibs to say that 'Baker had made it plain by his demands that he is unlikely to play for Hibs next season, or any other Scottish club for that matter'.

Meanwhile Roma had arrived in Scotland after a 15-hour journey. Italian international and captain Egidio Guarnacci was still struggling to overcome injury and did not travel. After defeating Belgian side St Gilloise 4–1 at home after a goalless draw in the first leg, the Italians had met West German side

Cologne in the second round, with a third match needed to separate the sides after each had won their home game by the same 2–0 scoreline. Switzerland had been suggested by the competition organisers as the venue for the Play-off, but the Italians disagreed, and somewhat prophetically for Hibs, as it would turn out, the third tie went ahead in the Italian capital.

Earlier in the season, Roma had topped the League table for a short time, but lately their form had dipped. Still formidable opponents at home, their away record in the Championship was the worst of any of the sides still in the Fairs Cup, but on their day they were still an exceptionally skilful side containing eight or nine internationals with a hard-tackling defence, and they were considered a tough proposition. Full-back Joe McClelland had missed the match against Rangers because of injury and was not risked. He was replaced by Joe Davin, who was making his competitive European debut. Barcelona goal hero Bobby Kinloch was another absentee. After a successful run in the first team, his form had dipped somewhat in recent weeks and he was playing for the reserve side.

Fairs Cup semi-final (first leg), Wednesday 19 April 1961, Easter Road.
Hibernian: Simpson, Fraser, Davin, Grant, Easton, Baird, Scott, Preston, Baker, Baxter, McLeod.
AS Roma: Cudicini, Raimondi, Corsini, Fontana, Losi, Giuliano, Orlando, Pestrin, Schiaffino, Lojacono, Menichelli.
Referee: D. Mellet (Switzerland)

The red-shirted Latins began the game playing an unusual defensive formation for that time, with right-half Foniana allocated the job of man-marking Baker, who had obviously been earmarked the danger man, and centre-half Losi mopping up at the back. As had come to be expected from Italian sides then, Roma resorted to a display of bad-tempered and cynical fouling whenever things started to go against them, particularly Lojacono, who continually harassed the referee whenever a decision was awarded against his side.

For 90 minutes the game was almost Barcelona revisited without the riot, and once again a player who objected to decisions going against him repeatedly lost his head. Inside-left Lojacono, ironically probably the best player on the field, was the main culprit in handing out rough treatment, particularly when the home side started to gain the ascendancy after the interval, and he was repeatedly booed by the home supporters as he continually resorted to scenes of petulance when pulled up by the referee.

Notwithstanding the histrionics, the immensely talented Lojacono opened the scoring midway through the first half after several near misses in the Hibs goalmouth, a lead the visitors deservedly took into the interval. To the great disappointment of the massive crowd, the attempts by the home side had been few and far between in the opening 45 minutes, their best effort of the half ending with Baxter hitting the bar with a long-range shot.

Half-time: Hibernian 0 AS Roma 1
In the second half it was a different story. McLeod, causing all kinds of panic in the visitors' defence as Hibs attacked down the slope, took the game to the Italians and set up an equalising goal for Baker early in the half. The goal inspired Hibs, who were now well on top and seeking the lead that their magnificent fightback and brilliant play deserved, when they were stunned by an atrocious refereeing blunder. Temporarily down to 10 men while full-back Davin was off the field receiving treatment to an injury, Roma started a move deep into Hibs' half of the field. The ball was swept forward to Pastrin in a dangerous position just outside the penalty box, but a perfect tackle by Baird cleared the danger. To the amazement of almost everyone inside the ground, referee Mellet awarded a free-kick to Roma just two yards outside the area. Lojacono took the kick and scored his second goal of the evening with a vicious swerving drive that gave Simpson absolutely no chance.

Instead of deflating Hibs, the goal had the opposite effect, and merely encouraged a fighting home side to throw everything into attack. With the Italian side grimly hanging on to their lead in the later stages of the game, Hibs' Man of the Match Johnny McLeod scored a well-deserved leveller near the end.

Full-time: Hibernian 2 AS Roma 2

As in the previous round the visitors left the field to a background of jeers from a crowd who had been unimpressed by the display of petulance and sometimes violent tactics by several of the Italian players throughout the game.

Apart from McLeod, young Joe Davin had impressed on his European debut, as had full-back partner Fraser, who had to be at his very best in dealing with the tricky Menichelli. The prolific Baker, who had been carrying an injury for the final 30 minutes of the match, had been tightly marked throughout the proceedings by two men, making it extremely difficult for the player, although the extra space created by this tactic had undoubtedly created more room for the tantalising McLeod.

After a 4–0 victory over Clyde on the Saturday, the same XI that had faced Roma in the first leg, plus Ormond, McClelland, Kinloch, Stevenson and Gibson, who was then still on National Service, made their way to East Fortune Airport for the flight to Rome. Flying from East Fortune was somewhat unusual, but at that time Turnhouse was undergoing an extensive renovation to its main runway, and consequently all air traffic in the area had been diverted to the East Lothian airport, whose main claim to fame had been its use by the military during both wars, and also as the departure point for the giant dirigible R34 before it made the historic first crossing of the Atlantic by an airship in 1919.

Centre-half Losi, who had performed so impressively as sweeper at Easter Road, was considered doubtful for the return leg after picking up an injury playing for the Italian national team against Ireland only the day before the Fairs Cup game, but better news for the Roma fans was that the influential and elusive Manfredini, who missed the first match in Edinburgh, had fully recovered from injury. As it happened, the injured Losi passed a late fitness test and was included in the line up, which was another major boost for the home side. Hibs manager Shaw recalled the veteran Willie Ormond in place of the tricky but inexperienced Jim Scott. The now ageing outside-left would be asked to play in an unfamiliar deep-lying role, using all his experience to hold the ball when necessary before releasing it to the attackers up front. Joe McClelland, who had still not returned to first-team action after injury, was given a late fitness test before the game, but although the defender could well have played if necessary, it was decided not to risk the player because of the importance of the match.

At that time the Italian press were voicing grave concern at the escalating win bonuses then being paid to players in Italy. It was thought that the Roma players were in line to collect £300 each if they were to bypass Hibs and reach the Final, and only the week before it had been claimed that £600 per man had been paid to the Inter Milan players for beating Juventus in the League title decider, which, according to the local media, was nothing short of a scandal. In the same newspapers there were stories linking Joe Baker with three Italian clubs. Roma and Torino were known to be interested in the centre-forward, but according to reports they had now been joined in the race by Florence, who were rumoured to be willing to pay a fee in excess of £70,000 to secure the player's signature. There was also talk that several Italian clubs were showing an interest in Baker's teammate and current Scottish international Johnny McLeod.

Because of a cut-price ticket deal, a crowd of 50,000–60,000 was now expected to attend the match, many more than had first been thought, and consequently the game, originally earmarked for the smaller Flaminio Stadium in Rome, was switched to the 100,000 capacity Olympic Stadium.

Fairs Cup semi-final (second leg), Wednesday 26 April 1961, Olympic Stadium, Rome.
AS Roma: Cudicini, Fontana, Raimondi, Pestrin, Losi, Giuliano, Orlando, Lojacono, Manfredini, Schiaffino, Menichelli.
Hibernian: Simpson, Fraser, Davin, Baxter, Easton, Baird, McLeod, Kinloch, Baker, Gibson, Ormond.
Referee: M. Lequesne (France)

Played under a torrent of hail and unremitting rain that had fallen throughout the day, interspersed with bouts of thunder and lightning, the extreme conditions had restricted the attendance at the start to a disappointing 35,000.

After a suggestion by trainer Eddie Turnbull, Baker and Kinloch switched jerseys to confuse the Roma players. The ruse was so successful that the Italian defenders, who had discovered at Easter Road just what a handful Baker could be, spent most of their time giving the Englishman, or so they thought, their undivided attention. It was only midway through the second half that they realised that they had been tricked, but by that time they were trailing 3–1.

The early play was even as both teams tested each other out, but any potential danger from the Scottish side was, more often than not, stifled by an overzealous linesman who repeatedly, and often wrongly, flagged the speedy McLeod offside whenever Hibs threatened the Roma goal.

With 20 minutes gone the visitors were denied what appeared to be a blatant penalty when McLeod was brutally smashed to the ground inside the penalty area. The French official waved the frantic appeals of the Hibs players aside, and the ball was swept upfield to Manfredini, who gave Roma the lead from what may well have been an offside position.

Ten minutes later, the scoreboard informed the fans that a goal for the visiting side had been scored by Baker, after the Hibs number nine had ignored the close attention of his markers to burst through the middle to level the tie once more.

Half-time: AS Roma 1 Hibernian 1

Eighteen minutes after the break, the Easter Road side took the lead. A double shuffle and beautiful body swerve by number 10 Baker left three defenders stranded before he calmly dispatched a crisp low shot into the corner of the net past the helpless Cudicini.

Just minutes later, Gibson, who was having a fine game and not in the least intimidated or overawed by the occasion, sent over a perfect cross that eluded the Italian defence. Baker, relishing the extra space the switch with Kinloch had created, launched himself to crash a spectacular diving header into the net to give his side a 3–1 lead. Although they were now aware that they had been tricked, the Italians were panicking and the winning post seemed in sight for Hibs.

With the game apparently drifting away from the home side, as at Easter Road in the earlier game, the temperamental Lojacono became involved in several heated exchanges with the referee, and a teammate had even been allowed to push a linesman without punishment. Then disaster struck for Hibs with Roma scoring twice in a five-minute spell. In the 67th minute Manfredini scored his second of the night as he sliced through the Hibs defence Baker-style to place the ball behind Simpson, before hot head Lojacono levelled the tie with 18 minutes remaining. An already exciting game built up to a thrilling climax as Roma stepped up the pressure, and they should have scored twice in a tremendous finish. Hibs were not totally out of it, however, winning three corners in the final three minutes of the match, but over the piece a draw was a fair result and yet another memorable night for Scotland.

Full-time: AS Roma 3 Hibernian 3

During a hastily arranged meeting in the boardroom after the game, the Hibs directors recommended Paris as their preferred option for the third game play-off, while the Italians opted for

Switzerland. In the end both sides agreed that the toss of a coin should decide the venue, the winner playing at home. The coin spun in favour of the Italian side, and although the Fairs Cup committee would later voice their disapproval that the third game was not to be played at a neutral venue, Rome it was for the decider. That, however, is the official version. It has long been accepted that Harry Swan and Hibs accepted a substantial sum and an all-expenses-paid holiday in Italy for the players and officials if they agreed to hold the third game in Italy, and it can only be assumed that the same scenario had taken place during the previous round when Cologne had also played their deciding match in Rome.

A major problem for Hibs was the date for the third game. The match in Rome was earmarked for 27 May, which was almost a month after the end of the Scottish League season and Hibs' final League fixture against Third Lanark at Cathkin on 29 April. There seemed no way that the Hibs players could remain match fit for the play-off after such a delay, and so it would prove.

On the journey back to Scotland from the Italian capital, an unexpected technical problem meant Hibs' flight was diverted to Prestwick instead of landing at East Fortune as planned. A long and exhausting coach journey back to Edinburgh could perhaps go some way towards explaining Hibs' humiliating defeat at the hands of Third Lanark in the final League game of the season two days later at Easter Road, when they conceded six goals including a hat-trick by Hartley. McLeod scored Hibs' solitary counter. The scoreline meant that Third Lanark, who would end the season third in the League table, had incredibly now scored 100 League goals, 12 more than champions Rangers. Hibs could only manage to finish the season in seventh place, the same as the previous year, one place above former champions Hearts who finished eighth.

On 2 May 1961 Joe Baker was officially placed on the transfer list. Although it was made clear that he would not be allowed to leave until after the match in Rome, the following statement was released by the club: 'Hibernian Football Club and Joe Baker have had further discussions. The club finds it impossible to accede to Baker's demands, and under the circumstances, request that he should be made available for transfer'. It is understood that the player would have been paid around £20 per week at that time, excluding bonuses, and had asked for another £5 per week, approximately equal to a 25 per cent wage rise. Put into perspective, if he was on £2,400 a week – as some modern Scottish players are now – then he would be asking for a rise in the region of £600 per week.

After a 17-day break, Hibs resumed training on 16 May in preparation for their forthcoming European tie. Three days earlier it had been disclosed that, barring accidents or unexpected developments, Joe Baker would be wearing the colours of Torino the following season.

Rumours had been rife throughout the city for some time that the veteran Willie Ormond would not be re-signing for the 1961–62 season. The rumours were vigorously denied both by the club and the player himself, but on the eve of Hibs' flight to Italy the news broke that Ormond would be placed on the transfer list after refusing terms and demanding a move. Ormond had played his last-ever game for Hibs in the Olympic Stadium in Rome in the 3–3 draw. Six times capped at full level and a member of Scotland's 1954 World Cup Squad, Ormond had been the last remaining link with the glory days of the late 1940s and early 1950s. Since signing from Stenhousemuir in 1946, he had held his place unchallenged, barring injuries, until Johnny McLeod had become a regular in the 1959–60 season. The last remaining on-field member of the Famous Five, he too would leave the club with the particular disappointment that he had failed to win the Scottish Cup during his time at Easter Road. Eric Stevenson, making his first European appearance, would replace Ormond in the side to face Roma in the third game play-off.

Fairs Cup semi-final (replay), Saturday 27 May 1961, Flaminio Stadium, Rome.
AS Roma: Panetti, Fontana, Raimondi, Pestrin, Losi, Giuliano, Menichelli, Lojacono, Manfredini, Shiaffino, Selmosson.
Hibernian: Simpson, Fraser, McClelland, Baxter, Easton, Baird, McLeod, Kinloch, Baker, Gibson, Stevenson.
Referee: H. Othmar. (Switzerland)

In the four weeks since the end of the Scottish season, Hibs had been forced to rely solely on a week's extensive training just prior to the game in an attempt to regain full match fitness, while Roma, who had completed their League fixtures only the week before, still remained fresh. This would have a major bearing on the eventual result.

In a farce of a game considering the differing levels of fitness between the sides, Hibs found themselves a goal behind as early as the opening minute when Manfredini netted, and the Italians never looked back. Argentinian centre-forward Manfredini, who had performed so poorly in the second leg when he had missed a couple of easy chances, showed the enthusiastic home crowd just what he was capable of by scoring four times. The visitors fought back briefly after the first-minute disappointment, but their resistance was shattered when Manfredini scored a second after 20 minutes. Hibs were rarely seen as an attacking force after that, but they were given a glimmer of hope when they were awarded a penalty after centre-half Losi pulled down Stevenson inside the box. Panetti, who had quite obviously moved before the kick was taken, saved Kinloch's effort but, despite heated protests from the Scots, the referee refused to allow the kick to be retaken. Two minutes later Hibs themselves conceded a penalty after Selmosson was brought down by McLelland, but Lojacono, who had displayed his shooting power in the first match at Easter Road, hit the post with a ferocious drive with 'keeper Simpson well beaten. From then on until the end of the game Hibs were simply outclassed. Quite obviously struggling against the pace of the fitter Italians, eventually their spirit and confidence collapsed. Manfredini, who ironically would have been the player replaced had Roma's bid for Baker been successful, hit the post twice before scoring a third shortly before half-time after a brilliant solo run.

Half-time: AS Roma 3 Hibernian 0

Apart from a brief spell in the opening minutes of the half, Hibs' tactics of switching wingers was to no avail and they never seriously threatened to trouble the opposition defenders after the break. With Baker in particular being well held by Losi throughout the 90 minutes the visitors were a sorry and well-beaten team long before the end, and it was no surprise when further goals from Manfredini, Menichelli and Selmosson were scored before the finish. The final whistle came as an act of mercy for the visitors, but as it stood, they had the embarrassment of having conceded the highest number of goals ever in a European game by a Scottish side.

Full-time: AS Roma 6 Hibernian 0

As his now former teammates enjoyed an all-expenses-paid holiday in the Italian sunshine as part of the play-off deal, Joe Baker was putting the finishing touches to his £65,000 transfer to Torino. After scoring 163 goals in 190 first-team appearances in all games, the phenomenon was gone. Within a few weeks Denis Law, signed from Manchester City for £100,000, would join him at Torino. Jimmy Greaves, a member of the Chelsea side beaten by the Edinburgh Select at the start of the season, had only recently become part of the British exodus to Italy when he moved to AC Milan for a fee of £85,000.

Roma defeated Birmingham 2–0 in Rome in the return leg of the Fairs Cup Final to win the trophy after a 2–2 draw in England.

The Story So Far

It was the end of an era at Easter Road, the most successful in the club's 86-year history. After the success during the golden years of the late 1940s and early 1950s, Hibs were now in the middle of a serious decline that would culminate in near relegation at the end of the 1962–63 season.

Now inevitably accepting that they had lost favourite Joe Baker to Torino, the fans were stunned to discover that a close-season bid in the region of £40,000 from Arsenal for the rapidly improving Johnny McLeod had been successful, and the player travelled south to join his new colleagues at Highbury in time for the big kick-off. McLeod, the only ever present the previous season, had improved out of all recognition the longer the season went on, and after the Wembley débâcle against England in April he kept his place in the Scottish side, winning another three caps, against the Republic of Ireland home and away and Czechoslovakia. He did not feature in the full international set-up after leaving Easter Road.

Joe Baker would eventually come to regret his move to Italy, finding life extremely difficult in Turin both on and off the field. The defensive style did not suit him, and he was sent off on more than one occasion, as well as being on the receiving end of numerous club fines, usually for petty indiscretions. Brian Glanville, then widely regarded as Britain's leading authority on Italian football, was of the opinion that Joe Baker had made an error of judgement in joining Torino. The Turin side, according to Granville, was a middle-of-the-road outfit constantly living in the shadow of near-neighbours Juventus, and Baker would have been better off joining Fiorentina instead. Perhaps Baker should never have entertained the thought of playing in Italy at all. Surviving a late-night near-fatal car crash, Baker soon ended his unhappy time in Turin by joining former teammate Johnny McLeod at Arsenal at the start of the following season. After further moves to Nottingham Forest and Sunderland he would rejoin his first love Hibs in 1970, ending his illustrious goal-packed playing career with Raith Rovers in 1974. In later years he was a matchday host at Easter Road. Sadly, the likeable Baker, still a great favourite with the fans, died prematurely from a heart attack in 2003 aged just 63. Johnny McLeod would spend three seasons with the Gunners before moving to Aston Villa, then Belgian club Mechelen, finally ending his senior career with Raith Rovers in 1972.

Willie Ormond had played his last game for Hibs in the return leg of the Fairs Cup against Roma in Italy. Rejecting several offers from the club to re-sign for his 16th season in a green-and-white jersey, within weeks of the start of the new season he would move to home-town club Falkirk on a free transfer, leaving trainer Eddie Turnbull as the last surviving member of the celebrated Famous Five still at Easter Road. On his retirement the following season, Ormond first became trainer at Brockville before accepting the offer to manage St Johnstone in 1967. St Johnstone had struggled in the bottom half of the table since winning promotion to the top League in 1963, but under the guidance of the new manager there was an almost immediate improvement. Reaching the League Cup Final in 1969, the club's first major Cup Final, they lost only narrowly to the all-conquering Celtic. Their finest period under the former Hibs player came at the end of the 1970–71 season when they finished in third place, the highest-ever placing in the club's history. This was enough to qualify the Perth side for the following season's Fairs Cup, the club's very first venture into European competition.

Ormond's time with the unfashionable club did not go unnoticed for long and he replaced Tommy Docherty as manager of Scotland in 1973, leading the country to the World Cup Finals in Munich in 1974. Although failing to progress into the later stages of the competition, Scotland returned home as the only unbeaten side in the entire tournament, their best-ever performance in a World Cup. Resigning in May 1977 with a track record that was statistically the most successful of any Scotland manager, a short spell as manager of Hearts soon followed. Never universally popular with a section of the Tynecastle support for obvious reasons, he was sacked after a boardroom dispute in 1980. Ormond returned to his first love Hibs as assistant to manager Eddie Turnbull that same year, and took over the Easter Road hot seat when his former teammate was sacked near the end of the season after the club had been relegated for only the second time in its history. Sadly, he soon began to be plagued by ill health, and his stay at Easter Road was relatively short. He died on 4 May 1984 aged 57.

On Tuesday 7 November 1961, Hugh Shaw ended an association with the club that stretched back to 1918 when he resigned as manager of Hibs after an argument with Harry Swan during a heated board meeting the previous evening. Born in Islay, Shaw had joined Hibs from Clydebank juniors during the closing months of World War One and had quickly established himself in the first team. Originally a centre-forward, he found his best position at left-half in the great side of the 1920s that had contested the 1923 and 1924 Scottish Cup Finals, before joining Rangers after a dispute with the club. Moving on to Hearts, East Fife and Leith Athletic, he finally ended his playing days as player-coach at Highland League side Elgin City. Returning to Easter Road as assistant trainer to Johnny Halligan in 1934, Shaw succeeded Halligan as first-team trainer in 1936 and had been manager at Easter Road for 13 years. Hugely respected in the game and widely admired, his abilities had been recognised by the SFA when he was selected as trainer to several Scottish international sides and also the Great Britain team that defeated the Rest of the World at Hampden in 1947. During his time as trainer at Easter Road the determined Shaw had studied physiotherapy and modern training techniques, and used this knowledge wisely after succeeding Willie McCartney in 1948, guiding Hibs to three League Championship wins in five seasons to become in the process the most successful manager in the club's long history. Shaw's last few years at Easter Road had seen the club in steady decline, and he was replaced in the Easter Road hot seat by former Queen's Park player Walter Galbraith, who had achieved minor success with English lower League sides Tranmere Rovers and Accrington Stanley. Never entirely popular with either supporters or players, Galbraith's time at Easter Road would be both inconspicuous and relatively short, culminating in near relegation in 1963 when only a last-day victory at Raith Rovers guaranteed survival. His tenure at the club, however, would see the emergence of several Hibs stars of the future such as Pat Stanton, Jimmy O'Rourke and Peter Cormack, but he stayed only long enough to guide the team to safety the following season before he too was sacked.

Galbraith was replaced by former Dunfermline manager Jock Stein, whose arrival helped arrest the slide, before leading the club to a famous victory over Real Madrid and success in the Summer Cup in his first season, albeit as runners-up in the section games to top-placed Hearts, who were unable to continue in the tournament because of a previous commitment. During his short time at the club, Stein built a strong side with an all-international forward line in Cormack, Quinn, Scott, Hamilton and Martin. He returned to Parkhead as manager a few weeks before the end of the 1964–65 season, but many respected figures in the game, and almost all of the Hibs players at that time, remain convinced that had Stein stayed at Easter Road until the end of the season, the club would probably have won both the League Championship and the Scottish Cup. As it was, now under the reins of manager Bob Shankly, Hibs finished in fourth place as Kilmarnock pipped Hearts for the title on goal average, and lost at the semi-final stage of the Scottish Cup to third-placed Dunfermline.

Eddie Turnbull, thought by many to be the logical successor to manager Hugh Shaw, remained as trainer at Easter Road under Galbraith until the summer of 1963, when he suddenly resigned without explanation. It is widely accepted that Turnbull became disillusioned working under Galbraith, whose knowledge of the game, as far as he was concerned, fell far short of his own. Circumstances probably proved Turnbull right in this assumption. Within days of leaving Easter Road he had been offered the post of trainer at Queen's Park, and his time at Hampden would coincide with an almost immediate upturn in the form of the amateurs who ended the season in seventh place, their highest position for several years. Installed as manager of Aberdeen in March 1965, Turnbull's time with the Grampian club would be highly successful, leading his side into Europe for the first time, as well as winning the Scottish Cup in 1970, and only narrowly failing to secure the League title the following year by the narrowest of margins.

His surprise return to Easter Road as manager just prior to the start of the 1970–71 season stunned the football world, and within a few short months he would assemble one of the best sides in the club's history. Turnbull's Tornadoes, as they came to be known, would eventually challenge the great Celtic side of the 1970s. Winning the League Cup in 1972, and two Drybrough Cups around the same time, the Tornadoes played the best football seen at Easter Road since the days of the Famous Five. Turnbull's teams would be regulars in Europe during most of the following few seasons, but the latter part of the decade would witness a sharp decline in the quality of players compared to his early years at Easter Road, culminating in relegation and the sack in 1980 after a 5–0 semi-final humiliation by Celtic in the Scottish Cup. After leaving Easter Road, the disillusioned Turnbull turned his back on the game to enter the licensed trade, eventually running pubs in Easter Road and Leith until his retirement. At the time of writing, he attends most matches at Easter Road as a guest of the club.

After leaving Easter Road in the summer of 1959, Gordon Smith won both a League and a League Cup medal with rivals Hearts at the end of the season. Transferred to Dundee in 1961, incredibly Smith collected yet another Championship medal with the Dens Park club to add to the three won at Easter Road and the one at Tynecastle, a truly extraordinary feat. No other player in the history of the Scottish game had won League medals with three different clubs, and amazingly none of them had been with either Rangers or Celtic. Smith signed for Greenock Morton in 1963 but never actually appeared for the Cappielow side, and he would end his illustrious career with Irish side Drumcondra in 1964, just a few months short of his 40th birthday. The 'Gay Gordon' would spend the remainder of his working life helping to run his grocery and public house business in the east of the city until his retirement, spending the rest of his days quietly at his home in North Berwick with wife Joan and son Tony. He died in 2003 at the age of 80 and is buried in the local cemetery. Almost 50 years after he retired from the game, Gordon Smith remains a revered figure, recognised by all who were lucky enough to have seen the 'Prince of Wingers' in action as one of the truly greatest players to grace the Scottish game.

After 29 years at the helm at Easter Road, during which time he had led the club from a position of near mediocrity before the war to become one of the leading sides not only in this country, but in Europe, Harry Swan sold Hibernian to Edinburgh bookmaker William Harrower during the summer of 1963. Remaining as a director of the club until shortly before his death in 1966, Swan will always be remembered as the man who saved the club from possible extinction in the early 1930s, and as a visionary who foresaw the major changes that were vital to the development of the game, long before most. After his death, a plaque dedicated to his memory was unveiled in the boardroom by the then directors of the club, and Swan's daughter Betty recently rededicated the plaque in the new boardroom of the West Stand at Easter Road in a ceremony attended by all the current directors of the club.

The youngest of the Famous Five, Bobby Johnstone, was the last of the quintet to retire from the playing side of the game. A firm favourite wherever ever he played, 'Nicker' would remain with Oldham until finally hanging up his boots in the summer of 1965. Living and working in the Manchester area, Johnstone returned to live in his native Selkirk after retirement, dying in the border town in 2001 aged 71. He was buried in the town cemetery; the funeral was attended by former colleagues Lawrie Reilly, Eddie Turnbull and Gordon Smith, as well as several other teammates from the period.

At the time of writing only Eddie Turnbull and Lawrie Reilly survive from Hibs' three Championship-winning sides. Retiring almost obscenely prematurely at the age of 29 because of injury, like Smith and Turnbull Reilly also entered the licensed trade, becoming landlord of the Bowlers Rest pub in Leith. The pub became a popular haunt, not only for Hibs fans who wished to spend time with a true Easter Road legend, but for all true football fans. The club's most capped player, with an international goal ratio better than that of Dalglish and Law, and the scorer of the record number of League goals by a Hibs player, Reilly is now retired and is usually to be found at his beloved Easter Road on match days as a hospitality host.

By the beginning of the 1960s the game itself was changing rapidly. Long gone was the innocence of the immediate post-war years, to be replaced with the first signs of hard-nosed commercialism that would help shape the game as we know it today. As we have seen, the previous decade had witnessed many on-field advances, such as the general acceptance of floodlights and European competition, and now sweeping off-field changes that would have a lasting effect on the players themselves were about to come into operation. Not long before, the Football League had rejected demands from the Professional Players' Union that both the maximum wage agreement and the archaic retain and transfer system, which bonded a player to a club indefinitely, be abolished. The refusal would eventually lead to Ted Hill, chairman of the TUC, warning of possible strike action by the players if their demands were not met. According to Hill, 'the Football League had been playing with the players for years by promising to review matters with absolutely no intention of freeing them from the bondage of the maximum wage'. Describing the Football League's stance as 'old fashioned and autocratic', Hill felt that 'every trade union member should rally round the players and, if need be, take strike action.' The Football League had also refused to intervene in a recent dispute between Newcastle United player George Eastham and the club over the player's insistence that he be allowed to be transferred to Arsenal, who were keen to sign him. The grievance eventually ended up in a court of law, the case ending with a satisfactory conclusion for the player, who would get his desired move to London. Not only that, the court ruling had brought to a swift end the retain and transfer system that had been in use since the advent of professionalism. This one-sided system had tied a player to a club indefinitely as long as he was offered the minimum guaranteed wage at the start of each season. It would now be replaced by the option clause contract, which allowed a player to be signed for a fixed number of years, with the club retaining the option of renewing the contract for a similar length of time.

The maximum wage restriction then in operation in England would also be found to be illegal and abolished in the coming months, allowing Johnny Haynes of Fulham to become the first £100-a-week footballer. With only a few exceptions, particularly during the war, a maximum wage regulation had never been in force in Scotland, only a minimum, but top wages had usually been on par with those south of the border. Now the improved wage structure in England threatened the stability of football in Scotland by encouraging the better players to move south. In an attempt to modernise the game in Scotland, new contract terms and conditions had been recommended by the SFA during the summer. It was now suggested that from the start of the next season players should not be allowed to demand a transfer within the tenure of their yearly agreement, only at the end of the season, thereby avoiding such situations as the long-running Joe Baker saga of the previous campaign and the disruption caused to the team during that time. Transfers could still take place during the season, but only if agreed by both clubs. More importantly, players on the transfer list would now have to be paid, in contrast to the previous system that allowed a club to terminate a player's wages the moment he was placed on the list. Furthermore, players would now be allowed to receive a larger slice of any transfer fee, but only in a move authorised by the club. Only some of these recommendations would ultimately be implemented, but at least it was a step in the right direction.

At a meeting of the League Management Committee around that time, radical proposals to streamline the game in Scotland had failed to reach an agreement. With Hibs chairman Harry Swan as usual playing a prominent part, recommendations were made for changes that were drastically needed for the survival of the game, according to Swan, including the amalgamation of clubs in several areas of the country. It was suggested that Falkirk, Stenhousemuir, East Stirling and Stirling Albion should join forces, as should Montrose, Brechin, Forfar and Arbroath. With many clubs now finding it difficult to survive, not only on the field but also financially, it was also proposed that Dunfermline, Raith Rovers, East Fife and Cowdenbeath should follow suit, as should Queen of the South, Berwick Rangers and Stranraer. At the meeting it had also been suggested that there should be no automatic promotion and relegation between the divisions, but that this should be based solely on recommendation. In the past many clubs had won promotion to the top division but were then found to be out of their depth, both on and off the field. Often failing to attract a crowd large enough to generate even the visiting club's guarantee, smaller clubs usually returned immediately to the lower League. Not only that, but there was also the recommendation that there should not necessarily be automatic relegation for the bottom side, but perhaps only if they had finished in bottom place two years running. Swan, frank as usual, was angry that none of the proposals were accepted, stating firmly that if agreement could not be reached mutually then the move should be implemented by force. Regardless of any common sense surrounding the arguments, perhaps understandably none came to pass in the future.

The perceived threat to the game from the television cameras refused to go away, and during an end-of-season meeting in England, League clubs had voted overwhelmingly against the showing of live televised football the following season except for the Cup Final, international matches and European games, but only if the games took place in midweek. As we now know, those with a vested interest in the televising of live football would not be diverted from their aims, and although the change would occur slowly, it would surely happen. Today the incredible power that the television companies hold over the sport is not always for the long-term good of the game, but the money involved is far too tempting to refuse. I'm not sure Harry Swan would have approved, but that again is another story.